Microsoft SQL Server 2012 Performance Tuning Cookbook

80 recipes to help you tune SQL Server 2012 and achieve optimal performance

Ritesh Shah

Bihag Thaker

[PACKT] enterprise 88
PUBLISHING   professional expertise distilled

BIRMINGHAM - MUMBAI

Microsoft SQL Server 2012 Performance Tuning Cookbook

First published: July 2012

Production Reference: 1160712

Published by Packt Publishing Ltd.
Livery Place
35 Livery Street
Birmingham B3 2PB, UK.

ISBN 978-1-84968-574-0

www.packtpub.com

Cover Image by Asher Wishkerman (a.wishkerman@mpic.de)

Credits

Authors
Ritesh Shah

Bihag Thaker

Reviewers
Satya SK Jayanty

Maria Zakourdaev

Michael Zilberstein

Acquisition Editor
Dhwani Devater

Lead Technical Editor
Kedar Bhat

Technical Editors
Apoorva Bolar

Madhuri Das

Merin Jose

Copy Editor
Brandt D'Mello

Project Coordinator
Sai Gamare

Proofreader
Lesley Harrison

Indexer
Monica Ajmera Mehta

Graphics
Manu Joseph

Valentina Dsilva

Production Coordinator
Shantanu Zagade

Cover Work
Shantanu Zagade

About the Authors

Ritesh Shah is a data professional with over 10 years of experience with using Microsoft technology, from SQL Server 2000 to the latest version. He has worked with various technologies, from Visual Basic 6.0 to .NET Framework 4.0. He has deployed many medium-scale as well as large-scale projects, using Microsoft technology.

He shares his knowledge on his blog, `SQLHub.com`, and also helps the community, using different portals, such as `BeyondRelational.com`, `Experts-Exchange.com`, and Asp.Net forum.

Acknowledgement

It is really truer than ever that this is not an individual effort. The Packt team worked with me the whole time, so a really big thanks goes to them, especially Sai, Kedar, Apoorva, Madhuri, and many more. I cannot forget to mention Dhwani from the Packt team, as she is the one who presented the idea of this book to me. Seriously, I wouldn't have been able to author this book alone, so thanks should go to Mr. Bihag Thaker, as well, as he agreed to co-author this book with me and has worked even harder on it than I have myself.

I am really honored to have Satya, Michael, and Maria as the technical reviewers for this book. They are all well-known personalities in the world of SQL Server.

Apart from the team that worked on this book, I would also like to thank, on a personal note, two well-known personalities in the SQL Server community, who always inspire me to do more. In fact, they were the ones who diverted my interest from .NET technology to SQL Server. They are:

- Pinal Dave, who blogs at `SQLAuthority.com` and is an author of several SQL Server books. Currently, he is working as a Technology Evangelist at Microsoft.
- Jacob Sebastian, who blogs at `BeyondRelational.com` and is a SQL Server MVP, book author, well-known speaker in SQL Server technology, and much more.

Most important of all, my deepest gratitude goes to my parents, Mr. Ashwin Shah and Mrs. Divya Shah. It is because of their hard work, inspiration, and motivation that a small-town boy like me, who has grown up with very limited resources, has progressed so much in life, which in itself proves *where there's a will there's a way*. I would also like to thank my one-and-a-half-year-old son, Teerth, who used to often start crying at midnight, because of which I would lose my sleep and, not being able to get it back, started researching more on the subjects that helped me write this book. Finally, I would like to thank my wife, Alka Shah.

Bihag Thaker is a SQL Server enthusiast, an MCTS (SQL Server 2005), and an MCITP (SQL Server 2008), who has been working with SQL Server technology for the past few years. Initially he was into .NET technology, but his keen interest for SQL Server led him to be a database specialist.

He is currently working as a database administrator. He has worked on numerous performance tuning assignments and executed large-scale database migrations. He likes to share his knowledge and enjoys helping the SQL Server community. You will find him talking about SQL Server on his blog `MsSQLBlog.com`.

Acknowledgement

I had never thought that the dream of writing my first book on SQL Server would come true so early, and I must give full credit for this to Mr. Ritesh Shah and Packt Publishing.

I would sincerely like to thank Packt Publishing, for showing their confidence in me and providing the invaluable opportunity of being a part of this book. Individuals at Packt whom I am deeply grateful to, are Kedar Bhat, Sai Gamare, Madhuri Das, Ashwin Shetty, Apoorva Bolar, and Dhwani Devater. They have been very co-operative and supportive at all the stages of this book. I am extremely thankful to Michael Zilberstein and Maria Zakourdaev, the technical reviewers, for their excellent work of getting the accuracy of the technical details of the book in perfect shape.

I find it difficult to express, in words, my gratitude, to Ritesh, who has shared the priceless gift of writing this book with me. This was not at all attainable without his continuous support. Apart from being a TechMate, Ritesh is an all-time great friend of mine, who is always willing to help the SQL Server community.

Two individuals to whom I am indebted and whose disciple I have always been, are Mr. Paresh Vora and Mr. Mukesh Devmurari. I have learnt a lot from them, and they are the reason I'm part of the IT community today.

Without my family support, a task such as writing a book would not have been achievable. I would like to heartily thank my parents, Mr. Kanaiyalal Thaker and Mrs. Hema Thaker. It is because of them that I exist, and I cherish their blessings, which are always with me. I am very thankful to my wife, Khyati, who has always stood by me, helped me at all times, and has even smilingly got me cups of coffee during my sleepless nights of writing!

Last but not the least, I would like to thank my friends who helped me directly or indirectly by giving me moral support.

About the Reviewers

Satya SK Jayanty is a SQL Server MVP and Subject Matter Expert with consulting and technical expertise for D Bi A Solutions INc. Limited, with over 20 years of experience. His work experience includes a wide range of industries, including the stock exchange, insurance, tele-communications, financial, retail, and manufacturing sectors, among others.

He is a regular speaker and SME volunteer at major technology conferences such as Microsoft Tech-Ed (Europe, India, and North America), and SQL PASS (Europe and North America), SQL Bits - UK, and manages the Scottish Area SQL Server user group based in Scotland. He is also a moderator in a majority of web-based SQL Server forums (Microsoft Technet and `www.sql-server-performance.com`), writer, and contributing editor, and blogs at `www.sqlserver-qa.net`, `www.sql-server-performance.com`, and `www.beyondrelational.com` websites.

He is the author of *Microsoft SQL Server 2008 R2 Administration Cookbook, Packt Publishing*, and co-author of *SQL Server MVP Deep Dives, Volume 2, Manning Publications*.

Maria Zakourdaev has more than 10 years of experience with SQL Server. She is currently working with one of the most successful Israeli startup companies, called Conduit. She has extensive knowledge of Microsoft replication solutions, table partitioning, and advanced, query tuning techniques. Prior to Conduit she had worked with different companies, benchmarking different SQL Server features and flows, such as partitioning, data import, index impact on DML flows, star transformations in RDBMS, hierarchic queries, and custom OLAP-like aggregations. She was a speaker in Microsoft Teched (Israel) on the SQL Server track and is an active member of the Israel SQL Server Group.

Michael Zilberstein has more than 10 years of experience in the IT industry and database world, working with all the SQL Server versions from 6.5 to 2012 and with different Oracle versions as well. After working with several start-up companies during the first few years of his career, in 2007 Michael founded DBArt Ltd – SQL Server, a consulting services company.

Two of Michael's most distinctive interests (besides rappelling, homebrewing, playing chess, and reading history books) are performance tuning and architecture of large-scale systems. The biggest professional satisfaction for him is to take a young start-up company and build its product from schemas in scrapbook and Visio to a working and scalable terabyte-size system.

Michael is a frequent speaker at Israeli SQL Server Usergroup (ISUG) and other SQL Server events in Israel. He also writes a blog—`http://sqlblog.com/blogs/michael_zilberstein/default.aspx`.

www.PacktPub.com

Support files, eBooks, discount offers and more

You might want to visit www.PacktPub.com for support files and downloads related to your book.

Did you know that Packt offers eBook versions of every book published, with PDF and ePub files available? You can upgrade to the eBook version at www.PacktPub.com and as a print book customer, you are entitled to a discount on the eBook copy. Get in touch with us at service@packtpub.com for more details.

At www.PacktPub.com, you can also read a collection of free technical articles, sign up for a range of free newsletters and receive exclusive discounts and offers on Packt books and eBooks.

http://PacktLib.PacktPub.com

Do you need instant solutions to your IT questions? PacktLib is Packt's online digital book library. Here, you can access, read and search across Packt's entire library of books.

Why Subscribe?

- ▸ Fully searchable across every book published by Packt
- ▸ Copy and paste, print and bookmark content
- ▸ On demand and accessible via web browser

Free Access for Packt account holders

If you have an account with Packt at www.PacktPub.com, you can use this to access PacktLib today and view nine entirely free books. Simply use your login credentials for immediate access.

Instant Updates on New Packt Books

Get notified! Find out when new books are published by following @PacktEnterprise on Twitter, or the *Packt Enterprise* Facebook page.

Table of Contents

Preface

Microsoft SQL Server 2012 Performance Tuning Cookbook is divided into three major parts—Performance Monitoring, Performance Tuning, and Performance Management—that are mandatory for dealing with performance in any capacity.

Microsoft SQL Server 2012 Performance Tuning Cookbook offers a great way to manage performance with effective, concise, and practical recipes. You will learn how to diagnose performance issues, fix them, and take precautions to avoid common mistakes.

Each recipe given in this book is an individual task that will address different performance aspects to take your SQL Server's Performance to a higher level.

The first part of this book covers monitoring with SQL Server Profiler, DTA, system statistical functions, SPs with DBCC commands, Resource Monitor, Reliability and Performance Monitor, and execution plans.

The second part of the book offers execution plan, dynamic management views and dynamic management functions, SQL Server Cache, stored procedure recompilations, indexes, important ways to write effective T-SQL, statistics, table and index partitioning, advanced query tuning with query hints and plan guide, dealing with locking, blocking, and deadlocking, and configuring SQL Server for optimization to boost performance.

The third and final part gives you knowledge about performance management with the help of policy based management and management with Resource Governor.

What this book covers

Chapter 1, SQL Server Profiler, teaches you how to create and start your first SQL Trace, limit the trace data and capture only the events which are of interest, detect slow running and expensive queries, and create a trace with system stored procedures.

Chapter 2, Tuning with Database Engine Tuning Advisor, covers how to analyze queries using Database Engine Tuning Advisor, how to run Database Engine Tuning Advisor for Workload, and how to execute Database Tuning Advisor from the command prompt.

Chapter 3, System Statistical Functions, System Stored Procedures, and DBCC SQLPERF Command, starts with the monitoring of system health using system statistical functions and later on covers the monitoring of SQL Server processes and sessions with system stored procedures, and log space usage statistics with the DBCC SQLPERF command.

Chapter 4, Resource Monitor and Performance Monitor, teaches you how to do quick monitoring of server performance, followed by monitoring of CPU and memory (RAM) usage.

Chapter 5, Monitoring with Execution Plans, includes recipes for working with Estimated Execution Plan and Actual Execution Plan, monitoring the performance of queries by SET SHOWPLAN_XML, SET STATISTICS XML, and SET STATISTICS IO, finding the execution time of a query by SET STATISTICS TIME, and including and understanding Client Statistics.

Chapter 6, Tuning with Execution Plans, explains the Hash, Merge, and Nested Loop Join strategies, teaches how to find table/index scans in execution plans and how to fix them, introduces Key Lookups, and explains how to find them in execution plans and resolve them.

Chapter 7, Dynamic Management Views and Dynamic Management Functions, includes recipes to monitor current query execution statistics, manage and monitor index performance, monitor the TempDB database's performance with database-related dynamic management views, and monitor disk I/O statistics.

Chapter 8, SQL Server Cache and Stored Procedure Recompilations, covers monitoring of compilations and recompilations at instance level, using Reliability and Performance Monitor, and monitoring of recompilations using SQL Server Profiler.

Chapter 9, Implementing Indexes, explains how to improve performance by creating a clustered index, by creating a non-clustered index, by covering index, by including columns in an index, by a filtered index, and by a columnstore index.

Chapter 10, Maintaining Indexes, includes recipes to find fragmentation, to enhance index efficiency by using the REBUILD and REORGANIZE index, to find missing and unused indexes, to enhance performance by creating indexed views and creating an index on Computed Columns, and to determine disk space consumed by indexes.

Chapter 11, Points to Consider While Writing Query, covers how to improve performance by limiting the number of columns and rows and by using sargable conditions, how to use arithmetic operators wisely in predicate to improve performance, how to improve query performance by not using functions on predicate columns, how to improve performance by Declarative Referential Integrity (DRI), and how to gain performance by trusting your foreign key.

Chapter 12, Statistics in SQL Server, explains how to create and update statistics, effects of statistics on non-key columns, how to find out-of-date statistics and correct them, and effects of statistics on a filtered index.

Chapter 13, Table and Index Partitioning, covers partitioning of table with RANGE LEFT and RANGE RIGHT, and deleting and loading of bulk data by splitting, merging, and switching partitions (sliding window).

Chapter 14, Implementing Physical Database Structure, includes recipes for configuring a data file and log file on multiple physical disks, using files and filegroups, moving an existing large table to a separate physical disk, moving non-clustered indexes to a separate physical disk, and configuring the `TempDB` database on a separate physical disk.

Chapter 15, Advanced Query Tuning: Hints and Plan Guides, includes recipes for using the NOLOCK table query hint, using the FORCESEEK and INDEX table hints, optimizing a query using an object plan guide, and implementing a fixed execution plan using a SQL plan guide.

Chapter 16, Dealing with Locking, Blocking, and Deadlocking, covers determining long-running transactions, detecting blocked and blocking queries, detecting deadlocks with SQL Server Profiler, and detecting deadlocks with Trace Flag 1204.

Chapter 17, Configuring SQL Server for Optimization, includes recipes for configuring SQL Server to use more processing power, configuring memory in 32-bit versus 64-bit, configuring "Optimize for Ad hoc Workloads", and optimizing SQL Server instance configuration.

Chapter 18, Policy Based Management, explains how to evaluate database properties and restrict database objects.

Chapter 19, Management with Resource Governor, includes recipes for configuring Resource Governor with SQL Server Management Studio and T-SQL script, and monitoring Resource Governor.

What you need for this book

To work with the examples given in the book, you must have the following infrastructure:

- SQL Server Denail CTP version 3 or higher, or SQL Server 2012 RTM
- The AdventureWorks2012 database, which can be freely downloaded from the following link: http://msftdbprodsamples.codeplex.com/releases/view/55330
- A Windows administrator login and/or a SQL server login with the sysAdmin privilege

Who this book is for

Microsoft SQL Server 2012 Performance Tuning Cookbook is aimed at SQL Server Database Developers, DBAs, and Database Architects who are working in any capacity to achieve optimal performance. Basic knowledge of SQL Server is expected, and professionals who want to get hands-on with performance tuning and have not worked on tuning the SQL Server for performance will find this book helpful.

Conventions

In this book, you will find a number of styles of text that distinguish between different kinds of information. Here are some examples of these styles, and an explanation of their meaning.

Code words in text are shown as follows: "You may notice some `TextData` appearing multiple times in a trace for a single execution of a T-SQL statement."

A block of code is set as follows:

```
--creating table for demonstration
CREATE TABLE ordDemo (OrderID INT IDENTITY, OrderDate DATETIME, Amount
MONEY, Refno INT)
GO
```

Any command-line input or output is written as follows:

```
dta -D AdventureWorks2012 -s adventureworks2012FromDTA5 -S WIN-
SLYJ9UY3PKD\DENALICTP3 -E -if D:\test.sql -F -of D:\DTA.sql
```

New terms and important words are shown in bold. Words that you see on the screen, in menus or dialog boxes for example, appear in the text like this: "Connect object explorer with server and move to **Management | Policy Management | Policies** ".

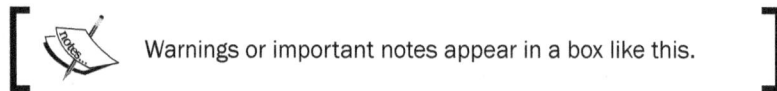

> Warnings or important notes appear in a box like this.

> Tips and tricks appear like this.

Reader feedback

Feedback from our readers is always welcome. Let us know what you think about this book—what you liked or may have disliked. Reader feedback is important for us to develop titles that you really get the most out of.

To send us general feedback, simply send an e-mail to feedback@packtpub.com, and mention the book title through the subject of your message.

If there is a topic that you have expertise in and you are interested in either writing or contributing to a book, see our author guide on www.packtpub.com/authors.

Customer support

Now that you are the proud owner of a Packt book, we have a number of things to help you to get the most from your purchase.

Downloading the example code

You can download the example code files for all Packt books you have purchased from your account at http://www.packtpub.com. If you purchased this book elsewhere, you can visit http://www.packtpub.com/support and register to have the files e-mailed directly to you.

Errata

Although we have taken every care to ensure the accuracy of our content, mistakes do happen. If you find a mistake in one of our books—maybe a mistake in the text or the code—we would be grateful if you would report this to us. By doing so, you can save other readers from frustration and help us improve subsequent versions of this book. If you find any errata, please report them by visiting http://www.packtpub.com/support, selecting your book, clicking on the **errata submission form** link, and entering the details of your errata. Once your errata are verified, your submission will be accepted and the errata will be uploaded to our website, or added to any list of existing errata, under the Errata section of that title.

Piracy

Piracy of copyright material on the Internet is an ongoing problem across all media. At Packt, we take the protection of our copyright and licenses very seriously. If you come across any illegal copies of our works, in any form, on the Internet, please provide us with the location address or website name immediately so that we can pursue a remedy.

Please contact us at copyright@packtpub.com with a link to the suspected pirated material.

We appreciate your help in protecting our authors, and our ability to bring you valuable content.

Questions

You can contact us at questions@packtpub.com if you are having a problem with any aspect of the book, and we will do our best to address it.

1
Mastering SQL Trace Using Profiler

In this chapter we will cover:

- ► Creating a trace or workload
- ► Filtering events
- ► Detecting slow running and expensive queries
- ► Creating trace with SQL Trace system stored procedures

Introduction

Welcome to the world of Performance Monitoring and Tuning with SQL Server 2012!

Let's assume that you are a database administrator in your organization. What, if one day one of your colleagues from your IT department calls you right away and complains that the production database server has abruptly started to run very slowly and applications that are accessing the production database are not responding the way they should? The issue needs immediate attention and for that you are required to investigate the issue and fix it in timely manner. What will be your approach to look at the problem and solve it? How would you be able to analyze the situation and identify where the problem is? What actions would you take once a particular problem is recognized in order to resolve it?

Installing and upgrading database servers, managing and maintaining database servers, managing database security, implementing disaster recovery plan, capacity planning, managing high-availability of databases, and performance tuning of databases and SQL server are some of the responsibilities of a DBA. Amongst these responsibilities, performance tuning of the database server is one of the prime responsibilities of DBA. The most common reason is, companies offering IT services are often engaged in signing **Service Level Agreements (SLAs)** and as per their SLAs they are committed to provide a certain level of services and up-time. Any additional down-time than what is allowed as per SLAs can cause them money loss or business loss. Even companies not engaged in SLAs might lose business because of their poor software systems caused by poor database systems. This is one of the reasons why skilled DBAs are required to keep the database performance up-to date by monitoring and tuning database performance.

In database centric application environment, it is very common for any DBA to face such database related performance issues at different levels. By means of different levels, it implies that performance problem can be found at query level, database level, server level or application level .There can be a number of reasons for a database centric application to be performing poorly. The troubleshooting skills and expertise in performance tuning of a DBA are tested out in recognizing such factors behind the performance degradation and taking the necessary corrective steps.

The first step towards performance tuning is monitoring. In data platform, monitoring something is the process of analyzing and identifying something. So, until you monitor something, you can't know for sure what and where the problem is. Until you know what and where the problem is, you can't analyze the problem. And until you can analyze the problem, you can't solve a problem! This also means that unless you understand performance monitoring, you cannot master performance tuning in a true sense. Thus, performance tuning always comes after performance monitoring. This is the reason why we have a few opening chapters that specifically concentrates on performance monitoring.

The troublesome situation that was just described earlier needs thorough monitoring and systematic analysis in order to identify the root problem accurately before a problem can be solved.

SQL Server Profiler is the most common but powerful tool for monitoring and auditing an instance of SQL server. By using this tool, a DBA is able to solve a large number of different types of database performance issues whether it is a query issue, index issue, locking issue or database, or server configuration issue. It is the tool that essentially any DBA must know. So, SQL Server Profiler will be the subject of this first chapter.

Creating a trace or workload

If you have never worked with SQL Server Profiler, this recipe will teach you how to create and start your first SQL Trace. There is some detailed information on SQL Trace in *There's more...* section of this recipe. This will help you in appreciating rest of the recipes quite easily, which employs SQL Trace in remaining chapters. The section covers the information that will help you in mastering core concepts of SQL Trace and thus mastering SQL Server Profiler. There are no major changes in SQL Server Profiler 2012 documented. In SQL Server 2012, the architecture and functionality of SQL Server Profiler is almost identical to that of SQL Server 2008.

Getting ready

In this recipe, we will create our first trace with SQL Server Profiler. The following are the prerequisites that you should fulfil:

▸ An instance of SQL Server 2012 Developer or Enterprise Evaluation edition.

▸ An SQL Server Login account with administrative rights.

▸ Sample AdventureWorks2012 database on the instance of SQL Server. For more details on how to install AdventureWorks2012 database, please refer to the *Introduction* section of this book.

How to do it...

To create a new trace, follow the steps provided here.

1. Start SQL Server Profiler. To start SQL Server Profiler, navigate through **Start | All Programs | Microsoft SQL Server 2012 Program Group | Performance Tools | SQL Server Profiler**.

2. Select **New Trace...** from the **File** menu. In the **Connect to Server** dialog box, provide connection details of SQL Server hosting AdventureWorks2012 database and click on **Connect**.

> Login name that you use to connect SQL Server Profiler must have the **ALTER TRACE** permission otherwise you will receive an error and cannot start a trace session.

3. In the **General** tab of the **Trace Properties** dialog box, specify CreatingTraceWorkload as trace name. Use the **Standard (default)** trace template for the **Use the template:** option.

4. Check the checkbox **Save to file:** and specify a path and file name in the **Save As** dialog box and then click on **Save**.

5. Keep **Enable file rollover** checked and **Set maximum file size (MB):** to its default value, that is, 128. The following screenshot shows the **General** tab of the **Trace Properties** dialog box:

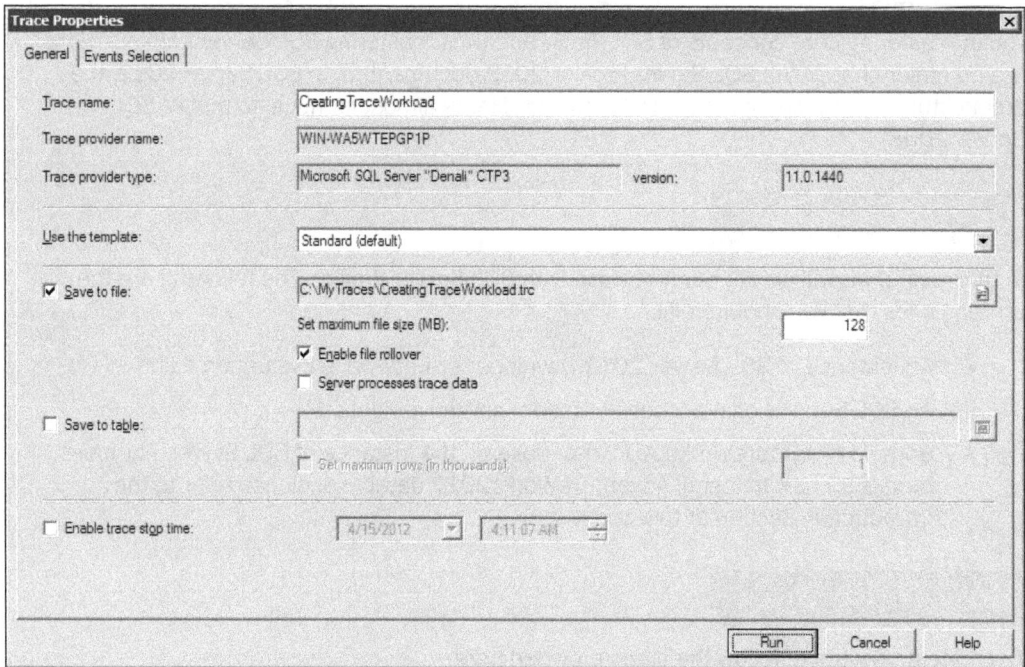

In the **Trace Properties** dialog box, there is a checkbox option in the **General** tab with the caption **Server processes trace data**, to specify whether trace data should be processed on the server. If not checked, trace data is processed at the client side.

When trace data is processed at the client side, it is possible for some events to be missed if the server load is high. If this option is checked, then trace data is processed on the server and all the events included in trace definition are guaranteed to be captured without miss. However, this guarantee comes with performance penalty, because processing trace data on server has an impact on the performance of SQL Server, and hence enabling this option is not recommended on production server.

Also, running SQL Server Profiler on production server itself should be avoided as running SQL Server Profiler is resource consuming. Instead, you should run SQL Server Profiler from a client computer and connect it to your SQL Server from there.

6. Click on the **Events Selection** tab. On this screen, the events that are predefined for the **Standard (default)** trace template are selected and shown in grid. Check the **Show all events** check box to show all events.

7. Navigate through the **Events** list until you find **Stored Procedures** event category. Expand **Stored Procedures** event category if it is collapsed. Uncheck the checkbox for **RPC:Completed** event and check the checkbox for **SP:Completed** event. Uncheck the **Show all events** checkbox to show only selected events. The screen should now look as shown in following screenshot:

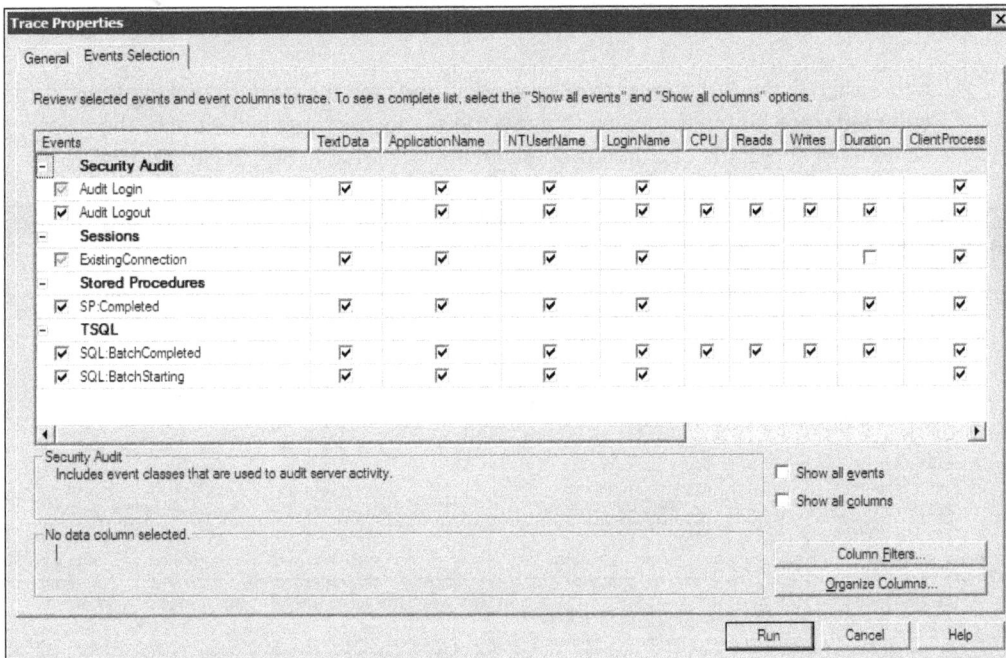

8. Click on the **Run** button to start the trace.

9. Now open SQL Server Management Studio and establish a connection to the same SQL Server.

10. In query window, type the sample T-SQL statements as shown in following script and then execute them by pressing the *F5* key:

```
USE AdventureWorks2012
GO

SELECT DB_ID()
GO

EXECUTE sp_helpdb
```

```
GO

SELECT
  P.FirstName + ' ' + P.LastName AS EmployeeName
  ,E.JobTitle
  ,E.BirthDate
  ,E.Gender
  ,E.BirthDate
FROM HumanResources.Employee AS E
INNER JOIN Person.Person AS P
ON E.BusinessEntityID = P.BusinessEntityID
GO
```

11. Now switch to the **SQL Server Profiler** window and stop the trace by clicking **Stop selected trace** button in toolbar. Observe the events captured in the trace. The following screenshot shows the captured events that are displayed in SQL Server Profiler:

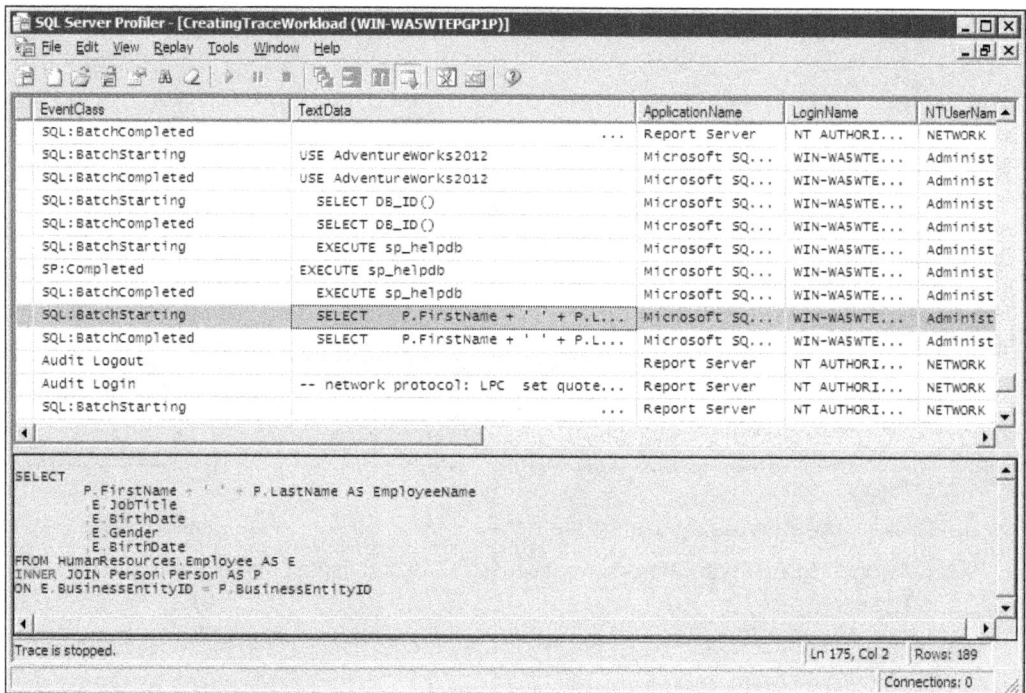

How it works...

We started to configure a trace by setting a few trace properties. To demonstrate how we can use one of the in-built trace templates to get a quick start, we used the default trace template **Standard (default)** in this example. When this template is used, the following events are selected by default:

- Audit Login
- Audit Logout
- ExistingConnection
- RPC:Completed
- SQL:BatchCompleted
- SQL:BatchStarting

> You may notice some TextData appearing multiple times in a trace for a single execution of a T-SQL statement. For instance, in the previous example, you will notice two events for SELECT DB_ID() statement even if we executed it only once. These two entries here do not represent two executions of the said statement. Rather, they represent two different related events associated to one single execution of the statement. For example, both events SQL:BatchStarting and SQL:BatchCompleted raised for a single execution of batch containing SELECT DB_ID() statement and they both show the same T-SQL command in TextData data column. This depends upon what events you have selected in trace definition.

In the **Trace Properties** dialog box, we have set the maximum file size for our trace to 128 MB. Option **Enable file rollover** was also enabled by default. Enabling this option is helpful while working with large amount of trace data.

When large amount of event data is captured, the trace file can grow very quickly and become very large. Enabling the **Enable file rollover** option can prevent a trace file from becoming very large by limiting a file to the maximum file size specified. When the file size is reached to the maximum file size specified, SQL Server creates a new roll-over file with the same name appended with a suffix of an incremental number for the same trace. Thus, when we have this option enabled and the size of trace data is greater than maximum file, we have multiple trace files for the same trace.

In this example, we are saving our trace file as C:\MyTraces\CreatingTraceWorkload. trc. A trace can also be started without having to save the trace data. In case a trace was started in this way without enabling the **Save to file:** checkbox, SQL Server manages to keep the captured data in queue temporarily. The unsaved trace data can be saved later on as well after gathering the required data. This can be done with the Save or Save As command from the **File** menu. With the **Save As** command, we can save trace data in our desired format. Selecting the **Trace Table...** option in the Save As command, asks for the SQL Server connection details and destination table details where the trace data will be stored.

It's best to store the trace file on a separate disk other than the one which is used to store data files and log files of SQL server databases. Storing the trace file on the same physical disk where database files are stored can degrade the performance of normal I/O operations of other databases.

> Configuring a trace by enabling the **Save to table** checkbox in the **Trace Properties** dialog box and saving trace data directly to trace table is less efficient. If you want your trace data to be saved in a trace table then consider saving the trace data first in a trace file; then export your trace data from trace file to trace table by opening the trace file in SQL Server Profiler and selecting the **Save As** command from the **File** menu with the **Trace Table...** option. When you want to save your trace in a trace table, always consider to save your trace in a separate database.

The **Events Selection** tab of **Trace Properties** dialog box displays the selected events only and does not show all events by default. So, we checked the **Show all events** option to list all the available events. Because we did not want to capture **RPC:Completed** event, we excluded this event by un-checking its checkbox from the event list and included **SP:Completed** event under **Stored Procedures** event category.

Once we finished configuring our trace, the trace was started. To demonstrate how the events are captured, we produced some events by executing a few T-SQL statements from another connection through SQL Server Management Studio.

In the final figure, we can see the trace data that is produced by the events included in trace definition. Look at the trace data that we captured. By looking at the values in different data columns, we can learn many different things. For example, for a given trace, by examining `LoginName`, `TextData`, and `HostName` we can tell who is running which query and from which machine. By examining `StartTime` and `EndTime` data columns we can determine when a particular query was executed and when it finished its execution.

> **Pausing and Stopping a trace**
>
> Once a trace is started, it can be either paused or stopped. To do this, select the **Run Trace**, **Pause Trace**, and **Stop Trace** commands from the **File** menu or click on the corresponding shortcut command buttons on standard toolbar.
>
> **Pausing and resuming trace**: When a trace is paused, event data stops from being captured temporarily. Once a trace is paused, it can be resumed by starting it again. Restarting a trace resumes and continues to capture event data again without wiping out any previously captured trace data.
>
> **Stopping and restarting trace**: When a trace is stopped, event data stops from being captured. If a trace is stopped, it can be restarted by starting it again. Restarting a stopped trace starts to capture event data again; but any previously captured trace data is lost.
>
> Remember that we cannot change the **Trace Properties** of a trace while it is running. To do this, we must have to pause or stop the trace.

There's more...

This section covers some essential information on SQL Trace that you must know if you want to master SQL Tracing. It is advised that even if you are an advanced user, you do not skip this section.

Some background of SQL Trace

Follow this section in order to have an in-depth understanding of SQL Trace and its architecture.

SQL Trace terms and concepts

Understanding the SQL Trace and its architecture by knowing its related terms and concepts is a prerequisite for working with SQL Server Profiler effectively. This section discusses the basic terminologies and concepts of SQL Trace in brief.

SQL Trace

SQL Trace is an event monitoring and capturing engine that comes with SQL Server. It provides the capability to capture the database events with event data and create traces that can be used for performance analysis afterwards.

SQL Server Profiler

SQL Server Profiler is a graphical user interface tool for working with SQL Trace. Behind the scene, it uses the same SQL Trace engine, but additionally provides graphical user interface to the user for working with traces. SQL Server Profiler provides functionalities, such as displaying collected event data on its graphical interface, saving traces either in a file or in an SQL Server table, opening previously saved traces, extracting T-SQL statements from a trace, and many more. Finding and analyzing long running or costly queries, finding deadlocks and their related information, looking for which indexes are scanned, and looking for database connection requests are some of the practical applications of SQL Server Profiler.

Event

In context of SQL Trace terminology, an **event** is the happening of a database activity that takes place within an instance of SQL Server. Execution of an ad-hoc query or T-SQL batch, a call to stored procedure, an attempt to log in or log out from database server are a few examples that raise specific SQL Server events.

Event class

An **event class** describes a specific type of event. There are many different types of events that can occur within the database engine and each type of event is represented by an event class. `Audit Login`, `Audit Logout`, `SP:Completed`, `SP:Recompile`, `SQL:BatchCompleted`, `Lock:Deadlock` are some of the examples of event classes. To get list of all available event classes, you can query `sys.trace_events` catalog view.

Event category

An event category is a subset of related event classes. Each event class belongs to a particular event category and each event category includes a subset of specific type of event classes. Locks, performance, scans, and stored procedures are some examples of the event categories. To get list of all available event categories,you can query `sys.trace_categories` catalog view. You can join `sys.trace_events` and `sys.trace_categories` catalog views on `category_id` column to make correlation between the two views.

Data column

A **data column** is an attribute that represents a particular characteristic of an event class. For example, event class `SQL:BatchCompleted` can have different characteristics, such as `TextData`, `LoginName`, `Duration`, `StartTime`, `EndTime`, and so on, where `TextData` represents T-SQL statement(s) whose execution raises a particular event. These characteristics of event classes are represented by different data columns.

Trace

A session that performs the activity of capturing database events and collecting events' data is typically called a **trace**. Loosely, the term Trace is also used by database professionals to refer the *Trace Data* that has been collected previously during a trace session and saved in a trace file or SQL Server table.

Trace properties and Trace definition

A set of configured settings for a trace that defines how event data should be collected or saved and which event classes or data columns should be collected as a part of trace data is called Trace properties or a Trace definition.

Filter

A **filter** is an optional logical condition that can be applied to a trace to limit the resulting trace data by capturing only the required trace events for which the filter condition is satisfied. For example, in a trace definition we can specify a filter condition so that SQL Trace collects event data only for a specific database by applying a filter on either `DatabaseID` data column or `DatabaseName` data column.

Trace file

This is a file with the extension `.trc` in which the captured trace data is saved.

Trace table

A table in SQL Server database in which the captured trace data is stored is a **trace table**.

Trace template

A file which saves the pre-configured trace definitions is called a **Trace Template**. This can be reused for creating new traces.

Architecture of SQL Trace

After learning the basic SQL Trace terms and concepts, it will be easier to understand the following architectural diagram of SQL Trace:

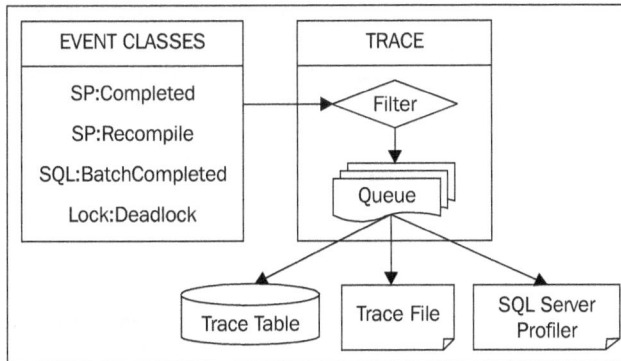

When events are raised in SQL Server database engine, SQL Trace captures event data only for those event classes that are included in trace definition and for which filter conditions if specified any are satisfied. Once the event data is captured, it is queued and then sent to its specified target location. The target location can be a Trace file, Trace table, or SQL Server Profiler. Trace data can also be viewed only in SQL Server Profiler without the need of saving a trace.

After understanding the basic concepts of SQL Trace, working with SQL Server Profiler and traces should be an easy task. As this is our first recipe of the book where we learn how to create a trace or workload with SQL Server Profiler, let's first discuss something about trace and workload.

Trace and workload

We now know that a trace is a session during which the events are captured and event data is collected. SQL Server supports few formats for saving this collected trace data. We can save trace data in one of the following formats:

▶ A trace file with `.trc` extension name

▶ A trace file in XML format with `.xml` extension name

▶ A trace table in an SQL Server database

A **trace** contains a series of events and every event has its associated event data. All the events of a trace and their event data collectively form trace data for a trace file. Data columns associated with trace events form the event data. T-SQL statements whose execution causes the events to be raised are also a part of this event data under `TextData` data column and are themselves included in trace data.

A **workload** or workload file basically contains a series of T-SQL statements. A T-SQL script is an example of a workload file. Because trace data also contains a series of T-SQL statements as a part of event data (as **TextData** Column), they are also used as workloads. Thus, a T-SQL script, trace file (.trc or .xml), trace table, all can be considered as workload. In other words, a trace file is also a workload file. This workload can be used to re-run on a database for workload or performance analysis. Usually, a workload file is provided as input file to **Database Engine Tuning Advisor** (**DTA**) for a tuning session. You will learn more about Database Engine Tuning Advisor in *Chapter 2, Tuning with Database Engine Tuning Advisor*.

Commonly-used event classes

The following list gives brief descriptions of commonly used event classes:

- ▶ Audit Login: This event occurs when a user connects and logs in to SQL Server
- ▶ Audit Logout: This event occurs when a users disconnects and logs out from SQL Server
- ▶ RPC:Starting: This event occurs when a **Remote Procedure Call** (RPC) starts executing
- ▶ RPC:Completed: This event occurs when a **Remote Procedure Call (RPC)** completes its execution
- ▶ SQL:BatchStarting: This event occurs when a T-SQL batch starts executing
- ▶ SQL:StmtStarting: This event occurs when a statement inside a T-SQL batch starts executing
- ▶ SQL:StmtCompleted: This event occurs when a statement inside a T-SQL batch completes its execution
- ▶ SQL:BatchCompleted: This event occurs when a T-SQL batch completes its execution
- ▶ SP:Starting: This event occurs when a stored procedure starts executing
- ▶ SP:StmtStarting: This event occurs when a statement inside a stored procedure starts executing
- ▶ SP:StmtCompleted: This event occurs when a statement inside a stored procedure completes its execution
- ▶ SP:Completed: This event occurs when a stored procedure completes its execution

Commonly-used data columns

The following list gives brief descriptions of commonly used event classes:

- ▶ ApplicationName: This data column represents the name of the client application causing a trace event to occur
- ▶ DatabaseID: This data column represents the internal system assigned ID of the database for which a trace event occurs

- ▶ `DatabaseName`: This data column represents the name of the database for which a trace event occurs

- ▶ `HostName`: This data column represents the name of the host or computer where the client component connecting to SQL Server causes a trace event to occur

- ▶ `LoginName`: This data column represents the name of the login under whose security context, particular T-SQL statement(s) executes that causes trace event to occur

- ▶ `ObjectID`: This data column represents the internal system assigned ID of an object for which a trace event occurs

- ▶ `ObjectName`: This data column represents the name of an object for which a trace event occurs

- ▶ `SessionLoginName`: This data column represents the name of the login who initiated the connection and under whose security context a trace event occurs

- ▶ `SPID`: This data column represents the Server Process ID or Session ID of the connection which causes a trace event to occur

> For a complete list of event classes and data columns of SQL Trace with their description, you can refer product documentation for SQL Server 2012 at `msdn.microsoft.com/en-us/library/bb418432(v=sql.10).aspx`.

Filtering events

Running a trace which is configured to collect large number of events is not best practice. While collecting trace data, SQL Trace itself can introduce overhead and affect the performance of SQL Server if trace is configured to collect too much trace information. This also depends on whether the trace is server-side trace or client-side trace. If the trace is client-side using profiler, then the performance overhead can be greater.

Also, if large number of trace data is captured, the size of the trace file immediately grows very big and it becomes a difficult job for us to look for the right data in the trace. Therefore, any unnecessary or irrelevant trace data should not be collected.

This is the reason why we should consider limiting the resulting trace data and capturing only the events which are of our interest. For this, we should identify what trace data we need to look at and based upon that we should identify the filters that are applied to our trace.

Collecting large amount of trace data can affect the performance of SQL Server. So, before creating a trace, we should identify the type of analysis we want to perform on trace information. A single trace should not be created for multiple types of analysis. For each analysis type, a separate trace should be created until and unless different types of analysis explicitly need to be combined into single trace for performing correlative analysis. For example, rather than creating a single trace that collects both scan events and lock events for index scan analysis and object locking analysis respectively, we should consider creating two separate traces; one for collecting only scan events and another for collecting lock events only.

Getting ready

In this recipe, we will see how to capture only those trace events that occurred for a specific database and from a specific SQL Server login.

Let's assume that sample database AdventureWorks2012 is our production database on our production server, which is hosting other databases also. One of the database users *James* complains that he faces some problems while running queries against database AdventureWorks2012. So, we want to trace his session only for database AdventureWorks2012. Because there are also other databases hosted on the same production server and many users are accessing AdventureWorks2012 database, we need to filter trace events based on session login name and database name in order to avoid any unwanted trace data from being collected.

To emulate this case practically, we need the following as prerequisites:

- An instance of SQL Server 2012 Developer or Enterprise Evaluation edition
- An SQL Server Login account with **sysadmin** rights
- The sample AdventureWorks2012 database on the instance of SQL Server. For more details on how to install AdventureWorks2012 database, please refer the *Introduction* section of this book.
- Two SQL Server logins named *James* and *Peter* with some permission on AdventureWorks2012 database.

How to do it...

We will be performing three main actions in this example. These are as follows:

- Creating the required logins and users in the AdventureWorks2012 database (*James* and *Peter*)
- Creating a trace by applying filters on the `DatabaseName` and `SessionLoginName` data columns

▶ Executing sample queries from two separate connections belonging to *James* and *Peter* respectively and observing the trace data

Because two SQL Server logins named *James* and *Peter* with permissions on AdventureWorks2012 database are required, create them by performing the following steps:

1. Open SQL Server Management Studio.

2. Connect to the instance of SQL Server with login account having sysadmin rights.

3. Execute the following T-SQL script to create the logins and their corresponding users in the AdventureWorks2012 database for James and Peter:

```
--Creating Login and User in
--AdventureWorks2012 database for James
USE [master]
GO
CREATE LOGIN [James] WITH PASSWORD=N'JamesPass123'
  ,DEFAULT_DATABASE=[AdventureWorks2012]
  ,CHECK_EXPIRATION=OFF
  ,CHECK_POLICY=OFF
GO
USE [AdventureWorks2012]
GO
CREATE USER [James] FOR LOGIN [James]
GO
ALTER ROLE [db_owner] ADD MEMBER [James]
GO


--Creating Login and User in AdventureWorks2012 database for Peter
USE [master]
GO
CREATE LOGIN [Peter] WITH PASSWORD=N'PeterPass123'
  ,DEFAULT_DATABASE=[AdventureWorks2012]
  ,CHECK_EXPIRATION=OFF
  ,CHECK_POLICY=OFF
GO
USE [AdventureWorks2012]
GO
CREATE USER [Peter] FOR LOGIN [Peter]
GO
ALTER ROLE [db_owner] ADD MEMBER [Peter]
GO
```

> Notice the new command syntax in this script introduced in SQL Server 2012 for adding members to a role.

Now, we will create a trace and capture only events that occur for AdventureWorks2012 database from *James'* session only. To do this, follow these steps:

1. Start SQL Server Profiler.

2. Select **New Trace...** from the **File** menu. In the **Connect to Server** dialog box, provide connection details of SQL Server hosting the AdventureWorks2012 database and click on **Connect**.

3. In the **General** tab of **Trace Properties**, enter FilteringEvents as the **Trace name** and select **Blank** template for the **Use the template:** drop-down menu as shown in following:

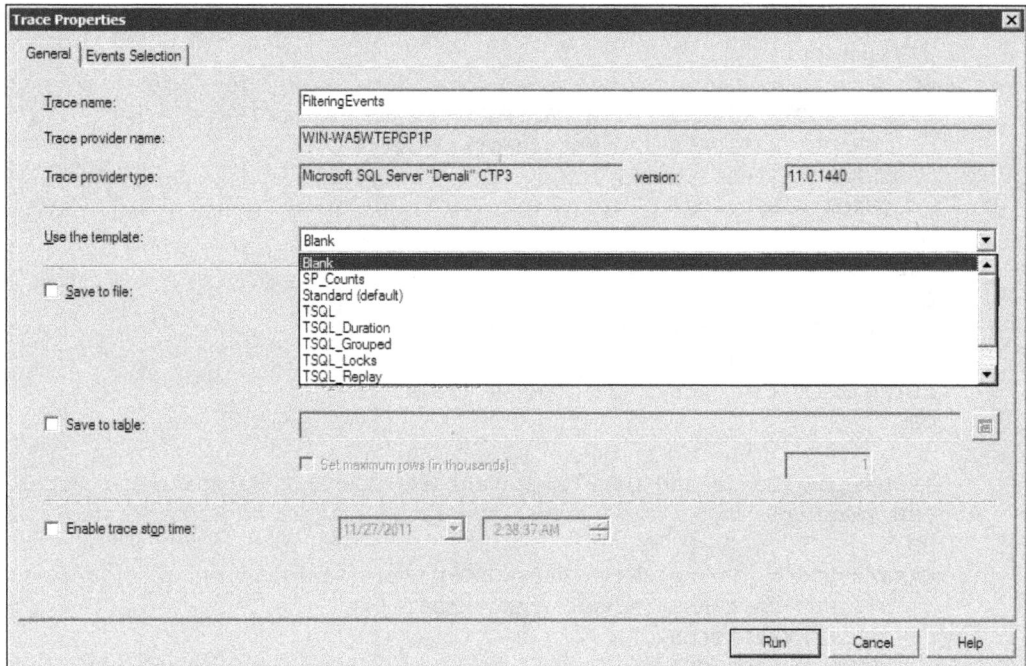

4. In **Events Selection** tab, check the checkbox for event class **SQL:BatchCompleted** under the **TSQL** event category as shown in following screenshot:

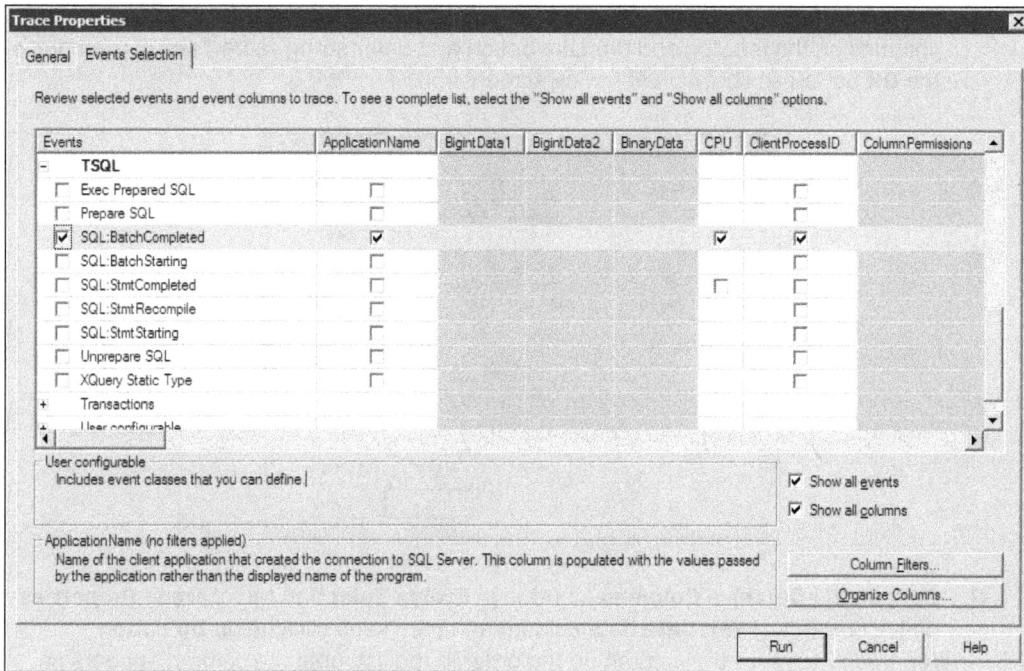

5. Click on **Column Filters...** button.

6. In the **Edit Filter** dialog box, select **DatabaseName** from the list of available data columns on the left. Expand the **Like** option and enter string value `AdventureWorks2012`; then press the **OK** button as shown in the following screenshot:

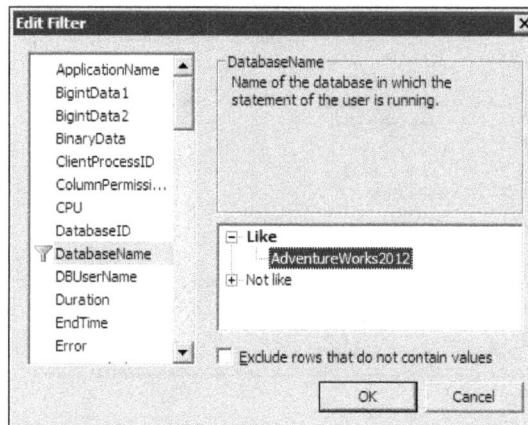

7. In the **Edit Filter** dialog box, select **SessionLoginName** from the list of available data columns on the left. Expand the **Like** option and enter string value James; then press the **OK** button as shown in following screenshot:

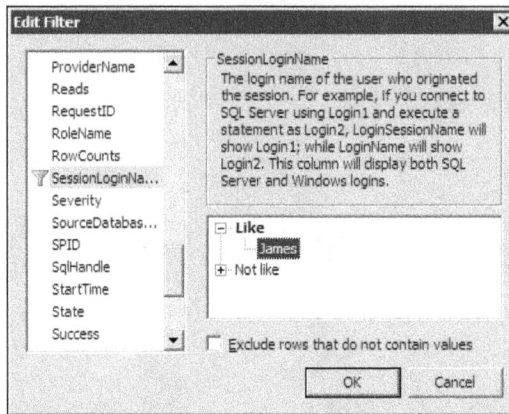

8. Click on the **Organize Columns...** button in **Events Selection** tab of **Trace Properties** dialog box. Select **TextData** data column and then keep clicking on **Up** button repeatedly to move the column up the order in the list, until the column appears as the second item, at the top of the list underneath **EventClass** data column. Do this same exercise also for the data columns **DatabaseName** and **SessionLoginName** so that the final order of the data columns should look like as shown in following screenshot. Press **OK** in the **Organize Columns** dialog box:

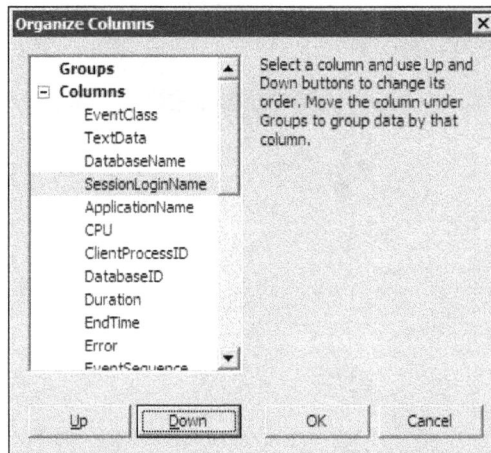

9. Click on the **Run** button to run the trace in the **Trace Properties** dialog box.

Now, we will open two instances of SQL Server Management Studio one by one that connect to SQL Server with the logins *James* and *Peter* respectively and run a few queries.

1. Open the first instance of SSMS and connect to SQL Server with the login credentials of *James*. In the query window, type and execute the T-SQL statements as shown in following script:

```
USE [AdventureWorks2012]
GO


SELECT * FROM [Sales].[Customer]
GO


USE [master]
GO


SELECT * FROM sys.databases
GO
```

2. Open a second instance of SSMS and connect to SQL Server with the login credentials of *Peter*. In the query window, type and execute the same T-SQL queries as shown in previous step.

3. Switch to SQL Server Profiler window that is running the trace. Examine the trace data as shown in following screenshot:

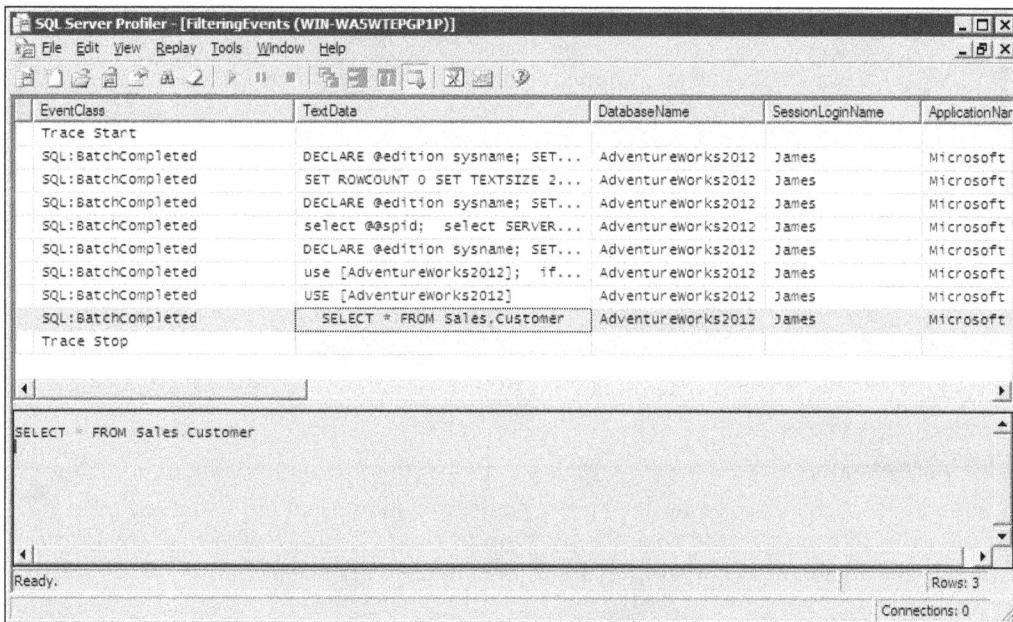

How it works...

In this recipe, we first created two SQL Server logins and their corresponding users in AdventureWorks2012 database to demonstrate how to apply a trace filter based on a specific SQL Server login, so that the events belonging to SQL Server logins other than the one for which the filter condition on **SessionLoginName** is satisfied are not captured. We executed a T-SQL script to create logins and users for *James* and *Peter*. For a login/user, the script first creates an SQL Server login account by the executing T-SQL statement—**CREATE LOGIN**. It then creates a user in the AdventureWorks2012 database for that login and adds the user to the **db_owner** database role by executing the T-SQL commands **CREATE USER** and **ALTER ROLE** respectively.

After creating logins and users, we started a new trace in SQL Server Profiler. We selected a **Blank** trace template and chose **SQL:BatchCompleted** event class as the only event that will be captured. Then we specified filters on **DatabaseName** and **SessionLoginName** data columns so that only the events which are occurred against AdventureWorks2012 database by user *James* are captured. We also organized the data columns in the **Organize Columns** dialog box, so that we can have better view of data columns we are interested in when trace data is displayed in SQL Server Profiler; we do not have to scroll much across the right side to see the values of **TextData**, **DatabaseName**, and **SessionLoginName**.

> **Use of DatabaseID**
>
> We can alternatively use **DatabaseID** data column instead of **DatabaseName** to specify a filter on a particular database. For this, we must know system assigned ID value for a specific database. This value can be retrieved by either calling DB_ID('AdventureWorks2012') metadata function or querying sys.databases catalog view.

After starting the trace, we opened two instances of SSMS out of which one instance connects with the login *James* and another one connects with the login *Peter*. In both the instances of SSMS, we run a few sample queries against the AdventureWorks2012 and master database.

We can see the resulting trace data as shown in final screenshot. Notice that events belonging to login *Peter* and the events occurred for master database were not captured.

There's more...

In a real world scenario, you may need to put filters on columns that are frequently used in trace filters to narrow down the data that you have to look at for troubleshooting. The following section lists some of data columns that are commonly used in trace filters:

▶ **ApplicationName**: A filter can be specified on this data column so that only trace events raised by a particular client application are captured

- ▸ **DatabaseID**: A filter can be specified on this data column so that only trace events raised for a specific database are captured

- ▸ **DatabaseName**: A filter can be specified on this data column so that only trace events raised for a specific database are captured

- ▸ **HostName**: A filter can be specified on this data column so that only trace events raised from a specific host or client machine are captured

- ▸ **LoginName**: A filter can be specified on this data column so that only trace events raised by a specific login are captured

- ▸ **ObjectID**: A filter can be specified on this data column so that only trace events raised for a specific object are captured

- ▸ **ObjectName**: A filter can be specified on this data column so that only trace events raised for a specific object are captured

- ▸ **SessionLoginName**: A filter can be specified on this data column so that only trace events raised by a specific login are captured

- ▸ **SPID**: A filter can be specified on this data column so that only trace events raised from a specific session connection are captured

LoginName and **SessionLoginName** may look identical at first. However, there is a small difference between them.

By using EXECUTE AS syntax in SQL Server, we can execute T-SQL statements in the same session under different security context other than the security context of the login who actually initiates the session/connection. For example, *James* can login to SQL Server and run a query under security context of *Peter* by using EXECUTE AS command. In this case, data column **SessionLoginName** returns **James**, while **LoginName** data column returns **Peter**. In other cases, where SQL Statements are not executed under different security context, data columns **SessionLoginName** and **LoginName** return the same value.

Detecting slow running and expensive queries

Quite a few times, you may come across database related performance issues that are caused by slow running and expensive queries. Slow running queries or expensive queries are queries that have longer execution time and consume more hardware resources, such as CPU, memory, and disk I/O. For instance, suppose that you are working for an organization having an enterprise application environment with high degree of database transaction activity against single production database that is used to support many applications, it is usual to face database performance issues due to a poorly designed application or poorly written queries.

For example, an application that processes one record at a time and makes a round trip to SQL server for each record is an example of poorly designed application when it is possible to process multiple records in batch and send them to database server in one go. Similarly, a query can be considered to be poorly written if is not optimized for efficient read/write operations, generates sub-optimum execution plan, and takes longer to execute. One common example of a poorly written query is the one which processes records row-by–row, using cursor to perform a task that can be accomplished by a set-based query.

When there are a few hundreds of query requests per second coming from different applications hitting the same database continuously, how would you identify those slow running and expensive queries?

Of course, you can use Dynamic Management Views or Activity Monitor to perform such an investigation. However, SQL Profiler will give you more insight into the execution flow of different applications because you can see the actual order and sequence of incoming query requests in real-time along with their execution statistics that can help you in identifying the performance related issues caused by any possible loopholes in application logic.

Getting ready

Remember that the objective of this recipe is not to teach you how to write efficient queries but instead how to identify expensive queries. Thus, for demonstration purposes, we ourselves will write a few expensive queries that take longer to execute in this example.

But before you can identify these slow running queries, you need to know what to look in SQL Server Profiler to identify those queries.

Whenever there is problem with the logic of the query, there is a possibility that the queries may start to take longer to execute as the database starts to grow. This results in holding locks on resources for a longer time, which can lead blockage to other queries. Poorly written queries also produce bad execution plans and can cause a high number of read/write operations that are expensive and take longer to execute.

So, when you are identifying long running queries, mostly you will be looking at time duration and CPU time that a query takes and the number of read/write operations that a query causes.

Therefore, in this recipe we will look at the following data columns:

- ▶ **CPU**: Amount of CPU processing time in milliseconds taken by an event
- ▶ **Duration**: Total amount of time in microseconds taken by an event
- ▶ **StartTime**: Time when an event starts
- ▶ **EndTime**: Time when an event ends
- ▶ **Reads**: Number of data pages that SQL Server has to read for an event
- ▶ **Writes**: Number of data pages that SQL Server has to write on disk for an event

The following are the prerequisites to do this recipe:

- An instance of SQL Server 2012 Developer or Enterprise Evaluation edition
- An SQL Server Login account with administrative rights
- Sample AdventureWorks2012 database on the instance of SQL Server

How to do it...

Follow the steps provided here for this recipe:

1. Start SQL Server Profiler. To start SQL Server Profiler, navigate through **Start | All Programs | Microsoft SQL Server 2012 Program Group | Performance Tools | SQL Server Profiler**.

2. Select **New Trace...** from the **File** menu. In the **Connect to Server** dialog box, provide connection details of SQL Server hosting the AdventureWorks2012 database and click on **Connect**.

3. In the **General** tab of **Trace Properties**, specify `IdentifyingExpensiveQueries` as trace name and select **Blank** template for the **Use the template:** drop-down menu.

4. Check the checkbox **Save to file:** and specify a trace file name and location in the **Save As** dialog box.

5. In the **Events Selection** tab, check the checkbox for event class **SQL:BatchCompleted** under TSQL event category.

6. Click on the **Column Filters...** button.

7. In the **Edit Filter** dialog box, select **DatabaseName** from the list of available data columns on the left. Expand the **Like** option and enter string value `AdventureWorks2012`; then click on the **OK** button.

8. Click on **Organize Columns...** button in **Events Selection** tab of **Trace Properties** dialog box. Select **TextData** data column and then keep clicking the **Up** button repeatedly to move the column up the order in the list until the column appears as the second item at the top of the list underneath **EventClass** data column. Do this same exercise also for data columns, such as **CPU**, **Duration**, **StartTime**, **Endtime**, **Reads**, and **Writes** so that they appear underneath the **TextData** column. Press **OK** in the **Organize Columns** dialog box.

9. Open SQL Server Management Studio and connect to SQL Server.

10. Click on the **Run** button to run the trace in **Trace Properties** dialog box.

11. Type and execute the following T-SQL script. The script creates a stored procedure `usp_calculateOrderTotals` in AdventureWorks2012 database and a table `tbl_SampleData` by generating and inserting five million sample records:

```
USE [AdventureWorks2012]
GO
```

```
--Drop the stored procedure if it exists.
IF OBJECT_ID('[dbo].[usp_CalculateOrderTotals]') IS NOT NULL
  DROP PROCEDURE [dbo].[usp_CalculateOrderTotals]
GO
--Creates the stored procedure.
CREATE PROCEDURE [dbo].[usp_CalculateOrderTotals] AS
BEGIN
  CREATE TABLE [tempdb].[dbo].[#tbl_OrderTotals]
  (
    SRNo INT IDENTITY(1,1) PRIMARY KEY CLUSTERED
    ,OrderID INT
    ,OrderDate DATETIME
    ,CustomerName NVARCHAR(200)
    ,SalesPersonName NVARCHAR(200)
    ,OrderTotal NUMERIC(38,6)
  )

  DECLARE @SalesOrderID INT
  DECLARE @OrderDate DATETIME
  DECLARE @CustomerName NVARCHAR(200)
  DECLARE @SalesPersonName NVARCHAR(200)
  DECLARE @OrderTotal NUMERIC(38,6)

  DECLARE curSalesOrders CURSOR FAST_FORWARD FOR
    SELECT
      SOH.SalesOrderID
      ,SOH.OrderDate
      ,UPPER(P2.FirstName + ' ' + P2.LastName) AS CustomerName
      ,UPPER(P1.FirstName + ' ' + P1.LastName) AS SalesPersonName
    FROM [Sales].[SalesOrderHeader] AS SOH
    LEFT OUTER JOIN [Sales].[SalesPerson] AS SP
    ON SOH.SalesPersonID = SP.BusinessEntityID
    LEFT OUTER JOIN [Sales].[Customer] AS C
    ON SOH.CustomerID = C.CustomerID
    LEFT OUTER JOIN [Person].[Person] AS P1
    ON SP.BusinessEntityID = P1.BusinessEntityID
    LEFT OUTER JOIN [Person].[Person] AS P2
    ON C.PersonID = P2.BusinessEntityID

  OPEN curSalesOrders

  FETCH NEXT FROM curSalesOrders INTO
    @SalesOrderID
    ,@OrderDate
```

```
        ,@CustomerName
        ,@SalesPersonName

    WHILE @@FETCH_STATUS=0
    BEGIN

        SELECT @OrderTotal=SUM(LineTotal) FROM [Sales].
[SalesOrderDetail]
        WHERE SalesOrderID = @SalesOrderID

        INSERT INTO [tempdb].[dbo].[#tbl_OrderTotals]
        VALUES
        (
          @SalesOrderID
          ,@OrderDate
          ,@CustomerName
          ,@SalesPersonName
          ,@OrderTotal
        )
        FETCH NEXT FROM curSalesOrders INTO
          @SalesOrderID
          ,@OrderDate
          ,@CustomerName
          ,@SalesPersonName
    END
    CLOSE curSalesOrders
    DEALLOCATE curSalesOrders

    SELECT * FROM [tempdb].[dbo].[#tbl_OrderTotals]
    ORDER BY OrderID DESC
END

GO
--Excutes stored procedure.
EXECUTE [dbo].[usp_CalculateOrderTotals]
GO
--Drop the table if it exists
IF OBJECT_ID('[dbo].[tblSampleData]') IS NOT NULL
  DROP TABLE [dbo].[tblSampleData]
GO
--Generate 5 million records and insert them into a table.
SELECT TOP 5000000 C1.*
INTO [dbo].[tblSampleData]
FROM sys.columns AS C1
```

```
CROSS JOIN sys.columns AS C2
CROSS JOIN sys.columns AS C3

GO
```

12. After executing the previous script, switch to SQL Server Profiler and stop the trace. Notice the **CPU**, **Duration**, **StartTime**, **EndTime**, **Reads**, and **Write** columns. The following screenshot shows the trace after execution of the script:

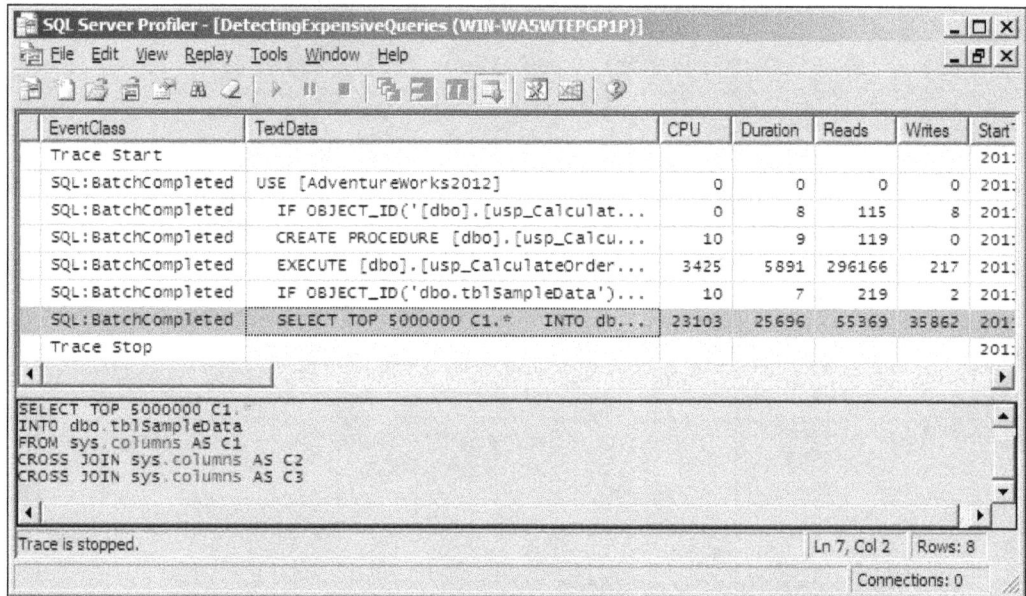

EventClass	TextData	CPU	Duration	Reads	Writes	Start
Trace Start						201:
SQL:BatchCompleted	USE [AdventureWorks2012]	0	0	0	0	201:
SQL:BatchCompleted	IF OBJECT_ID('[dbo].[usp_Calculat...	0	8	115	8	201:
SQL:BatchCompleted	CREATE PROCEDURE [dbo].[usp_Calcu...	10	9	119	0	201:
SQL:BatchCompleted	EXECUTE [dbo].[usp_CalculateOrder...	3425	5891	296166	217	201:
SQL:BatchCompleted	IF OBJECT_ID('dbo.tblSampleData')...	10	7	219	2	201:
SQL:BatchCompleted	SELECT TOP 5000000 C1.* INTO db...	23103	25696	55369	35862	201:
Trace Stop						201:

```
SELECT TOP 5000000 C1.*
INTO dbo.tblSampleData
FROM sys.columns AS C1
CROSS JOIN sys.columns AS C2
CROSS JOIN sys.columns AS C3
```

Trace is stopped.   Ln 7, Col 2   Rows: 8   Connections: 0

Notice in the figure, how some of the **SQL:BatchCompleted** events caused high number of CPU usage counts, duration counts, and reads/writes counts. These queries are resource consuming and thus expensive queries.

How it works...

We started a new trace in SQL Server Profiler. We selected **Blank** trace template and **SQL:BatchCompleted** event class that is the only event we wanted to capture. We then specified a trace filter on **DatabaseName** data column so that only the events which are occurred against AdventureWorks2012 database are captured.

We organized data columns in the **Organize Columns** dialog box so we can have a better view of data columns that we are interested in when trace data is displayed in SQL Server Profiler; we do not have to scroll much across the right side to see the values of **TextData**, **CPU**, **Duration**, **StartTime**, **Endtime**, **Reads**, and **Writes** data columns.

Trace Filter on CPU or Duration

We could also have put a trace filter on **CPU** or **Duration** data column with > (greater than) operator in order to capture only those events whose CPU or duration count is higher than the value specified in trace filter. With this, let's say for example, if you want to find out the queries that are taking total execution time of 10 seconds or more, then you can define a filter on **Duration** column and only those queries running for 10 seconds or more will be captured.

After starting trace, we opened SSMS and connected to SQL Server. We then run sample script against AdventureWorks2012 database. The script creates and executes a sample stored procedure named [AdventureWorks2012].[dbo].[usp_CalculateOrderTotals] that loops through a cursor to calculate the total for an order and inserts it in a temporary table. Looking at **CPU** and **Duration** data columns, it can be noticed that stored procedure took almost around six seconds to execute. Also, the **Reads** data column has high value and suggests that SQL Server had to read **296166** data pages to run this stored procedure. Higher the reads and writes counts are, slower the query will be. When the stored procedure [AdventureWorks2012].[dbo].[usp_CalculateOrderTotals] is executed to retrieve the requested data with required columns along with the required calculation, it performed a read operation on the following tables:

- ▸ Sales.SalesOrderHeader
- ▸ Sales.SalesPerson
- ▸ Sales.Customer
- ▸ Person.Person
- ▸ #tbl_OrderTotals

The script also generates five million sample records by cross joining sys.columns catalog view with itself multiple times and inserting the resulting data in tblSampleData table by SELECT...INTO command. This demonstrates how the writes count gets high when large amount of data is inserted. You can see that it caused **55369** reads and **35862** writes counts.

Remember that value in **CPU** data column is reported in milliseconds and the value in **Duration** data column is reported in microseconds. However, when SQL Server Profiler shows the value of **Duration** on its GUI, it shows the value in milliseconds by default. But when you save the trace in a trace file or trace table the value is stored in microseconds and not in milliseconds. Thus, for the **Duration** data column SQL Server behaves differently when it displays and stores the value.

You can change the way SQL Server displays the value of Duration so that it is reported in microsecond instead of millisecond on GUI if you wish so. You can change this setting from **Tools | Options....**

There's more...

If you are performing the task of identifying expensive queries on frequent basis, you may want to use the same trace definition each time you run a trace. It's convenient to save our trace definition as a trace template and use that template each time we run a trace.

Trace templates

Trace templates are the files that save the trace definition and trace properties. SQL Server Profiler comes with some default trace templates. They are as follows:

- **Blank**
- **SP_Counts**
- **Standard**
- **TSQL**
- **TSQL_Duration**
- **TSQL_Grouped**
- **TSQL_Locks**
- **TSQL_Replay**
- **TSQL_SPs**
- **Tuning**

Each of the above trace templates has its own trace definition that can be used to start a new trace. However, there are chances that the in-built templates may not have the settings which you require for your regular task.

In this type of situation, creating and using trace template should be a practical thing. The trace definition and settings that you normally use on regular basis or frequently can be saved in a trace template file. For this, you just need to save a trace file as trace template in order to create it. Once a trace template is created, it can be used for other trace sessions later on and you do not need to perform the tedious task of playing with trace properties each time.

Creating trace with system stored procedures

What if you have no SQL Server Profiler installed on your machine and want to create a trace? What if you have SQL Server Profiler installed but the executable binary file of SQL Server Profiler is corrupted and cannot be run? What if you want to automate completely the process of capturing trace data as per your defined schedules so that you do not have to be physically present to start and stop the traces? Is it possible to create a trace in this manner without SQL Server Profiler?

The answer is yes. You can do this. SQL Server provides T-SQL system stored procedures to deal with SQL Trace. This capability enables us to write code that can create traces programmatically. By using SQL Trace system stored procedures along with SQL Agent, it is possible to automate and schedule the traces so that they run in background and capture event data during only certain period of time on a regular basis.

In this recipe, we will see how to create a trace without SQL Server Profiler by using SQL Trace system stored procedures. The trace that we will create in this recipe can be used to monitor the file growth of data files and log files of all databases on an instance of SQL Server. Monitoring file growth event for data files and log files will tell you how frequently your database files are grown that helps further in determining appropriate values for FILEGROWTH attribute of database files. If the size of files is increased by a smaller amount (for example, by 1 MB), SQL Server has to increase and extend the size of database files very frequently, which degrades the performance of write operations while working with large amount of data. It may also degrade the performance of read operations due to physical file fragmentation caused by small file chunks that are spread all over on the disk which makes a possible sequential read a random read. Thus, you should consider setting an appropriate FILEGROWTH value for your databases.

Getting ready

Before you start with the recipe, it is necessary that you have some background of basic system stored procedures provided in SQL Server which are used to work with traces. Following are the stored procedures which you should know:

- ▶ sp_trace_create: This stored procedure is used to create a trace and returns the ID of newly created trace
- ▶ sp_trace_setevent: This stored procedure is used to add or remove event classes and data columns to and from a given trace
- ▶ sp_trace_setfilter: This stored procedure is used to set a filter condition on desired data column for a given trace
- ▶ sp_trace_setstatus: This stored procedure is used to start, stop, or close a given trace

In this example, we will capture only two event classes:

- ▶ Data File Auto Grow
- ▶ Log File Auto Grow

For these mentioned event classes, we will be capturing the following data columns:

- ▶ **DatabaseName**
- ▶ **FileName**
- ▶ **StartTime**
- ▶ **EndTime**

By collecting these data columns, we can know which database file is automatically grown for which database and when.

We will not apply any filter in this trace because we want to capture and audit the database file growth events for all databases on the server. Thus, stored procedure `sp_trace_setfilter` will not be used in our example.

How to do it...

Follow the steps provided here to create a trace with system stored procedures:

1. Start SQL Server Management Studio and connect to SQL Server.

2. In the query window, type and execute the following T-SQL script to create a new trace through system stored procedures:

```
DECLARE @ReturnCode INT
DECLARE @TraceID INT
DECLARE @Options INT = 2
DECLARE @TraceFile NVARCHAR(245) = 'C:\MyTraces\MyTestTrace'
DECLARE @MaxFileSize INT = 5
DECLARE @Event_DataFileAutoGrow INT = 92
DECLARE @Event_LogFileAutoGrow INT = 93
DECLARE @DataColumn_DatabaseName INT = 35
DECLARE @DataColumn_FileName INT = 36
DECLARE @DataColumn_StartTime INT = 14
DECLARE @DataColumn_EndTime INT = 15

DECLARE @On BIT = 1
DECLARE @Off BIT = 0

--Create a trace and collect the returned code.
EXECUTE @ReturnCode = sp_trace_create
  @traceid = @TraceID OUTPUT
  ,@options = @Options
  ,@tracefile = @TraceFile

--Check returned code is zero and no error occurred.
IF @ReturnCode = 0
BEGIN
  BEGIN TRY
    --Add DatabaseName column to DataFileAutoGrow event.
    EXECUTE sp_trace_setevent
    @traceid = @TraceID
    ,@eventid = @Event_DataFileAutoGrow
    ,@columnid = @DataColumn_DatabaseName
```

```
  ,@on = @On

  --Add FileName column to DataFileAutoGrow event.
  EXECUTE sp_trace_setevent
    @traceid = @TraceID
    ,@eventid = @Event_DataFileAutoGrow
    ,@columnid = @DataColumn_FileName
    ,@on = @On

  --Add StartTime column to DataFileAutoGrow event.
  EXECUTE sp_trace_setevent
    @traceid = @TraceID
    ,@eventid = @Event_DataFileAutoGrow
    ,@columnid=@DataColumn_StartTime
    ,@on = @On

  --Add EndTime column to DataFileAutoGrow event.
  EXECUTE sp_trace_setevent
    @traceid = @TraceID
    ,@eventid = @Event_DataFileAutoGrow
    ,@columnid = @DataColumn_EndTime
    ,@on = @On

  --Add DatabaseName column to LogFileAutoGrow event.
  EXECUTE sp_trace_setevent
    @traceid = @TraceID
    ,@eventid = @Event_LogFileAutoGrow
    ,@columnid = @DataColumn_DatabaseName
    ,@on = @On

  --Add FileName column to LogFileAutoGrow event.
  EXECUTE sp_trace_setevent
    @traceid = @TraceID
    ,@eventid = @Event_LogFileAutoGrow
    ,@columnid = @DataColumn_FileName
    ,@on = @On

  --Add StartTime column to LogFileAutoGrow event.
  EXECUTE sp_trace_setevent
    @traceid = @TraceID
    ,@eventid = @Event_LogFileAutoGrow
    ,@columnid=@DataColumn_StartTime
    ,@on = @On
```

```
        --Add EndTime column to LogFileAutoGrow event.
        EXECUTE sp_trace_setevent
          @traceid = @TraceID
          ,@eventid = @Event_LogFileAutoGrow
          ,@columnid = @DataColumn_EndTime
          ,@on = @On

        --Start the trace. Status 1 corresponds to START.
        EXECUTE sp_trace_setstatus
          @traceid = @TraceID
          ,@status = 1
    END TRY
    BEGIN CATCH
      PRINT 'An error occurred while creating trace.'
    END CATCH
  END
  GO
```

> It is possible that the stored procedure sp_trace_create may
> fail if the windows account under which the SQL Server Service
> is running has no write permission on the directory where the
> trace file is created. If this is the case, then you will need to assign
> proper permissions to the login account so that it can write to the
> specified directory.

3. By executing the following query and observing the result set, make sure that the trace has been created successfully. This query should return a record for the trace that we created:

```
--Verify the trace has been created.
SELECT * FROM sys.traces
GO
```

4. The previous query will give you the list of traces that are currently running on the system. You should see your newly created trace listed in the result set of the previous query. If the trace could be created successfully, execute the following T-SQL script to create a sample database and insert one million records:

```
--Creating Sample Database keeping Filegrowth Size
--to 1 MB for Data and Log file.
CREATE DATABASE [SampeDBForTrace] ON  PRIMARY
(
  NAME = N'SampeDB'
  ,FILENAME = N'C:\MyTraces\SampeDBForTrace_Data.mdf'
  ,SIZE = 2048KB , FILEGROWTH = 1024KB
)
```

```
LOG ON
(
  NAME = N'SampeDBForTrace_log'
  ,FILENAME = N'C:\MyTraces\SampeDBForTrace_log.ldf'
  ,SIZE = 1024KB , FILEGROWTH = 1024KB
)
GO

USE SampeDBForTrace
GO

--Creating and Inserting one million records tbl_SampleData table.
SELECT TOP 1000000 C1.*
INTO tbl_SampleData
FROM sys.columns AS C1
CROSS JOIN sys.columns AS C2
CROSS JOIN sys.columns AS C3
GO
```

5. After executing the previous script, execute the following T-SQL script to stop and close the trace:

```
DECLARE @TraceID INT
DECLARE @TraceFile NVARCHAR(245) = 'C:\MyTraces\MyTestTrace.trc'

--Get the TraceID for our trace.
SELECT @TraceID = id FROM sys.traces
WHERE path = @TraceFile

IF @TraceID IS NOT NULL
BEGIN
  --Stop the trace. Status 0 corroponds to STOP.
  EXECUTE sp_trace_setstatus
    @traceid = @TraceID
    ,@status = 0

  --Closes the trace. Status 2 corroponds to CLOSE.
  EXECUTE sp_trace_setstatus
    @traceid = @TraceID
    ,@status = 2
END
GO
```

6. Execute the following query to verify that the trace has been stopped and closed successfully. This query should not return a record for our trace if it is stopped and closed successfully.

```
--Verify the trace has been stopped and closed.
SELECT * FROM sys.traces
GO
```

7. The previous query will not return the row for the trace that we created because the trace has now been stopped and closed. Inspect the resulting trace data collected in our trace file by executing the following query:

```
--Retrieve the collected trace data.
SELECT
   TE.name AS TraceEvent
   ,TD.DatabaseName
   ,TD.FileName
   ,TD.StartTime
   ,TD.EndTime
FROM fn_trace_gettable('C:\MyTraces\MyTestTrace.trc',default) AS
TD
LEFT JOIN sys.trace_events AS TE
ON TD.EventClass = TE.trace_event_id
GO
```

How it works...

In this recipe, we first created and configured our trace by executing a T-SQL script. The script first declares some required variables whose values are passed as parameters to system stored procedures. It creates a trace by executing the `sp_trace_create` stored procedure that returns ID of the newly created trace. The stored procedure `sp_trace_create` accepts the following parameters:

- ▸ `@traceid OUTPUT`
- ▸ `@options`
- ▸ `@tracefile`

The `@Options` parameter is passed to specify the trace options. The following are the predefined values for the `@Options` parameter:

- ▸ 2: `TRACE_FILE_ROLLOVER`
- ▸ 4: `SHUTDOWN_ON_ERROR`
- ▸ 8: `TRACE_PRODUCE_BLACKBOX`

The parameter `@TraceFile` specifies the location and file name where the trace file should be saved. `@TraceID` is the output variable and the returned ID value of the trace will be stored in this variable. If the stored procedure can create a trace file successfully, it returns `0` that gets stored in variable `@ReturnCode`.

Remember that all SQL Trace system stored procedures are strictly typed. By saying strictly typed, it means that the data types of the parameters that you pass to these stored procedures must match exactly with the data types of stored procedures' parameter definition. So, you cannot pass a parameter of type INT when BIGINT is required.

If trace is created successfully and `@ReturnCode` is zero, then we add event classes and data columns by calling stored procedure `sp_trace_setevent` for each combination of event class and data column one-by-one for following event classes and data columns:

▶ `DataFileAutoGrow` event class and **DatabaseName** data column

▶ `DataFileAutoGrow` event class and **FileName** data column

▶ `DataFileAutoGrow` event class and **StartTime** data column

▶ `DataFileAutoGrow` event class and **EndTime** data column

▶ `LogFileAutoGrow` event class and **DatabaseName** data column

▶ `LogFileAutoGrow` event class and **FileName** data column

▶ `LogFileAutoGrow` event class and **StartTime** data column

▶ `LogFileAutoGrow` event class and **EndTime** data column

Stored procedure accepts the following parameters:

▶ `@traceid`

▶ `@eventid`

▶ `@columnid`

▶ `@on`

`@TraceID` is the ID of the trace we add event classes and data columns to.

Note that every event classes and data columns have their associated event IDs and column IDs. We have to pass these ID values corresponding to event classes and data columns that we want to include in our trace. These values are passed by appropriate variables declared for each event class and data column. For example, for `DataFileAutoGrow` event class and **FileName** data column we have stored their appropriate ID values in `@Event_DataFileAutoGrow` and `@DataColumn_FileName` variables respectively.

> **How to get IDs for all event classes and data columns?**
>
> ID values for required event classes and data columns must be passed to the stored procedure `sp_trace_setevent`. You can get a list of EventIDs for all event classes by querying `sys.trace_events` system catalog view. To get a list of column IDs for all data columns, use `sys.trace_columns` system catalog view. Also, you can retrieve list of column IDs for all available columns for a given event by querying `sys.trace_event_bindings` system catalog view and by joining it with `sys.trace_events` and `sys.trace_columns` system catalog views on `trace_event_id` and `trace_column_id` columns respectively.

The value of @ on parameter value can be either 0 or 1 where the value 1 means that event data for specified event class and data column should be captured otherwise not.

After adding the required event classes and data columns, the stored procedure `sp_trace_setstatus` is used to set the status of the trace to START. Any trace that is created with system stored procedure is always in STOP state by default, and needs to be started explicitly by calling `sp_trace_setstatus` stored procedure. This stored procedure accepts the following parameters:

- ▸ `@traceid`
- ▸ `@status`

@TraceID is the ID of the trace we created and need to be started. @Status specifies the state of the trace. Possible values for @Status parameter are as follows:

- ▸ 0: Stops a trace
- ▸ 1: Starts a trace
- ▸ 2: Closes a trace

Because we wanted to start our trace, we are passing a value of 1 to this parameter.

SQL Server keeps track of currently opened trace sessions. This list of traces can be retrieved by querying `sys.traces` system catalog view. We just make sure by querying this view that the trace is indeed created.

Next, we create a sample database named `SampleDBTrace`. We deliberately keep the value of FILEGROWTH attribute smaller in order to be able to produce Data File Auto Growth and Log File Auto Growth events. The script also creates a sample table named `tbl_SampleData` though SELECT ... INTO statement in which we insert one million sample records by cross joining `sys.columns` system catalog view with itself multiple times. This operation requires additional space in data and log files to make room for inserting new records. For this, SQL Server has to increase the size of data and log files when required by one MB (specified value for the FILEGROWTH attribute). This causes DataFileAutoGrowth and LogFileAutoGrowth events to be raised.

> We deliberately kept the value of the `FILEGROWTH` attribute as smaller as 1 MB in order to demonstrate this recipe. Setting value of the `FILEGROWTH` attribute this small is just for the sake of being able to produce the desired file growth events. Such small value for the `FILEGROWTH` attribute is not recommended and should not be used on production server with heavy DML operations.

Once the record insertion operation is completed, the script is executed to stop and close the trace by again calling the stored procedure `sp_trace_setstatus` twice with the appropriate status value for each call. Remember that to close a trace, it should be stopped first. So, a trace should be stopped first before it can be closed.

After closing a trace, we make sure that the trace stopped and closed successfully by querying `sys.traces` system catalog view again.

Once our trace is stopped, we use `fn_trace_gettable()` function to query the captured trace data saved in specified trace file whose full file path is also being passed to the function for the first parameter `filename`. We also pass the default value for the second parameter `number_files` of the function which specifies that the function should read all rollover files to return trace data. Because this function does not return any column for the event class' name, we join it with `sys.trace_events` system catalog view on IDs of event classes in order to fetch the names of event classes.

> If you want to analyze large size of trace data containing large number of trace files, then you should specify 1 for `number_files` parameter. If you specify default, the SQL Server tries to load all trace files into memory and then inserts them into a table in a single operation, which may crash your system.

2

Tuning with Database Engine Tuning Advisor

In this chapter we will cover:

- ▶ Analyzing queries using Database Engine Tuning Advisor
- ▶ Running Database Engine Tuning Advisor for Workload
- ▶ Executing Database Tuning Advisor from command prompt

Introduction

Database Engine Tuning Advisor (**DTA**) suggests ways to tune the database by analyzing the Workload provided. DTA helps in creating an efficient index, an indexed view (if it's supported by the SQL Server Edition you are using), statistics, and partitions. DTA can give efficient suggestions only if you have created proper workload with sufficient data. For further details of creating workload, refer *Creating a trace or workload* recipe of *Chapter 1, Mastering SQL Trace Using Profiler*.

Studying an Estimated execution plan (covered in *Chapter 5, Monitoring with Execution Plans*) of query from Query Editor to find out the bottleneck and resolve it needs knowledge of the database structure as well as good command over performance tuning, whereas DTA offers a very simple solution to this. Just collect the proper workload, give it to DTA and it will analyze that Workload for you and suggests you the ways for tuning.

Sometimes it happens that we tune one query by creating/removing an index, which helps that query for performance but on the other hand, other SELECT or DML queries get hurt in terms of their performance. (More about indexes and their behavior is explained in *Chapter 9, Implementing Indexes* and *Chapter 10, Maintaining Indexes.)* DTA offers suggestion to this situation if you have collected proper workload of the queries that execute against the database we want to tune. By analysing the query included in workload, DTA suggests changes to index, the indexed view, statistics, and partitions to improve the overall performance

DTA won't provide efficient suggestions if an incomplete workload is provided to DTA. So make sure to include every possible query in workload before you load it to DTA for analyzing.

Workload is simply a collection of SQL statements that executes against the database(s). Refer *Creating a trace or workload* section of *Chapter 1* to know more about workload.

Analyzing queries using Database Engine Tuning Advisor

There are few different ways that can help you in providing workload to DTA. One of the popular ways is to ask DTA about the query you are designing at the moment for performance point of view, so that DTA can analyze the query and provide suggestions, if any.

Getting ready

We will need two tables to demonstrate this recipe. Here is the script to create the same:

```
USE AdventureWorks2012
GO

IF OBJECT_ID('ProductDemo') IS NOT NULL
  DROP TABLE ProductDemo
GO

IF OBJECT_ID('ProductModelDemo') IS NOT NULL
  DROP TABLE ProductModelDemo
GO

select * into ProductModelDemo from Production.ProductModel
select * into ProductDemo from Production.Product
GO
```

We have just created two tables, named `ProductDemo` and `ProductModelDemo`, which don't have any index or statistics right now.

How to do it...

Now here is the query we want to execute and tune if possible:

```
SELECT
    P.ProductID
    ,P.ProductModelID
FROM
    ProductDemo AS P
JOIN
    ProductModelDemo AS PM
ON
    P.ProductModelID=PM.ProductModelID
WHERE
    P.ProductID=680
GO
```

Here is the list of steps that we should follow in order to analyze the given query in DTA.

1. Write down the query in SSMS. Click on **Start | All Program | Microsoft SQL Server 2012 | SQL Server Management Studio (SSMS)** and try to execute it by pressing the *F5* key or the **execute** button from standard toolbar.

2. Select the query in SSMS and right-click on it.

3. Select the option **Analyze Query in Database Engine Tuning Advisor** from the pop up menu:

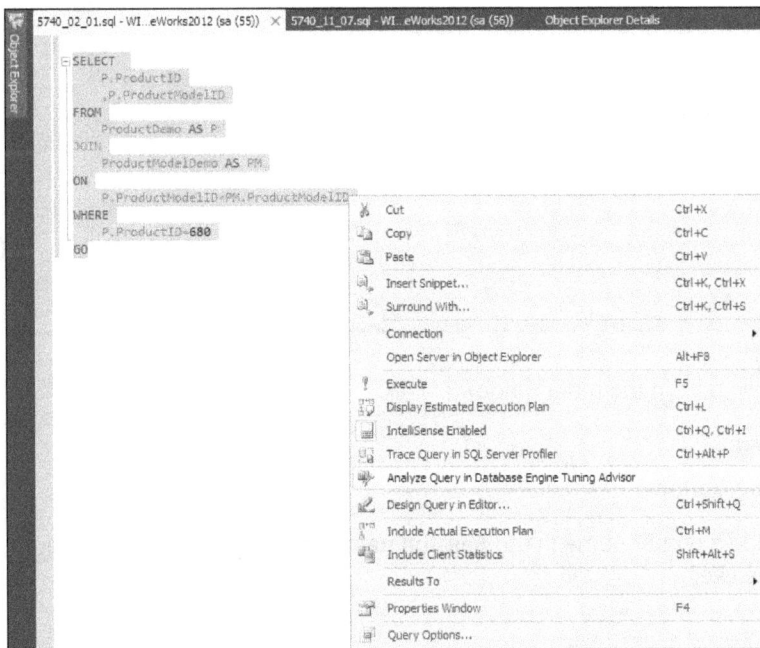

4. DTA opens and asks for the credentials to run the tool; provide the same credential, that is, Windows authentication or SQL authentication you use and open DTA. A piece of advise is to use Windows authentication. There could be long debate regarding pro and cons of each but let us make long story short by showing some key advantages of using Windows authentication. Windows authentication will shield your SQL Server installation from most Internet-based attacks by restricting connections to Microsoft Windows user and domain user accounts. Your server will also benefit from Windows security enforcement mechanisms, such as stronger authentication protocols, mandatory password, complexity, and expiration:

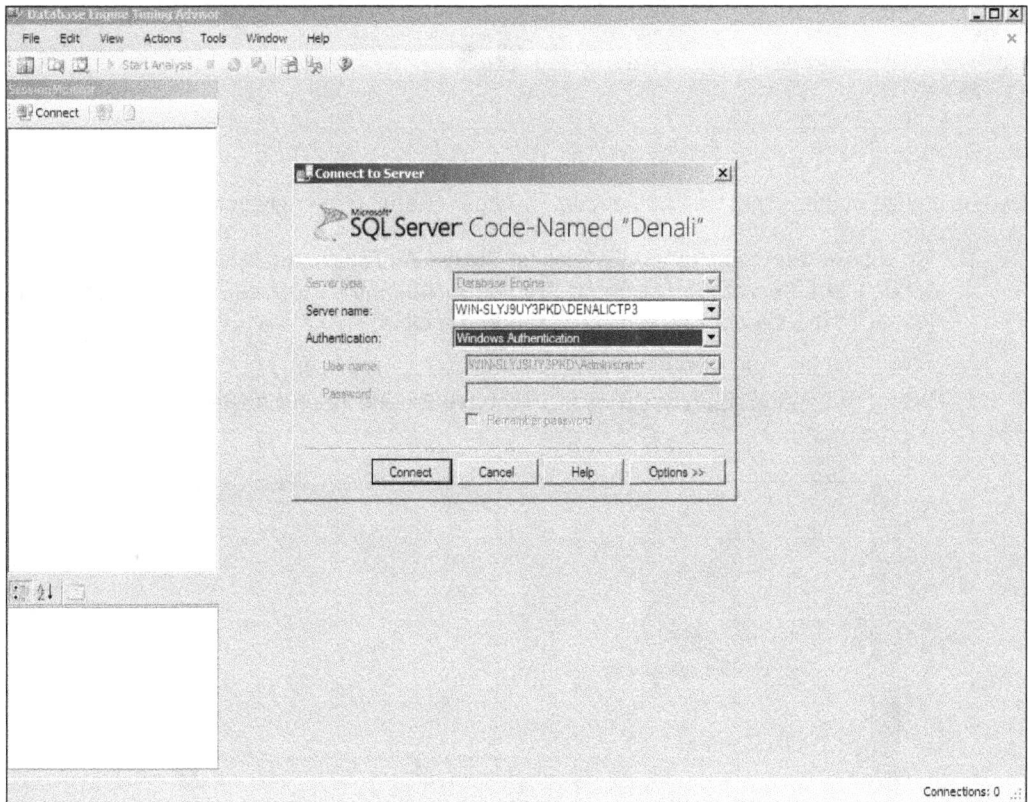

You will find two tabs in the main window of DTA:

▶ **General**

▶ **Tuning Options**

1. Provide a proper name in the **Session name** box for documentation purposes for future use:

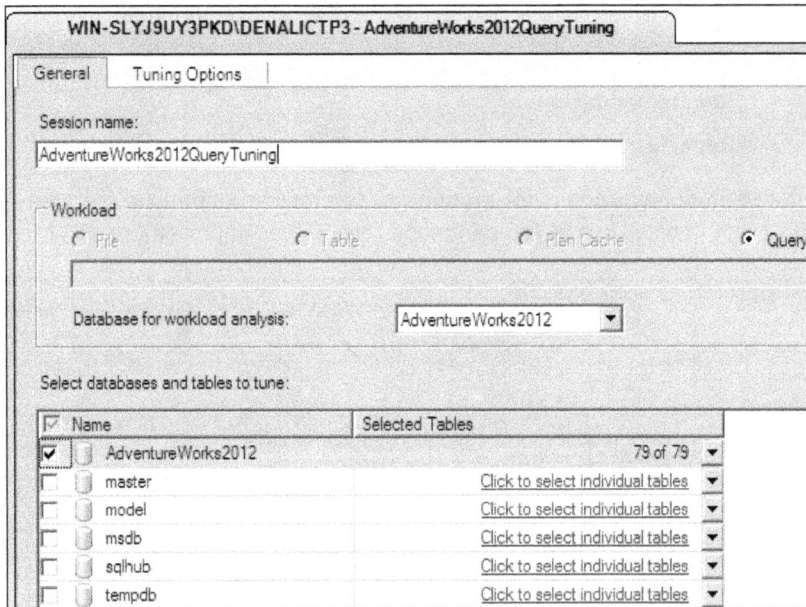

2. Now, click on the **Start Analysis** button under the **View** menu:

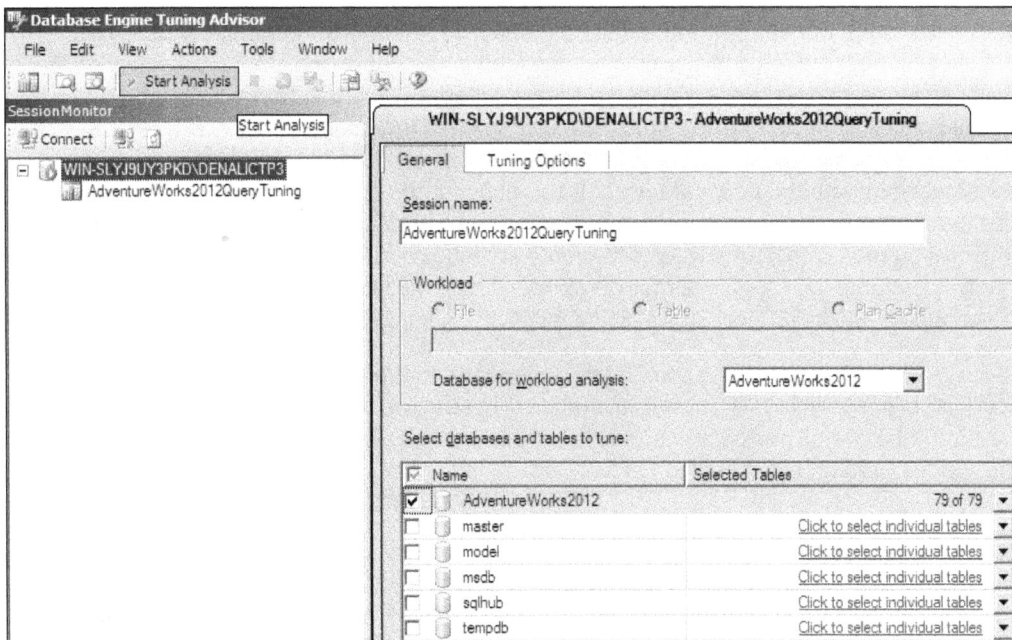

3. Once it finishes progress, you can see three new tabs on the main screen:

    ▶   **Progress**

    ▶   **Recommendations**

    ▶   **Reports**

4. In the **Recommendations** tab, it is showing two recommendations and also saying that by implementing all two recommendations, we will get improvement of 84 percent:

WIN-SLYJ9UY3PKD\DENALICTP3 - Administrator 29-03-2012 15:28:10								

General | Tuning Options | Progress | Recommendations | Reports

Estimated improvement: 84%

Partition Recommendations

Index Recommendations

✓	Database Name ▼	Object Name ▼	Recommendation	Target of Recommendation	D...	P...	Size (KB)	Definition
✓	AdventureWorks2...	[dbo].[ProductDemo]	create	_dta_index_ProductDemo_6_1684201050__K1_K...			8	[ProductID] asc, [ProductModelID] asc)
✓	AdventureWorks2...	[dbo].[ProductModelDemo]	create	_dta_index_ProductModelDemo_6_1668200993_...			8	[ProductModelID] asc)

5. There is a column **Definitions** on the right, which gives the exact syntax for creating index or statistics DTA suggests. In this case, it has suggested one statistics and two indexes.

How it works...

DTA analyzes the workload submitted to it; in our case, there is only one query provided. DTA checks the table structure, predicate provided in the query and statistics/histogram if available for predicates, and try to find out best suited way to execute the query, if it finds anything missing (such as index, statistics, and so on), DTA recommends it to create. Basically after submitting workload (or query), DTA goes through each table and view available in workload along with the predicate used. It searches for the available index, statistics, and partition scheme too (if selected) in order to prepare the suggestion list. If it doesn't find statistics on predicate, DTA suggests to create statistics and if statistic is out of date on a predicate column, DTA suggests that we update it. DTA also look for all available indexes on the predicate and if DTA finds any missing index, it will suggest to create it.

All suggestions given by DTA is completely dependent on the workload provided. If incomplete workload is provided to DTA, there is a chance that DTA would suggest something wrong that may harm the overall performance. So it's highly recommended that we check the suggestions carefully before implementing it.

> A word of caution: Before creating any index suggested by DTA, it is recommended to check the table and column that DTA suggests because index comes with little overhead on DML statement and index needs space to maintain itself. So it is better to first check whether the column that DTA suggests is worth the index or not.

Actually there is no index created at the moment on both the sample table we have created. So DTA is suggesting to create one composite non-clustered index on the **ProductDemo** table on **ProductID** and **ProductModelID** column so that both the predicate used from this table can get benefit of leaf pages of index, return the resultset faster and; that is how DTA calculated a performance improvement of 84 percent in the **Recommendations** tab. DTA is also suggesting to create one non-clustered index on the **ProductModelDemo** table so the **ProductModelID** column used as a predicate with join clause, can get benefit of fast searching from the index tree.

Running Database Engine Tuning Advisor for workload

Trace is a session during which the events are captured and event data is collected. SQL Server supports a few formats for saving this collected trace data, which is known as a workload. We can save trace data (a workload) in one of the following formats:

▸ A trace file with `.trc` extension name

▸ A trace file in XML format with `.xml` extension name

▸ A trace table in an SQL Server database

We are going to use trace file `.trc` for this recipe. For detailed information regarding trace, workload, and different events of trace in profiler, refer *Creating a trace or workload* recipe in *Chapter 1*.

In this recipe, we will create a trace with SQL Server Profiler; execute some queries that will be captured in running profiler trace file and load that trace file in Database Engine Tuning tool to analyze the workload.

> It is recommended to use server-side trace over profiler use on a production server as profiler can consume lot of network bandwidth resources whereas server-side trace consumes no network bandwidth resources, which is an ideal situation to go for in-production server, where many users and/or applications are connected.

Getting ready

Following are the prerequisites that you should fulfill:

▸ An instance of SQL Server 2012

▸ SQL Server Login account with administrative rights

▸ Sample AdventureWorks2012 database on the instance of SQL Server

▸ An instance of Database Engine Tuning Advisor

DTA can analyze workload or even a single query but analyzing a workload is one of the famous ways in DTA because a properly created workload has all different queries that we use to execute in the database, and wide range of query helps DTA to make good decision, based on the workload provided.

How to do it...

Follow the ensuing steps to create some sample tables in the AdventureWorks2012 database for demonstration:

1. Create a table `ordDemo` and insert some records into that table with the following script:

```
Use AdventureWorks2012
GO

--if orders table is already there. you can delete it than
--create new one with name "Orders"
IF OBJECT_ID('ordDemo', 'U') IS NOT NULL
BEGIN
        DROP TABLE ordDemo
END
GO

--creating table for demonstration
CREATE TABLE ordDemo (OrderID INT IDENTITY, OrderDate DATETIME,
Amount MONEY, Refno INT)
GO

--inserting 100000 sample rows into table
INSERT INTO ordDemo (OrderDate, Amount, Refno)
SELECT TOP 100000
        DATEADD(minute, ABS(a.object_id % 50000 ), CAST('2011-11-04'
AS DATETIME)),
        ABS(a.object_id % 10),
        CAST(ABS(a.object_id % 13) AS VARCHAR)
FROM sys.all_objects a
CROSS JOIN sys.all_objects b
GO
```

2. Create two more tables `ProductDemo` and `ProductModelDemo` from the existing table of our database AdventureWorks2012 with the help of the following script.

```
IF OBJECT_ID('ProductDemo') IS NOT NULL
  DROP TABLE ProductDemo
GO

IF OBJECT_ID('ProductModelDemo') IS NOT NULL
  DROP TABLE ProductModelDemo
GO
```

```
select * into ProductModelDemo from Production.ProductModel
select * into ProductDemo from Production.Product
GO
```

Follow the steps provided here to create a new trace:

1. Start SQL Server Profiler.

2. Select **New Trace...** from the **File** menu. In the **Connect to Server** dialog box, provide connection details of SQL Server hosting AdventureWorks2012 database and click on **Connect**.

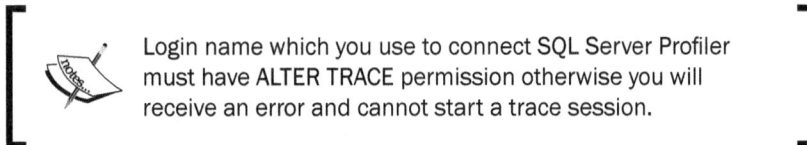

> Login name which you use to connect SQL Server Profiler must have ALTER TRACE permission otherwise you will receive an error and cannot start a trace session.

3. In the **General** tab of **Trace Properties** dialog box, specify `AdventureWorks2012Trace` as trace name. Use the **Standard (default)** trace template for **Use the template:** option.

4. Enable the checkbox **Save to file:** and specify a path, file name in the **Save As** dialog box; then click on Save, save file name as `AdventureWorks2012Trace.trc` file in the D drive.

5. Keep **Enable file rollover** checked and **Set maximum file size (MB):** to its default value 5. Refer the following screenshot, which shows the **General** tab of **Trace Properties** dialog box:

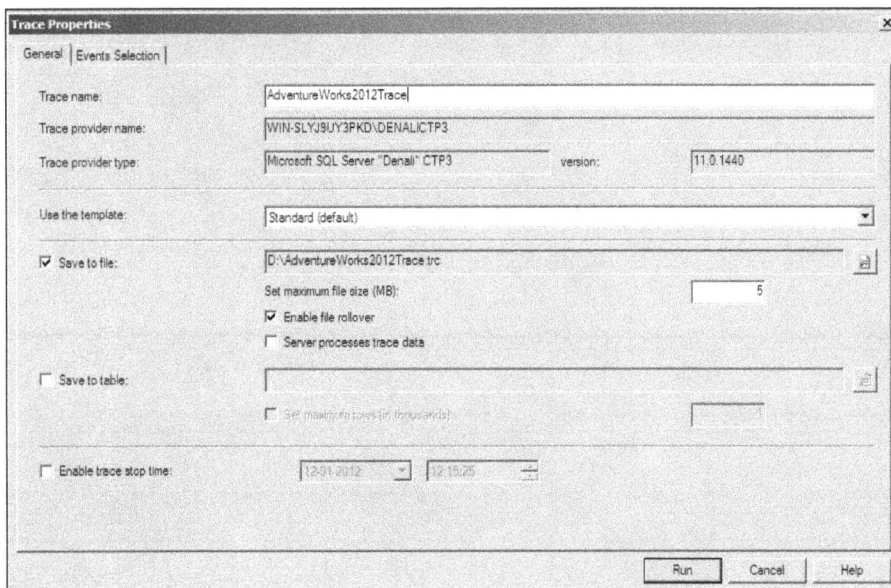

In the **Trace Properties** dialog box, there is a checkbox option in the **General** tab with the caption **Server processes trace data** to specify whether trace data should be processed on server. If not checked, trace data is processed on client.

When trace data is processed on client, it is possible for some events to be missed if the server load is high. If this option is checked, then trace data is processed on the server, and all the events included in trace definition are guaranteed to be captured without miss. However, this guarantee comes with performance penalty because processing trace data on server has an impact on performance of SQL Server and therefore, enabling this option is not recommended for production servers. Also, running SQL Server Profiler on production server itself should be avoided.

6. Click on the **Events Selection** tab. On this screen, the events that are predefined for **Standard (default)** trace template are selected and shown in grid. Enable the **Show all events** checkbox to show all events. Navigate through the event list until you find the **Stored Procedures** event category. Expand **Stored Procedures** event category if it is collapsed. Uncheck the checkbox for **RPC:Completed** event and enable the checkbox for **SP:Completed** event. Disable the **Show all events** checkbox to show only the selected events. The screen should now look similar to the following screenshot:

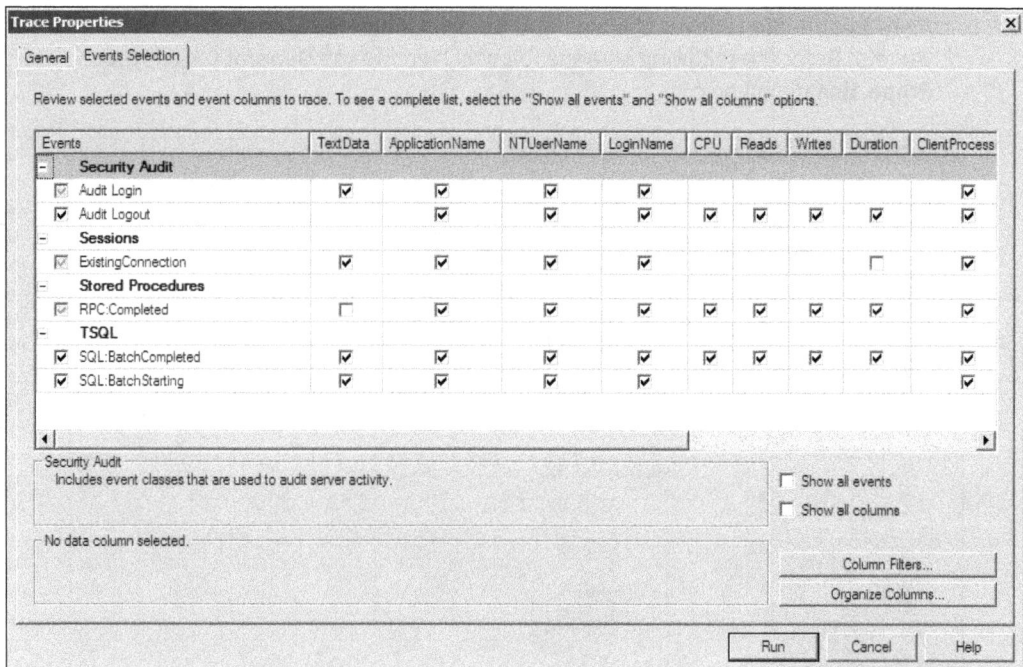

7. Details about **SP:Completed** event could be found in the following screenshot:

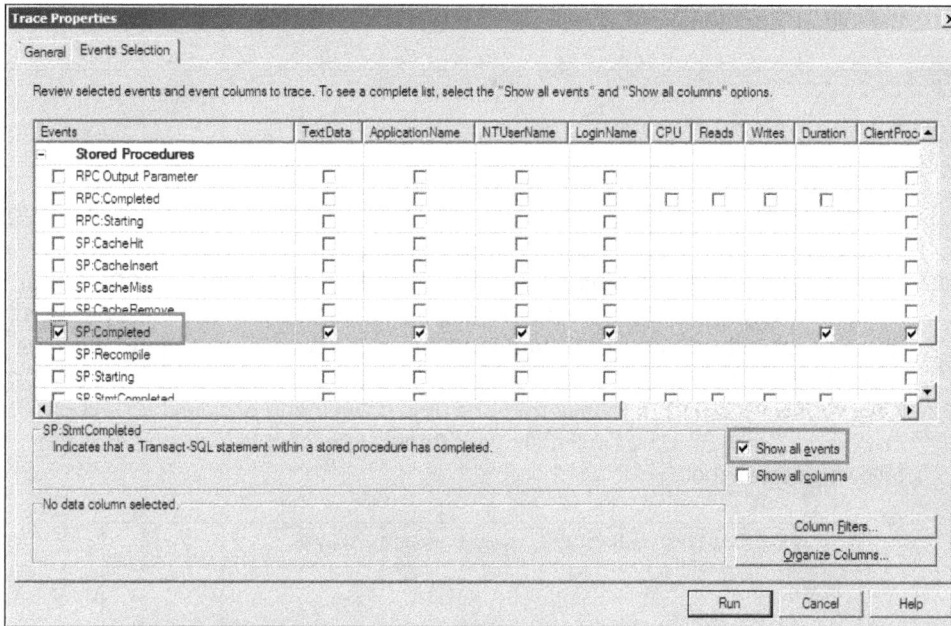

8. Click on the **Run** button to start the trace.

9. Now open SQL Server Management Studio and establish a connection to the same SQL Server.

10. In the query window, type the sample T-SQL statements as shown in the following code snippet and then execute them by pressing *F5* key:

```
Use AdventureWorks2012
GO

SELECT OrderDate,Amount,Refno FROM ordDemo WHERE Refno>8
GO

SELECT
  P.ProductID
  ,P.ProductModelID
FROM
  ProductDemo AS P
JOIN
  ProductModelDemo AS PM
ON
  P.ProductModelID=PM.ProductModelID
WHERE
  P.ProductID=680
GO
```

11. After executing this T-SQL statement, it's time to stop the trace that is currently running by pressing the **Stop** button on the toolbar as shown in the following screenshot:

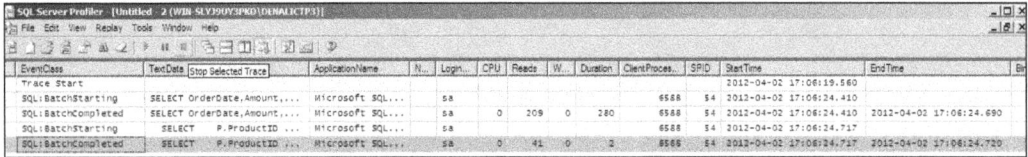

12. Open Database Engine Tuning Advisor tool from **Start | All Program | SQL Server 2012 | Performance Tool | Database Engine Tuning Advisor**. Enter the **Session name** as **AdventureWorks2012WorkloadFile**. In the **Workload** section, select the **File** radio button and select the .trc file that we have saved in D drive. Select **Adventureworks2012** database from the drop-down menu besides Database for workload analysis. Finally, your **General** tab should look similar to the following screenshot:

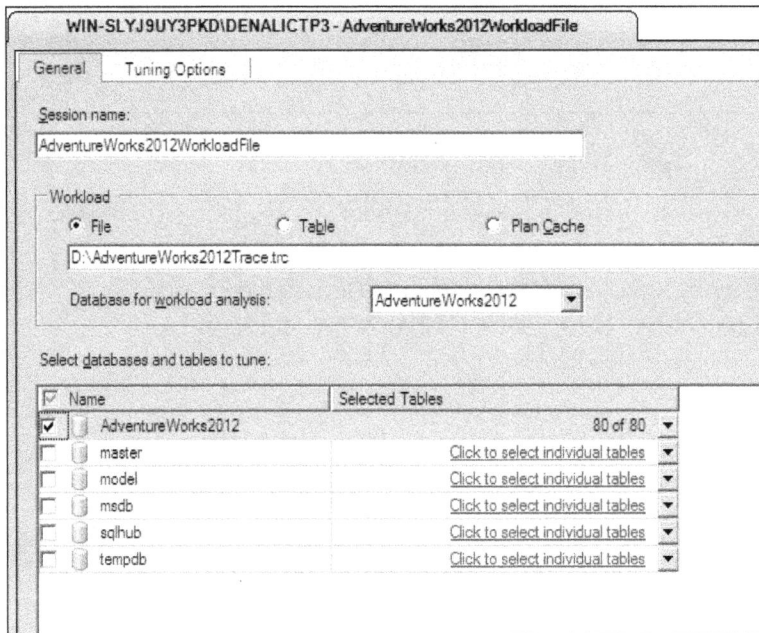

13. Now, in the **Tuning Options** tab, select the **Indexes** radio button and enable the **Include filter index** checkbox. The **Tuning Options** screen should look similar to the following screenshot:

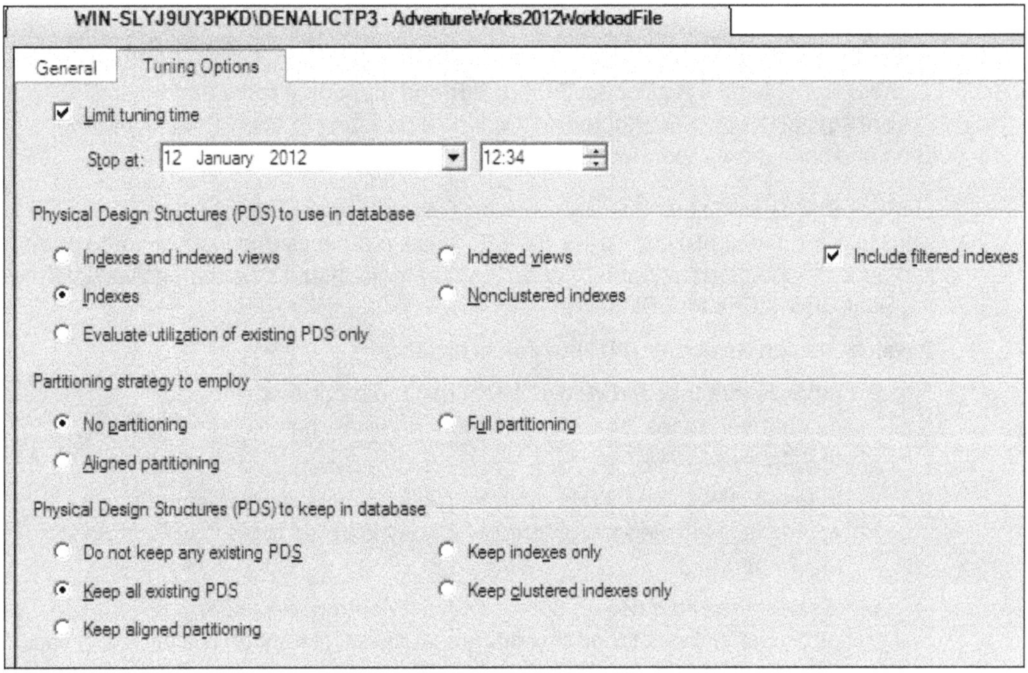

14. Now, click on the **Start Analysis** button from toolbar under the **Action** menu.

15. As soon as the analysis will be completed, DTA will show its recommendation in the **Recommendations** tab as shown in the following screenshot. Carefully read each recommendations and if you think it is worth to go for, select the syntax to follow the steps given in the **Definition** column:

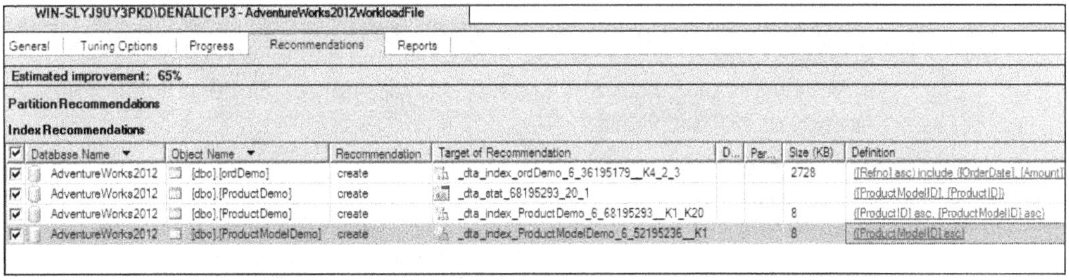

How it works...

The .trc file is a bunch of T-SQL statement(s) that we have executed while generating the .trc file. After submission of the .trc file to DTA, DTA goes through each and every T-SQL statement to read its ways of execution (execution plan), start time of execution, end time of execution. Once the data is read, it starts measuring performance based on the option selection that we made in the **Tuning Options** tab.

There's more...

In step 12, there is a screenshot given for **Tuning Options** tab. Some radio buttons and checkboxes are suggested to select there but it will be interesting to know the use of other radio buttons and checkboxes too. Here is the list of the same:

-   **Limit Tuning Time**: Select this checkbox and insert proper data and time when you want to finish the analyses of trace file. DTA takes resources and locks on objects so it is better to mention appropriate date/time there. It should stop the analyses before the peak hour starts for SQL Server instance.

-   **Physical Design Structure (PDS) to use in database**:

    -   **Indexes and indexed views**: Select this radio button to include recommendations for adding clustered indexes, non-clustered indexes, and indexed views.

    -   **Indexed views**: Select this radio button to include recommendations for adding indexed views. Clustered and non-clustered indexes will not be recommended.

    -   **Include filtered indexes**: Select this radio button to include recommendations for adding filtered indexes. This option is available if you select one of these physical design structures—indexes and indexed views, indexes, or non-clustered indexes.

    -   **Indexes**: Select this radio button to include recommendations for adding clustered and non-clustered indexes. Indexed views will not be recommended.

    -   **Non-clustered indexes**: Select this radio button to include recommendations for only non-clustered indexes. Clustered indexes and indexed views will not be recommended.

    -   **Evaluate utilization of existing PDS only**: This option will evaluate the effectiveness of the current indexes but does not recommend additional indexes or indexed views.

-   **Partitioning strategy to employ**:

> To know more about what the partition is? And what is the role partition plays? Refer *Chapter 13, Table and Index Partitioning*.

    -   **No partitioning**: Does not recommend partitioning.

    -   **Full partitioning**: Include recommendations for partitioning.

    -   **Aligned partitioning**: New recommended partitions will be aligned to make partitions easy to maintain.

▶ **Physical Design Structure (PDS) to keep in database:**

> To know more about what the index is? And what is the role index plays? Refer*Chapter-9, Implementing Indexes* and *Chapter-10, Maintaining Indexes*.

- ❏ **Do not keep any existing PDS**: Recommend dropping unnecessary existing indexes, views, and partitioning. If an existing **Physical Design Structure (PDS)** is useful to the workload, Database Engine Tuning Advisor does not recommend dropping it.

- ❏ **Keep indexes only**: Keep all existing indexes but recommend dropping unnecessary indexed views and partitioning.

- ❏ **Keep all existing PDS**: Keep all existing indexes, indexed views, and partitioning.

- ❏ **Keep clustered indexes only**: Keep all existing clustered indexes but recommend dropping unnecessary indexed views, partitions, and non-clustered indexes.

- ❏ **Keep aligned partitioning**: Keep partitioning structures that are currently aligned, but recommend dropping unnecessary indexed views, indexes, and non-aligned partitioning. Any additional partitioning recommended will align with the current partitioning scheme.

Executing Database Tuning Advisor from command prompt

There is a command prompt version of Database Engine Tuning Advisor, which is known as **DTA**. Like a Database Engine Tuning Advisor, DTA also analyses the workload given to it in the form of trace file, table, or query. There is no difference in tuning activity or the suggestions it provides. The visible difference is that Database Engine Tuning Advisor provides GUI and DTA provides a traditional approach. Apart from that, DTA gives you the liberty to provide XML file, if you don't like to type down all parameter on command line.

If you have the same database structure in your development environment as you have in production server with very less data in development environment, you can copy the production instance's index statistics and metadata. This effectively recreates a target environment without the need to migrate a volume of data onto a development server. DTA creates a shell database that you can tune by using the `TestServer` sub-element and the tuning options element in XML file. This is the advantage of DTA utility over Database Engine Tuning Advisor.

For more information regarding XML file in DTA, please have a look at the following links:

- `http://msdn.microsoft.com/en-us/library/ms190389.aspx`
- `http://technet.microsoft.com/en-us/library/ms174202.aspx`

Getting ready

Like the previous recipe (Running Database Engine Tuning Advisor for Workload), we can load the `AdventureWorks2012Trace.trc` trace file in DTA. But we are going to create one `test.sql` file in D drive with few `SELECT` statements, which we will load in DTA utility. Open SQL Server Management Studio and write down the following SQL statement:

```
SELECT OrderDate,Amount,Refno FROM AdventureWorks2012.dbo.ordDemo
WHERE Refno>8
GO

SELECT
  P.ProductID
  ,P.ProductModelID
FROM
  AdventureWorks2012.dbo.ProductDemo AS P
JOIN
  AdventureWorks2012.dbo.ProductModelDemo AS PM
ON
  P.ProductModelID=PM.ProductModelID
WHERE
  P.ProductID=680
GO
```

Now, save this SSMS file in D drive with the name `test.sql`.

How to do it...

Execute the following command on command line utility:

```
dta -D AdventureWorks2012 -s adventureworks2012FromDTA5 -S WIN-
SLYJ9UY3PKD\DENALICTP3 -E -if D:\test.sql -F -of D:\DTA.sql
```

After successful execution of this command, the command prompt would look similar to the following screenshot:

```
Administrator: Command Prompt                                       _ □ ×
C:\Program Files (x86)\Microsoft SQL Server\110\Tools\Binn>dta -D AdventureWo
2012 -s adventureworks2012FromDTA5 -S WIN-SLYJ9UY3PKD\DENALICTP3 -E -if D:\te
sql -F -of D:\DTA.sql
Microsoft (R) SQL Server Microsoft SQL Server Database Engine Tuning Advisor
mand line utility
Version 11.0.1440.19 ((SQL_PreRelease).110624-1701 )
Copyright (c) Microsoft Corporation. All rights reserved.

Tuning session successfully created. Session ID is 11.

Total time used: 00:00:00
Workload consumed:   100%, Estimated improvement:   65%




Tuning process finished.
Successfully generated recommendations script: D:\DTA.sql.

C:\Program Files (x86)\Microsoft SQL Server\110\Tools\Binn>
```

How it works...

Just like DTA, we can submit the workload with necessary parameter to DTA and it analyses
each query that exists in the workload submitted to generate recommendations in the
output file.

Here is an explanation of the parameters that can be used in conjunction with the command:

- ► -D: It represents our database AdventureWorks2012

- ► -s: It is a session name

- ► -S: It represents server name/instance name (in our server, it is WIN-
  SLYJ9UY3PKD\DENALICTP3, you can replace it with your own server name/
  instance name)

- ► -E: It connects DTA with secure windows authentication, if you wish to run DTA with
  SQL authentication and you have sysadmin account, you can provide -U username
  and -P password instead of -E

- ► -if: It is the input file that could be the .sql file we have saved in D drive

- ► -of: It represents the path where we want to save the recommendation of DTA after
  it analyses the workload

- ► -F: It will overwrite any file that has the same name and path as our output file

There's more...

DTA needs each object name has three part naming convention, that is, `ProductDemo` table should be referred as `AdventureWorks2012.dbo.ProductDemo` (`DatabaseName.SchemaName.TableName`) otherwise it would generate an error.

> All the events in the workload were ignored due to syntax errors. The most common reason for this error is that the database to connect has not been set correctly.

The following is a screenshot of the error:

```
Administrator: Command Prompt                                            _ □ ×
C:\Program Files (x86)\Microsoft SQL Server\110\Tools\Binn>dta -D AdventureWorks
2012 -s adventureworks2012FromDTA4 -S WIN-SLYJ9UY3PKD\DENALICTP3 -U sa -P upgrad
e1 -if D:\AdventureWorks2012Trace.trc
Microsoft (R) SQL Server Microsoft SQL Server Database Engine Tuning Advisor com
mand line utility
Version 11.0.1440.19 ((SQL_PreRelease).110624-1701 )
Copyright (c) Microsoft Corporation. All rights reserved.

Tuning session successfully created. Session ID is 10.

Total time used: 00:00:00
Workload consumed:     0%, Estimated improvement:     0%




Tuning process finished.
All the events in the workload were ignored due to syntax errors.The most common
 reason for this error is that the database to connect has not been set correctl
y.
```

This screenshot has used the same `.trc` file, which we generated in the previous recipe *Running database engine tuning Advisor for workload,* even DTA throws an error because the `SELECT` statement we had executed to generate the `.trc` file did not have three part naming for the table. You can also observe `-U` and `-P` parameter are used instead of `-E`. The `-E` parameter works as Windows authentication and `-U` and `-P` works as SQL authentication.

3
System Statistical Functions, Stored Procedures, and the DBCC SQLPERF Command

In this chapter we will cover:

- ▶ Monitoring system health using system statistical functions
- ▶ Monitoring SQL Server processes and sessions with system stored procedures
- ▶ Monitoring log space usage statistics with the DBCC SQLPERF command

Introduction

There are a few system statistical functions, stored procedures, and DBCC commands that can be useful while analysing performance-related issues. However, even though most of the statistical information that these commands provide can be retrieved by using dynamic management views and dynamic management functions, many database professionals use these features because they have been a part of SQL Server for a long time and are popular and handy while monitoring and looking into performance-related statistics.

You would often use these commands in real life as a quick tool to check the health of the server and the status of SQL Server processes.

Monitoring system health using system statistical functions

SQL Server has a set of few useful **system statistical functions** that provide certain statistics related to SQL Server health. These functions are useful for checking and monitoring the health of the server.

Suppose that, in your database environment, one of the web applications is processing records row-by-row. In order to process each row, the application makes a round trip to the database. This means that to process each row there is a new connection. In order to troubleshoot the issue, you want to monitor at regular intervals the number of connections that are taking place. This example will describe how to perform the said task.

Getting ready

In this recipe we will use following functions:

- @@CONNECTIONS
- @@TIMETICKS
- @@CPU_BUSY
- @@IDLE
- @@IO_BUSY
- @@PACK_RECEIVED
- @@PACK_SENT
- @@PACKET_ERRORS
- @@TOTAL_READ
- @@TOTAL_WRITE
- @@TOTAL_ERRORS

In this example, we will use all these functions, and create and execute a script several times that will insert the output of these functions into a table and query that table by comparing the number of connections between every two consecutive rows.

The following is the prerequisite for this recipe:

- An instance of SQL Server 2012 Developer or Enterprise Evaluation edition

How to do it...

Follow the steps given here to perform this recipe:

1. Open SQL Server Management Studio and connect to an instance of SQL Server.
2. In a new query window, type and execute the following T-SQL script several times to monitor and capture the health of the SQL server:

```
--Creating a table to store server health
--statistics data if the table does not exist.
IF OBJECT_ID('[dbo].[tbl_ServerHealthStatistics]') IS NULL
BEGIN
    CREATE TABLE [dbo].[tbl_ServerHealthStatistics]
    (
        ID INT IDENTITY(1,1)
        ,StatDateTime DATETIME DEFAULT GETDATE()
        ,TotalConnections INT
        ,TimeTicks INT
        ,TotalCPUBusyTime INT
        ,TotalCPUIdleTime INT
        ,TotalIOBusyTime INT
        ,TotalReceivedPackets INT
        ,TotalSentPackets INT
        ,TotalErrorsInNetworkPackets INT
        ,TotalPhysicalReadOperations INT
        ,TotalWriteOperations INT
        ,TotalReadWriteErrors INT
    )
END

GO

--Collect and store server health statistics
--data in our table.
INSERT INTO [dbo].[tbl_ServerHealthStatistics]
(
        TotalConnections
        ,TimeTicks
        ,TotalCPUBusyTime
        ,TotalCPUIdleTime
        ,TotalIOBusyTime
        ,TotalReceivedPackets
        ,TotalSentPackets
        ,TotalErrorsInNetworkPackets
```

```
        ,TotalPhysicalReadOperations
        ,TotalWriteOperations
        ,TotalReadWriteErrors
    )
    SELECT
        @@CONNECTIONS AS TotalConnections
        ,@@TIMETICKS AS  TimeTicks
        ,@@CPU_BUSY AS TotalCPUBusyTime
        ,@@IDLE AS TotalCPUIdleTime
        ,@@IO_BUSY AS TotalIOBusyTime
        ,@@PACK_RECEIVED AS TotalReceivedPackets
        ,@@PACK_SENT AS TotalSentPackets
        ,@@PACKET_ERRORS AS TotalErrorsInNetworkPackets
        ,@@TOTAL_READ AS TotalPhysicalReadOperations
        ,@@TOTAL_WRITE AS TotalWriteOperations
        ,@@TOTAL_ERRORS AS TotalReadWriteErrors

    GO
```

3. Next, run the query, as shown in the following script, to display the collected server health statistics data:

```
--Display the collected server health
--statistics data.
WITH cteStatistics AS
(
    SELECT
        ID
        ,StatDateTime
        ,TotalConnections
        ,TotalCPUBusyTime*CAST(TimeTicks AS BIGINT)
            AS TotalCPUBusyTime
        ,TotalCPUIdleTime*CAST(TimeTicks AS BIGINT)
            AS TotalCPUIdleTime
        ,TotalIOBusyTime*CAST(TimeTicks AS BIGINT)
            AS TotalIOBusyTime
        ,TotalReceivedPackets
        ,TotalSentPackets
        ,TotalErrorsInNetworkPackets
        ,TotalPhysicalReadOperations
        ,TotalWriteOperations
        ,TotalReadWriteErrors
    FROM [dbo].[tbl_ServerHealthStatistics]
)
SELECT
```

```
      Cur.TotalConnections AS CurrentConnections
      ,Cur.StatDateTime AS CurrentStatDateTime
      ,Prev.TotalConnections AS PreviousConnections
      ,Prev.StatDateTime AS Previous_StatDateTime
      ,Cur.TotalConnections - Prev.TotalConnections AS
   ConnectionsIncreamentedBy
      ,DATEDIFF(millisecond, Prev.StatDateTime, Cur.StatDateTime)
         AS ConnectionsIncreamentedIn
   FROM cteStatistics AS Cur
   LEFT OUTER JOIN cteStatistics AS Prev
      ON Cur.ID = Prev.ID + 1
```

How it works...

We first created a table called `dbo.tbl_ServerHealthStatistics`. Before creating the table, the script checks for its existence with the help of the `OBJECT_ID()` function. The script creates the table only if `OBJECT_ID()` returns `NULL` and the table does not exist. This will ensure that the same script can be executed multiple times without any problem. When this script is executed for the first time, it will create the table. In all the subsequent executions, the `IF` condition will not be satisfied and table creation logic will be skipped.

The next batch in the script gathers server health statistics data with the `INSERT...SELECT` statement. In the `SELECT` statement, multiple system statistical functions are called and the result set is inserted into table `dbo.tbl_ServerHealthStatistics`.

Finally, we query the table `dbo.tbl_ServerHealthStatistics`, which contains the collected statistics. Because we need to compare the values for a row with the values of its previous row, we are using a **Common Table Expression** (**CTE**) here by declaring it with the `WITH` syntax. After creating CTE, we use the two instances of CTE in our query by using `LEFT JOIN`. The first instance is aliased as `Cur`, which becomes the left table of the join and represents the current rows. The second instance is aliased as `Prev`, which becomes the right table of the join and represents the previous rows. This is achieved using the join condition `Cur.ID = Prev.ID + 1`. You can see that we derived the difference between the connections, and time interval between a row and its previous row, so that we can tell how many new connections have been created in what time frame.

Note how we convert the time values of `TotalCPUBusyTime`, `TotalCPUIdleTime`, and `TotalIOBusyTime` columns from tick to microseconds. We multiply these values by `Timeticks`. While multiplying, we need to watch out for results for which the value falls beyond the integer limit. This is the reason why we convert one of the operands (`TimTicks`) by multiplication to `BIGINT`, to avoid arithmetic overflow.

There's more...

The following is a list of system statistical functions, along with their descriptions, that you will find useful in monitoring SQL Server. All these system statistical functions return an aggregate value that most of them have cumulatively calculated since SQL Server starts or restarts.

Let us briefly discuss all of them one by one and see what they will return:

-   **@@CONNECTIONS**: This function returns an integer value that represents the number of connections that have been attempted since the SQL Server service was last started. These connection attempts may either be successful or unsuccessful.
-   **@@MAX_CONNECTIONS**: This function returns an integer value that represents the number of maximum connections that are allowed simultaneously. The value depends on the current setting that has been configured for `'Max Connections'` with `sp_configure`, the version of SQL Server, and also the limitations of applications and hardware.
-   **@@TIMETICKS**: This function returns an integer value that represents the number of microseconds that make up a tick. A tick is system-dependent time unit. A tick in an operating system is generally 31.50 milliseconds.
-   **@@CPU_BUSY**: This function returns an integer value that represents the CPU time in ticks that SQL Server has taken to perform its tasks since the SQL Server service was last started. Remember that on machines with multiple processors, this value is cumulative for all CPUs used by SQL Server.
-   **@@IDLE**: This function returns an integer value that represents the CPU time in ticks that SQL Server has been idle for, since the SQL Server service was last started. Remember that on machines with multiple processors, this value is cumulative for all CPUs used by SQL Server.
-   **@@IO_BUSY**: This function returns an integer value that represents the CPU time in ticks that SQL Server has taken to perform input/output operations since the SQL Server service was last started. Remember that on machines with multiple processors, this value is cumulative for all CPUs used by SQL Server.
-   **@@PACK_RECEIVED**: This function returns an integer value that represents the total number of network packets that SQL Server has received since the SQL Server service was last started.
-   **@@PACK_SENT**: This function returns an integer value that represents the total number of network packets that SQL Server has sent since the SQL Server service was last started.
-   **@@PACKET_ERRORS**: This function returns an integer value that represents the total number of erroneous network packets that SQL Server has encountered since the SQL Server service was last started.
-   **@@TOTAL_READ**: This function returns an integer value that represents the total number of physical read operations that SQL Server has performed since the SQL Server service was last started.

▶ **@@TOTAL_WRITE**: This function returns an integer value that represents the total number of write operations that SQL Server has performed since the SQL Server service was last started.

▶ **@@TOTAL_ERRORS**: This function returns an integer value that represents the total number of errors in input/output operations that SQL Server has encountered since the SQL Server service was last started.

> Functions `@@CPU_BUSY`, `@@IDLE`, and `@@IO_BUSY`, return time value in ticks and not in milliseconds or microseconds. To retrieve time values in microseconds, multiply the returned values by time ticks (`@@TIMETICKS`).

The script in this recipe provides the SQL Server health statistics for a given point of time. With SQL Server Agent, you can schedule this particular script, so that it executes at a particular time interval on a regular basis and this task can be automated. This populates our table `[dbo].[tbl_ServerHealthStatistics]` regularly and builds a history of statistical data, which can then be used later for analysis.

▶ **sp_monitor**: There is one system stored procedure named `sp_monitor`, which provides the same statistical data that we retrieved in this recipe by system statistical functions. It returns results in multiple result sets. You are advised to experiment this stored procedure and observe its results.

Monitoring with system stored procedure

SQL Server provides a few system stored procedures that can be used to monitor SQL Server by getting details on current processes, sessions, requests, locking information, and so on. In this recipe, you will see how you can use some system stored procedures to monitor current SQL Server processes, sessions, requests, and blocking information.

If you suddenly experience that database requests coming from applications are not being served normally and applications have to wait normally for database responses, you may want to do a quick check to see whether the requests are blocked by other requests or whether the processes are getting suspended very frequently.

Getting ready

In this example, we will use following system stored procedures to get the status of current processes:

▶ `sp_who`
▶ `sp_who2`

The following is the prerequisite for this recipe:

▶ An instance of SQL Server 2012 Developer or Enterprise Evaluation edition.

How to do it...

Follow the steps provided here to perform this recipe:

1. Open SQL Server Management Studio and connect to an instance of SQL Server.
2. In a new query window, type and execute the query, as shown in following script, to monitor the SQL Server processes and sessions:

```
USE tempdb
GO

--Check if the table exists. If it does,
--drop it first.
IF OBJECT_ID('tempdb.dbo.#tbl_SPWho') IS NOT NULL
BEGIN
     DROP TABLE tempdb.dbo.#tbl_SPWho
END

--Creating table to store the output
--sp_who stored procedures.
CREATE TABLE dbo.#tbl_SPWho
(
     spid SMALLINT
     ,ecid SMALLINT
     ,status NVARCHAR(30)
     ,loginame NVARCHAR(128)
     ,hostName NVARCHAR(128)
     ,blk CHAR(5)
     ,dbname NVARCHAR(128)
     ,cmd NVARCHAR(16)
     ,request_id INT
)

--Insert the result of sp_who stored procedure
--into table.
INSERT INTO dbo.#tbl_SPWho
EXECUTE sp_who
GO

--Check if the table exists. If it does,
--drop it first.
```

```
IF OBJECT_ID('tempdb.dbo.#tbl_SPWho2') IS NOT NULL
BEGIN
    DROP TABLE tempdb.dbo.#tbl_SPWho2
END

CREATE TABLE dbo.#tbl_SPWho2
(
    SPID SMALLINT
    ,Status NVARCHAR(30)
    ,Login NVARCHAR(128)
    ,HostName NVARCHAR(128)
    ,BlkBy CHAR(5)
    ,DBName NVARCHAR(128)
    ,Command NVARCHAR(16)
    ,CPUTime INT
    ,DiskIO INT
    ,LastBatch NVARCHAR(50)
    ,ProgramName NVARCHAR(100)
    ,SPID2 SMALLINT
    ,REQUESTID INT
)
INSERT INTO dbo.#tbl_SPWho2
EXECUTE sp_who2

--Looking at only processes for
--a particular database.
SELECT
    spid AS SessionID
    ,ecid AS ExecutionContextID
    ,status AS ProcessStatus
    ,loginame AS LoginName
    ,hostName AS HostName
    ,blk AS BlockedBy
    ,dbname AS DatabaseName
    ,cmd AS CommandType
    ,request_id AS RequestID
FROM dbo.#tbl_SPWho
WHERE dbname = 'AdventureWorks2012'
GO

--Looking at only blocked requests.
SELECT
    spid AS SessionID
    ,ecid AS ExecutionContextID
```

```
    ,status AS ProcessStatus
    ,loginame AS LoginName
    ,hostName AS HostName
    ,blk AS BlockedBy
    ,dbname AS DatabaseName
    ,cmd AS CommandType
    ,request_id AS RequestID
FROM dbo.#tbl_SPWho
WHERE blk > 0

--Looking at only suspended processes.
SELECT
    SPID AS SessionID
    ,Status AS ProcessStatus
    ,CPUTime
    ,DiskIO
    ,ProgramName
    ,Login AS LoginName
    ,HostName AS HostName
    ,BlkBy AS BlockedBy
    ,DBName AS DatabaseName
    ,Command AS CommandType
    ,REQUESTID AS RequestID
FROM dbo.#tbl_SPWho2
WHERE status = 'suspended'
```

How it works...

In this example, we created a temporary table named #tbl_SPWho. We first checked if the table exists, with the IF condition. If one exists, we drop the table first. Note that the table structure is identical to the set of columns that sp_who returns.

Next, the stored procedure sp_who is executed and its output is collected in the #tbl_SPWho table by the INSERT...EXECUTE statements.

We also created another table called #tbl_SPWho2 and inserted the output of sp_who2 in the same way that we did for sp_who.

The reason why we created temporary tables and stored the output of sp_who and sp_who2 is that we cannot directly filter the result set returned by sp_who and sp_who2, based on certain columns. We query the table by filtering the dbname, blk, and status columns to view the processes that are only targeted to a specified database, the processes that are blocked, and the processes that are suspended.

There's more...

Let's discuss briefly the system stored procedures that we used in our recipe. The following are some useful system stored procedures that were commonly used before dynamic views were introduced for troubleshooting performance issues:

- sp_monitor
- sp_who2
- sp_who

Though most performance-related statistics that these stored procedures provide can be retrieved by dynamic management views and functions, they are still widely used by many database professionals.

We saw in the earlier recipe that we can use sp_monitor to check server health, and we can get the same statistics information that we retrieve by using system statistical functions. They can be used interchangeably.

Because we have used the sp_who system stored procedure in this recipe, we will now discuss this stored procedure in detail.

sp_who is a system stored procedure that provides detailed information on current SQL Server processes, sessions, and requests. This information can be used to know: what operations/commands are being performed by whom and the processes that block other processes and introduce blocking issues.

sp_who accepts optional parameters, which are @loginame(type sysname), session ID (type smallint), and ACTIVE. By supplying login name, only processes belonging to a specific login are returned. If a session ID is supplied for the session ID parameter, only processes belonging to a specific session are returned. If no parameters are supplied to this stored procedure, it returns processes for all sessions in the instance. If you don't have VIEW SYSTEM STATE permissions, you will see information regarding your session only. If ACTIVE is passed as a parameter, only processes that are active are returned.

The following are the columns that `sp_who` returns:

Column Name	Description
spid	This column represents the session ID. Values in this column starting from 1 to 50 are reserved for system threads. Value 51 and onwards are used for user connections.
ecid	Sometimes you might see several sessions with the same `spid` value. This can happen in case of query parallel processing. This column represents the execution context ID for a session ID. This column will have the value 0 for the main parent thread, and rest of the values represent subthreads.
status	This column represents the status of the process. The status can be one of the following: ▸ Dormant: A session is being reset ▸ Running: A session is running the process ▸ Background: A session is running a background task such as deadlock detection ▸ Rollback: A transaction within a session is being rolled back ▸ Pending: A session is waiting for the worker thread to become available ▸ Runnable: A task within a session is in the runnable queue of scheduler while waiting to get a time quantum ▸ Spinloop: A task within a session is waiting for spinlock to become free ▸ Suspended: The session is waiting for an event, for example, I/O completion
loginame	This column represents the login name associated with a session.
hostname	This column represents the machine name associated with a session.
blk	This column represents the ID of the session that is blocking the request of the current session. If session is not blocked, this column will have the value 0.
dbname	This column represents the database name involved in a request for a particular session request.
cmd	This column represents the type of database engine command.
request_id	This column represents the request ID within a session.

Apart from `sp_who`, there is another stored procedure that we have used in our recipe and that is popular among database professionals—`sp_who2`. This stored procedure provides additional columns, such as `CPUTime`, `DiskIO`, `LastBatch`, and `ProgramName`. `sp_who2` is undocumented. This means that you will not find this stored procedure documented in SQL Server Books online.

Monitoring log space usage statistics with DBCC command

Every database has a transaction log associated with it. A transaction log records every DML activity that can be used by SQL Server to recover a database. If the recovery model of the database is full and the frequency of DML operations is very high on the database, this transaction log file can grow very quickly. Even if the recovery model is simple and the database is published for transactional or merge replication; this can cause the log to blow up as well. If the transaction log is not backed up regularly and the transaction file has been allowed to grow unlimitedly, then it can even occupy all your hard disk space and turn your databases down, which prevents all DML operations from functioning on databases and your application goes down as well. As a DBA, you should regularly monitor log space usage statistics to prevent any situation that can cause such downtime issues.

When you are working as a DBA, it should be one of your important responsibilities to monitor the size of log files of your database to make sure that you do not run out of space and your database server is not down.

SQL Server provides different DBCC commands for database administration. **DBCC SQLPERF** is one of those commands that can be helpful in monitoring the size of the log files. In this recipe, to get log space usage statistics on all databases, we will use the DBCC SQLPERF command. Apart from retrieving log space usage statistics, the DBCC SQLPERF command is also used to reset wait and latch statistics.

DBCC SQLPERF accepts one argument, LOGSPACE, when it is used to get log space usage statistics. However, it also accepts other arguments; they are used to reset the wait and latch statistics.

Useful columns that the DBCC SQLPERF command returns for log space usage statistics are as follows:

▶   Database Name
▶   Log Size (MB)
▶   Log Space Used (%)

Getting ready

This recipe will show you how to monitor log space usage statistics for all databases using the DBCC SQLPERF command.

The following is the prerequisite for this recipe:

▶   An instance of SQL Server 2012 Developer or Enterprise Evaluation edition

How to do it...

Follow the steps provided here to perform this recipe:

1. Open SQL Server Management Studio and connect to an instance of SQL Server.

2. In a new query window, type and execute the query, as shown in following script, to retrieve the log space usage statistics:

```
USE tempdb
GO

--Check if the table exists. If it does,
--Drop it first.
IF OBJECT_ID('dbo.#tbl_DBLogSpaceUsage') IS NOT NULL
BEGIN
    DROP TABLE dbo.#tbl_DBLogSpaceUsage
END

--Creating table to store the output
--DBCC SQLPERF command
CREATE TABLE dbo.#tbl_DBLogSpaceUsage
(
    DatabaseName NVARCHAR(128)
    ,FileGroupName NVARCHAR(128)
    ,LogSize NVARCHAR(25)
    ,LogSpaceUsed NVARCHAR(25)
    ,Status TINYINT
)

INSERT INTO dbo.#tbl_DBLogSpaceUsage
EXECUTE ('DBCC SQLPERF(LOGSPACE)')

--Retriving log space details for
-- all databases.
SELECT
    DatabaseName
    ,LogSize
    ,LogSpaceUsed
    ,Status
FROM dbo.#tbl_DBLogSpaceUsage
GO
```

```
--Retriving log space details for
-- a specific databases.
SELECT
    DatabaseName
    ,LogSize AS LogSizeInMB
    ,LogSpaceUsed As LogspaceUsed_In_Percent
    ,Status
FROM dbo.#tbl_DBLogSpaceUsage
WHERE DatabaseName = 'AdventureWorks2012'
GO
```

How it works...

In this example, we created a temporary table named #tbl_DBLogSpaceUsage. We first checked if the table exists, with the IF condition. If one exists, we first drop the table. The table structure that we have created should be identical to the set of columns that DBCC SQLPERF returns.

Next, DBCC SQLPERF is executed and its output is collected in the #tbl_DBLogSpaceUsage table by INSERT...EXECUTE statements. Note that we have used a dynamic SQL statement here in the EXECUTE statement, as we cannot directly redirect the output of the DBCC command into the table.

Next, we queried the table and retrieved the log space usage statistics information for all databases. The very next query returns the log space usage statistics for the AdventureWorks2012 database by creating a filter on the DatabaseName column.

From the output, you can know the size of the log for every database and if you see any alarming statistics, you can immediately take the necessary steps, such as backing up the log files.

There's more...

You can use the logic of the script provided in this recipe to accumulate the log space usage statistics for all databases and populate these details in a table. Over time, the table becomes a history of log space usage details, which you can use in trend analysis of how fast a log file is growing.

4
Resource Monitor and Performance Monitor

In this chapter we will cover:

- ▸ Monitoring of server performance
- ▸ Monitoring CPU usage
- ▸ Monitoring memory (RAM) usage

Introduction

If you encounter database performance problems caused by poorly written queries, lack of necessary indexes, or anything else at database level, you can troubleshoot such issues and investigate the root cause by using execution plans, DMVs and DMFs, SQL Traces, or Database Engine Tuning Advisor (DTA).

However, if the performance issues are at hardware or operating system level, you need a sophisticated tool that gives you an idea about the performance of your hardware resources (such as CPU, memory, I/O, or network adapters) with respect to the processes that might be running on the system. If the instance of your SQL Server suffers from lack of adequate hardware resources or bad hardware performance, you need to identify that particular hardware component and the reason behind its poor performance in order to fix the issue.

In the days of Windows Server 2003 or Windows Server 2000, prior to Window Server 2008 R2 and Windows 7, you might have worked with **Performance Monitor** with SQL Server Performance Objects and Counters to troubleshoot hardware-related issues. In Windows Server 2008 R2 and Windows 7, you will find a similar Performance Monitor tool, but with enhanced features. Microsoft calls it **Performance Monitor** or **Reliability and Performance Monitor**.

Basically, in Windows, there are three tools for monitoring performance:

1. Resource Monitor
2. Performance Monitor
3. Reliability Monitor

Resource Monitor has a Resource View that provides a quick, real-time, graphical view of hardware usage that includes CPU usage, memory usage, disk I/O usage, and network usage. You can monitor and examine all the processes that are currently running on the machine. From there, you can even kill a process that you might suspect to be the cause of a bottleneck. You might want to replace the usage of Task Manager with Resource Monitor to accomplish the tasks that you used to perform with Task Manager.

Performance Monitor is another tool that gives us a real-time graphical view of performance counter data. We can specify required performance counters from hundreds of available performance counters to trace performance data. The performance data can also be saved to a log file, which can then be used for performance analysis.

Reliability Monitor provides a graphical report view of how stable the system is, by calculating a system stability index over a period of time. The calculation of this system stability index is based on system failures that might have occurred in the system. Any problem or system failure reduces the system stability index.

All these three tools share a common interface, the **Microsoft Management Console** (**MMC**), where they all can be viewed altogether. **Reliability and Performance Monitor** combines functionalities of all these three tools at one place.

In this chapter, we will get familiar with Resource Monitor, and Reliability and Performance Monitor, and see how we can use these tools to check and monitor the performance of hardware resources. We will not cover Reliability Monitor in this chapter.

Monitoring of server performance

If you are approached by someone and told that the server hosting the instance of SQL Server is running and responding very slowly, which tool would you prefer to first open to have a quick review of server performance?

You may have used Task Manager in the past, to quickly check the health of the server. We have yet another, similar, but new and powerful tool in our pocket that can be used to quickly check the health of the server resources. Yes, we are talking about Resource Monitor! As its name suggests, we can use Resource Monitor to monitor the various resources of the system.

In this recipe, we will have an overview of how we can use Resource Monitor to quickly monitor hardware resources and server performance.

Getting ready

The following are the prerequisites for this recipe:

- ▸ An instance of SQL Server 2012 Developer or Enterprise Evaluation edition
- ▸ Resource Monitor, as installed with Windows OS
- ▸ A sample `AdventureWorks2012` database on the instance of SQL Server

> Resource Monitor is a new tool and you may not find this tool available in previous releases of Windows, prior to Windows Server 2008 R2 and Windows 7. To have Resource Monitor, you need Windows 2008 Server R2 or Windows 7.

How to do it...

To monitor server performance, follow the steps given here:

1. In order to start **Resource Monitor**, press the Windows + *R* key combination to display the **Run** dialog box. In this dialog box, type `resmon.exe` and press *Enter*.

2. **Resource Monitor** will start and you will see five tabs at the top of the window, below the menu bar. Click on the first tab captioned **Overview**, to look at the overview of overall system health. The following screenshot depicts the **Overview** tab in **Resource Monitor**.

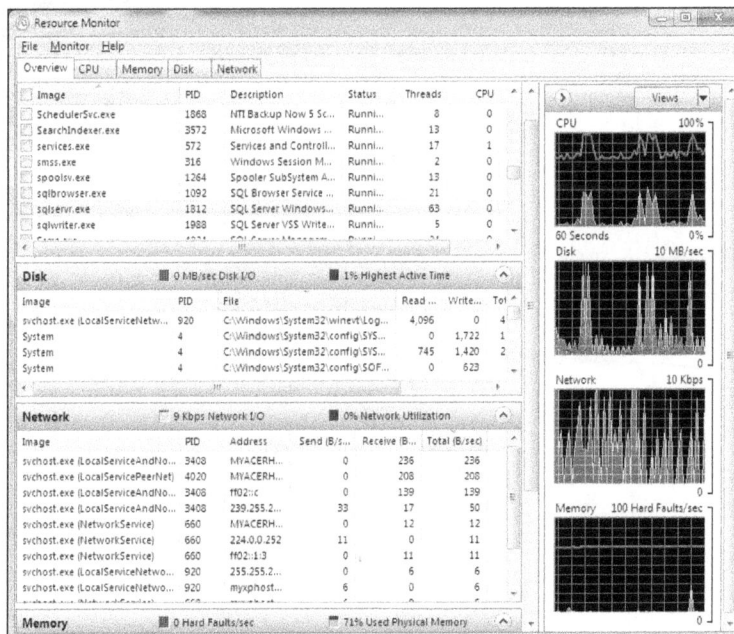

3. To see CPU usage for only the SQL Server service, click on the second tab captioned **CPU** and in list of processes, locate the process **sqlservr.exe**; check its associated checkbox in the **Image** column. Based on the amount of activity that your SQL Server is performing, you will see the CPU usage for the available CPUs, as shown in following screenshot:

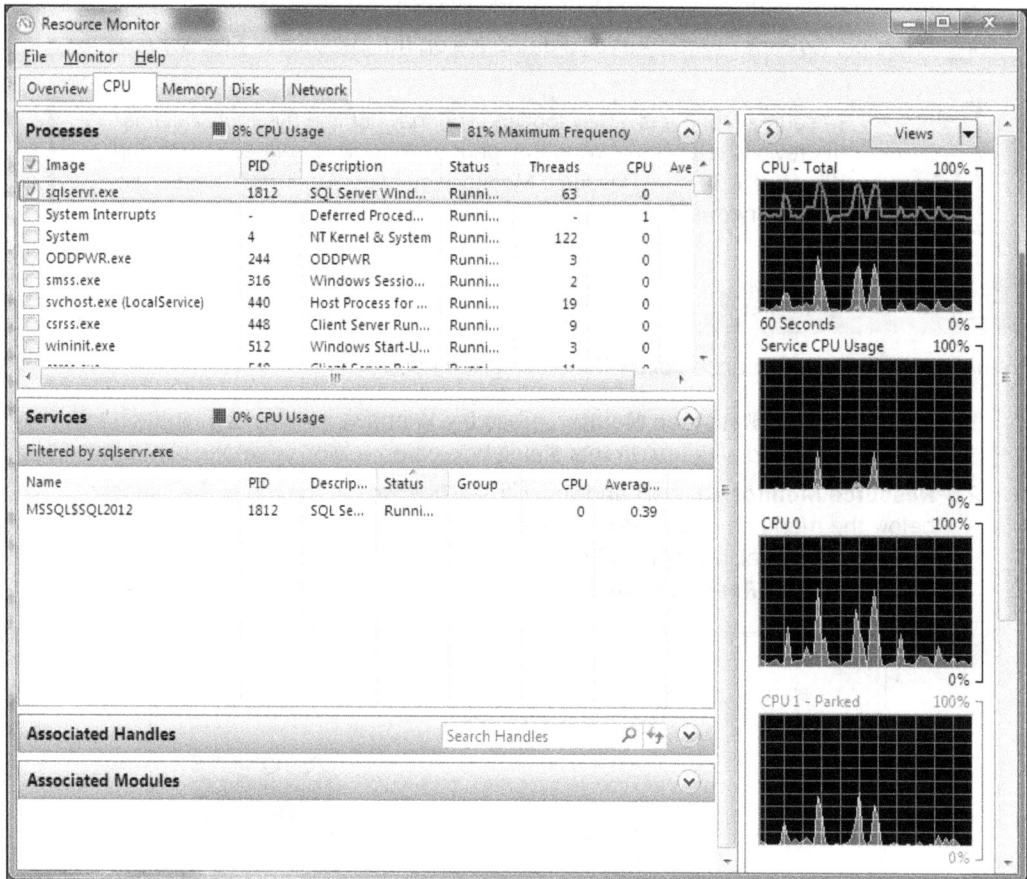

4. To check the memory usage of your server, click on the tab captioned **Memory**, and you will see the screen shown in the following screenshot:

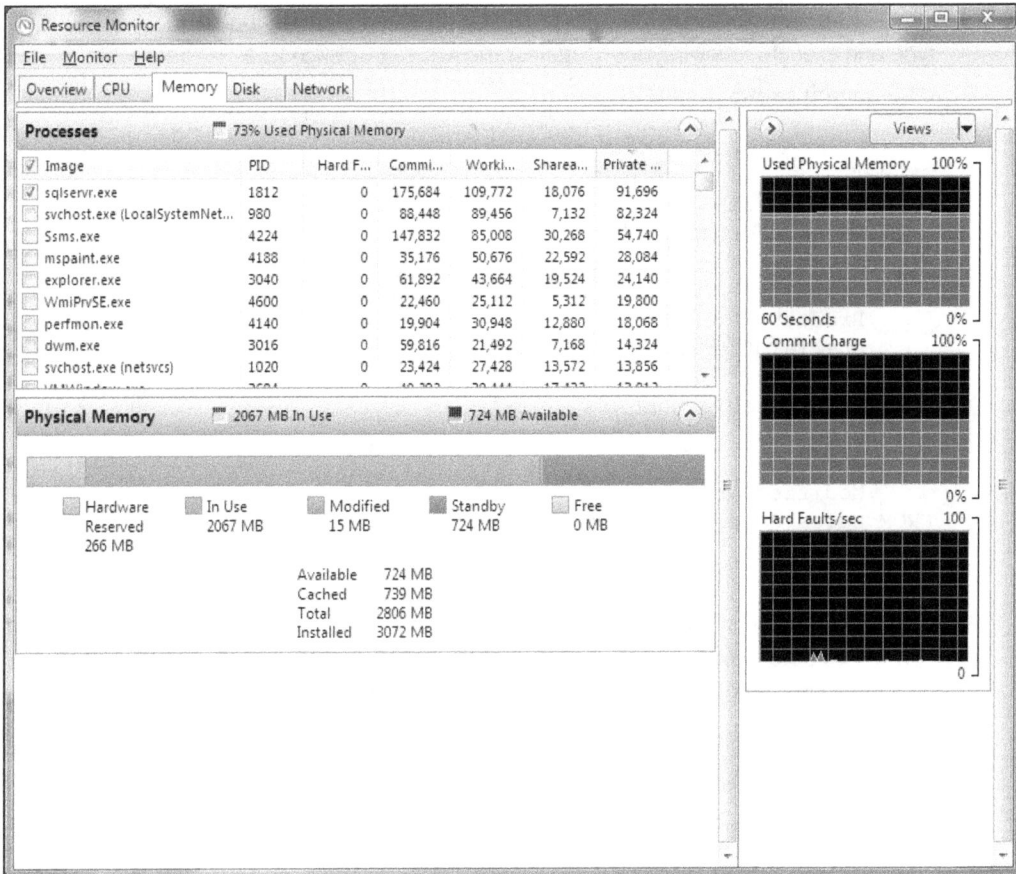

5. To check the disk I/O activity on the server, click on the tab captioned **Disk**. Because we have already selected **sqlservr.exe** from the list of available processes, we will see disk I/O activity that is caused by only the SQL Server service. Let's run a query to cause some I/O activity to occur. Connect SSMS to SQL Server, and in a new query window, type and execute following query against the `AdventureWorks2012` database:

```
USE AdventureWorks2012
GO

SELECT
    SalesOrderID
    ,SalesOrderDetailID
    ,CarrierTrackingNumber
    ,OrderQty
    ,ProductID
    ,SpecialOfferID
    ,UnitPrice
    ,UnitPriceDiscount
    ,LineTotal
    ,rowguid
    ,ModifiedDate
FROM Sales.SalesOrderDetail WITH (NOLOCK)

GO
```

6. After running the preceding query, immediately switch to **Resource Monitor**, and you will be able to monitor disk I/O activity performed on `AdventureWorkk2012` database files, along with few others, as shown in the following screenshot:

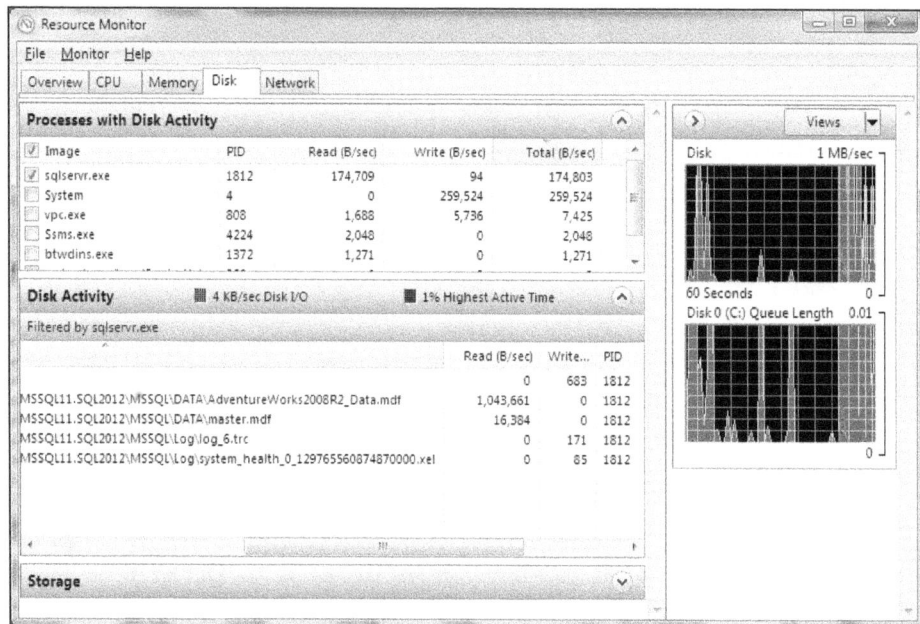

How it works...

The usage of Resource Monitor was straightforward in this recipe. Resource Monitor basically provides resource usage information for CPU, memory, disk I/O, and network. The main screen of **Resource Monitor** divides this resource usage information into the following five tabs:

- ▸ **Overview**: This tab gives you an overview of usage statistics for all four main server resources—CPU, memory, disk, and network—in their separate sections and in real-time graphs as well. The top section on the screen also displays the list of all processes that are currently in action. If you identify a problematic process that could be causing performance issues, you can kill that process from here.

- ▸ **CPU**: This tab provides the CPU usage information, in percentage, and details for each process that we saw on the **Overview** tab. From here, for any given process, we can identify its associated services, handles, and modules. On the right-hand side, we have a real-time graphical usage view of all the available CPUs. If you find that CPU usage is very high, you can look at the list of processes, to identify the process that is using more CPU by examining the **CPU** column.

- ▸ **Memory**: This tab provides memory usage information. From here, you can tell how much memory has been installed, how much has been used, and how much memory is free. It also displays the same list of processes, from where you can identify which processes consume how much memory and which processes consume most of the memory resources.

  The best and most helpful feature of Resource Monitor is that you can select particular process(es) by checking the corresponding checkbox(es) from the list of processes, to monitor the hardware resource usage information for only that particular process(es).

  Notice that in this recipe we have selected the **sqlservr.exe** process, to monitor the resource usage information for SQL Server service only.

- ▸ **Disk**: This tab provides usage information for the disk I/O activity of various processes. By looking at the **Read (B/Sec)** and **Write (B/Sec)** columns, you can identify disk I/O activity for a given process. It also displays the list of files upon which the disk I/O activity (read/write operation) is performed for the processes. The real-time graphical view of disk usage information is also displayed on the right-hand side of the window.

  In our example, to cause some disk I/O activity, we executed a query on the `Sales. SalesOrderDetail` table in the `AdventureWorks2012` database. Note the entry for **AdventureWorks2008R2_Data.mdf** in **Disk Activity**. This file is the physical data file for the `AdventureWorks2012` database. Also, look at the **Read (B/sec)** column for this file and examine the number of bytes that have been read from this file when we executed the query.

▶ **Network**: This tab provides information regarding current network usage. The real-time graphical view is displayed on the right-hand side along with available network adapters installed on your machine. You will see all the TCP connections that are associated with different processes and can filter the network activity by a given process also, in order to identify network usage by a particular process.

There's more...

By using Resource Monitor, you can quickly identify the processes that are swallowing your hardware resources. In Resource Monitor, You can also check network usage information and identify the processes that generate more network traffic.

On a production SQL Server, if you find any processes/applications other than SQL Server that are consuming more hardware resources and affecting the SQL Server's performance, you probably would like to move those processes or applications to a different server, so that the performance of SQL Server does not get affected.

Monitoring CPU usage

The CPU is the most important resource on a server. On a database server, CPU usage should be monitored from time to time to make sure that the performance of the database server is optimized.

In this recipe, we will use Reliability and Performance Monitor to capture CPU-related usage statistics.

You may have used **Performance Monitor** (where you could add different performance counters that need to be traced) in the past. **Reliability and Performance Monitor** is an enhanced version of the old Performance Monitor tool. In **Reliability and Performance Monitor** also, we can use performance objects and counters to analyse system performance by different parameters.

Performance Counters provide statistical data for various system activities. You will find hundreds of performance counters that belong to the Windows OS or third-party applications. SQL Server has hundreds of performance counters of its own that provide useful performance-statistics information to the DBA.

In this recipe, we will trace the following CPU-related performance counters in our recipe:

▶ Processor:% Processor Time

▶ System:Processor Queue Length

Getting ready

Before you continue with this recipe, you should know what data the **Processor:% Processor Time** and **System:Processor Queue Length** performance counters gather.

Processor:% Processor Time: This provides the percentage of CPU time that has been used by a thread. Remember that if you have multiple CPUs or multiple CPU cores installed on your system, you will find multiple instances of this performance counter. For example, if you have two Intel Xeon processors installed on your machine with four CPU cores on each processor, then you will have a total of 8 instances of this performance counter. You can add this counter either for all CPU/core instances or for a specific CPU/core instance.

System:Processor Queue Length: This provides you with the number of threads that are waiting for their turn to use the CPU.

The following are the prerequisites for this recipe:

▶ An instance of SQL Server 2012 Developer or Enterprise Evaluation edition

▶ Performance Monitor, as installed with Windows OS

How to do it...

To monitor CPU usage statistics, follow the steps given here:

1. To start **Reliability and Performance Monitor**, press the Windows + R key combination to display the **Run** dialog box. In this dialog box, type **perfmon.exe** and press *Enter*.

2. When **Reliability and Performance Monitor** is started, to switch to **Performance Monitor** view, click the **Performance Monitor** node under the **Monitoring Tools** node in the left-hand-side console tree.

3. Press the *Delete* key or click on the **X** button in the toolbar to delete any existing performance counter. Click on the **+** button in the toolbar to add counters.

4. In the **Add Counters** dialog box, type the name of the computer that you are going to monitor, or let it be **<Local computer>**, if you are monitoring a local machine under the **Select counters from computer:** drop-down list.

5. In the list of available performance counter objects, expand **Processor** and select **% Processor Time**.

6. In the list under **Instances of selected object:**, select **<All instances>**, and then click on the **Add > >** button. This will add the **% Processor Time** counter to the list of **Added counters** on the right-hand side.

7. Now to add another performance counter, in the list of available performance counter objects, expand **System** and select **Processor Queue Length**; click on the **Add > >** button to add it.

8. After adding these two counters, your screen should look like as shown in the following screenshot:

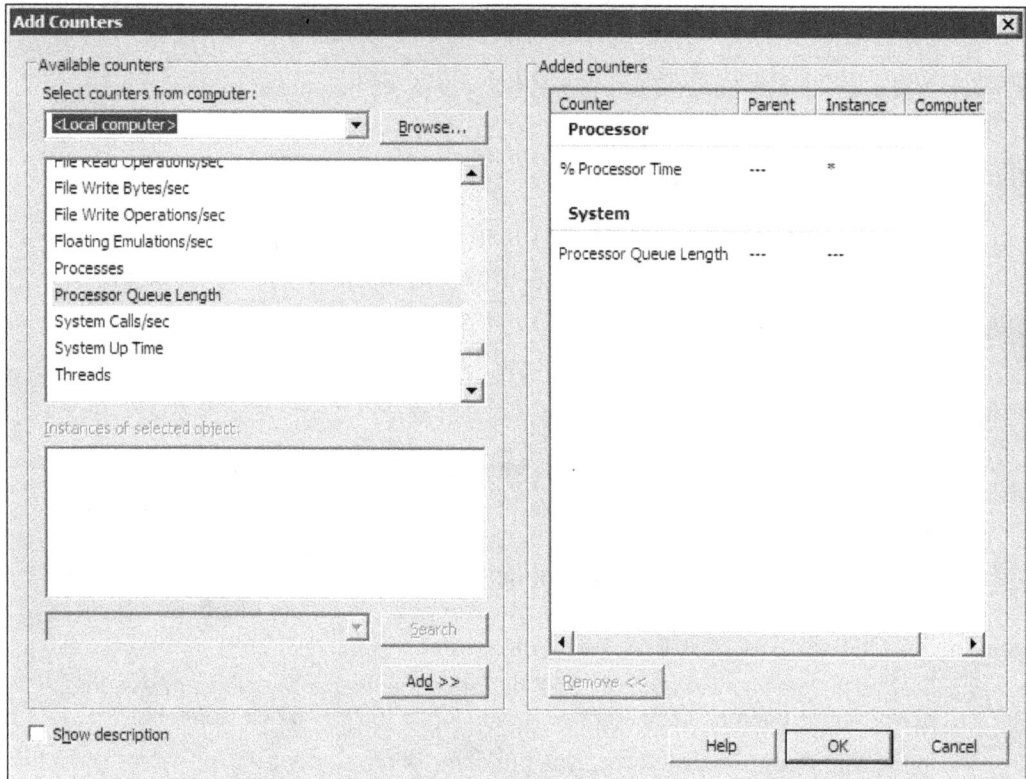

9. Click the **OK** button in the **Add Counter** dialog box.

10. **Performance Monitor** will start to monitor performance data for the added performance counters and will show you that data in a running chart. Select **% Processor Time** from the list of added performance counters, which can be located beneath the performance monitor graph, and observe the various values in the value bar. Based on the activity your machine is carrying out, you should see a screen similar to the one shown in the following screenshot:

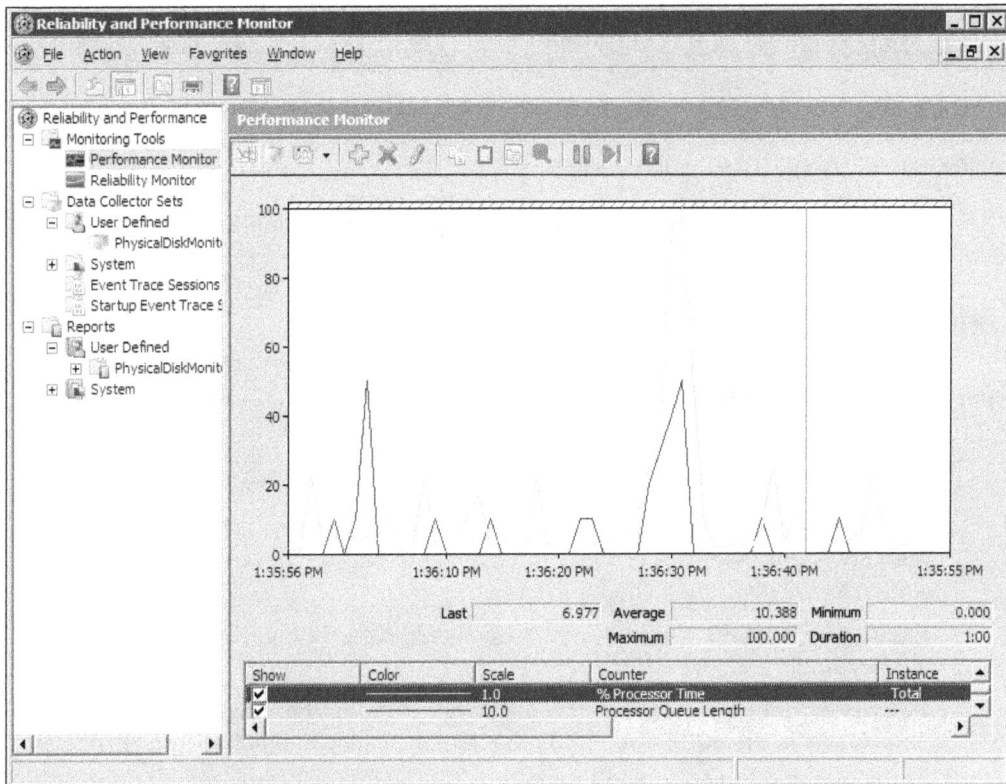

How it works...

Using performance counters in **Reliability and Performance Monitor** is very straightforward. We started the **Reliability and Performance Monitor** tool, and in **Performance Monitor** view, we added the **% Processor Time** performance counter to **Processor** counter and **Processor Queue Length** performance counter to the **System** counter.

Note the graphical representation of collected data for a specific counter that has been selected in the counter list. The data is collected at every second, and based on the timeline, a real-time graph is created. To see the graph for different performance counters, select one from the counter list located at bottom of the window.

Below the graph is a "Value Bar", which provides the **Last**, **Average**, **Minimum**, and **Maximum** values for a performance counter that has been selected in the counter list.

If you notice that the average value of **Processor:% Processor Time** consistently remains above 80 percent and the value of **System:Processor Queue Length** consistently remains above 2, it should indicate that your processor is not fast enough to bear the burden of all the processes running on the server and you either need to upgrade your CPU or add more CPU cores to your system.

Monitoring memory (RAM) usage

Monitoring the memory (RAM) usage of your database server is very important. There are a number of factors that can cause all your memory to be consumed. This is why you should monitor memory usage on a regular basis.

In this recipe, we will use **Reliability and Performance Monitor** to capture memory (RAM)-related usage statistics.

Getting ready

Before starting the recipe, it's important for you to know how to interpret the values of the following performance counters that we will be using in this example:

- **Memory:Available MBytes**: This provides the amount of memory available on the system.
- **Memory:Pages/sec**: This provides the number of pages that were read from, or written to, the disk, due to hard page faults.
- **Paging File:% Usage**: This provides the amount, in percentage, of the paging that has occurred.
- **SQL Server:Buffer Manager:Buffer cache hit ratio**: This provides the amount, in percentage, of the SQL Server data read from the cache and not from the disk.
- **SQL Server:Buffer Manager:Page life expectancy**: This provides the average number of seconds during which data pages reside in memory.
- **SQL Server:Memory Manager:Memory Grants Pending**: This provides the number of processes that are waiting for the workplace memory grant.

The following are the prerequisites for this recipe:

- An instance of SQL Server 2012 Developer or Enterprise Evaluation edition
- Performance Monitor, as installed with Windows OS

How to do it...

To monitor memory usage statistics, follow the steps given here:

1. To start **Reliability and Performance Monitor**, go to **Control Panel | Administrative Tools** and double-click on the icon for Reliability and Performance Monitor.
2. When **Reliability and Performance Monitor** is started, to switch to Performance Monitor view, click on the **Performance Monitor** node under the **Monitoring Tools** node in the left-hand side console tree.

3. To remove all previously added counters, right-click the list of counters and click on **Remove All Counters**, in the shortcut menu.

4. To add required counters, right-click the list of counters and click on **Add Counters...**, in the shortcut menu. This will display the **Add Counters** dialog box.

5. In the **Add Counters** dialog box, type the name of the computer (or let it be **<Local computer>** if you are monitoring a local machine under the **Select counters from computer:** drop-down list).

6. Select and add the following performance counters from the available list:

   ❑ **Memory:Available MBytes**

   ❑ **Memory:Pages/sec**

   ❑ **Paging File:% Usage**

   ❑ **SQL Server:Buffer Manager:Buffer cache hit**

   ❑ **SQL Server:Buffer Manager:Page life expectancy**

   ❑ **SQL Server:Memory Manager:Memory Grants Pending**

7. After adding these performance counters, your screen should look like the one shown in the following screenshot:

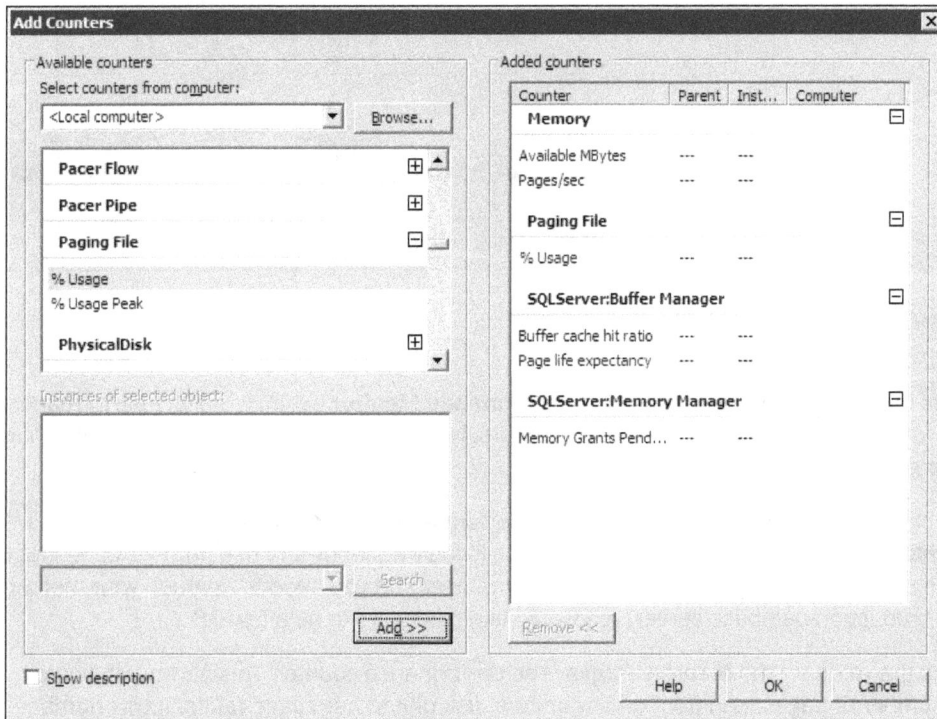

8. Click on the **OK** button to start performance monitoring. The following is the screenshot that shows the gathered performance data for the selected performance counters:

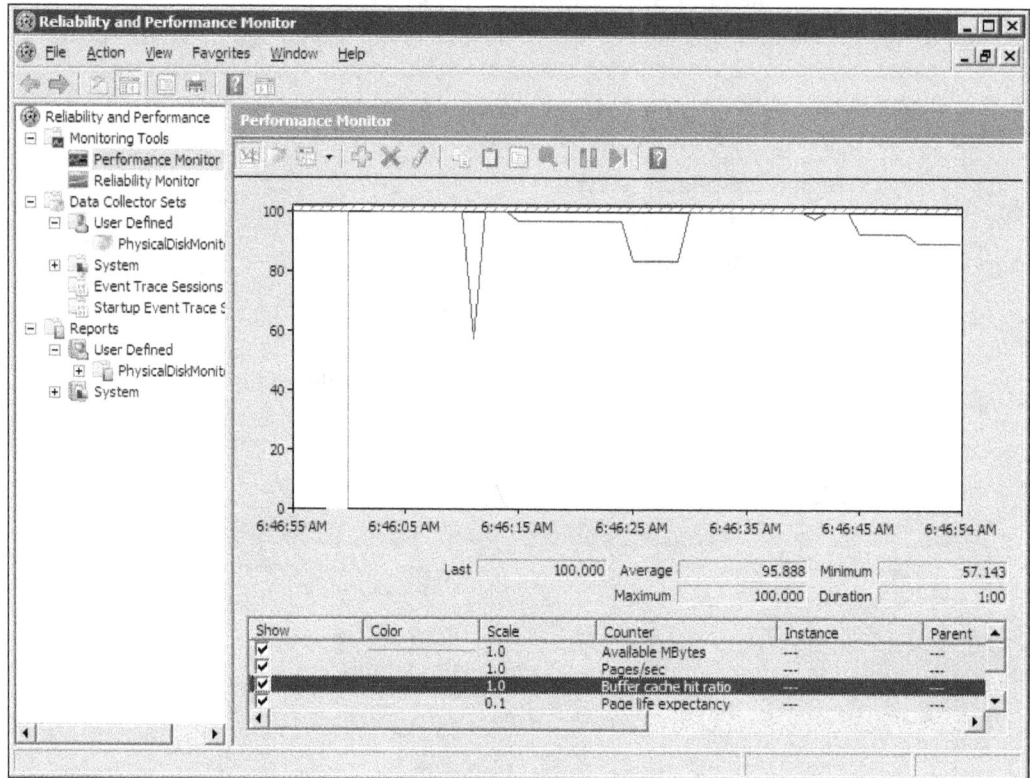

How it works...

In this recipe, we used **Reliability and Performance Monitor** again, to collect performance data for memory-related performance counters. Note the values of each performance counter in the graph.

First check the **Memory:Available MBytes** performance counter. This is the value that indicates the memory available in the system. If you frequently find this number to be low, it is possible that your server is running short of memory and you need to upgrade your memory. On a production database server, you would like this figure to be a few GB.

Check the value for the **Memory:Pages/sec** performance counter. This number indicates the number of pages read from or written to a disk due to hard page faults. If this number is frequently higher than 20 then it may indicate a shortage of memory that causes the application to use virtual memory, resulting in paging.

Along with **Memory:Pages/sec**, also check the **Paging File:% Usage** performance counter to estimate paging usage. If you frequently find this value to be more than 20 percent, you are probably falling short of memory.

SQL Server:Buffer Manager:Buffer cache hit ratio indicates the number of times SQL Server reads data from the cache. It is desired that this be more than 90 percent. If this number is frequently low, either you have a memory shortage or you need to check your query and indexes. If you fetch a large amount of data, it alone may occupy much of the memory and can cause SQL Server to read data from disk instead of from the memory. Check indexes. Make sure that large tables are not getting scanned. Try to limit the number of rows in your queries.

Check the value of the **SQL Server:Buffer Manager:Page life expectancy** performance counter. This value represents the life of data pages in seconds. Microsoft recommends this value to be at least 300 seconds. For instance, if this value is less than 300 very often, it means life of the data pages is less than 5 minutes, that they don't stay longer than this duration in memory, and that they are removed from memory once the duration has elapsed.

If the **SQL Server:Memory Manager:Memory Grants Pending** performance counter frequently suggests waiting processes, you should probably increase your memory.

For any reason if you find that there is a shortage of memory and paging is occurring quite frequently, you should first check if there are any other services or applications other than SQL Server that are heavily taking up the memory. If you find any such applications or services, try to move them to a different server. If you can't do this, then add more memory to the server and allocate the required amount of memory to SQL Server.

If the server is dedicated to SQL Server only and there are no other services or applications, then you should analyze your queries and indexes to make sure that they are optimized. If you find that the queries and indexes are optimized but all the memory is still used up by SQL Server, you may probably need to add more memory to your server.

Correlating performance data with SQL Trace

You can also correlate the results of Performance Monitor with SQL Server Profiler. For this, you need to create a user-defined data collector set and save it to a file. When you gather performance data in Performance Monitor, SQL Server Profiler also needs to be running simultaneously. Once you are done with collecting data, you can import performance data into SQL Server Profiler by selecting **Import Performance Data** from the **File** menu. Importing performance data into SQL Server Profiler will allow you to correlate SQL Trace events with performance data for a given point of time on the system monitor graph.

5
Monitoring with Execution Plans

In this chapter we will cover:

- ► Working with an Estimated Execution Plan
- ► Working with an Actual Execution Plan
- ► Monitoring the performance of a query by SET SHOWPLAN_XML
- ► Monitoring the performance of a query by SET STATISTICS XML
- ► Monitoring the performance of a query by SET STATISTICS IO
- ► Finding the Execution Time of a query by SET STATISTICS TIME
- ► Including and understanding Client Statistics

Introduction

An execution plan is one of the most important feature shipped with SQL Server since long. This feature is not only for DBA or SQL developer, but this is useful for everybody who is dealing with **T-SQL** (**Transact-SQL**) in any capacity.

An execution plan guides you to understand what has happened with the query, which was getting executed, with the help of estimated execution plan/actual execution plan. It helps you to identify how your JOIN statements are behaving, whether Index is being used or not, what was the estimation of query optimizer for your query, what are the actual costs taken by the query executed, and much more such as data flow, sampling of rows, reads, writes, logical I/O, physical constraints of query, operators.

> When we see questions related to slow query performance, in any technical forum about SQL Server; we used to ask, *Can you please provide us with the execution plan of the query?* This is the best way to get an insight about the path taken by optimizer and storage engine while executing the query, even without physically accessing the production server of the person who has asked the question.

There are a few different ways to see the execution plan provided by SQL Server; some of the important ways are listed here:

- Graphical execution plan
- Text execution plan
- XML execution plan

We will see each of these in detail in this chapter, but even before you start looking at different ways of seeing the execution plan, we would like to explain some fundamentals about how query is being processed in SQL Server.

We want to keep the long story short as a detailed understanding of the internals would need a few chapters or maybe a whole book. Kindly note that the steps which are being performed during the execution of the query are beyond the scope of this book, so only the necessary steps are mentioned, along with some important terminology which is useful to understand the chapter correctly.

- **Relational engine**: The relational engine, also known as **query processor** (**QP**) manages execution of the query, requests data from the storage engine, and processes result set.
- **Command parser**: The command parser checks for proper syntax and translates T-SQL command into query tree. If there is any syntax error, parser immediately pops up the error.
- **Query optimizer**: Query optimizer takes the *query tree* from the command parser and if it is a **Data Manipulation Language** (**DML**) statement, it tries to optimize it. The query optimizer first dismantles the batch it has received in form of query tree into small pieces, and then tries to optimize each piece by finding different ways and then choosing the best suited way to execute the query. Query optimizer is a cost-based optimizer as the optimizer chooses the plan that it determines would cost the least, based on its finding which is based on estimated memory requirements, index(es) and statistics available on table, number of required I/O, and CPU utilization. Based on all these analyses, query optimizer generates the estimated execution plan.
- **Storage engine**: As the name suggests, storage engine takes care of data access, modification, and caching. Storage engine also takes responsibility to read data from disk or from memory and retains data integrity. The storage engine receives information regarding the query from the query processor along with the execution plan in the form of a query tree.

▸ **Plan cache**: SQL Server 2012 is equipped with memory pool which is used to save execution plan. Plan cache will not store more than two copies of the execution plan for a single query.

    ❑ For serial execution

    ❑ For parallel execution

▸ **Lazy writer**: Lazy writer reads buffer pool memory, finds out dirty pages (pages which has some data but have not written into the disk at the moment; so in time of server crash, we might loose data in dirty pages), and writes them up into the disk in order to clear the pool.

Understanding of relation between the relational engine and storage engine is described in following diagram:

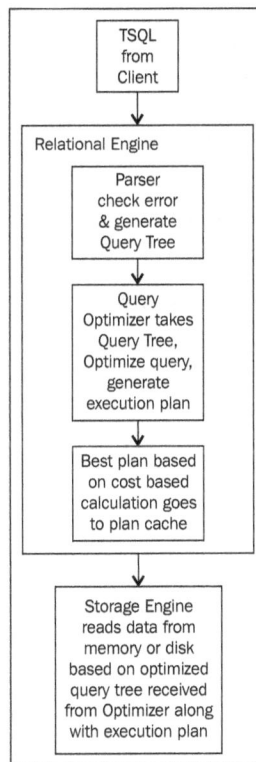

```
┌──────────────────────────────────────────┐
│            ┌─────────────┐                │
│            │    TSQL     │                │
│            │    from     │                │
│            │   Client    │                │
│            └─────────────┘                │
│                   │                       │
│  ┌────────────────▼────────────────────┐ │
│  │ Relational Engine                    │ │
│  │      ┌─────────────────┐             │ │
│  │      │     Parser      │             │ │
│  │      │   check error   │             │ │
│  │      │   & generate    │             │ │
│  │      │   Query Tree    │             │ │
│  │      └─────────────────┘             │ │
│  │               │                      │ │
│  │      ┌─────────────────┐             │ │
│  │      │     Query       │             │ │
│  │      │ Optimizer takes │             │ │
│  │      │  Query Tree,    │             │ │
│  │      │ Optimize query, │             │ │
│  │      │    generate     │             │ │
│  │      │ execution plan  │             │ │
│  │      └─────────────────┘             │ │
│  │               │                      │ │
│  │      ┌─────────────────┐             │ │
│  │      │ Best plan based │             │ │
│  │      │  on cost based  │             │ │
│  │      │ calculation goes│             │ │
│  │      │  to plan cache  │             │ │
│  │      └─────────────────┘             │ │
│  └──────────────────────────────────────┘ │
│                   │                       │
│          ┌─────────────────┐              │
│          │ Storage Engine  │              │
│          │ reads data from │              │
│          │ memory or disk  │              │
│          │ based on optimized│            │
│          │ query tree received│           │
│          │ from Optimizer along│          │
│          │ with execution plan │          │
│          └─────────────────┘              │
└──────────────────────────────────────────┘
```

Working with estimated execution plan

Estimated execution plan is the result of query optimizer, it is generated even before the query execution. Hence, it might have some or more changes when compared with the actual execution plan, but in most cases the actual and estimated execution plan remain almost the same.

Getting ready

As a DBA, many times you might come across a situation where you come to the office in the morning, somebody comes to you complaining that one of the page is taking a long time to display data which was working just fine and fast some days back. What would you do in the first step? How do you determine where the problem is?

This is the time where the estimated execution plan comes into picture. You take the query or stored procedure from the page which is showing the data very slowly (though there could be other reasons too, but let us assume that it is because of SQL Server only, as of now.) and check the execution plan of the query or stored procedure in order to find the bottleneck of the issue.

In this recipe, we will execute one `select` query which will display information regarding the purchase order made by each vendor. It will consists of purchase order ID, purchase order date, employee login ID (who has made a deal with the vendor), total order quantity, and amount from the `AdventureWorks2012` database.

How to do it...

To see the effect of the estimated execution plan, let us go through the steps given as follows:

1. Write down following query in SSMS from **Start |All Programs | SQL Server 2012 | SQL Server Management Studio (SSMS)**:

```
Use AdventureWorks2012
GO

SELECT
  POH.PurchaseOrderID
  ,POH.OrderDate
  ,EMP.LoginID
  ,V.Name AS VendorName
  ,SUM(POD.OrderQty) AS OrderQty
  ,SUM(POD.OrderQty*POD.UnitPrice) AS Amount
  ,COUNT_BIG(*) AS Count
FROM
  [Purchasing].[PurchaseOrderHeader] AS POH
JOIN
  [Purchasing].[PurchaseOrderDetail] AS POD
ON
  POH.PurchaseOrderID = POD.PurchaseOrderID
JOIN
  [HumanResources].[Employee] AS EMP
ON
```

```
    POH.EmployeeID=EMP.BusinessEntityID
JOIN
    [Purchasing].[Vendor] AS V
ON
    POH.VendorID=V.BusinessEntityID
GROUP BY
    POH.PurchaseOrderID
    ,POH.OrderDate
    ,EMP.LoginID
    ,V.Name
GO
```

2. Go to the **Query** menu and click on **Display Estimated Execution Plan** or press *Ctrl+L* which will display the estimated execution plan. Look at the screenshot given as follows:

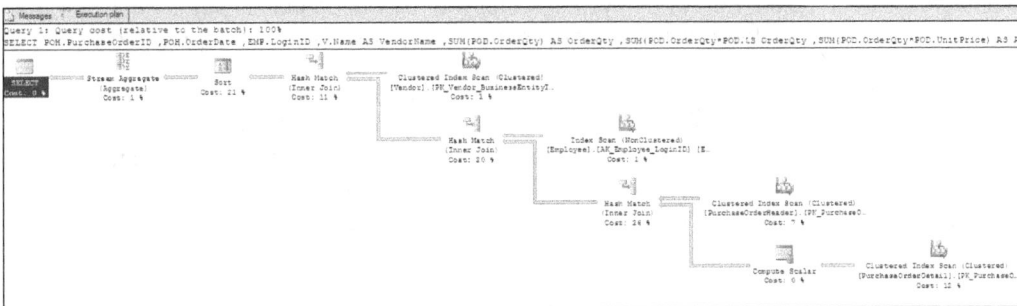

How it works...

When we execute any T-SQL statement, it first goes to a relational engine which does two tasks for us.

▶ Parse the query with help of the parser

▶ After getting the response from the parser, query optimizer processes the query and generates the estimated execution plan

Once the query comes to the query optimizer, it finds out the optimal way to execute the query by looking at the predicate given in the query. It finds out the statistics, if available, and indexes to decide the path of execution in form of estimated execution plan which will be available to the storage engine before it finally executes the query.

Query optimizer is a smart tool in SQL Server 2012 which is used to find the best optimal way to execute the query in most cases. But, it may address the sub-optimal way sometimes, due to lack of information such as out dated statistics or over indexing.

Working with actual execution plan

The actual execution plan is one of the most important features provided by SQL Server, as it tells us how the query has actually performed. We can find the bottleneck in query, if any, and find out the way to resolve it.

Getting ready

In the previous recipe, *Working with estimated execution plan*, we have already discussed about the importance of estimated execution plan, which shows how your query should be processed, with the way it should get executed.

Most of the time, your query runs exactly in the same way as it has been mentioned in estimated execution plan. But, what if you find that your execution plan is perfect and still your query execution seems slow? Well, in that case the actual execution plan comes into picture.

Execute your query with actual execution plan and see whether it is following the ways we saw in estimated execution plan. In most cases, both the plans should be the same (except that the estimated execution plan is based on sampling data stored in the histogram and the actual execution plan is based on real table in database), but in some scenarios, especially in case of out of date statistics and/or over indexing, both executions follow different paths. This is called a bottleneck and we should fix it.

How to do it...

To generate and study the actual execution plan, refer the following steps:

1. Write down the following query which we have used in the previous recipe, *Working with estimated execution plan*, so that we can compare both the plans.

    ```
    USE AdventureWorks2012
    GO

    SELECT
      POH.PurchaseOrderID
      ,POH.OrderDate
      ,EMP.LoginID
      ,V.Name AS VendorName
      ,SUM(POD.OrderQty) AS OrderQty
      ,SUM(POD.OrderQty*POD.UnitPrice) AS Amount
      ,COUNT_BIG(*) AS Count
    FROM
      [Purchasing].[PurchaseOrderHeader] AS POH
    JOIN
    ```

```
   [Purchasing].[PurchaseOrderDetail] AS POD
ON
   POH.PurchaseOrderID = POD.PurchaseOrderID
JOIN
   [HumanResources].[Employee] AS EMP
ON
   POH.EmployeeID=EMP.BusinessEntityID
JOIN
   [Purchasing].[Vendor] AS V
ON
   POH.VendorID=V.BusinessEntityID
GROUP BY
   POH.PurchaseOrderID
   ,POH.OrderDate
   ,EMP.LoginID
   ,V.Name
GO
```

2. Go to the **Query** menu and click on **Include Actual Execution Plan** or press *Ctrl+M*
   which will display the estimated execution plan.

3. Now, execute the query, you will get the output of the query in the **Result** tab and
   the graphical actual execution plan in **Execution Plan** tab. Have a look at the
   following screenshot:

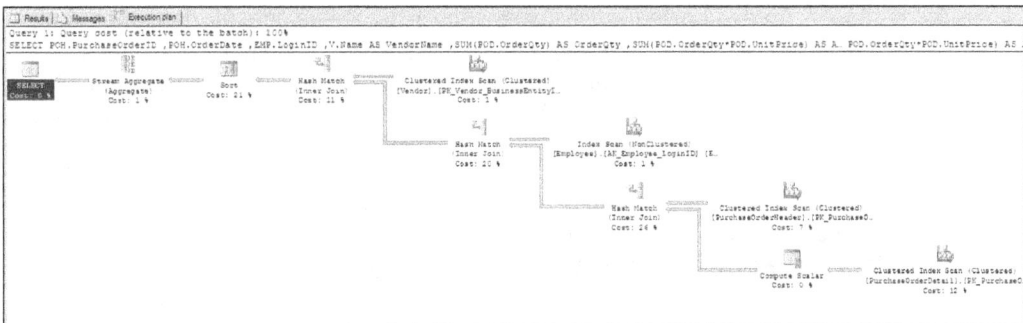

The same execution plan as shown in the previous screenshot is presented in text format as
follows with the help of SHOWPLAN_TEXT:

```
   |--Stream Aggregate(GROUP BY:([POH].[PurchaseOrderID], [EMP].
[LoginID], [V].[Name]) DEFINE:([Expr1010]=Count(*), [Expr1008]=SUM([
AdventureWorks2012].[Purchasing].[PurchaseOrderDetail].[OrderQty] as
[POD].[OrderQty]), [Expr1009]=SUM([Expr1011]), [POH].[Or
        |--Sort(ORDER BY:([POH].[PurchaseOrderID] ASC, [EMP].[LoginID]
ASC, [V].[Name] ASC))
```

```
                    |--Hash Match(Inner Join, HASH:([V].
[BusinessEntityID])=([POH].[VendorID]))
                         |--Clustered Index Scan(OBJECT:([AdventureWorks2012].
[Purchasing].[Vendor].[PK_Vendor_BusinessEntityID] AS [V]))
                         |--Hash Match(Inner Join, HASH:([EMP].
[BusinessEntityID])=([POH].[EmployeeID]))
                              |--Index Scan(OBJECT:([AdventureWorks2012].
[HumanResources].[Employee].[AK_Employee_LoginID] AS [EMP]))
                              |--Hash Match(Inner Join, HASH:([POH].
[PurchaseOrderID])=([POD].[PurchaseOrderID]))
                                   |--Clustered Index Scan(OBJECT:([AdventureW
orks2012].[Purchasing].[PurchaseOrderHeader].[PK_PurchaseOrderHeader_
PurchaseOrderID] AS [POH]))
                                   |--Compute Scalar(DEFINE:([Expr101
1]=CONVERT_IMPLICIT(money,[AdventureWorks2012].[Purchasing].
[PurchaseOrderDetail].[OrderQty] as [POD].[OrderQty],0)*[AdventureWor
ks2012].[Purchasing].[PurchaseOrderDetail].[UnitPrice] as [POD].[U
                                        |--Clustered Index Scan(OBJECT
:([AdventureWorks2012].[Purchasing].[PurchaseOrderDetail].[PK_
PurchaseOrderDetail_PurchaseOrderID_PurchaseOrderDetailID] AS [POD]))
```

How it works...

As we already discussed, the optimizer generates the estimated execution plan and sends it to the storage engine in a binary format to actually execute the query. Actual execution plan is the feature of storage engine which conveys to you what has actually happened while executing the query. We can compare both the estimated execution plan and the actual execution plan to see whether there is any difference in both. In most cases both remain the same, but in some situations we can find some differences in the actual execution plan and the estimated execution plan; as explained in the *Getting ready* section of this recipe.

The estimated execution plan and actual execution plan should be the same if the situation is normal, but there are some cases which create differences in both the execution plans. For example, if you have old statistics for your index or column, estimated execution plan selects the wrong path to execute the query, in this situation when query is actually going to execute, the storage engine changes the path of query execution, to gain performance, which will be reflected in the actual execution plan. This is how we see the difference between the execution plans.

Generating an execution plan is one of the big overheads; that is why SQL Server stores generated execution plan in **plan cache**.

Saving the execution plan in the plan cache will save it permanently. Once it is aged or is out of date, it is removed by the **Lazy Writer** process.

There's more...

After reading the last paragraph of the *How It works* section, you might have a question regarding when and how the saved execution plan gets out of date and removed by SQL Server 2012.

SQL Server 2012 has very smart way to remove aged, old, and unused execution plan from the memory. Each query plan and execution context has an associated cost factor that indicates how expensive the structure is to compile. These data structures also have an age field. Every time the object is referenced by a connection, the age field is incremented by the compilation cost factor.

To explain in more detail; if your query plan has a cost factor of four and it is referenced two times, age of plan becomes eight now. The lazywriter process periodically scans the list of objects in the plan cache. The lazywriter then decrements the age field of each object by one on each scan. The age of the query plan is decremented to zero after 8 scans of the plan cache if the same plan is not referenced even a single time in the duration of these eight scans by lazywriter. The lazywriter process deallocates an object if the following conditions are met:

 ▸ The age field for the object is zero
 ▸ The memory manager requires memory and all available memory is currently being used
 ▸ The object is not currently referenced by a connection

To know more about out of date statistics refer to the *Finding out-of-date statistics and correct them* recipe in *Chapter 12, Statistics in SQL Server*.

Monitoring performance of a query by SET SHOWPLAN_XML

SHOWPLAN_XML is an XML version of the estimated execution plan. It provides all the information in XML format which we used to get in graphical format in estimated execution plan, more details about information which is provided by XML execution plan is given in the *How it works* section of this recipe. XML execution plan is nothing more than one XML file, so it is really very easy to save for future reference or for comparing it with other execution plan. The XML Execution plan becomes even more useful in a shared database hosting environment, as in that case you don't have enough permissions on the server to determine the bottleneck.

Getting ready

I have already mentioned in the introduction section that the execution plan is the obvious first step when we start looking into any performance issue in the query. Many times, in a community portal, I have been asked a question regarding query performance tuning but in that case I neither have access to the database nor have the server access of the person who has asked the question. So, I usually ask them to post the execution plan in XML format because it happens many times that the query has a big execution plan and it is not possible to capture complete graphical execution plan in one screen.

How to do it...

SET SHOWPLAN_XML is small but powerful, let us see the usage by performing the following steps:

1. Write down the following query in SSMS from **Start | All Programs | SQL Server 2012 | SQL Server Management Studio (SSMS)**:

```
USE AdventureWorks2012
GO

SET SHOWPLAN_XML ON
GO

SELECT
  POH.PurchaseOrderID
  , POH.OrderDate
  , EMP.LoginID
  , V.Name AS VendorName
  , SUM(POD.OrderQty) AS OrderQty
  , SUM(POD.OrderQty*POD.UnitPrice) AS Amount
  , COUNT_BIG(*) AS Count
FROM
  [Purchasing].[PurchaseOrderHeader] AS POH
JOIN
  [Purchasing].[PurchaseOrderDetail] AS POD
ON
  POH.PurchaseOrderID = POD.PurchaseOrderID
JOIN
  [HumanResources].[Employee] AS EMP
ON
  POH.EmployeeID=EMP.BusinessEntityID
JOIN
  [Purchasing].[Vendor] AS V
ON
```

```
      POH.VendorID=V.BusinessEntityID
GROUP BY
   POH.PurchaseOrderID
   ,POH.OrderDate
   ,EMP.LoginID
   ,V.Name
GO

SET SHOWPLAN_XML OFF
GO
```

2. As it is explained that **SHOWPLAN_XML** is an XML version of the estimated execution plan, it will not execute the previous query, instead it will generate the estimated execution plan and display one row as a result; as shown in the following screenshot:

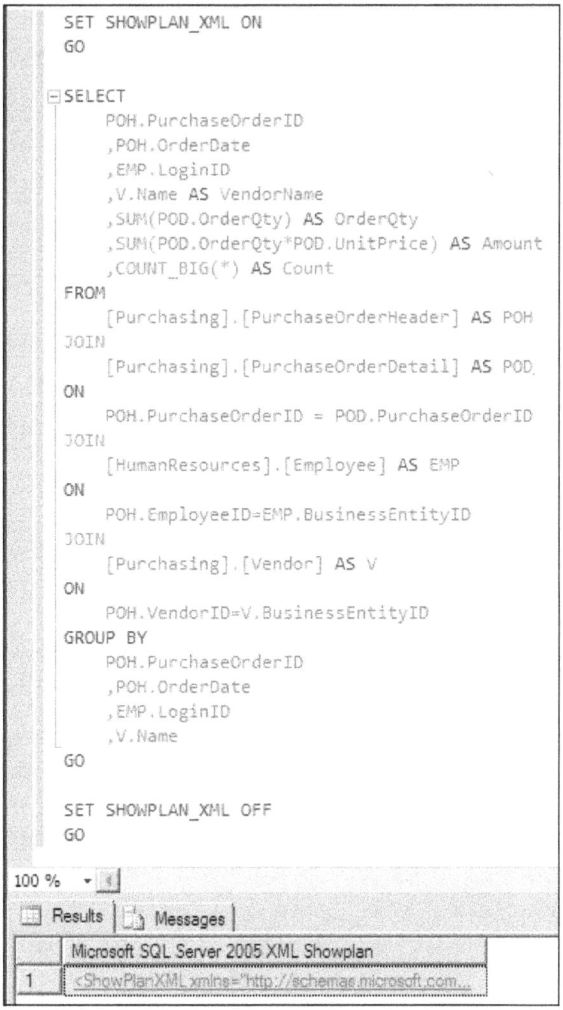

```
SET SHOWPLAN_XML ON
GO

SELECT
      POH.PurchaseOrderID
      ,POH.OrderDate
      ,EMP.LoginID
      ,V.Name AS VendorName
      ,SUM(POD.OrderQty) AS OrderQty
      ,SUM(POD.OrderQty*POD.UnitPrice) AS Amount
      ,COUNT_BIG(*) AS Count
FROM
      [Purchasing].[PurchaseOrderHeader] AS POH
JOIN
      [Purchasing].[PurchaseOrderDetail] AS POD
ON
      POH.PurchaseOrderID = POD.PurchaseOrderID
JOIN
      [HumanResources].[Employee] AS EMP
ON
      POH.EmployeeID=EMP.BusinessEntityID
JOIN
      [Purchasing].[Vendor] AS V
ON
      POH.VendorID=V.BusinessEntityID
GROUP BY
      POH.PurchaseOrderID
      ,POH.OrderDate
      ,EMP.LoginID
      ,V.Name
GO

SET SHOWPLAN_XML OFF
GO
```

100 %

Results | Messages

	Microsoft SQL Server 2005 XML Showplan
1	<ShowPlanXML xmlns="http://schemas.microsoft.com...

3. When you click on the **Result** tab where you can see **<ShowPlanXML......**, you will be redirected to the graphical estimated execution plan file which has .SqlPlan extension, as given in the following screenshot. Right-click on that window and click on the **Show Execution Plan XML...** option.

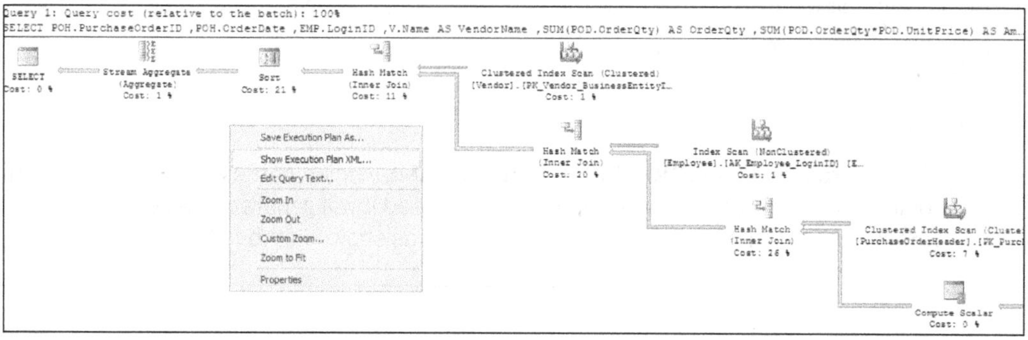

4. The **Show Execution Plan XML...** option will forward you to the XML screen in your SSMS which you can even save to get your XML file for future use. The following is a screenshot of XML file:

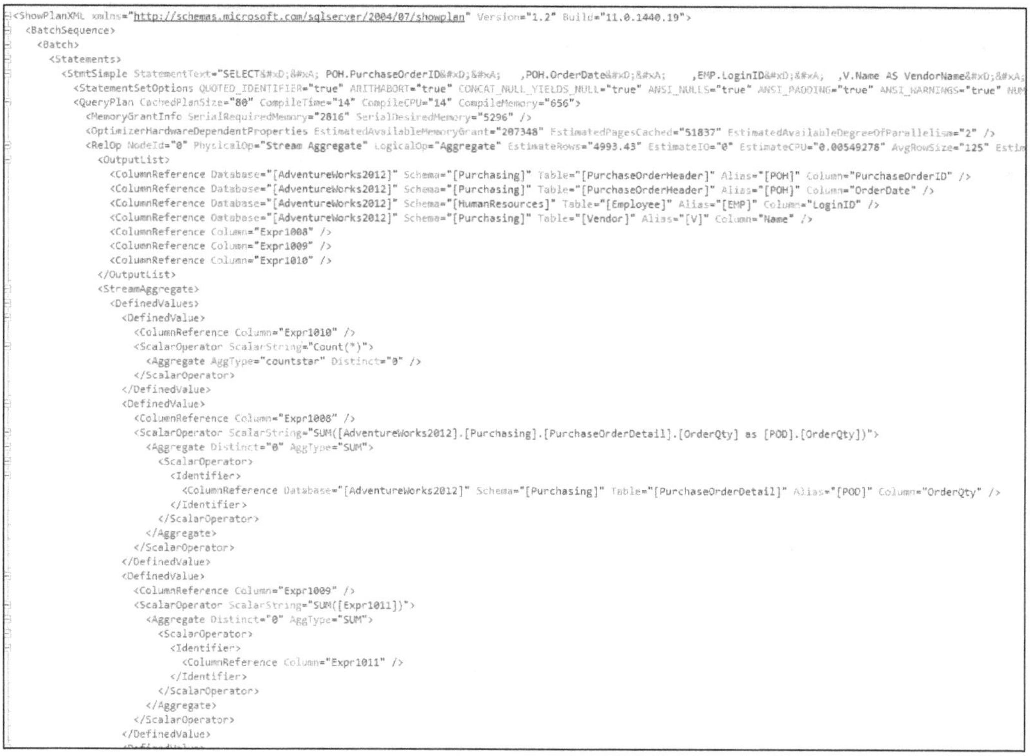

> You can download the full XML execution plan, `5740_05_01.xml`, with the code snippet of this chapter.

How it works...

XML execution plan provides a lot of crucial information to dig in. We will look at a few of the important tags from XML file:

```
<BatchSequence>
  <Batch>
    <Statements>
      <StmtSimple StatementText="SELECT&#xD;&#xA; POH.PurchaseOrderID&#xD;&#xA;     ,POH.OrderDate&#xD;&#xA;       ,EMP.LoginID&#xD;&#xA;
        ,V.Name AS VendorName&#xD;&#xA; ,SUM(POD.OrderQty) AS OrderQty&#xD;&#xA;     ,SUM(POD.OrderQty*POD.UnitPrice) AS Amount&#xD;&#xA;
        ,COUNT_BIG(*) AS Count&#xD;&#xA;FROM &#xD;&#xA; [Purchasing].[PurchaseOrderHeader] AS POH &#xD;&#xA;JOIN &#xD;&#xA; [Purchasing].[PurchaseOrderDetail] AS
        POD&#xD;&#xA;ON&#xD;&#xA;   POH.PurchaseOrderID = POD.PurchaseOrderID&#xD;&#xA;JOIN &#xD;&#xA; [HumanResources].[Employee] AS EMP&#xD;&#xA;ON&#xD;&#xA;
        POH.EmployeeID=EMP.BusinessEntityID&#xD;&#xA;JOIN &#xD;&#xA;   [Purchasing].[Vendor] AS V&#xD;&#xA;ON&#xD;&#xA;   POH.VendorID=
        V.BusinessEntityID&#xD;&#xA;GROUP BY&#xD;&#xA;  POH.PurchaseOrderID&#xD;&#xA;   ,POH.OrderDate&#xD;&#xA;       ,EMP.LoginID&#xD;&#xA;   ,V.Name &#xD;&#xA;"
        StatementId="1" StatementCompId="1" StatementType="SELECT" RetrievedFromCache="true" StatementSubTreeCost="0.508986" StatementEstRows="4993.43"
        StatementOptmLevel="FULL" QueryHash="0x7593A4FA9923191B" QueryPlanHash="0xC487CCF9199D02BA" StatementOptmEarlyAbortReason="TimeOut">

        <StatementSetOptions QUOTED_IDENTIFIER="true" ARITHABORT="true" CONCAT_NULL_YIELDS_NULL="true" ANSI_NULLS="true" ANSI_PADDING="true" ANSI_WARNINGS="true" N

        <QueryPlan CachedPlanSize="80" CompileTime="14" CompileCPU="14" CompileMemory="656">

          <MemoryGrantInfo SerialRequiredMemory="2816" SerialDesiredMemory="5296" />

          <OptimizerHardwareDependentProperties EstimatedAvailableMemoryGrant="207348" EstimatedPagesCached="51837" EstimatedAvailableDegreeOfParallelism="2" />
          <RelOp NodeId="0" PhysicalOp="Stream Aggregate" LogicalOp="Aggregate" EstimateRows="4993.43" EstimateIO="0" EstimateCPU="0.00549278" AvgRowSize="125"
            EstimatedTotalSubtreeCost="0.508986" Parallel="0" EstimateRebinds="0" EstimateRewinds="0" EstimatedExecutionMode="Row">
```

The previous screenshot shows the **BatchSequence**, **Batch**, and **Statement** elements which are the starting tags of the XML file.

- ▶ If we have multiple batch or statement in execution, we would have more then one **Batch** and **Statement** element in XML.

- ▶ The **StmtSimple** element displays information about the query we ran and some physical attribute value at the time of executing the query.

- ▶ The **Statement SetOption** elements make us aware with the value of the SET environment variables.

- ▶ The **QueryPlan** element gives you an insight regarding the resources and memory consumed by plan generation task.

- ▶ The **RelOp** elements provide information regarding the operation that is going to be performed on a statement. An operation such as a table scan, index scan, index seek, aggregation, sorting, or others would come under these elements along with more details.

Monitoring performance of a query by SET STATISTICS XML

SET STATISTICS XML is an XML version of the actual execution plan. It provides all the information in XML format which we used to get in graphical format in the actual execution plan.

Getting ready

We are going to use the SELECT query given in the previous recipe's *How to do it...* section by replacing SHOWPLAN_XML with SET STATISTICS XML. The main intention to use the same query from the previous recipe *Monitoring performance of query by SET SHOWPLAN_XML* is to see the difference between two execution plan. Generally, if an index and statistics' histogram is updated, then the execution plan on sampling (estimated execution plan) and execution plan on real table (actual execution plan) remain the same. If you find any difference between these two plans, then it is a time to investigate that.

How to do it...

Perform the following steps to use SET STATISTICS XML:

1. Write down the following query in SSMS from **Start |All Programs | SQL Server 2012 | SQL Server Management Studio (SSMS)**:

```
Use AdventureWorks2012
GO

SET STATISTICS XML ON
GO

SELECT
  POH.PurchaseOrderID
  ,POH.OrderDate
  ,EMP.LoginID
  ,V.Name AS VendorName
  ,SUM(POD.OrderQty) AS OrderQty
  ,SUM(POD.OrderQty*POD.UnitPrice) AS Amount
  ,COUNT_BIG(*) AS Count
FROM
  [Purchasing].[PurchaseOrderHeader] AS POH
JOIN
  [Purchasing].[PurchaseOrderDetail] AS POD
ON
```

```
    POH.PurchaseOrderID = POD.PurchaseOrderID
JOIN
    [HumanResources].[Employee] AS EMP
ON
    POH.EmployeeID=EMP.BusinessEntityID
JOIN
    [Purchasing].[Vendor] AS V
ON
    POH.VendorID=V.BusinessEntityID
GROUP BY
    POH.PurchaseOrderID
    ,POH.OrderDate
    ,EMP.LoginID
    ,V.Name
GO
SET STATISTICS XML OFF
GO
```

2. As it is explained that SET STATISTICS XML is an XML version of the actual execution plan, it will execute the previous query and generate the actual execution plan also. Have a look at the following screenshot:

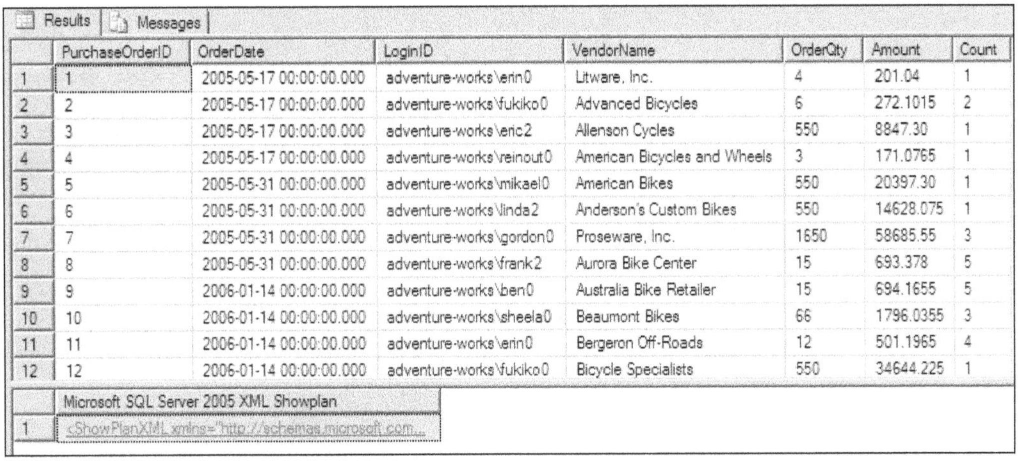

	PurchaseOrderID	OrderDate	LoginID	VendorName	OrderQty	Amount	Count
1	1	2005-05-17 00:00:00.000	adventure-works\erin0	Litware, Inc.	4	201.04	1
2	2	2005-05-17 00:00:00.000	adventure-works\fukiko0	Advanced Bicycles	6	272.1015	2
3	3	2005-05-17 00:00:00.000	adventure-works\eric2	Allenson Cycles	550	8847.30	1
4	4	2005-05-17 00:00:00.000	adventure-works\reinout0	American Bicycles and Wheels	3	171.0765	1
5	5	2005-05-31 00:00:00.000	adventure-works\mikael0	American Bikes	550	20397.30	1
6	6	2005-05-31 00:00:00.000	adventure-works\linda2	Anderson's Custom Bikes	550	14628.075	1
7	7	2005-05-31 00:00:00.000	adventure-works\gordon0	Proseware, Inc.	1650	58685.55	3
8	8	2005-05-31 00:00:00.000	adventure-works\frank2	Aurora Bike Center	15	693.378	5
9	9	2006-01-14 00:00:00.000	adventure-works\ben0	Australia Bike Retailer	15	694.1655	5
10	10	2006-01-14 00:00:00.000	adventure-works\sheela0	Beaumont Bikes	66	1796.0355	3
11	11	2006-01-14 00:00:00.000	adventure-works\erin0	Bergeron Off-Roads	12	501.1965	4
12	12	2006-01-14 00:00:00.000	adventure-works\fukiko0	Bicycle Specialists	550	34644.225	1

	Microsoft SQL Server 2005 XML Showplan
1	<ShowPlanXML xmlns="http://schemas.microsoft.com...

3. Since this is not like an estimated execution plan, SET STATISTICS XML will execute the query and will generate the actual execution plan in XML format, so you will find two result sets in the **Results** tab. The first result set shows the result of the query and the second result set shows link to open the plan. Click on the link and you will be forwarded to the graphical actual execution plan window:

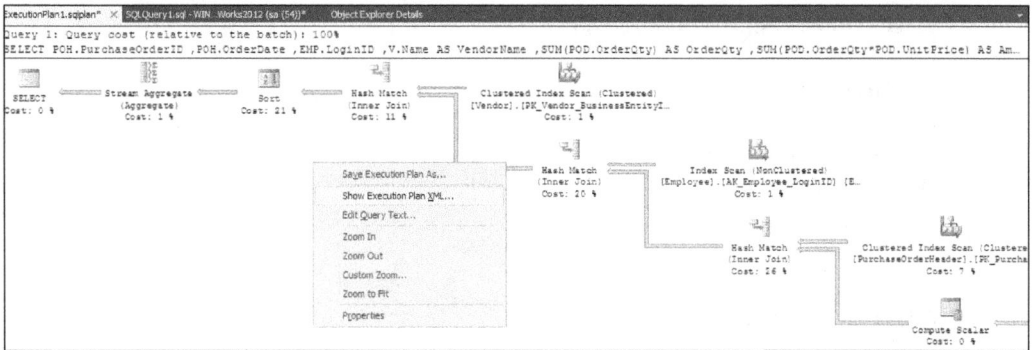

4. Right-click on the graphical plan and select the **Show Execution Plan XML...** option and you will be forwarded to the XML plan:

[✎ You can download the full XML execution plan, `5740_05_02.xml`, with the
code snippet of this chapter.]

How it works...

XML actual execution plan provides a lot of crucial information to dig in. We will understand a
few of the important tags from the XML file:

```
<BatchSequence>
  <Batch>
    <Statements>
      <StmtSimple StatementText="SELECT&#xD;&#xA; POH.PurchaseOrderID&#xD;&#xA;    ,POH.OrderDate&#xD;&#xA;    ,EMP.LoginID&#xD;&#xA;
      ,V.Name AS VendorName&#xD;&#xA; ,SUM(POD.OrderQty) AS OrderQty&#xD;&#xA;    ,SUM(POD.OrderQty*POD.UnitPrice) AS Amount&#xD;&#xA;
      ,COUNT_BIG(*) AS Count&#xD;&#xA;FROM &#xD;&#xA; [Purchasing].[PurchaseOrderHeader] AS POH &#xD;&#xA;JOIN &#xD;&#xA; [Purchasing].[PurchaseOrderDetail] AS
      POD&#xD;&#xA;ON&#xD;&#xA;   POH.PurchaseOrderID = POD.PurchaseOrderID&#xD;&#xA;JOIN &#xD;&#xA; [HumanResources].[Employee] AS EMP&#xD;&#xA;ON&#xD;&#xA;
      POH.EmployeeID=EMP.BusinessEntityID&#xD;&#xA;JOIN &#xD;&#xA;    [Purchasing].[Vendor] AS V&#xD;&#xA;ON&#xD;&#xA;    POH.VendorID=
      V.BusinessEntityID&#xD;&#xA;GROUP BY&#xD;&#xA;  POH.PurchaseOrderID&#xD;&#xA;    ,POH.OrderDate&#xD;&#xA;    ,EMP.LoginID&#xD;&#xA;    ,V.Name &#xD;&#xA;"
        StatementId="1" StatementCompId="1" StatementType="SELECT" RetrievedFromCache="true" StatementSubTreeCost="0.508986" StatementEstRows="4993.43"
        StatementOptmLevel="FULL" QueryHash="0x7593A4FA99231918" QueryPlanHash="0xC487CCF91990028A" StatementOptmEarlyAbortReason="TimeOut">

        <StatementSetOptions QUOTED_IDENTIFIER="true" ARITHABORT="true" CONCAT_NULL_YIELDS_NULL="true" ANSI_NULLS="true" ANSI_PADDING="true" ANSI_WARNINGS="true" N

        <QueryPlan CachedPlanSize="80" CompileTime="14" CompileCPU="14" CompileMemory="656">

          <MemoryGrantInfo SerialRequiredMemory="2816" SerialDesiredMemory="5296" />

          <OptimizerHardwareDependentProperties EstimatedAvailableMemoryGrant="207348" EstimatedPagesCached="51837" EstimatedAvailableDegreeOfParallelism="2" />
          <RelOp NodeId="0" PhysicalOp="Stream Aggregate" LogicalOp="Aggregate" EstimateRows="4993.43" EstimateIO="0" EstimateCPU="0.00549278" AvgRowSize="125"
            EstimatedTotalSubtreeCost="0.508986" Parallel="0" EstimateRebinds="0" EstimateRewinds="0" EstimatedExecutionMode="Row">
```

The previous screenshot shows the **BatchSequence**, **Batch**, and **Statement** elements which
are the starting tags of the XML file.

▸ If we have multiple batch or statement in execution, we would have more then one
  Batch and **Statement** element in XML.

▸ The **StmtSimple** element displays information about the query we ran and some
  physical attribute value at the time of executing the query.

▸ The **Statement SetOption** elements make us aware with the value of the SET
  environment variables.

▸ The **QueryPlan** element gives you an insight regarding the resources and memory
  consumed by plan generation task.

▸ The **RelOp** elements provide information regarding the operation that is going to
  be performed on a statement. Operations such as a table scan, index scan, index
  seek, aggregation, sorting, and others would come under these elements along
  with more details.

Monitoring performance of a query by SET STATISTICS IO

> There are so many weapons in the world, but it depends on the person what to choose. Everybody has their own choice which may or may not change with the situation. Some people like to use Stilettos whereas some would like to go for Swords. Some people love Nunchucks whereas some would like to use Spartan Spearhead.

Microsoft has also provided many weapons in SQL Server 2012 to monitor and deal with performance issue; you can choose your weapon and use it. SET STATISTICS IO is one of the light weight weapon that can be used very easily to get some of the important information regarding input and output resources consumed by the batch we have executed.

SET STATISTICS IO is an evergreen weapon and most DBA never forget to give it a shot as the first step on the enemy (slow performance). SQL Server used to provide this weapon from the initial versions of SQL Server and it is still available in SQL Server 2012 without change. This is really light weight and very effective in helping you to find the weakness of your enemy (slow performance), once you find the weakness, you can deal with it.

Performance is affected by so many different factors. Out of them, a few are listed here which are major:

- Memory
- CPU
- Disk I/O
- Network
- (Logical/Physical) Read

All these factors are important in performance tuning and each has their own significance. All other factors may have variance (fluctuation) depends on the situation such as in pick hour, factors are in heavy pressure so might show you a higher number of CPU or memory utilization; and in off hours, you will find idle resources.

While dealing with bad performance, it is highly important that we first see non-fluctuating cost reference so we can decide query performance increment or decrement, after we have taken the steps to improve query performance and re-executed the same query multiple times.

[CPU and memory value may fluctuate significantly when re-executing the same query with no change in the base table schema or indexes or even data.]

It happens because background applications running on the SQL Server machine continuously affects the processing time of the under observation query. So these values are not something we can depend on, at the same time `reads` remains the same when a similar query with the same table schema and data is executed multiple times.

Getting ready

Use the `SELECT` query we have used in previous recipe *Monitoring performance of query by SET STATISTICS XML* by adding `SET STATISTICS IO`.

If there is a difference found in the estimated execution plan and the actual execution plan, we would definitely like to see what is the current `reads` status with `SET STATISTICS IO` and we can observe the same after we take some action resolving the bottleneck.

How to do it...

`SET STATISTICS IO` is one of the favorite commands for anybody who is dealing with performance tuning in SQL Server. Let us see the usage of the same by performing the following steps:

1. Write down the following query in SSMS from **Start | All Programs | SQL Server 2012 | SQL Server Management Studio (SSMS)**.

```
Use AdventureWorks2012
GO

SET STATISTICS IO ON
GO

SELECT
  POH.PurchaseOrderID
  ,POH.OrderDate
  ,EMP.LoginID
  ,V.Name AS VendorName
  ,SUM(POD.OrderQty) AS OrderQty
  ,SUM(POD.OrderQty*POD.UnitPrice) AS Amount
  ,COUNT_BIG(*) AS Count
FROM
  [Purchasing].[PurchaseOrderHeader] AS POH
JOIN
```

```
      [Purchasing].[PurchaseOrderDetail] AS POD
ON
    POH.PurchaseOrderID = POD.PurchaseOrderID
JOIN
    [HumanResources].[Employee] AS EMP
ON
    POH.EmployeeID=EMP.BusinessEntityID
JOIN
    [Purchasing].[Vendor] AS V
ON
    POH.VendorID=V.BusinessEntityID
GROUP BY
    POH.PurchaseOrderID
    ,POH.OrderDate
    ,EMP.LoginID
    ,V.Name
GO
SET STATISTICS IO OFF
GO
```

2. The `SELECT` query will be executed and the output is displayed in the **Results** panel and the result of `SET STATISTICS IO` will come in the **Message** tab. The following is the screenshot of the same:

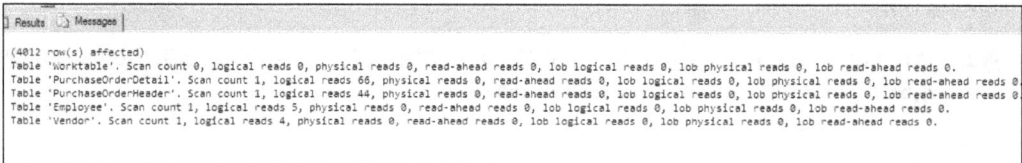

Here is the message in text format to make it more readable:

```
(4012 row(s) affected)
Table 'Worktable'. Scan count 0, logical reads 0, physical reads 0,
read-ahead reads 0, lob logical reads 0, lob physical reads 0, lob
read-ahead reads 0.
Table 'PurchaseOrderDetail'. Scan count 1, logical reads 66, physical
reads 0, read-ahead reads 0, lob logical reads 0, lob physical reads
0, lob read-ahead reads 0.
Table 'PurchaseOrderHeader'. Scan count 1, logical reads 44, physical
reads 0, read-ahead reads 0, lob logical reads 0, lob physical reads
0, lob read-ahead reads 0.
Table 'Employee'. Scan count 1, logical reads 5, physical reads 0,
read-ahead reads 0, lob logical reads 0, lob physical reads 0, lob
read-ahead reads 0.
```

```
Table 'Vendor'. Scan count 1, logical reads 4, physical reads 0, read-
ahead reads 0, lob logical reads 0, lob physical reads 0, lob read-
ahead reads 0.
```

How it works...

While executing the query in SQL Server, it has to read the data from data cache which is represented by Logical Read and if the data is not available in data cache then the storage engine reads the data from the disk which is represented by Physical Read. These are really useful while doing performance tuning, which you can get by SET STATISTICS IO.

You can see one more important information in message tag for each table used in query, which is Scan count.

> The number that comes in Scan count represents the number of index or table scan performed on a particular table while executing the query. If you have a unique clustered index on primary key and you are searching for one particular value on that column, then obviously clustered index seek will happen and you will get 0 as the value of Scan count.

There's more...

To keep SET STATISTICS IO always on, go to the **Query** menu | **Query Options** and select **Advanced** from the tree-view on left-hand side and select the checkbox of **SET STATISTICS IO**. Look at the following screenshot for more information:

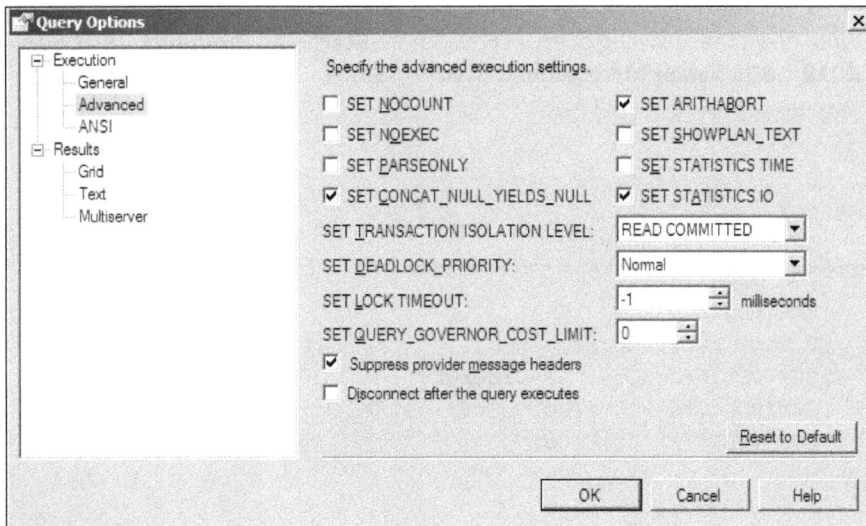

Monitoring performance of a query by SET STATISTICS TIME

SET STATISTICS TIME is also one of the light weight weapons which can be used to get some of the important information regarding CPU resources consumed by the batch we have executed.

Getting ready

In order to know the real CPU usage statistics of the query you execute, we will use the same SELECT query that we have used in the previous recipe *Monitoring performance of query by SET STATISTICS IO* by adding SET STATISTICS TIME.

After comparing the different execution plan, check the statistics IO of the query, it is now time for further digging by looking at CPU resources consumed by query or batch which displays the number of milliseconds required by the CPU to parse, compile, and execute query or batch. This time doesn't include the time which SQL Server 2012 spends to deliver the result set to client.

Every database professional wants to tune the query and make it faster than before, but how could you measure whether query is working faster after the tuning action you have taken?

This is the time when SET STATISTICS TIME comes into picture.

How to do it...

Let us have a look at SET STATISTICS TIME by performing the following steps:

1. Write down the following query in SSMS from **Start | All Programs | SQL Server 2012 | SQL Server Management Studio (SSMS)**.

```
SET STATISTICS TIME ON
GO

SELECT
  POH.PurchaseOrderID
  ,POH.OrderDate
  ,EMP.LoginID
  ,V.Name AS VendorName
  ,SUM(POD.OrderQty) AS OrderQty
  ,SUM(POD.OrderQty*POD.UnitPrice) AS Amount
  ,COUNT_BIG(*) AS Count
FROM
```

```
   [Purchasing].[PurchaseOrderHeader] AS POH
JOIN
   [Purchasing].[PurchaseOrderDetail] AS POD
ON
   POH.PurchaseOrderID = POD.PurchaseOrderID
JOIN
   [HumanResources].[Employee] AS EMP
ON
   POH.EmployeeID=EMP.BusinessEntityID
JOIN
   [Purchasing].[Vendor] AS V
ON
   POH.VendorID=V.BusinessEntityID
GROUP BY
   POH.PurchaseOrderID
   ,POH.OrderDate
   ,EMP.LoginID
   ,V.Name
GO
SET STATISTICS TIME OFF
GO
```

2. The SELECT query will be executed and the output is displayed in the **Results** panel and the result of SET STATISTICS TIME will appear in the **Message** tab. The following is screenshot illustrates this:

```
(4012 row(s) affected)

SQL Server Execution Times:
   CPU time = 46 ms,  elapsed time = 140 ms.
```

How it works...

To check the query execution time, are you going to look at your watch after start execution and count it till end of execution of the query? This is not the best way. The query execution time from start to end, according to your watch, may misguide you as query execution is affected by many different things such as load on the server, usage of the SQL Server instance, and many more things. To check how much CPU resources (CPU time) is consumed by the query we can use the SET STATISTICS TIME option.

More CPU resources means slow query. It would be a nice combo to use SET STATISTICS IO and SET STATISTICS TIME together, so that you can get information regarding how much heavy load on CPU is coming from SET STATISTICS TIME and what table(s) is creating that load from SET STATISTICS IO.

To keep SET STATISTICS TIME always on, go to the **Query** menu | **Query Options** and select **Advanced** from the tree view on the left-hand side and select the checkbox of SET STATISTICS TIME. Here is a screenshot for more information:

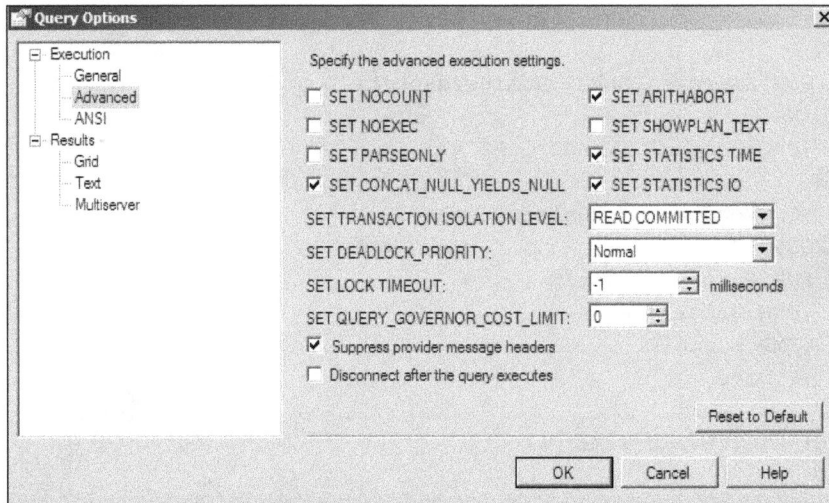

Including and understanding client statistics

Client statistics collects information of query execution by considering your computer as a client. Because of this, you can see all those information and statistics which generally don't come into picture if you execute query on the same server such as, network traffic and its effect. Sometimes we feel query is running slower than what it suppose to. DBA might feel to enhance the performance of the query by a different route such as create missing index, update statistics, using proper predicate, and so on. DBA loves to see how much improvement came in performance by looking at the facts which are given in client statistics.

Getting ready

Let us create one big table which will be used in this recipe. After a creating table with thousands of row, we can check performance in client statistics and trying to improve its performance. After performance tuning, we will compare the results.

```
USE AdventureWorks2012
GO

--if ordDemo table is already there. you can delete it than
--create new one with name " ordDemo"
IF OBJECT_ID('ordDemo', 'U') IS NOT NULL BEGIN
```

```
      DROP TABLE ordDemo
END
GO


--creating table for demonstration
CREATE TABLE ordDemo (OrderID INT IDENTITY, OrderDate DATETIME, Amount
MONEY, Refno INT)
GO


--inserting 100000 sample rows into table
INSERT INTO ordDemo (OrderDate, Amount, Refno)
SELECT TOP 100000
      DATEADD(minute, ABS(a.object_id % 50000 ), CAST('2011-11-04' AS
DATETIME)),
      ABS(a.object_id % 10),
      CAST(ABS(a.object_id % 13) AS VARCHAR)
FROM sys.all_objects a
CROSS JOIN sys.all_objects b
GO
```

How to do it...

Client Statistics are very helpful to compare query execution and cost. Let us study them by performing the following steps:

1. Select the **Include Client Statistics** option from **Query** menu or press _Shift+Alt+S_.

2. Execute the following query:

    ```
    SELECT OrderDate,Amount,Refno FROM ordDemo WHERE Refno<3
    ```

3. Open a new query window and create the following index from that new query window, if you use the same query window in which we have executed the previous query, index creation statistics will also be included in client statistics; which obviously we would not want.

    ```
    --creating clustered index on column refno without discussing
    --whether refno is right field to be a part of clustered index or
    not
    CREATE CLUSTERED INDEX idx_refno ON ordDemo(Refno)
    GO
    ```

4. Go to the same query window where we have executed the SELECT query and execute it again.

    ```
    SELECT OrderDate,Amount,Refno FROM ordDemo WHERE Refno<3
    ```

5. You will get a comparison of both `SELECT` query executions in **Client Statistics** tab, as shown in the following screenshot:

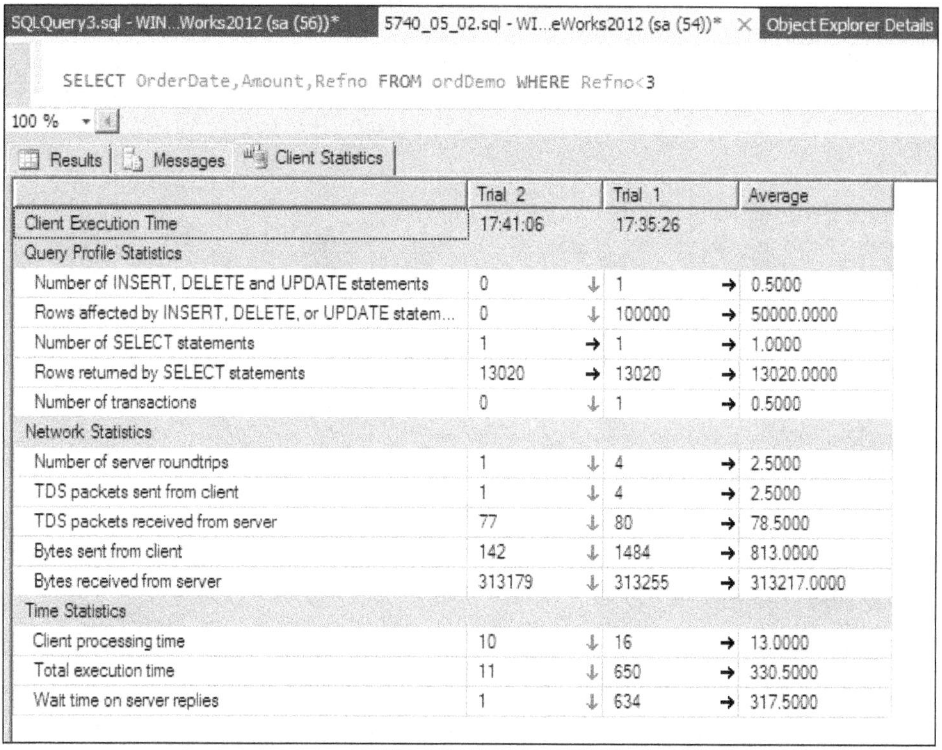

	Trial 2		Trial 1		Average
Client Execution Time	17:41:06		17:35:26		
Query Profile Statistics					
Number of INSERT, DELETE and UPDATE statements	0	↓	1	→	0.5000
Rows affected by INSERT, DELETE, or UPDATE statem...	0	↓	100000	→	50000.0000
Number of SELECT statements	1	→	1	→	1.0000
Rows returned by SELECT statements	13020	→	13020	→	13020.0000
Number of transactions	0	↓	1	→	0.5000
Network Statistics					
Number of server roundtrips	1	↓	4	→	2.5000
TDS packets sent from client	1	↓	4	→	2.5000
TDS packets received from server	77	↓	80	→	78.5000
Bytes sent from client	142	↓	1484	→	813.0000
Bytes received from server	313179	↓	313255	→	313217.0000
Time Statistics					
Client processing time	10	↓	16	→	13.0000
Total execution time	11	↓	650	→	330.5000
Wait time on server replies	1	↓	634	→	317.5000

The query text shown above the results is:
```
SELECT OrderDate,Amount,Refno FROM ordDemo WHERE Refno<3
```

How it works...

It gives you the time of query execution in **Client Execution Time** row along with many other important details such as **Client processing time**, **Total execution time** of query, different important **Network Statistics**, and much more. The beautiful thing is that you can find an up, down, or horizontal arrow in result which gives you an idea about whether both the trials had the same result and the processing time was increased or decreased (there is no up arrow in this case).

There's more...

The **Client Statistics** window can contain a maximum number of 10 trials and follows **FIFO** (**First In First Out**) method. While executing the 11th query, the first trial will be removed.

You can reset client statistics by selecting **Reset Client Statistics** from the **Query** menu.

6
Tuning with Execution Plans

In this chapter we will cover:

- ▸ Understanding Hash, Merge, and Nested Loop Join strategies
- ▸ Finding Table/Index Scans in execution plan and fixing them
- ▸ Introducing Key Lookups, finding them in execution plans, and resolving them

Introduction

Performance tuning needs concentration in the following areas:

- ▸ Deciding the performance baseline of your environment
- ▸ Monitoring current performance and finding bottleneck
- ▸ Resolving the bottleneck to get good performance

An **Estimated Execution Plan** is a kind of blue-print that defines how a query should actually perform, whereas an **Actual Execution Plan** is like a mirror that tells you what happened while executing the query. By looking at this fact you can find the bottleneck and try to resolve it. By comparing both execution plans, you can find out whether the query is actually performed as per the blue-print (Estimated Execution Plan) or not.

There are some important parts (operator) that we should refer to in the execution plan in the order to understand it and to find the pain point. Some of the very important operators in execution plan, which we are going to cover in this chapter, are as follows:

- Join strategies: There are three physical join operators in SQL Server 2012, which are as follows:

    - Hash Join
    - Merge Join
    - Nested Loop Join

    Each join operator has its own pros and cons, which we are going to discuss in this chapter.

- Scan and seek are two ways that SQL Server 2012 uses to read the data. Scan looks at each and every row available in the table/index, whereas seek has address of each row based on the key field value. So seek directly goes to that data page and fetches the row if your predicate matches with the key field. This is an essential concept while working with performance tuning and will be covered in this chapter.

- Key Lookups sometimes become a major performance issue. As in the situation of Key Lookup, storage engine has to go to clustered index from non-clustered index, in order to fetch the value of non-key field of non-clustered index. This round-trip always consumes time.

Understanding Hash, Merge, and Nested Loop Join strategies

SQL Server uses three physical join operators, listed as follows, to interpret the query you execute:

- Hash Join
- Merge Join
- Nested Loop Join

None of the physical join operators are the "best" or "worst" for all situations. SQL Server 2012 chooses appropriate operator to perform query in an appropriate way. Join operators are being used in SQL Server from earlier versions and is still available in SQL Server 2012 without any change.

Let us have short introduction of each join operator:

- ▸ **Hash Join**: SQL Server chooses Hash Join as a physical operator for query in case of high volume of data that is not sorted or indexed. Two processes together make the Hash Join, which are **Build** and **Probe**. In Build process, it reads all rows from Build input (left-hand side input table) and creates an in-memory hash table based on the equijoin keys. In the Probe process, it reads all rows from the Probe input (right-hand side input table) based on equijoin keys and matches those rows in hash table created by Build process. Hash Join operator looks like the following screenshot in the execution plan:

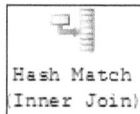

- ▸ **Merge Join**: SQL Server chooses Merge Join as a physical operator for query in case of a sorted join expression. Merge Join requires one equijoin predicate along with a sorted input. It works better if the data is not as bulky as we have in the Hash Join; it is not a heavy-weight champion like Hash Join. A Merge Join operator looks like the following screenshot in the execution plan:

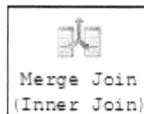

- ▸ **Nested Loop Join**: The Nested Loop Join operator works well with at least two result sets, and out of these, one is relatively small that is used as an outer loop input, and another result set with efficient index works as inner loop set. It supports equijoin and inequality operator. This is a simple form to understand as it is used to compare each row of left-hand side table with every row of right-hand side table. So if the dataset is big, nested loop process consumes more time. Nested Loop Join operator looks like the following screenshot in the execution plan:

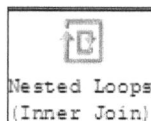

Getting ready

We are going to create two tables to see the different effects of physical join operator in the execution plan. Execute the following query to create those tables. We are going to make some schema-level changes in the tables. As it is not a good idea to change the schema of the original AdventureWorks2012 database, we will create two sample tables from the table of AdventureWorks2012:

```
USE AdventureWorks2012
GO

if object_id('SalesOrdHeaderDemo') is not null
begin
drop table SalesOrdHeaderDemo
end
GO

if object_id('SalesOrdDetailDemo') is not null
begin
drop table SalesOrdDetailDemo
end
GO

Select * Into SalesOrdHeaderDemo
from Sales.SalesOrderHeader
GO

Select * Into SalesOrdDetailDemo
from Sales.SalesOrderDetail
GO
```

How to do it...

Perform the following given steps to understand the Hash, Merge, and Nested Loop Join strategies:

1. Execute the following query with the execution plan (press *Ctrl* + *M* to enable **Execution plan**):

```
SELECT
sh.*
FROM
SalesOrdHeaderDemo AS sh
JOIN
SalesOrdDetailDemo AS sd
ON
sh.SalesOrderID=sd.SalesOrderID
GO
```

2. The **Execution plan** shows a Hash Join, the following is a screenshot of the query:

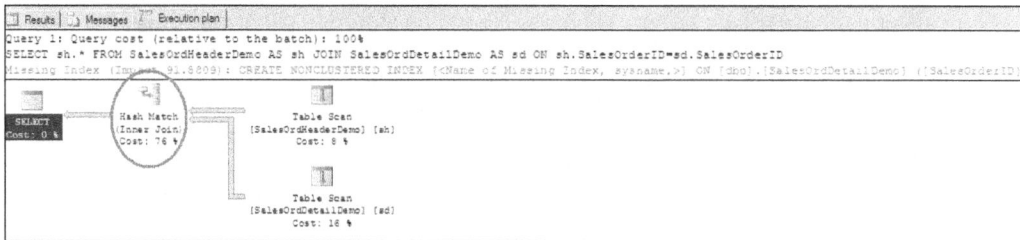

3. Now create a unique clustered index on both tables with the following T-SQL statements. As both the tables created before are meeting with table scan, as shown in the previous screenshot, let us consider creating clustered index so that data gets stored in sorted manner inside the clustered index.

```
CREATE UNIQUE CLUSTERED INDEX idx_salesorderheaderdemo_
SalesOrderID ON SalesOrdHeaderDemo (SalesOrderID)
GO

CREATE UNIQUE CLUSTERED INDEX idx_SalesDetail_SalesOrderlID ON
SalesOrdDetailDemo (SalesOrderID,SalesOrderDetailID)
GO
```

4. Next, execute the same SELECT query we ran previously along with the **Execution plan**:

```
SELECT
sh.*
FROM
SalesOrdHeaderDemo AS sh
JOIN
SalesOrdDetailDemo AS sd
ON
sh.SalesOrderID=sd.SalesOrderID
```

5. The **Execution plan** shows Merge Join in the same query, as we have not sorted the dataset in both tables. You can also see clustered index scan for both tables instead of table scan, as now we have all records stored in clustered index in a sorted manner. As there is no predicate in the SELECT query, there is no scope for executing clustered index seek.

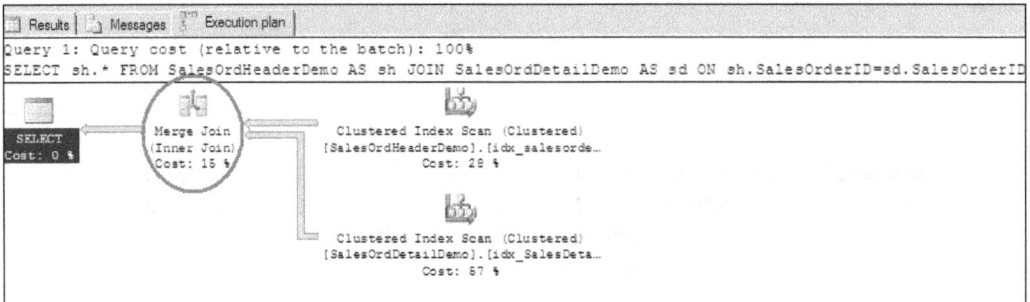

6. Now to see the Nested Loop Join, we are moving towards retrieving a small dataset by providing WHERE clause with equality predicates. Execute the following SELECT query:

```
SELECT
sh.*
FROM
SalesOrdHeaderDemo AS sh
JOIN
SalesOrdDetailDemo AS sd
ON
sh.SalesOrderID=sd.SalesOrderID
WHERE
sh.SalesOrderID=43659
```

7. The **Execution plan** shows a Nested Loop Join operator, as shown in the following screenshot:

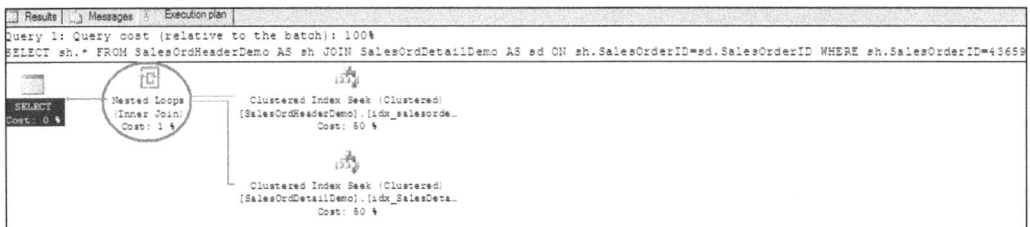

How it works...

As discussed in the _Introduction_ section, the Hash Join works with heavy data that is not sorted on predicate column. So obviously when we execute our first `SELECT` query in step 1, it shows Hash Join operator in the **Execution plan** as a high volume of data is generated, which is not sorted or indexed.

In step 3, we have created unique clustered index on key fields in both the tables. So obviously our data will be sorted physically as well as indexed in table. So when we execute same `SELECT` query in step 5, we will see a Merge Join operator rather than a Hash Join, as our data is now sorted and we also have equijoin operator.

In step 6 we have provided predicate in `WHERE` condition, so dataset from `SalesOrderHeaderDemo` table becomes smaller than it used to be in step 3. As dataset becomes small with sorted data, it performs as outer loop along with inner loop of `SalesOrderDetailDemo` table to perform a Nested Loop Join.

A Nested Loop Join works well with at least two result sets and out of those, one is a relatively small dataset which is used as an outer loop input and another result set with an efficient index works as an inner loop set. It fetches each record from the left-hand side dataset and loops through the second dataset to find a match, so we have reduced the dataset by providing a `WHERE` clause and the Nested Loop comes into the picture.

As each join operator has its own pros and cons, no single one is the "best" or "worst" for all situation. It depends on the task we are performing. Quite a few times I have been asked why the Hash Join is there in SQL Server as it is consuming lots of CPU time?

I always answer that a Hash is not bad, it is good for situations where we have heavy datasets that are not sorted or indexed. If it is possible in your environment, try to make a unique clustered index on each table so that you can meet with a Merge Join operator. If it is not possible, never try to advise optimizer to use a Merge or a Nested Loop by providing an `OPTION` query hint, as it may degrade the performance. A Nested Loop works best only with a small dataset, as described in this recipe.

There's more...

SQL Server chooses best physical operator for your join, but there is one option called `OPTION` clause which helps you to change SQL Server 2012's decision with your preferred way.

You can specify which physical operator (Loop, Merge, or Hash) should be used in your query. For example:

```
--use
--OPTION(LOOP JOIN) for Nested Loop Join
--OPTION(HASH JOIN)for HashJoin
--OPTION(MERGEJOIN) for Merge Join
SELECT
sh.*
FROM
SalesOrdHeaderDemo AS sh
JOIN
SalesOrdDetailDemo AS sd
ON
sh.SalesOrderID=sd.SalesOrderID
WHERE
sh.SalesOrderID=43659
OPTION(HASH JOIN)
```

A word of caution, worth mentioning here, is that SQL Server 2012's optimizer is very smart and it always makes a good choice for your query, so it is better to let the optimizer do its work. Query hint OPTION should be used as a last resort by expert database developer or administrator who knows what actually is going to be done with the query hint. You can use OPTION in your development environment to check the effect of different joins while working on performance tuning, but it is not recommended on the production server. If UNION is involved in the query, OPTION will go with the last query only.

Finding table/index scans in execution plan and fixing them

In most cases, especially while working with small amount of data from big tables, table scan/index scan should not be the desired way to go for. It becomes mandatory to find and resolve it in order to improve the performance, because scanning process goes through each and every row available in table/index, looks for match with the criteria provided, and returns the result set. This is really a time and resource consuming, heavy process. While working on performance tuning, people are afraid of several major bottleneck issues, mentioned as follows:

- CPU
- Network
- Disk I/O

Table/index scan creates all three types of bottleneck. Scanning every row of a table/index creates a lot of disk I/O due to heavy CPU usage. As it is scanning the whole table/index and preparing a big dataset, it takes heavy network resources and/or bandwidth to deliver the big dataset.

Getting ready

We are going to create two tables to see different effects of physical join operator in execution plan. Execute the following query to create those tables.

Actually these are the objects we have used in the previous recipe, _Understanding Hash, Merge, and Nested Loop Join strategies_, as well, and have looked at different join operators with these objects. But now we are going to find and resolve a major pain point scan with the same tables.

```
USE AdventureWorks2012
GO

if object_id('SalesOrdHeaderDemo') is not null
begin
drop table SalesOrdHeaderDemo
end
GO

if object_id('SalesOrdDetailDemo') is not null
begin
drop table SalesOrdDetailDemo
end
GO

Select * Into SalesOrdHeaderDemo
from Sales.SalesOrderHeader
GO

Select * Into SalesOrdDetailDemo
from Sales.SalesOrderDetail
GO
```

How to do it...

Follow the given steps to find table/index scans in execution plan and fix them:

1. Execute the following query by keeping the **Execution plan** on:

```
SELECT
sh.SalesOrderID
FROM
SalesOrdHeaderDemo AS sh
JOIN
SalesOrdDetailDemo AS sd
ON
sh.SalesOrderID=sd.SalesOrderID
WHERE
sh.OrderDate='2005-07-01 00:00:00.000'
GO
```

    You will find a table scan operator on both the tables, as shown in the following screenshot.

> The **Execution plan** suggests a missing index in the query, so check the worthiness of this index also by looking at the key field of the index to decide whether it is worth creating or not.

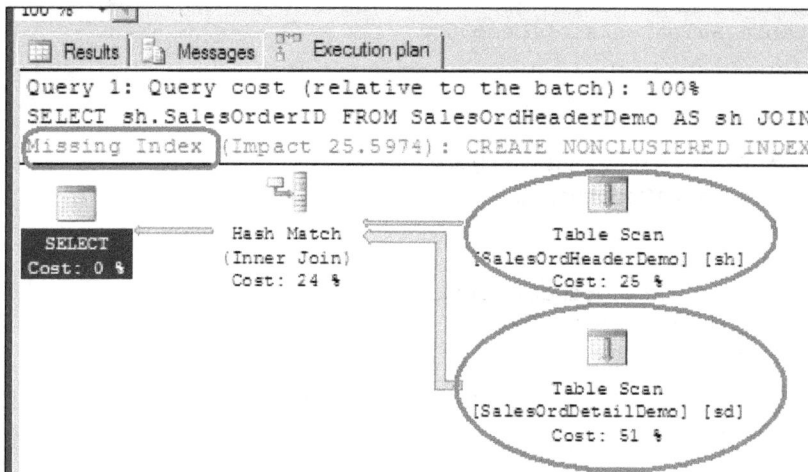

2. To remove the table scan, create one clustered index on the table
   `SalesOrdHeaderDemo` with the following query:

```
CREATE UNIQUE CLUSTERED INDEX idx_salesorderheaderdemo_
SalesOrderID ON SalesOrdHeaderDemo (SalesOrderID)
GO
```

3. Now execute the following `SELECT` query to see whether the table scan is removed
   or not:

```
SELECT
sh.SalesOrderID
FROM
SalesOrdHeaderDemo AS sh
JOIN
SalesOrdDetailDemo AS sd
ON
sh.SalesOrderID=sd.SalesOrderID
WHERE
sh.OrderDate='2005-07-01 00:00:00.000'
GO
```

4. The following is the screenshot of the **Execution plan** that is now showing **Clustered
   Index Scan** on the **SalesOrdHeaderDemo** table but is still showing **Table Scan**
   operator on the second table. As we had clustered index on `SalesOrdHeaderDemo`
   table, it is scanning from the index rather than table, so there is no major gain
   in performance.

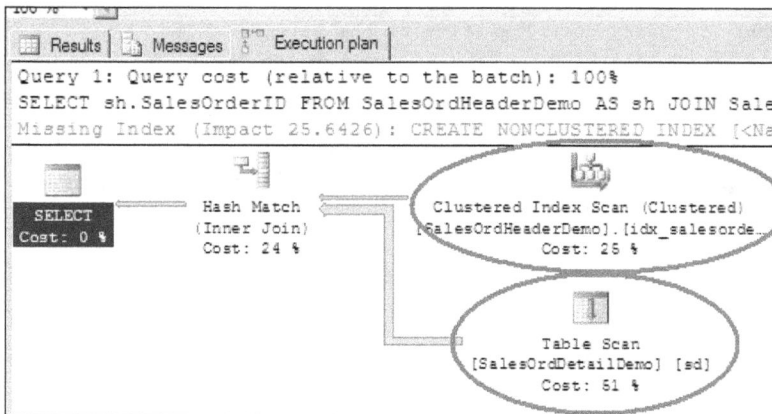

5. After creating clustered index on `SalesOrdHeaderDemo` table, table scan disappears from the **Execution plan** but it is still there in `SalesOrdDetailDemo` table. Let us try to remove table scan from the second table as well, by creating a clustered index on `SalesOrdDetailDemo` table using the following query:

```
CREATE UNIQUE CLUSTERED INDEX idx_SalesDetail_SalesOrderlID ON
SalesOrdDetailDemo (SalesOrderID,SalesOrderDetailID)
GO
```

6. Again execute the same `SELECT` query to analyze the behavior of the operator:

```
SELECT
sh.SalesOrderID
FROM
SalesOrdHeaderDemo AS sh
JOIN
SalesOrdDetailDemo AS sd
ON
sh.SalesOrderID=sd.SalesOrderID
WHERE
sh.OrderDate='2005-07-01 00:00:00.000'
GO
```

7. Analyze the **Execution plan** given in the next screenshot, which shows **Clustered Index Seek** on the second table:

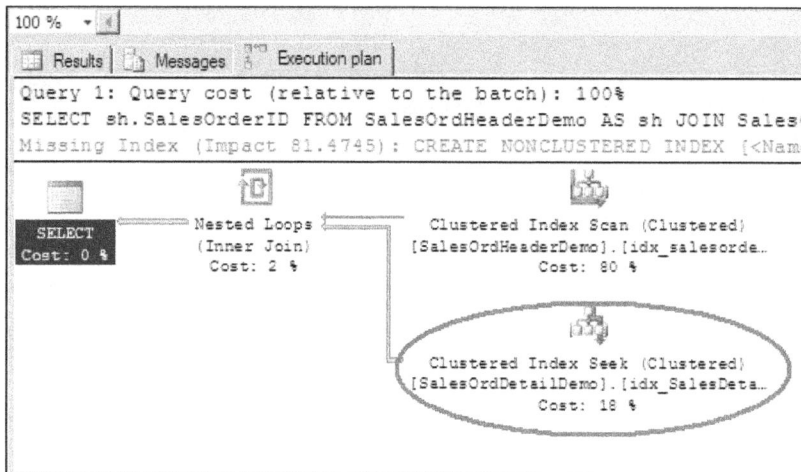

How it works...

Before we move further, let us clarify that scan is not always bad and seek is not always good, but in most cases, especially while working with small dataset from big table, seek is going to be the preferred way. Also, it is not always possible to remove scan in each and every query. If there is any performance issue occurring in the query and if the query is making scan, which is consuming more resource, then it will be better to remove scan, if possible, otherwise look for another alternative. Suppose your table has 10 million rows out of which you are retrieving only 100 rows, then you would use seek. But from the same table, for any reason, if you are returning 9.5 million rows, then it is better to have scan rather than seek.

In step 1, when we have executed query with join, there were no indexes defined on both tables and so table scan was the only option for optimizer to go for.

In step 3, we have created clustered index on `SalesOrdHeaderDemo` table and executed the same `SELECT` query that we have used in step 1, but **Execution plan** was giving Clustered index scan on first table as against table scan. Clustered index seek is desired, but we don't have any predicate on the first table so it is not possible for the index to seek for any particular record, so it scans the complete index.

In step 6, we had created clustered index on second table with non-key fields, `SalesOrderID` and `SalesOrderDetailID`, out of which `SalesOrderID` is used as a predicate in the `ON` clause to compare records with a parent table which resulted in clustered index seek.

There's more...

For more details about different types of indexes, refer to *Chapter 9, Implementing Index* and *Chapter 10, Maintaining Index*.

As this chapter discusses the execution plan, we have not covered details about indexes here.

Introducing Key Lookups, finding them in execution plans, and resolving them

Key Lookup is a bookmark lookup on a table with a clustered index. Key Lookup is used by SQL Server while retrieving information regarding non-key column. All the queries that use non-clustered index wouldn't have Key Lookup but all Key Lookup occurrences are accompanied by a non-clustered index. One more thing to remember is that Key Lookup always enjoys the company of Nested Loop operator.

Getting ready

We are going to create a table to see different effects of Key Lookup operator in execution plan. In order to generate the case of Key Lookup, we need two essential things to be present on the table:

- Clustered index
- Non-clustered index

When you have predicate based on key field of non-clustered index, which meets seek on the same index and goes to clustered index to retrieve the data for non-key field of non-clustered index, it generates Key Lookup, which we will achieve by creating `SalesOrdDetailDemo` table. Execute the following query to create the table:

```
USE AdventureWorks2012
GO

if object_id('SalesOrdDetailDemo') is not null
begin
drop table SalesOrdDetailDemo
end
GO

Select * Into SalesOrdDetailDemo
from Sales.SalesOrderDetail
GO
```

How to do it...

Follow the steps given here to perform this recipe:

1. Create one clustered index and one non-clustered index on `SalesOrdDetailDemo` table with the following query:

   ```
   CREATE UNIQUE CLUSTERED INDEX idx_SalesDetail_SalesOrderlID ON
   SalesOrdDetailDemo (SalesOrderID,SalesOrderDetailID)
   GO

   CREATE NONCLUSTERED INDEX idx_non_clust_SalesOrdDetailDemo_
   ModifiedDate ON SalesOrdDetailDemo(ModifiedDate)
   GO
   ```

2. Execute the following `SELECT` query with **Execution plan**:

   ```
   SELECT
   ModifiedDate
   FROM SalesOrdDetailDemo
   WHERE ModifiedDate='2005-07-01 00:00:00.000'
   GO
   ```

3. The following screenshot shows non-clustered index seek, as we have a non-clustered index on `ModifiedDate` and we have that field in the predicate:

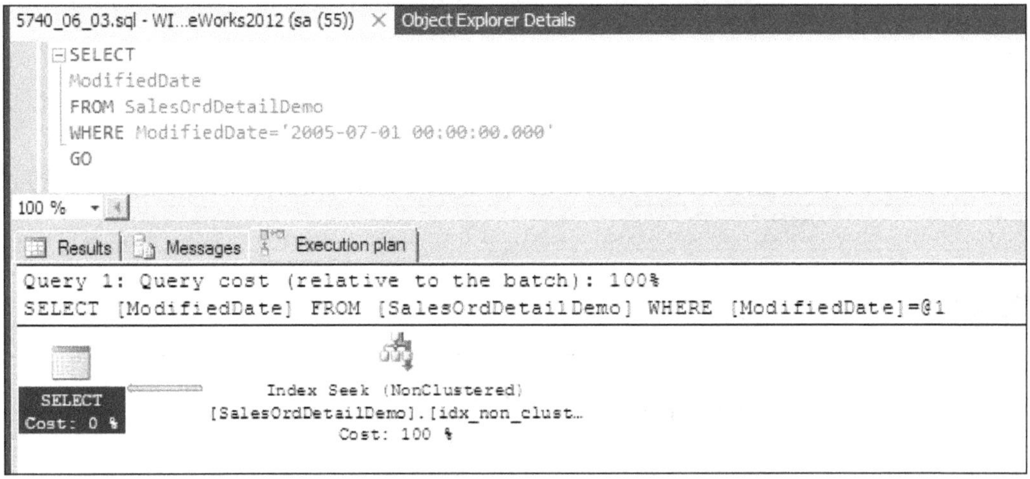

Details of the execution plan in text format for the previous screenshot are as follows:

```
StmtText
---------------------------
  |--Index Seek(OBJECT:([AdventureWorks2012].[dbo].
[SalesOrdDetailDemo].[idx_non_clust_SalesOrdDetailDemo_
ModifiedDate])), SEEK:([AdventureWorks2012].[dbo].
[SalesOrdDetailDemo].[ModifiedDate]=CONVERT_
IMPLICIT(datetime,[@1],0)) ORDERED FORWARD)
```

4. Execute the previous `SELECT` query with small changes in `SELECT` column section. Previously we had an index on `ModifiedDate` field only and also, it was the only field in the `SELECT` list, but now we will add more fields (`SalesOrderID`, `SalesOrderDetailID`) to the `SELECT` list.

```
SELECT
ModifiedDate,
SalesOrderID,
SalesOrderDetailID
FROM SalesOrdDetailDemo
WHERE ModifiedDate='2005-07-01 00:00:00.000'
GO
```

5. The following screenshot shows a non-clustered index seek:

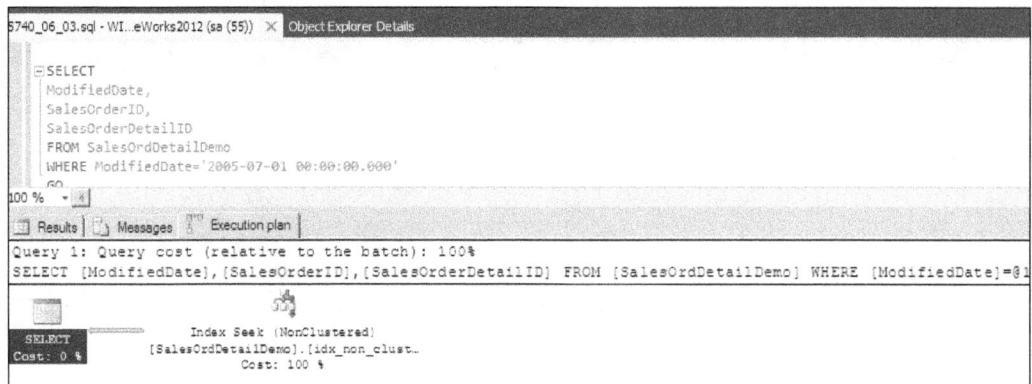

Details of the execution plan in text format for the previous screenshot are as follows:

```
StmtText
------------------------
  |--Index Seek(OBJECT:([AdventureWorks2012].[dbo].
[SalesOrdDetailDemo].[idx_non_clust_SalesOrdDetailDemo_
ModifiedDate]), SEEK:([AdventureWorks2012].[dbo].
[SalesOrdDetailDemo].[ModifiedDate]=CONVERT_
IMPLICIT(datetime,[@1],0)) ORDERED FORWARD)
```

6. In the previous SELECT query, we had three fields and all were either belonging to clustered index or non-clustered index. Now add two more fields (ProductID, UnitPrice) to the SELECT query.

```
SELECT
ModifiedDate,
SalesOrderID,
SalesOrderDetailID,
ProductID,
UnitPrice
FROM SalesOrdDetailDemo
WHERE ModifiedDate='2005-07-01 00:00:00.000'
GO
```

7. We can see the index seek operator on a non-clustered index, but two new operators also come up, Key Lookup and Nested Loop, as shown in the following screenshot:

Details of the execution plan in text format for the previous screenshot are given as follows:

```
StmtText
----------------------------------------
  |--Nested Loops(Inner Join, OUTER REFERENCES:([Adventu
reWorks2012].[dbo].[SalesOrdDetailDemo].[SalesOrderID],
[AdventureWorks2012].[dbo].[SalesOrdDetailDemo].
[SalesOrderDetailID], [Expr1004]) WITH UNORDERED PREFETCH)
       |--Index Seek(OBJECT:([AdventureWorks2012].[dbo].
[SalesOrdDetailDemo].[idx_non_clust_SalesOrdDetailDemo_
ModifiedDate]), SEEK:([AdventureWorks2012].[dbo].
[SalesOrdDetailDemo].[ModifiedDate]='2005-07-01 00:00:00.000')
ORDERED FORWARD)
       |--Clustered Index Seek(OBJECT:([AdventureWorks2012].
[dbo].[SalesOrdDetailDemo].[idx_SalesDetail_SalesOrderlID]),
SEEK:([AdventureWorks2012].[dbo].[SalesOrdDetailDemo].[SalesOrder
ID]=[AdventureWorks2012].[dbo].[SalesOrdDetailDemo].[SalesOrderID]
AND
```

8. As it is showing heavy Key Lookup operator now, we might want to remove it by guiding query optimizer to use clustered index by providing the table hint index with the WITH keyword, as shown in the following query:

```
SELECT
ModifiedDate,
SalesOrderID,
SalesOrderDetailID,
ProductID,
UnitPrice
FROM SalesOrdDetailDemo WITH(INDEX=idx_SalesDetail_SalesOrderlID)
WHERE ModifiedDate='2005-07-01 00:00:00.000'
GO
```

9. As per our guidance, SQL Server optimizer has used clustered index but it is not able to make seek on clustered index, so it is showing scan on the clustered index.

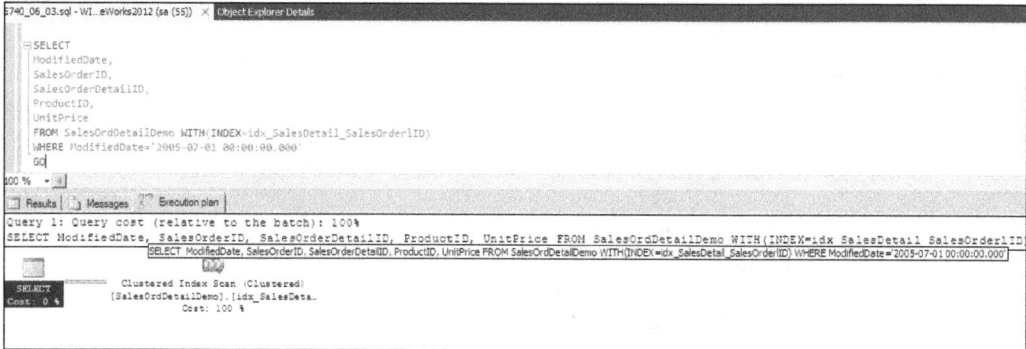

10. **Clustered Index Scan** is shown in the previous screenshot, which is not good for returning only a few records of date. So it would be interesting to know which one is better, Key Lookup or clustered index scan. Let us compare the load by keeping execution plan (press *Ctrl + M*) on in the following query and also keeping SET STATISTICS IO ON to measure IO load:

```
SET STATISTICS IO ON
GO

SELECT
ModifiedDate,
SalesOrderID,
SalesOrderDetailID,
ProductID,
UnitPrice
FROM SalesOrdDetailDemo
WHERE ModifiedDate='2005-07-01 00:00:00.000'
GO

SELECT
ModifiedDate,
SalesOrderID,
SalesOrderDetailID,
ProductID,
UnitPrice
FROM SalesOrdDetailDemo WITH(INDEX=idx_SalesDetail_SalesOrderlID)
WHERE ModifiedDate='2005-07-01 00:00:00.000'
GO

SELECT
```

```
ModifiedDate,
SalesOrderID,
SalesOrderDetailID,
ProductID,
UnitPrice
FROM SalesOrdDetailDemo WITH(INDEX=idx_non_clust_
SalesOrdDetailDemo_ModifiedDate)
WHERE ModifiedDate='2005-07-01 00:00:00.000'
GO
```

11. Our suggestion of using the clustered index in the query seems heavy compared to other options. Look at the following screenshot to confirm the query cost:

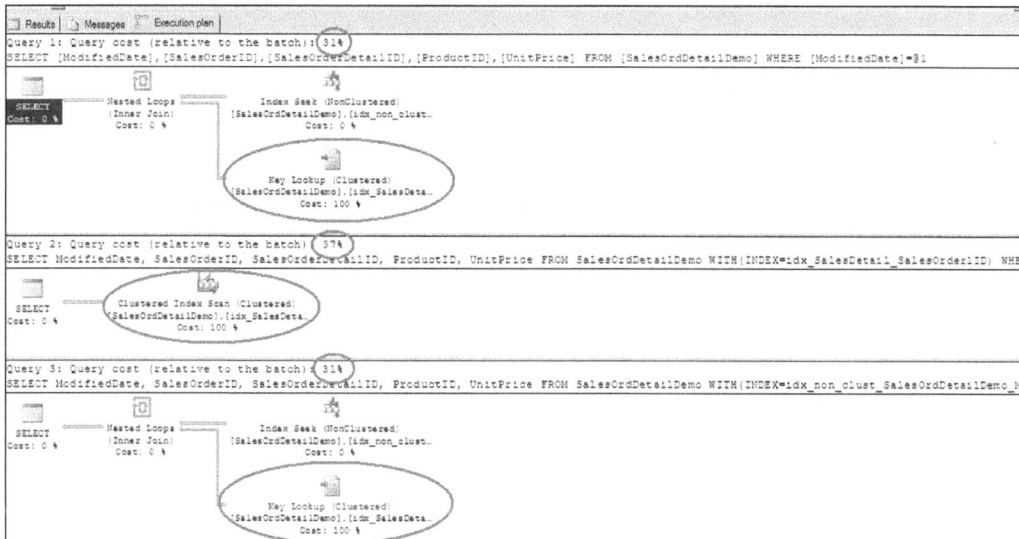

Details of the execution plan in text format for the previous screenshot are given as follows:

```
StmtText
---------------------------------------------------------
  |--Nested Loops(Inner Join, OUTER REFERENCES:([Adventu
reWorks2012].[dbo].[SalesOrdDetailDemo].[SalesOrderID],
[AdventureWorks2012].[dbo].[SalesOrdDetailDemo].
[SalesOrderDetailID], [Expr1004]) WITH UNORDERED PREFETCH)
       |--Index Seek(OBJECT:([AdventureWorks2012].[dbo].
[SalesOrdDetailDemo].[idx_non_clust_SalesOrdDetailDemo_
ModifiedDate]), SEEK:([AdventureWorks2012].[dbo].
[SalesOrdDetailDemo].[ModifiedDate]='2005-07-01 00:00:00.000')
ORDERED FORWARD)
       |--Clustered Index Seek(OBJECT:([AdventureWorks2012].[dbo].
[SalesOrdDetailDemo].[idx_SalesDetail_SalesOrderlID]),
```

```
SEEK:([AdventureWorks2012].[dbo].[SalesOrdDetailDemo].[SalesOrderI
D]=[AdventureWorks2012].[dbo].[SalesOrdDetailDemo].[SalesOrderID]
AND
```

```
StmtText
-----------------------------------------------------------
    |--Clustered Index Scan(OBJECT:([AdventureWorks2012].
[dbo].[SalesOrdDetailDemo].[idx_SalesDetail_SalesOrderlID]),
WHERE:([AdventureWorks2012].[dbo].[SalesOrdDetailDemo].
[ModifiedDate]='2005-07-01 00:00:00.000'))
```

```
StmtText
-----------------------------------------
    |--Nested Loops(Inner Join, OUTER REFERENCES:([Adventu
reWorks2012].[dbo].[SalesOrdDetailDemo].[SalesOrderID],
[AdventureWorks2012].[dbo].[SalesOrdDetailDemo].
[SalesOrderDetailID], [Expr1003]) WITH UNORDERED PREFETCH)
         |--Index Seek(OBJECT:([AdventureWorks2012].[dbo].
[SalesOrdDetailDemo].[idx_non_clust_SalesOrdDetailDemo_
ModifiedDate]), SEEK:([AdventureWorks2012].[dbo].
[SalesOrdDetailDemo].[ModifiedDate]='2005-07-01 00:00:00.000')
ORDERED FORWARD)
         |--Clustered Index Seek(OBJECT:([AdventureWorks2012].
[dbo].[SalesOrdDetailDemo].[idx_SalesDetail_SalesOrderlID]),
SEEK:([AdventureWorks2012].[dbo].[SalesOrdDetailDemo].[SalesOrder
ID]=[AdventureWorks2012].[dbo].[SalesOrdDetailDemo].[SalesOrderID]
AND
```

SET STATISTICS IO result of all the three queries are given here, out of which the second query, in which we have guided the optimizer to use the clustered index, has the highest logical reads.

```
(357 row(s) affected)
Table 'SalesOrdDetailDemo'. Scan count 1, logical reads 1105,
physical reads 0, read-ahead reads 0, lob logical reads 0, lob
physical reads 0, lob read-ahead reads 0.

(357 row(s) affected)
Table 'SalesOrdDetailDemo'. Scan count 1, logical reads 1502,
physical reads 0, read-ahead reads 0, lob logical reads 0, lob
physical reads 0, lob read-ahead reads 0.

(357 row(s) affected)
```

```
Table 'SalesOrdDetailDemo'. Scan count 1, logical reads 1105,
physical reads 0, read-ahead reads 0, lob logical reads 0, lob
physical reads 0, lob read-ahead reads 0.
```

12. As compared to clustered index scan, non-clustered index with Key Lookup seems good, but it would be better if we can remove Key Lookup from non-clustered index scan. Let us try to do that by either creating covering index or INCLUDE column index. Let us also clear the cache memory so that the optimizer doesn't use the plan already saved in the cache or buffer.

```
DROP INDEX idx_non_clust_SalesOrdDetailDemo_ModifiedDate ON
SalesOrdDetailDemo
GO

CREATE NONCLUSTERED INDEX idx_non_clust_SalesOrdDetailDemo_
ModifiedDate ON SalesOrdDetailDemo(ModifiedDate)
INCLUDE
(
ProductID,
UnitPrice
)
GO

--don't use these commands on live environment, it gives you
--temporary slow performance for all stored procedure whose
--plan are saved and being in use. This is just for testing or
--development environment.
DBCC FREEPROCCACHE
DBCC DROPCLEANBUFFERS
GO
```

13. Try to execute the SELECT query again:

```
SELECT
ModifiedDate,
SalesOrderID,
SalesOrderDetailID,
ProductID,
UnitPrice
FROM SalesOrdDetailDemo
WHERE ModifiedDate='2005-07-01 00:00:00.000'
GO
```

14. The following screenshot confirms that we have successfully removed the Key Lookup from the non-clustered index:

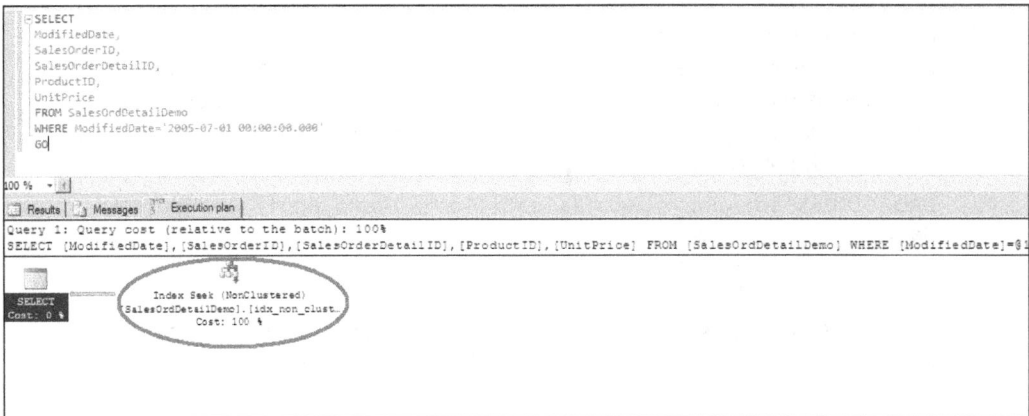

How it works...

In step 2, we had `ModifiedDate` in predicate as well as in `SELECT` list, so we have non-clustered index seek as index doesn't need to go anywhere else to find other values. All the values could be searched within the index key.

In step 4, we had `SalesOrderID` and `SalesOrderDetailID` along with `ModifiedDate` in `SELECT` list; even then it showed non-clustered index seek as the value of `ModifiedDate` is there in the non-clustered index key. `SalesOrderID` and `SalesOrderDetailID` are part of the clustered index key so it would be there in the non-clustered index as well, as a reference of the clustered index.

In step 6, we have introduced two more fields, `UnitPrice` and `ProductID`, which are not a part of any index. So non-clustered index has to go through the clustered index leaf pages to find the values of `UnitPrice` and `ProductID`, and that is why Key Lookup operator comes in picture along with Nest Loop operator. Key Lookup is a heavy process, so we have instructed the optimizer to use clustered index with `INDEX` hint and `WITH` keyword in step 8. So it is using clustered index but making scan rather then seek. So now we have the question: which query works faster?

To get the answer to this question, we ran three queries together in step 10. The first query is running without any query hint, so obviously it is showing non-clustered index seek along with Key Lookup operator, the second query has a hint to use clustered index, and the third query works like first query as we have instructed to use non-clustered index, which would be the default way of SQL Server.

If you observe the screenshot provided in step 11, you will come to know that SQL Server is having proper instruction of using non-clustered index with Key Lookup as against clustered index scan, because the second query with clustered index scan has taken 37 percent of query cost as against 31 percent load in first and third query each.

It is now clear that non-clustered index seek along with Key Lookup is faster in current situation, but it works more efficiently if we remove Key Lookup.

If we remove `UnitPrice` and `ProductID` from `SELECT` list, Key Lookup will be removed from execution plan, but it may not be a desirable situation as we might need those fields in the result set. So, now we can go for one of the other options, either create covering index or create `INCLUDE` column non-clustered index rather than simple non-clustered index. We decided to go for `INCLUDE` column index in step 12 and executed the same `SELECT` query in step 13 which worked even better and removed the Key Lookup successfully.

One of the major reasons that invites Key Lookup is to have predicate that meets criteria to call non-clustered index, and to have fields in `SELECT` section which neither belong to the non-clustered index or clustered index. The clustered index has to make the Key Lookup to find value of those non-key fields.

There's more...

For more details on different types of indexes, please refer to *Chapter 9, Implementing Index* and *Chapter 10, Maintaining Index*.

In this chapter only the execution plan is discussed, so we have not covered details about Indexes here.

7

Dynamic Management Views and Dynamic Management Functions

In this chapter we will cover:

- ▶ Monitoring current query execution statistics
- ▶ Monitoring index performance
- ▶ Monitoring performance of TempDB database
- ▶ Monitoring disk I/O statistics

Introduction

With the inception of SQL Server 2005, Microsoft has introduced a very helpful feature in SQL Server known as **Dynamic Management Views(DMV)** and **Dynamic Management Functions(DMF)**. These views and functions are used to retrieve internal statistics of an SQL Server instance for performance monitoring. They provide real-time statistics about a variety of the internal working details of the SQL Server that can be used for performance analysis to identify performance bottlenecks and hardware bottlenecks, and tune the performance of SQL Server. Some of the performance issues can be identified and the necessary steps to be taken can be determined easily just by looking at the statistics returned by DMVs and DMFs. This feature is a real blessing for database administrators.

All DMVs and DMFs are located in the `sys` schema and all DMVs and DMFs have a common naming convention, which is `dm_*`. This prefix is generally followed by a category prefix to which a DMV or DMF belongs, which is followed by the name of DMV or DMF.

> Executing these DMVs and DMFs requires `VIEW SERVER STATE` and `VIEW DATABASE STATE` permissions.

The following section discusses some of the categories of DMVs and DMFs that we will cover in this book:

- **Execution-specific DMVs and DMFs** (`sys.dm_exec_*`): This category provides the statistics related to query execution. These DMVs and DMFs can be used to monitor statistics pertaining to the cached queries, execution plans, active connections/ sessions, and currently running queries along with their execution plans.

- **Index-specific DMVs and DMFs** (`sys.dm_db_index_*` and `sys.dm_db_ missing_*`): This category provides the statistics related to indexes. These DMVs and DMFs can be used to monitor and troubleshoot the performance of the indexes by finding missing indexes, unused indexes and examining the index usage statistics.

- **Database-specific DMVs and DMFs** (`sys.dm_db_*`): This category provides the statistics related to databases. These DMVs and DMFs can be used to monitor and troubleshoot the performance of databases by analyzing the database-specific file statistics, session statistics, and task statistics.

- **I/O-specific DMVs and DMFs** (`sys.dm_io_*`): This category provides the statistics related to I/O operations. These DMVs and DMFs can be used to monitor and troubleshoot the I/O performance of SQL Server.

- **OS-specific DMVs and DMFs** (`sys.dm_os_*`): This category provides the statistics related to SQL OS internals. These DMVs can be used to monitor and troubleshoot the server configuration issues.

- **Transaction-specific DMVs and DMFs** (`sys.dm_tran_*`): This category provides the statistics related to transactions. These DMVs and DMFs can be used to monitor and troubleshoot the locking and blocking issues caused by long-running transactions.

> The statistics provided by dynamic management views and dynamic management functions are not persistent. These statistics, for most of the DMVs and DMFs, are reset when SQL Server is restarted or `DBCC SQLPERF ('sys.dm_os_wait_stats', CLEAR)` command is executed.

Monitoring current query execution statistics

In order to perform query tuning on production database server, you need to identify those resource-consuming queries and the source from where they are coming. For this, you need to monitor the incoming query requests and examine their execution time, number of read/write operations, and so on.

SQL Server has dedicated a separate category of DMVs and DMFs to query execution statistics. These DMVs and DMFs provide a wide range of statistics on query execution requests. The names of these execution-related DMVs and DMFs are generally prefixed by `sys.dm_exec_`. By examining the results returned by these DMVs and DMFs, you can find out long-running and resource-consuming queries, and pick them up for query tuning.

In this recipe, we will see how to monitor current incoming query requests made on SQL Server by using DMVs and DMFs in order to find out the queries with higher execution time. We will also learn how to monitor currently opened cursors in a database that are expensive in nature.

Getting ready

In this recipe, using DMVs and DMFs, we will write a query that will be used to monitor current query requests by examining some of the useful columns of a request, such as database name, login name, program name, query start time, reads, and writes.

As we know cursors are very resource-consuming objects that affect the query performance and should be avoided, we will also see how to monitor the currently executing cursors on SQL Server instance.

The following are the prerequisites for this recipe:

▸ An instance of SQL Server 2012 Developer or Enterprise Evaluation edition.

▸ Sample `AdventureWorks2012` database on the instance of SQL Server. For more details on how to install `AdventureWorks2012` database, please refer the *Preface* of this book.

How to do it......

The following are the steps you should follow to do this recipe:

1. Open SQL Server Management Studio and connect to the instance of SQL Server.

2. In a new query window, type and execute the query as shown in the following script to monitor currently running queries:

```
--Monitoring currently executing queries
--and listing them in the order of
--most resource-consuming to
--least resource-consuming
SELECT
    DB_NAME(R.database_id) AS DatabaseName
    ,S.original_login_name AS LoginName
    ,S.host_name AS ClientMachine
    ,S.program_name AS ApplicationName
    ,R.start_time AS RequestStartTime
    ,ST.text AS SQLQuery
    ,QP.query_plan AS ExecutionPlan
    ,R.cpu_time AS CPUTime
    ,R.total_elapsed_time AS TotalTimeElapsed
    ,R.open_transaction_count AS TotalTransactionsOpened
    ,R.reads
    ,R.logical_reads
    ,R.writes AS TotalWrites
    ,CASE
        WHEN R.wait_type IS NULL THEN 'Request Not Blocked'
        ELSE 'Request Blocked'
    END AS QueryBlockInfo
    ,blocking_session_id AS RequestBlockedBy
FROM sys.dm_exec_requests AS R
INNER JOIN sys.dm_exec_sessions AS S
    ON R.session_id = S.session_id
CROSS APPLY sys.dm_exec_sql_text(R.sql_handle) AS ST
CROSS APPLY sys.dm_exec_query_plan (R.plan_handle) AS QP
ORDER BY TotalTimeElapsed DESC
GO
```

3. Now execute the query as shown in the following script to monitor currently opened cursors:

```
--Monitoring currently executing cursors
--and listing them in the order of
--most expensive to least expensive
```

```
SELECT
     S.host_name AS ClientMachine
     ,S.program_name AS ApplicationName
     ,S.original_login_name AS LoginName
     ,C.name AS CursorName
     ,C.properties AS CursorOptions
     ,C.creation_time AS CursorCreatinTime
     ,ST.text AS SQLQuery
     ,C.is_open AS IsCursorOpen
     ,C.worker_time/1000 AS DurationInMiliSeconds
     ,C.reads AS NumberOfReads
     ,C.writes AS NumberOfWrites
FROM sys.dm_exec_cursors(0) AS C
INNER JOIN sys.dm_exec_sessions AS S
       ON C.session_id = S.session_id
CROSS APPLY sys.dm_exec_sql_text(C.sql_handle) AS ST
ORDER BY DurationInMiliSeconds DESC
GO
```

How it works...

In this recipe the first query uses the following DMVs and DMFs:

- `sys.dm_exec_requests`
- `sys.dm_exec_sessions`
- `sys.dm_exec_sql_text`
- `sys.dm_exec_query_plan`

In this query, we specified numerous columns that provide great amount of details on current requests. The following are the questions whose answers we can determine about a particular request by examining the result of the query:

- Which database is supposed to handle the request?
- Which login is executing the request?
- From which computer has the request arrived?
- From which application has the request been initiated?
- When did the request arrive?
- What SQL statements are being executed in the request?
- What is the execution plan for the SQL statements?
- What is the time duration since the request has been running?
- Did the request open any transaction?

> ▶ What are the read/write counts made by the request?

> ▶ Is the request blocked? If so, by which session?

To retrieve the session-specific information for the current request, we joined the output of `sys.dm_exec_requests` with `sys.dm_exec_sessions` on `session_id` column.

We applied `CROSS APPLY` to the result set with `sys.dm_exec_sql_text()` function to retrieve the SQL text for the request and with `sys.dm_exec_query_plan()` function to retrieve the execution plan of the current query. We pass `sql_handle` of the current row to `sys.dm_exec_sql_text()` function as a parameter and `plan_handle` parameter of the current row to `sys.dm_exec_query_plan()` DMF as parameter. The output of the query is sorted in descending order on the `TotalTimeElapsed` column so that we get the most resource-consuming query at the top of the list.

The second query uses `sys.dm_exec_cursors()` function and returns a list of cursors with the cursor details that are currently in use. The `sys.dm_exec_cursors()` function accepts `session_id` as a parameter. If `session_id` is specified, then only the cursors that are created by that specific session are returned. If `0` is passed to the `session_id` parameter, then the details of all the cursors across all the sessions are returned. Because we wanted to retrieve the details of all the cursors running on the server, we passed `0` to `sys.dm_exec_cursors()` function.

We used the same `sys.dm_exec_sessions` DMV and `sys.dm_exec_sql_text` DMF that we used in the first query. To retrieve session-specific details for the cursor, we joined the output of `sys.dm_exec_cursors()` function with `sys.dm_exec_sessions` on `session_id` column and applied `CROSS APPLY` to the result set with `sys.dm_exec_sql_text()` function to retrieve the SQL text for the SQL batch that declared the cursor. The output of the query is sorted in descending order on `DurationInMiliSeconds`, so that we get the most resource-consuming cursor at the top of the list. Note that we divided `worker_time` by 1000 to calculate `DurationInMiliSeconds` because `worker_time` is reported in microseconds.

There's more...

The following section discusses the DMVs and DMFs that we used in this recipe, in more detail.

sys.dm_exec_connections (DMV)

`sys.dm_exec_connections` is a dynamic management view. This DMV returns a list of currently active connections established to SQL Server with their connection details. This DMV can be used to learn which applications or users are currently connected to SQL Server. Some of the important columns of this DMV are as follows:

Column name	Description
session_id	This column represents the ID of the session, which is associated with the connection.
most_recent_session_id	This column represents the ID of the session for the most recent request that is associated with the connection.
connect_time	This column represents the time when this connection was established.
endpoint_id	This column represents the type of the connection. Value in this column can be mapped with sys.endpoints catalog view.
client_net_address	This column represents the IP address of the client machine that is connected to the server.
connection_id	This column represents a unique ID of the connection. This column is very important because it connects this DMV to other useful DMVs such as sys.dm_exec_requests and sys.dm_broker_connections.
most_recent_sql_handle	This column represents the handle of the T-SQL text that was executed last on this connection.

sys.dm_exec_sessions (DMV)

sys.dm_exec_sessions is a dynamic management view. This DMV returns a list of currently active sessions on SQL Server. This DMV can be used to retrieve session-specific details, such as host name, application name, login name, and login time. Some of the important columns of this DMV are as follows:

Column name	Description
session_id	This column represents the ID of the session.
login_time	This column represents the time when the session was started.
host_name	This column represents the name of the host machine associated with the session.
program_name	This column represents the application that started the session.
host_process_id	This column represents the windows-specific process ID of the client program that started the session. This is very important column as you can investigate the source windows process associated with the session. You will find this process in Task Manager under the column **PID** (process identifier) on the machine associated with the system.

Column name	Description
login_name	This column represents the login name under whose security context the current session is running.
status	This column represents the state of the session. It can be Running, Sleeping, Dormant or Preconnect.
cpu_time	This column represents the total CPU time in milliseconds used by the session.
memory_usage	This column represents the total number of 8 KB pages used by the session.
total_elapsed_time	This column represents the time in milliseconds since the session has been running.
last_request_start_time	This column represents the time when the last request associated with this session was made.
last_request_end_time	This column represents the time when the last request associated with this session was ended.
reads	This column represents the number of reads by requests for the session.
writes	This column represents the number of writes by requests for the session.
logical_reads	This column represents the number of logical reads by requests for the session.

sys.dm_exec_requests (DMV)

sys.dm_exec_requests is a dynamic management view. This DMV returns a list of requests that are currently executing on the server. This DMV can be used to monitor the current query requests to identify long-running and resource-intensive queries. This view is rich in terms of information that it returns and offers a lot of details which can be used for performance analysis. Some of the important columns of this DMV are as follows:

Column name	Description
session_id	This column represents the ID of the session which the request belongs to.
request_id	This column represents the unique ID of the request within a session.
start_time	This column represents the time when the request arrives.
Status	This column represents the status of the request.

Column name	Description
command	This column represents the type of command that is executed by the request.
sql_handle	This column represents the handle of the T-SQL query text of the request.
plan_handle	This column represents the handle of the execution plan of the request.
database_id	This column represents the ID of the database against which the request is made.
connection_id	This column represents the ID of the connection this request belongs to.
blocking_session_id	This column represents the ID of the session that is blocking the request.
wait_type	This column represents the type of lock if the request is blocked.
wait_time	This column represents the time duration in milliseconds that the request waited.
open_transaction_count	This column represents the number of transactions that are opened by the request.
transaction_id	This column represents the ID of the transaction under which the request is running.
cpu_time	This column represents the CPU time in milliseconds that the request took.

sys.dm_exec_sql_text (DMF)

sys.dm_exec_sql_text is a table-valued dynamic management function. This DMF returns the SQL text for the T-SQL query or batch for a specified sql_handle or plan_handle that is passed to this function as a parameter. The following are some of the columns of this DMF:

Column name	Description
dbid	This column represents the ID of the database.
objectid	This column represents the ID of the object.
encrypted	This column represents whether the SQL text is encrypted.
text	This column represents the SQL text for specified sql_handle or plan_handle.

sys.dm_exec_query_plan (DMF)

`sys.dm_exec_query_plan` is a table-valued dynamic management function. This DMF returns the query execution plan for a specified `plan_handle` that is passed to this function as a parameter. The following are some of the columns of this DMF:

Column name	Description
dbid	This column represents the ID of the database.
objected	This column represents the ID of the object.
encrypted	This column represents whether the SQL text is encrypted.
query_plan	This column represents the actual query execution plan for specified plan_handle.

sys.dm_exec_cursors (DMF)

`sys.dm_exec_cursors` is a table-valued dynamic management function. This DMF returns the list of cursors that are currently open for a given `session_id` or all sessions (for all sessions, `session_id` should be 0). The following are some of the useful columns of this DMF:

Column name	Description
session_id	This column represents the ID of the session that executes the cursor.
cursor_id	This column represents the ID of the cursor object.
name	This column represents the name of the cursor object.
properties	This column represents the cursor options with which the cursor was created.
sql_handle	This column represents the sql_handle of the SQL batch that declared the cursor object.
creation_time	This column represents the time when the cursor was created.
is_open	This column represents the status of the cursor to indicate whether the cursor is open or not.
fetch_status	This column represents the last fetch status that was returned by @@FETCH_STATUS.
worker_time	This column represents the time duration in milliseconds that the worker has taken to execute the cursor.
reads	This column represents the number of reads caused by the cursor.
writes	This column represents the number of writes caused by the cursor.

There is more to execution-related DMVs and DMFs. The following is a list of some more DMVs and DMFs that are frequently used in query tuning that you may like to explore:

- ▸ `sys.dm_exec_cached_plans` (DMV)
- ▸ `sys.dm_exec_procedure_stats` (DMV)
- ▸ `sys.dm_exec_query_stats` (DMV)
- ▸ `sys.dm_exec_cached_plan_dependent_objects` (DMF)

These DMVs and DMFs deal with providing caching details of the queries and objects, and are helpful in query tuning as well.

Monitoring index performance

As you may know, index is a key to improve the query performance. Even if you have appropriate indexes on your tables, you need to perform index-maintenance tasks from time-to-time.

SQL Server has specialized DMVs and DMFs that provide useful index-related statistics which can be helpful in evaluating the performance metrics of existing indexes and usage patterns. By analyzing the statistics data returned by these DMVs and DMFs, you can do the following things:

- ▸ Examining the index usage patterns
- ▸ Finding the missing indexes
- ▸ Finding the unused indexes
- ▸ Finding the fragmented indexes
- ▸ Analyzing the index page allocation details

In this recipe, we will use some of these DMVs and DMFs to determine the missing indexes in our database, number of seek and scan operations performed on indexes, and identify the fragmented indexes that may need to be reorganized or rebuilt.

Getting ready

This example will show you how you can find the missing indexes using DMVs and DMFs. Missing indexes are the indexes that are not present but can improve the performance of the queries if created.

We will also see how to retrieve the index usage details and fragmentation details using certain DMVs and DMFs so that you can easily perform the index-maintenance tasks on your database.

The following are the prerequisites for this recipe:

▸ An instance of SQL Server 2012 Developer or Enterprise Evaluation edition.

▸ Sample `AdventureWorks2012` database on the instance of SQL Server. For more details on how to install `AdventureWorks2012` database, please refer to the *Preface* of this book.

How to do it...

To do this recipe practically, perform the following steps:

1. Open SQL Server Management Studio and connect to the instance of SQL Server hosting `AdventureWorks2012` database.

2. In a new query window, type and execute the queries as shown in the following script:

```
USE AdventureWorks2012
GO


--Retrieving records from Sales.SalesOrderDetail
--table based on ModifiedDate column.
SELECT
    SalesOrderID
    ,SalesOrderDetailID
    ,OrderQty
    ,ProductID
FROM Sales.SalesOrderDetail
WHERE ModifiedDate >='20080101'
GO


--Retrieving records from Sales.SalesOrderDetail
--for which the ProductId is 921
SELECT
    SalesOrderDetailID
    ,UnitPrice
    ,UnitPriceDiscount
FROM Sales.SalesOrderDetail
WHERE ProductID = 921
GO
```

3. To retrieve the missing index details, type and run the query as shown in the following script:

```
--Retrieving Missing Index Details
SELECT
    MID.Statement AS ObjectName
    ,MID.equality_columns
```

```
    ,MID.inequality_columns
    ,MID.included_columns
    ,MIGS.avg_user_impact As ExpectedPerformanceImprovement
    ,(MIGS. user_seeks + MIGS. user_scans) * MIGS.avg_total_user_
cost * MIGS.avg_user_impact As PossibleImprovement
FROM sys.dm_db_missing_index_details AS MID
INNER JOIN sys.dm_db_missing_index_groups AS MIG
ON MID.index_handle = MIG.index_handle
INNER JOIN sys.dm_db_missing_index_group_stats AS MIGS
ON MIG.index_group_handle = MIGS.group_handle
GO
```

4. To retrieve the index usage details, type and run the query as shown in the following script:

```
USE AdventureWorks2012
GO


--Retrieving Index Usage Information
SELECT
    O.Name AS ObjectName
    ,I.Name AS IndexName
    ,IUS.user_seeks
    ,IUS.user_scans
    ,IUS.last_user_seek
    ,IUS.last_user_scan
FROM sys.dm_db_index_usage_stats AS IUS
INNER JOIN sys.indexes AS I
ON IUS.object_id = I.object_id AND IUS.index_id = I.index_id
INNER JOIN sys.objects AS O
ON IUS.object_id = O.object_id
GO
```

5. To retrieve the information related to index fragmentation, type and run the query as shown in the following script:

```
USE AdventureWorks2012
GO


--Retrieving Index Fragmentation Details.
SELECT
    O.name AS ObjectName
    ,I.name AS IndexName
    ,IPS.avg_page_space_used_in_percent AS AverageSpaceUsedInPages
    ,IPS.avg_fragmentation_in_percent AS AverageFragmentation
    ,IPS.fragment_count AS FragmentCount
```

```
        ,suggestedIndexOperation = CASE
            WHEN IPS.avg_fragmentation_in_percent<=30 THEN 'REORGANIZE
Index'
            ELSE 'REBUILD Index' END
FROM sys.dm_db_index_physical_stats(DB_
ID(),NULL,NULL,NULL,'DETAILED') AS IPS
INNER JOIN sys.indexes AS I
ON IPS.object_id = I.object_id AND IPS.index_id = I.index_id
INNER JOIN sys.objects AS O
ON IPS.object_id = O.object_id
WHERE IPS.avg_fragmentation_in_percent > 5
ORDER BY AverageFragmentation DESC
GO
```

The previous query should return a result similar to the one shown in the
following screenshot:

	ObjectName	IndexName	AverageSpaceUsedInPages	AverageFragmentation	Fragment
1	WorkOrderRouting	PK_WorkOrderRouting_WorkOrderI...	81.3133185075365	100	2
2	Store	PXML_Store_Demographics	98.4627996046454	98.4375	64
3	ProductModel	PXML_ProductModel_CatalogDescri...	86.182357301705	80	5
4	ProductVendor	PK_ProductVendor_ProductID_Busi...	81.8136891524586	80	5
5	DatabaseLog	PK_DatabaseLog_DatabaseLogID	88.7632814430442	75	4
6	ProductModelProduc...	PK_ProductModelProductDescriptio...	87.0583148010872	75	4
7	Store	AK_Store_rowguid	75.0350135903138	66.6666666666667	3
8	ProductCostHistory	PK_ProductCostHistory_ProductID_...	73.1776624660242	66.6666666666667	3
9	ProductDescription	AK_ProductDescription_rowguid	81.5665925376822	66.6666666666667	3
10	ProductListPriceHistory	PK_ProductListPriceHistory_ProductI...	73.1776624660242	66.6666666666667	3
11	SpecialOfferProduct	PK_SpecialOfferProduct_SpecialOff...	90.8162466024216	66.6666666666667	3

How it works...

In this recipe, we first executed sample queries on `Sales.SalesOrderDetail` table
against `Adventureworks2012` database. The first query retrieves data from `Sales.
SalesOrderDetail` based on `ModifiedDate`, while the second query retrieves data
from `Sales.SalesOrderDetail` table for which the `ProductID` is 921.

`sys.dm_db_missing_index_details` provides details for missing indexes. Missing
indexes are the indexes that do not exist in the database, but by creating these missing
indexes, the queries could have benefited and executed faster. We then executed a query
that used `sys.dm_db_missing_index_details` by joining it with two other DMVs, `sys.
dm_db_missing_index_groups` and `sys.dm_db_missing_index_group_stats`. The
`sys.dm_db_missing_index_group_stats` returns the details regarding any possible
improvement in query performance if missing indexes are created. Note that to retrieve
the `avg_user_impact` column from this view, we indirectly joined it with `sys.dm_db_
missing_index_details` through `sys.dm_db_missing_index_groups`.

> Like DTA, DMVs also may recommend wide indexes with many INCLUDE columns. It does not mean that you should create every index that DMVs recommend. Practically, creating many indexes with many INCLUDE columns also put overhead on your DML statements, such as INSERT, UPDATE, and DELETE statements.

Then we executed a query that provides index usage statistics. It gives the number of seek and scan operations performed on a particular index, and the time when seek or scan operation was last performed on a particular index. To retrieve the index name and object name, we joined the output of sys.dm_db_index_usage_stats with sys.indexes and sys.objects catalog views respectively.

Then we retrieved the fragmentation details with the query that uses the sys.dm_db_index_physical_stats() function. This DMF accepts the following parameters:

Parameter name	Description
database_id	This parameter specifies the ID of the database for which the index details are to be returned. If the value of this parameter is NULL, 0, or DEFAULT, then the index details for all databases is returned.
object_id	This parameter specifies the ID of the object for which the index details are to be returned. If the value of this parameter is NULL, 0, or DEFAULT, then the index details for all objects for a given database is returned.
index_id	This parameter specifies the ID of the index for which the index details are to be returned. If the value of this parameter is NULL, 0, or DEFAULT, then the index details for all indexes for a given object is returned.
partition_number	This parameter specifies the partition number for which the index details are to be returned. If the value of this parameter is NULL, 0, or DEFAULT, then the index details for all partitions for a given index is returned.
mode	This parameter specifies the mode of scan level that is used to gather the statistics. DEFAULT, NULL, LIMITED, SAMPLED, and DETAILED are the possible values that can be specified for this parameter. The default is LIMITED. The LIMITED mode scans a smaller number of pages to collect statistics. The SAMPLED mode scans one percent of all pages. The DETAILED mode scans all the pages and is the heavier operation.

Notice that we are passing the value of DB_ID() as the database_id parameter and NULL for the rest of the parameters because we want to retrieve the fragmentation details for all indexes of the current database. To retrieve the index name and object name, we joined the output of the sys.dm_db_index_physical_stats() function with the sys.indexes and sys.objects catalog views respectively. Note that we also included a column named SuggestedIndexOperation in the query that can suggest us, based on the level of fragmentation, whether a particular index should be rebuilt or reorganized.

There's more...

The following section discusses the DMVs and DMFs that we used in the recipe, in more detail.

sys.dm_db_missing_index_details (DMV)

sys.dm_db_missing_index_details is a dynamic management view. This DMV returns missing index details. The following are some of the useful columns of this DMV:

Column name	Description
index_handle	This column represents the identifier used to identify a missing index.
database_id	This column represents the ID of the database where missing index should be created.
object_id	This column represents the ID of the table to which the missing index is applicable.
equality_columns	This column represents a comma separated list of the columns that contribute to equality predicates.
inequality_columns	This column represents a comma separated list of the columns that contribute to inequality predicates.
included_columns	This column represents a comma separated columns that are suggested to be included in missing index.
Statement	This column shows the name of the table for which the missing index is applicable.

sys.dm_db_missing_index_groups (DMV)

`sys.dm_db_missing_index_groups` is a dynamic management view. This DMV returns information about which missing indexes belong to which missing index group. The following are the columns of this DMV:

Column name	Description
index_group_handle	This column represents the identifier used to identify the missing index group.
index_handle	This column represents the identifier used to identify a missing index.

sys.dm_db_missing_index_group_stats (DMV)

`sys.dm_db_missing_index_group_stats` is a dynamic management view. This DMV returns statistical details for missing index groups. This DMV can be used to analyze approximately how much a missing index might have benefited the queries. The following are some of the useful columns of this DMV:

Column name	Description
group_handle	This column represents the identifier of the missing index group.
unique_compiles	This column suggests the number of compilation and recompilation that could have been benefited from the missing index.
user_seeks	This column suggests the number of seek operations that the missing index could have been used for.
user_scans	This column suggests the number of scan operations that the missing index could have been used for.
last_user_seek	This column suggests the time when the missing index could have been last used for seek operation.
last_user_scan	This column suggests the time when the missing index could have been last used for scan operation.
avg_total_user_cost	This column suggests the average cost of the queries that can be reduced by the missing index.
avg_user_impact	This column suggests the improvement in percentage that could have been achieved by the missing index.

sys.dm_db_index_usage_stats (DMV)

`sys.dm_db_index_usage_stats` is a dynamic management view. This DMV returns the index usage statistics for the different types of index operations. The DMV can be used to analyze which indexes are used most frequently and which indexes are not. The following are some of the columns of this DMV:

Column name	Description
database_id	This column represents the ID of the database where the index is located.
object_id	This column represents the ID of the object to which the index is applicable.
index_id	This column represents the ID of the index.
user_seeks	This column represents the number of seek operations performed on the index.
user_scans	This column represents the number of scan operations performed on the index.
user_lookups	This column represents the number of Bookmark Lookup operations performed on the index.
user_updates	This column represents the number of update operations performed on the index.
last_user_seek	This column represents the time when the last seek operation was performed on the index.
last_user_scan	This column represents the time when the last scan operation was performed on the index.
last_user_lookup	This column represents the time when the last Bookmark Lookup operation was performed on the index.
last_user_update	This column represents the time when the last update operation was performed on the index.

sys.dm_db_index_physical_stats (DMF)

`sys.dm_db_index_physical_stats` is a dynamic management function. This DMF returns the fragmentation details of all indexes for all the databases or specified index(s) for a specified database. The following are some of the useful columns of this DMF:

Column name	Description
database_id	This column represents the ID of the database where the index is located.
object_id	This column represents the ID of the object the index belongs to.

Column name	Description
index_id	This column represents the ID of the index.
partition_number	This column represents the partition number of a table, view, or index.
index_type_desc	This column represents the type of the index.
avg_fragmentation_in_percent	This column represents the percentage of the logical fragmentation for indexes or the extent fragmentation for HEAP in IN_ROW_DATA allocation unit.
fragment_count	This column represents the number of fragments in leaf-level pages belonging to the IN_ROW_DATA allocation unit.
avg_fragment_size_in_pages	This column represents the average number of pages in a fragment belonging to the IN_ROW_DATA allocation unit.
page_count	This column represents the total number of pages in an index.
avg_page_space_used_in_percent	This column represents the percentage of average space used by all pages. This column is very important as it tells you how much of your pages are filled, on average.
record_count	This column represents total number of records in an index or HEAP.

There are two more index-related dynamic management functions that provide useful index-related statistics that you would like to explore. These views are as follows:

- sys.dm_db_index_operational_stats (DMF)
- sys.dm_db_missing_index_columns (DMF)

Monitoring performance of TempDB database

We know that the `TempDB` database is one of the system databases in SQL Server and SQL Server heavily depends on `TempDB` for its normal functioning. Therefore, monitoring performance-related statistics of `TempDB` database is very important. Quite a few times, we see that people just don't care about `TempDB` database and tend to ignore looking after its performance. This is not a good idea because the reasons for SQL Server's inefficient performance may be hiding behind the suboptimal performance of `TempDB` database. That's why you should consider monitoring `TempDB` database time-to-time.

You should know that SQL Server uses `TempDB` database while performing certain kinds of operations on a large data. Some of them perform grouping or sorting operations in query, cursor operations, version store operation, online index creations, and storing user objects, such as local or global temporary tables and table variable data. As a DBA, you may need to keep a watch on certain statistics for `TempDB` database to find out the usage pattern of the `TempDB` database to identify resource-consuming operations. You can get this information by using database-related dynamic management views.

But, to work with most of the database-related dynamic management views, it's important that you know the basic concept of how SQL Server internally organizes its data physically. So, let's first do some groundwork by understanding the role of **pages** and **extents**.

As you may know, SQL Server stores its database primarily in two types of files. These are data file (`.mdf` and `.ndf` file) and log file (`.ldf` file). Here, our discussion on pages and extents is applicable to, and is in context of, data files only. So, do not get confused between pages and extents, and log files, as they are not applicable to log files.

Data file is a type of database file where SQL Server stores its data for a database in the form of database objects such as tables and indexes. This data file is composed of smaller storage units called pages. A page is a block of 8 KB in size that actually stores the data.

On the other hand, extents are composed of pages. An extent is a series of 8 contiguous pages. So, the size of an extent is 64 KB and there are 16 extents per MB.

Objects that contain data are allocated pages from these extents for data storage. There are two types of extents and these are, uniform extent and mixed extent. A uniform extent is the one whose data pages are dedicatedly allocated to a single object only, whereas a mixed extent is the extent whose data pages can be allocated to up to 8 different objects. Mixed extents are also called shared extents because they are shared amongst multiple objects. Smaller tables are usually allocated to mixed extents initially and as soon as they get large, they are allocated to their own uniform extents.

Following diagram depicts the logical concept of the page, extent, uniform extent, and mixed extent:

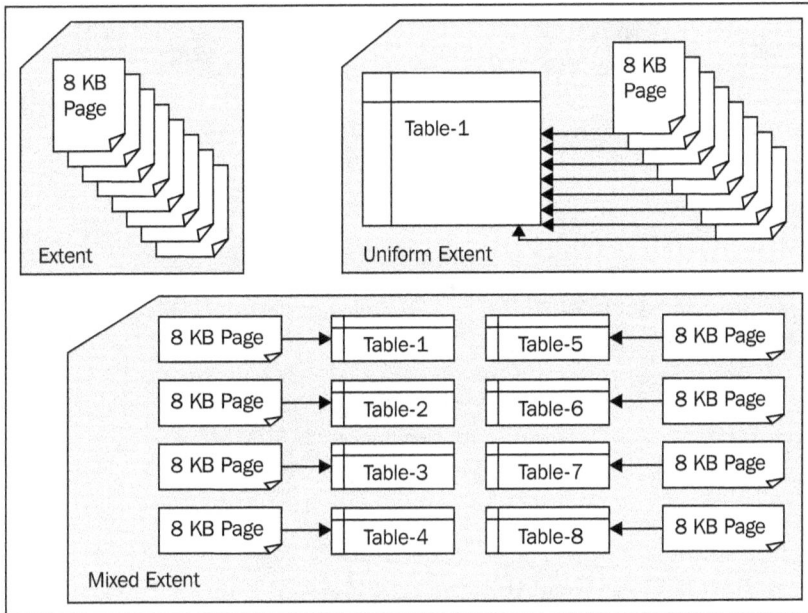

In this recipe, we will learn how to monitor the performance of `TempDB` database. We will learn how to identify the sessions and tasks that cause an increase in space usage on the `TempDB` database.

Getting ready

In this recipe, we will run a sample query that generates 10 million rows and stores them in a local temporary table in `TempDB` database. We will record and notice the difference in page allocation and deallocation statistics for `TempDB` database, before and after running our sample query.

Following is the prerequisite for this recipe:

▶ An instance of SQL Server 2012 Developer or Enterprise Evaluation edition

How to do it...

Follow the steps provided here to perform this example practically:

1. Open SQL Server Management Studio and connect to the instance of SQL Server.

2. In a new query window, type and execute the following T-SQL script:

```
USE tempdb
GO

--Checking if the table exists
--and dropping if it exists
IF OBJECT_ID('[dbo].[tbl_TempDBStats]') IS NOT NULL
    DROP TABLE [dbo].[tbl_TempDBStats]

--Creating a table to store
--page allocation details
CREATE TABLE [dbo].[tbl_TempDBStats] (
    session_id SMALLINT
    ,database_id SMALLINT
    ,user_objects_alloc_page_count BIGINT
    ,user_objects_dealloc_page_count BIGINT
    ,internal_objects_alloc_page_count BIGINT
    ,internal_objects_dealloc_page_count BIGINT
)
GO

--Collect page allocation details for
--current session before executing
--sample query.
INSERT INTO [dbo].[tbl_TempDBStats]
SELECT
    session_id
    ,database_id
    ,user_objects_alloc_page_count
    ,user_objects_dealloc_page_count
    ,internal_objects_alloc_page_count
    ,internal_objects_dealloc_page_count
FROM sys.dm_db_session_space_usage WHERE session_id = @@SPID
GO

--Checking if the table exists
--and dropping if it exists
IF OBJECT_ID('TempDB.dbo.#tbl_SampleData') IS NOT NULL
    DROP TABLE TempDB.dbo.#tbl_SampleData
GO

--Generating 10 million records and inserting
--them into temporary table
SELECT TOP 10000000
    SC1.object_id
    ,SC1.column_id
```

```
    ,SC1.name
    ,SC1.system_type_id
INTO TempDB.dbo.#tbl_SampleData
FROM sys.columns AS SC1
CROSS JOIN sys.columns AS SC2
CROSS JOIN sys.columns AS SC3
ORDER BY SC1.column_id
GO

--Collect page allocation details for
--current session after executing
--sample query.
INSERT INTO [dbo].[tbl_TempDBStats]
SELECT
    session_id
    ,database_id
    ,user_objects_alloc_page_count
    ,user_objects_dealloc_page_count
    ,internal_objects_alloc_page_count
    ,internal_objects_dealloc_page_count
FROM sys.dm_db_session_space_usage WHERE session_id = @@SPID
GO
```

3. Now, run the following query and notice the difference in the statistics before and after executing of the sample query:

```
USE tempdb
GO

--Notice the difference in page allocation
--and deallocation statistic details by looking at
--collected data.
SELECT * FROM [dbo].[tbl_TempDBStats]
GO
```

4. You should see a result similar to the one given in the following screenshot. Note that the figures may vary on your system compared to what the following screenshot is showing:

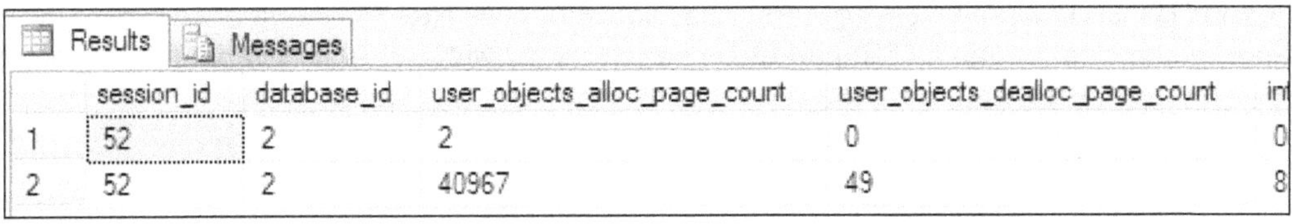

	session_id	database_id	user_objects_alloc_page_count	user_objects_dealloc_page_count	in
1	52	2	2	0	0
2	52	2	40967	49	8

5. Run the query as shown in the following script to retrieve the space usage statistics of `TempDB` database files:

```
--Get file space usage statistics by calculating
--space of unallocated and allocated pages
SELECT
    DB_NAME(FSU.database_id) AS DatabaseName
    ,MF.Name As LogicalFileName
    ,MF.physical_name AS PhysicalFilePath
    ,SUM(FSU.unallocated_extent_page_count)*8.0/1024
    AS Free_Space_In_MB,
    SUM(
            FSU.version_store_reserved_page_count
          + FSU.user_object_reserved_page_count
          + FSU.internal_object_reserved_page_count
          + FSU.mixed_extent_page_count
        )*8.0/1024 AS Used_Space_In_MB

FROM sys.dm_db_file_space_usage AS FSU
INNER JOIN sys.master_files AS MF
ON FSU.database_id = MF.database_id
    AND FSU.file_id = MF.file_id
GROUP BY FSU.database_id,FSU.file_id,MF.Name,MF.physical_name
```

6. Observe the result returned by the query.

How it works...

At the beginning of the first script, we first create a table `tbl_TempDBStats` in order to be able to collect page allocation and deallocation statistic data for the current session. Before creating the table, we first check if the table already exists. If it exists, we simply drop the existing table and create a new one.

Next, page allocation statistics for `TempDB` database are collected for the current session and we store them in our newly created table `tbl_TempDBStats`. To do this, we query `sys.dm_db_session_space_usage`. We fetch total number of allocated and deallocated pages by both user-defined objects and internal system objects. The result set returned by the DMV is inserted into `tbl_TempDBStats`. Notice how we filter the result of `sys.dm_db_session_space_usage` by comparing the `session_id` with `@@SPID` metadata function. `@@SPID` returns the session ID for the current connection. So, only statistics data for our current session is recorded and stored in the table.

Next is a sample query that simply generates 10 million records by cross-joining `sys.columns` catalog view with itself multiple times, and inserts the resulting data into temporary table, `#tbl_SampleData`, by using `SELECT INTO` syntax. Because we inserted records into temporary table, it required I/O operation to be performed on `TempDB` database and SQL Server performed allocation and deallocation of space at page-level in order to complete the request. SQL Server updates the internal statistics which are returned by `sys.dm_db_session_space_usage` once the request is completed.

After the execution of the sample query is completed, the updated page allocation and deallocation statistics are collected by querying `sys.dm_db_session_space_usage` and inserting them into `tbl_TempDBStats` table.

Once the statistics data is gathered into the table, we then review the table data by executing a query to examine how many pages were allocated and deallocated in `TempDB` database by current session when the sample query was executed.

Finally, we fetch the space usage statistics for the file using a query that uses `sys.dm_db_file_space_usage`. This view returns the number of unallocated pages, and pages reserved by version store, user-defined objects, and internal objects. We calculate free space and used space in MB by calculating all the deallocated and allocated pages across all the files.

There's more...

The following section discusses the DMVs and DMFs that we used in this recipe in more detail.

sys.dm_db_session_space_usage (DMV)

`sys.dm_db_session_space_usage` is a the dynamic management view. This DMV returns the total number of pages that have been allocated to and deallocated from `TempDB` database by each session. Pages can be allocated to or deallocated from user-defined objects or system objects. This DMV can be used to find the session that is making most of the `TempDB` database. Following are some of the useful columns of this DMV:

Column name	Description
session_id	This column represents the ID of the session.
database_id	This column represents the internal ID of the database assigned by SQL Server. For TempDB database, database_id is always 2.
user_objects_alloc_page_count	This column represents the total number of pages that have been allocated to or reserved for user-defined objects by the session.

Column name	Description
user_objects_dealloc_page_count	This column represents the total number of pages that have been deallocated or/and are no longer reserved for user-defined objects by the session.
internal_objects_alloc_page_count	This column represents the total number of pages that have been allocated to or reserved for internal objects by the session.
internal_objects_dealloc_page_ count	This column represents the total number of pages that have been deallocated or/and are no longer reserved for internal objects by the session.

sys.dm_db_file_space_usage (DMV)

sys.dm_db_file_space_usage is a dynamic management view. This DMV returns space usage details by providing page allocation and deallocation details for each TempDB file. This DMV can be used to monitor the number of unallocated, allocated, or reserved pages in TempDB database. The following are some of the useful columns of this DMV:

Column name	Description
file_id	This column represents the internal ID of the file assigned by SQL Server. This file_id can be associated and used in Joins with sys.master_files system catalog view along with database_id.
unallocated_extent_page_count	This column represents the total number of pages in unallocated extents. This column can be used to calculate free space in TempDB database.
version_store_reserved_page_count	This column represents the total number of pages in uniform extents that have been allocated or reserved for version store mechanism.
user_object_reserved_page_count	This column represents the total number of pages in uniform extents that have been allocated or reserved for user-defined objects.
internal_object_reserved_page_ count	This column represents the total number of pages in uniform extent that have been allocated or reserved for internal objects.

Remember that these dynamic management views are used and are applicable only for TempDB database.

This recipe demonstrated how we can monitor the usage of TempDB database by a particular session.

Sometime we need to investigate further. Just finding out the session that is using TempDB database heavily may not be enough. It may be required to discover the queries that are resource-intensive and put load on TempDB database.

There is another dynamic management view that can be used for this purpose. This is sys. dm_db_task_space_usage. With this DMV, you can know which task is consuming how many resources in TempDB database. It returns total number of pages that have been allocated to and deallocated from TempDB database by each task. Pages can be allocated or deallocated for user-defined objects or system objects. This DMV can be used to find out the individual task which consumes TempDB database a lot. The following is a brief overview of this DMV:

Column name	Description
session_id	This column represents the ID of the session.
request_id	This column represents the ID of the request within a session. This request_id can be mapped with sys.dm_exec_requests.
exec_context_id	This column represents the execution context ID of the task.
database_id	This column represents the internal ID of the database assigned by SQL Server. For TempDB database, database_id is always 2.
user_objects_alloc_page_count	This column represents the total number of pages that have been allocated to or reserved for user-defined objects by the task.
user_objects_dealloc_page_count	This column represents the total number of pages that have been deallocated or are no longer reserved for user-defined objects by the task.
internal_objects_alloc_page_count	This column represents the total number of pages that have been allocated or reserved for internal objects by the task.
internal_objects_dealloc_page_count	This column represents the total number of pages that have been deallocated or are no longer reserved for internal objects by the task.

Discovering responsible T-SQLquery or T-SQL batch

To discover a query or query batch associated with a task that is consuming high resources of `TempDB` database, join `sys.dm_db_task_space_usage` with `sys.dm_exec_requests` on `session_id` and `request_id`, and then `CROSS APPLY` the result set with `sys.dm_exec_sql_text()` function by passing `sql_handle` column of `sys.dm_exec_requests`. `sys.dm_exec_sql_text()` function will return the SQL text of the request associated with a task.

Monitoring disk I/O statistics

As a DBA, you often have to face disk I/O-related problems with your databases that might have been introduced due to a number of reasons, and you have to analyze and troubleshoot I/O performance of your databases. SQL Server provides certain DMVs and DMFs that can be specifically used for troubleshooting such I/O-related performance issues.

This recipe will teach you how you can monitor your disk I/O subsystem for your databases to identify any possible I/O bottlenecks. By monitoring how your databases consume disk subsystem, you can distinguish the I/O usage patterns across different databases and can make your decisions related to physical structure of the databases. You can identify those databases that are causing or demanding high number of I/O operations. Then, you may either want to move the databases having justified high number of I/O operations on separate disks, or you may want to investigate databases further for high number of I/O operations.

Getting ready

This example will show you how you can monitor database files for I/O operations. We will execute a sample query against `AdventureWorks2012` database and monitor the I/O operations by using DMVs and DMFs.

The following are the prerequisites for this recipe:

 ▶ An instance of SQL Server 2012 Developer or Enterprise Evaluation edition.

 ▶ Sample AdventureWorks2012 database on the instance of SQL Server. For more details on how to install AdventureWorks2012 database, please refer to the *Preface* of this book.

How to do it...

The following are the steps to perform the tasks of this recipe:

1. Open SQL Server Management Studio and connect to the instance of SQL Server hosting `AdventureWorks2012` database.

2. In a new query window, type and execute the query as shown in the following script to monitor the data files and log files of all databases on the instance of the SQL Server:

```
--Monitor the database files for all databases.
SELECT
DB_NAME(VFS.database_id) AS DatabaseName
    ,MF.name AS LogicalFileName
    ,MF.physical_name AS PhysicalFileName
    ,CASE MF.type
        WHEN 0 THEN 'Data File'
        WHEN 1 THEN 'Log File'
    END AS FileType
    ,VFS.num_of_reads AS TotalReadOperations
    ,VFS.num_of_bytes_read TotalBytesRead
    ,VFS.num_of_writes AS TotalWriteOperations
    ,VFS.num_of_bytes_written AS TotalBytesWritten
    ,VFS.io_stall_read_ms AS TotalWaitTimeForRead
    ,VFS.io_stall_write_ms AS TotalWaitTimeForWrite
    ,VFS.io_stall AS TotalWaitTimeForIO
    ,VFS.size_on_disk_bytes AS FileSizeInBytes
FROM sys.dm_io_virtual_file_stats(NULL,NULL) AS VFS
INNER JOIN sys.master_files AS MF
    ON VFS.database_id = MF.database_id AND VFS.file_id = MF.file_id
ORDER BY VFS.database_id DESC
GO
```

3. Next, open a second instance of query window. In this query window, type and execute the sample query on the `AdventureWorks2012` database as shown in the following script:

```
USE [AdventureWorks2012]
GO

--Clear the data cache.
DBCC DROPCLEANBUFFERS
GO
```

```
--Exceute a sample query.
SELECT *
FROM [Sales].[SalesOrderDetail]
GO
```

4. Now, run the following query in the first query window to notice the number of read operations and number of bytes read after running the sample query in the previous step:

```
USE [AdventureWorks2012]
GO


--Monitor the database files for AdventureWorks2012.
--Observe the read operations.
SELECT
    DB_NAME(VFS.database_id) AS DatabaseName
    ,MF.name AS LogicalFileName
    ,MF.physical_name AS PhysicalFileName
    ,CASE MF.type
        WHEN 0 THEN 'Data File'
        WHEN 1 THEN 'Log File'
    END AS FileType
    ,VFS.num_of_reads AS TotalReadOperations
    ,VFS.num_of_bytes_read TotalBytesRead
    ,VFS.num_of_writes AS TotalWriteOperations
    ,VFS.num_of_bytes_written AS TotalBytesWritten
    ,VFS.io_stall_read_ms AS TotalWaitTimeForRead
    ,VFS.io_stall_write_ms AS TotalWaitTimeForWrite
    ,VFS.io_stall AS TotalWaitTimeForIO
    ,VFS.size_on_disk_bytes AS FileSizeInBytes
FROM sys.dm_io_virtual_file_stats(DB_ID(),NULL) AS VFS
INNER JOIN sys.master_files AS MF
    ON VFS.database_id = MF.database_id AND VFS.file_id = MF.file_
id
ORDER BY VFS.database_id DESC
GO
```

5. Execute the query as shown in the following script to inspect if there are any pending I/O operations to be performed on any database files on SQL server:

```
--Monitor database files for any
--pending I/O requests.
SELECT
    DB_NAME(VFS.database_id) AS DatabaseName
    ,MF.name AS LogicalFileName
    ,MF.physical_name AS PhysicalFileName
```

```
      ,CASE MF.type
            WHEN 0 THEN 'Data File'
            WHEN 1 THEN 'Log File'
      END AS FileType
      ,PIOR.io_type AS InputOutputOperationType
      ,PIOR.io_pending AS Is_Request_Pending
      ,PIOR.io_handle
      ,PIOR.scheduler_address
FROM sys.dm_io_pending_io_requests AS PIOR
INNER JOIN sys.dm_io_virtual_file_stats(DB_ID('[AdventureWorks2012
]'),NULL) AS VFS
ON PIOR.io_handle = VFS.file_handle
INNER JOIN sys.master_files AS MF
ON VFS.database_id = MF.database_id AND VFS.file_id = MF.file_id
GO
```

How it works...

In the first query, we examined the data and log files for all the databases by using the `sys.dm_io_virtual_file_stats()` function. It accepts the following two parameters:

Parameter name	Description
database_id	This is the internal ID of a database assigned by SQL Server. If `database_id` is specified, then this function returns I/O statistics details for specified database only. If `database_id` is NULL then I/O statistics details for all databases is returned.
file_id	This is the internal ID of a database file assigned by SQL Server. If `file_id` is specified then this function returns I/O statistics details for specified file of a particular database. If `file_id` is NULL then I/O statistics details for all databases is returned.

Because we are passing NULL value for both parameters I/O statistics details for all the files of all the databases will be returned. We joined the output of the `sys.dm_io_virtual_file_stats()` function with the `sys.master_files` system catalog view on `database_id` to retrieve database file details. The `sys.master_files` returns the list of data and the log file details of all the databases. We determine whether a file is a data file or a log file by checking the `type` column of `sys.master_files`.

We then executed the sample query shown against `AdventureWorks2012` that simply retrieves the records from `Sales.SalesOrderDetails` table. Before running this query we cleared the data cache by running the DBCC DROPCLEANBUFFERS command to make sure that the query reads data from the disk and not from the data cache.

> Remember that you should not run the DBCC DROPCLEANBUFFERS command on the production database server. Doing so clears the data cache of SQL Server and forces subsequent queries to read data from disk, which hits the performance. However, you may want to use the DBCC DROPCLEANBUFFERS command while performing query tuning in the development environment.

After running the sample query against the AdventureWorks2012 database, we again reviewed the IO statistics details by running sys.dm_io_virtual_file_stats() function, but this time by specifying the database_id of the current database by calling DB_ID() system metadata function. This query returns the IO statistics details only for the current database, which happens to be AdventureWorks2012 in our case. You can notice that the values of num_of_reads and num_of_bytes_read have been increased after we run our sample query. This is due to the physical read operation caused by the query in the previous step. It increased the count of num_of_reads and added the number of bytes to num_of_bytes_read that it had read.

Finally we executed query that uses sys.dm_io_pending_io_requests. This query helps us to track any pending I/O operations. Column io_handle represents the internal handle of the file on which I/O operation is supposed to be performed. To retrieve file-specific details from sys.master_files system catalog view, we first joined the output of sys.dm_io_pending_io_requests with the output of sys.dm_io_virtual_file_stats() function by having a join condition on io_handle and file_handle columns and then eventually joined the resulting output with sys.master_files on database_id column.

For this simple example, it is unlikely that sys.dm_io_pending_io_requests reports any pending I/O request if you are running these queries on standalone SQL Server. On standalone environment, where there are no other queries running on SQL server, there is hardly any contention between I/O requests and the query gets executed immediately that we can hardly notice any pending I/O request. However, on production server, where there are a number of I/O resource-consuming queries running, you may frequently notice pending I/O requests reported by sys.dm_io_pending_io_requests.

There's more...

The following section discusses the DMVs and DMFs that we used in the recipe in more detail.

dm_io_virtual_file_stats (DMF)

dm_io_virtual_file_stats is a dynamic management function and provides disk input/output statistics for the read/write operations performed on data files and log files of all or a given database. It accepts two parameters, which are database_id and file_id. The following are some of the useful columns of this DMF:

Column name	Description
num_of_reads	This column represents the total number of read operations that have been performed on the file.
num_of_bytes_read	This column represents the total number of bytes that have been read from the file.
num_of_writes	This column represents the total number of write operations that have been performed on the file.
num_of_bytes_written	This column represents the total number of bytes that have been written to the file.
io_stall_read_ms	This column represents the total time duration in milliseconds during which processes waited for performing read operations on the file.
io_stall_write_ms	This column represents the total time duration in milliseconds during which processes waited for performing write operations on the file.
io_stall	This column represents the total time duration in milliseconds during which the processes waited for performing both, read and write operations on the file.
size_on_disk_bytes	This column represents the size in bytes of a file on the disk.

dm_io_pending_io_requests (DMV)

dm_io_pending_io_requests is a dynamic management view that returns a list of requests that are pending for input/output operations on a file. Following are some of the columns of this DMV:

Column name	Description
io_type	This column represents the type of I/O request that is pending.
io_pending	This column represents whether the request is indeed pending for I/O operation or the I/O request has been completed but SQL Server is yet to remove it from the list of pending I/O requests.
io_handle	This column represents the file handle of the file on which I/O operation is to be performed.
scheduler_address	This column represents the address of the scheduler to which a particular I/O request belongs.

The I/O statistics provided by `sys.dm_io_virtual_file_stats()` function and `sys.dm_io_pending_io_requests` are very useful in troubleshooting the issues with disk subsystem. You can monitor I/O operations being performed on files by looking at their usage statistics. You can easily find out database files having high degree of disk usage, with frequent resource-intensive read/write operations being performed on them, degrading the disk I/O throughput and thus causing I/O bottlenecks. Once you identify the files and databases responsible for the degradation of the I/O performance, you can either investigate the root cause of such a high degree of I/O operations or move those databases/files to different physical disks.

8
SQL Server Cache and Stored Procedure Recompilations

In this chapter we will cover:

► Monitoring compilations and recompilations at instance level, using Reliability and Performance Monitor

► Monitoring recompilations using SQL Server Profiler

Introduction

When a query, a batch, or a stored procedure is submitted to SQL Server for execution for the first time, the query gets parsed and then compiled. The result of a compiled query is a query plan that is cached in the **procedure cache**. The procedure cache is a portion of memory that SQL Server allocates to cache its query plans.

When the query is executed, an execution plan with its execution context is derived from the cached query plan, in order to save time during query execution, because query compilation is quite a heavy and long process. If multiple users execute the same reusable query from multiple sessions, the same query plan is used with different execution contexts. Each execution plan has its own execution context (user and session-specific information) details with it. Eventually, these execution plans get executed. Subsequent execution of the same query can reuse the cached version of the plan, and the compilation step is skipped.

People often get confused between "query compilation" and "query recompilation". However, there is a difference between the two.

Query compilation can be defined as the process of compiling a query and generating its query plan, for query execution, for those queries that don't already have a query plan present in the procedure cache.

Query recompilation can be defined as the process of compiling a query and generating a new, different query plan for the query whose query plan is already present in the procedure cache but cannot be used because the query plan is no longer valid for query execution. A query or stored procedure can also be explicitly marked for recompilation with T-SQL command options.

Query plan reusability refers to the ability of a query to be executed by reusing an existing execution plan from cache without the query being recompiled. So, a query whose execution plan is already cached does not have to pass through the phase of compilation or recompilation and execution plan generation. Thus, plan reusability is an ideal factor for improved performance in SQL Server, when a large number of query requests is processed at a time. So, in your database environment, if you see frequent compilations and recompilations for common queries, you are most probably having a recompilation issue and that harms SQL Server performance. However, it's important to know that in some specific situations, query recompilation can be beneficial. For example, to avoid the parameter sniffing problem, you would want to force a *recompile* to a specific query. Parameter sniffing occurs when a query executes and generates a good execution plan for a particular parameter value based on its selectivity and number of returning rows but uses the same execution plan for a subsequent query with different parameter values, which can be sub-optimal for that specific parameter value, based on its selectivity and number of returning rows.

Don't underestimate the overhead of compilation/recompilation on your SQL server. A query compilation or recompilation may take a few milliseconds and it may seem trivial at first. However, if you have a recompiling query that is hitting your database hundreds of times in a few seconds, continuously, and if you have several recompiling queries of this type, in your database application, your CPU will quite frequently be busy just compiling/recompiling and generating query plans. In this type of scenario, the degradation of your SQL server performance becomes quite obvious. Therefore, always consider minimizing recompilation issues and maximizing the query plan reusability in your SQL server environment.

However, we cannot evade recompilation issues completely. So, let's see some of the possible factors of query compilation and query recompilation:

▶ The query is executed for the first time, it has to be compiled to generate its query plan.

▶ The `DBCC FREEPROCCACHE` command is executed on SQL Server, it clears the plan cache or procedure cache of SQL Server and removes all cached query plans from memory. This causes any query to be compiled the next time it is run.

- The DBCC FLUSHPROCINDB command is issued on SQL Server, it removes all cached query plans for a particular database. If, after executing this command on a particular database, any query execution request comes for that particular database, it becomes essential for the query to be compiled again due to non-existence of its query plan in cache.

- Restarting the SQL Server service also clears the procedure cache of SQL Server and removes all cached query plans from the memory.

- While performing other memory-consuming tasks, or if the procedure cache is full and requests to execute some new queries whose query plans do not exist in the procedure cache, SQL Server may need to remove few query plans (generally old query plans that are reused infrequently) from memory to make room for new query plans.

- The schema of the object that is referenced by a query has been changed, for example, if the definition of a column in a table is changed, if a column is dropped from the table, or if an index is created or rebuilt.

- The statistics of tables referenced by the query are updated. Statistics can be updated by the sp_createstats, sp_updatestats, or UPDATE STATISTICS T-SQL commands, by rebuilding an index, or automatically by SQL Server if statistics are outdated.

- An object does not exist at query compile time. For example, definitions of temporary tables in a stored procedure may cause a recompilation issue.

- A stored procedure has been declared with the WITH RECOMPILE option.

- A stored procedure is executed with the WITH RECOMPILE option.

- A stored procedure is recompiled with the sp_recompile system stored procedure.

- A query is executed with the OPTION (RECOMPILE) query hint.

- The following SET options may also cause recompilation of stored procedures in which they are used:

    - ANSI_NULL_DFLT_OFF
    - ANSI_NULL_DFLT_ON
    - ANSI_NULLS
    - ANSI_PADDING
    - ANSI_WARNINGS
    - ARITHABORT
    - CONCAT_NULL_YIELDS_NULL
    - DATEFIRST
    - DATEFORMAT
    - FORCEPLAN

- ❑ LANGUAGE

- ❑ NO_BROWSETABLE

- ❑ NUMERIC_ROUNDABORT

- ❑ QUOTED_IDENTIFIER

> **DBCC FREEPROCCACHE and DBCC FLUSHPROCINDB**
>
> Never run the DBCC FREEPROCCACHE and DBCC FLUSHPROCINDB commands on a production server. DBCC FREEPROCCACHE clears the entire SQL Server procedure cache, whereas DBCC FLUSHPROCINDB clears the procedure cache for a given database. Clearing the procedure cache causes queries to compile again in their subsequent executions, which degrades the performance of SQL Server.

As we saw, there can be a number of reasons for compilations and recompilations; we must identify the correct reasons for a recompilation issue.

In this chapter, we will see how we can investigate and analyze recompilation issues.

Monitoring compilations and recompilations at instance level using Reliability and Performance Monitor

Imagine that you have set up your production SQL server that is hosting several databases used by different applications. Initially your SQL server responds smoothly, but as the number of query requests increases, becoming larger day by day, and when it reaches several hundred per second, you notice that queries take a little longer to execute and your SQL server CPU usage is higher than what you expected.

As you may know, there can be a number of reasons for SQL server to respond poorly, such as:

- ▸ Your physical database design and database file placement is not optimized

- ▸ Databases are missing proper indexes

- ▸ Queries are not optimized and are poorly written

- ▸ Statistics are out-of-date, and query optimizer is not able to generate an optimum plan

- ▸ Queries face blocking issues

- ▸ You need to upgrade the CPU or increase the number of CPU cores

- ▸ The server does not have enough memory

- ▸ There is a problem with the disk I/O system

This is not a complete list of reasons!

Recompilation can be one of the issues to cause slow query response. If the recompilation issue is severe, it can constantly keep the CPU busy. If you want to verify that your database server is not facing a recompilation issue, monitoring the SQL Server instance for compilation and recompilation events can be useful.

In this recipe, we will learn how to monitor compilation and recompilation events at server-level with Reliability and Performance Monitor.

Getting ready

In this recipe, we will gather compilation- and recompilation-related statistics for the following performance counters, using Reliability and Performance Monitor:

- **SQL Server:SQL Statistics:SQL Compilations/sec**
- **SQL Server:SQL Statistics:SQL Re-Compilations/sec**

For this, we will execute a script that will create a stored procedure named `usp_GetSalesOrderDetail_ProductID`. This stored procedure will accept `ProductID`, and based on `ProductID`, it will return records from the `Sales.SalesOrderDetail` table.

We will call this stored procedure twice. However, before we call the stored procedure a second time, we will rebuild the index defined on the `ProductID` column, so that it causes recompilations.

Before you can continue with the recipe, here are the prerequisites that you should fulfill:

- An instance of SQL Server 2012 Developer or Enterprise Evaluation edition
- A sample `AdventureWorks2012` database on the SQL Server instance

How to do it...

Follow the ensuing steps to capture compilation and recompilation events through Reliability and Performance Monitor:

1. To start Reliability and Performance Monitor:
    i. Press the Windows **+** R key combination to display the **Run** dialog box.
    ii. In this dialog box, type `perfmon.exe` and press *Enter*.
2. When Reliability and Performance Monitor is started, to switch to Performance Monitor view, click on the **Performance Monitor** node, under the **Monitoring Tools** node, in the left-hand side console tree.

3. Press the *Delete* key or click on the **X** button in the toolbar, to delete any existing performance counter. Click on the **+** button in the toolbar to add counters.

4. In the **Add Counters** dialog box, under the **Select counters from computer:** dropdown list, type the name of the computer or let it be **<Local computer>** if you are monitoring a local machine.

5. In the list of available performance counter objects, expand **SQL Server:SQL Statistics** and select **SQL Compilations/sec** and **SQL Re-Compilations/sec**, with the mouse, while holding down the *Ctrl* key.

6. Click on the **Add > >** button. This will add the **SQL Compilations/sec** and **SQL Re-Compilations/sec** counters to the **Added counters** list, on the right-hand side. After adding these two counters, your screen should look as shown in the following screenshot:

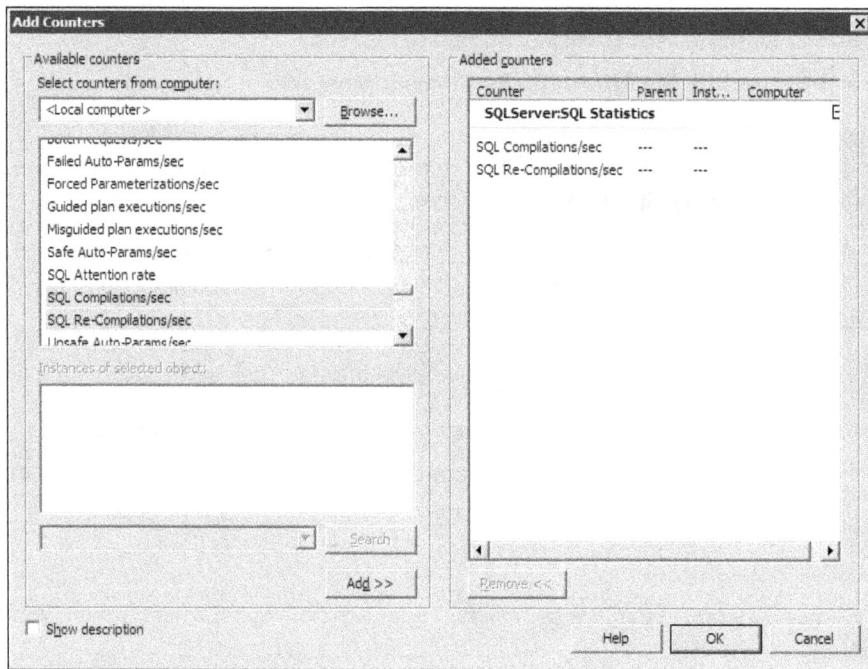

7. In **Reliability and Performance Monitor**, click on the **Action** menu and select **Properties**.

8. In the **General** tab of the **Performance Monitor Properties** dialog box, change the value of **Duration** to 60 **seconds** in the **Graph elements** section. The following screenshot shows the **Performance Monitor Properties** dialog box with an updated **Duration** value:

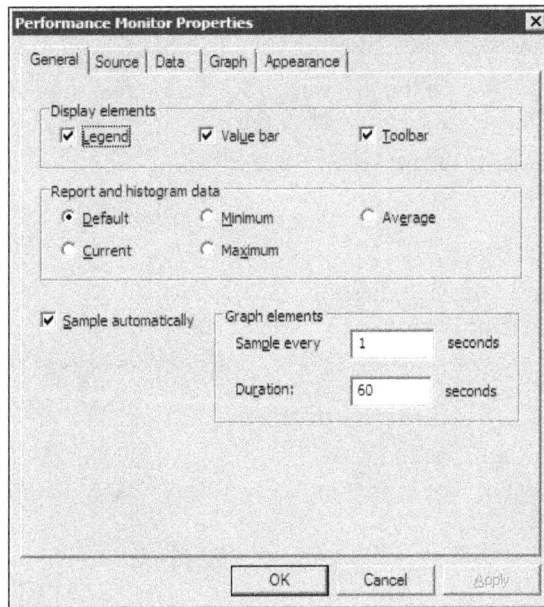

9. Click on the **Graph** tab of the **Performance Monitor Properties** dialog box, and change the value of **Maximum** to 25 in the **Vertical scale** section. The following screenshot shows the **Performance Monitor Properties** dialog box with an updated **Maximum** value:

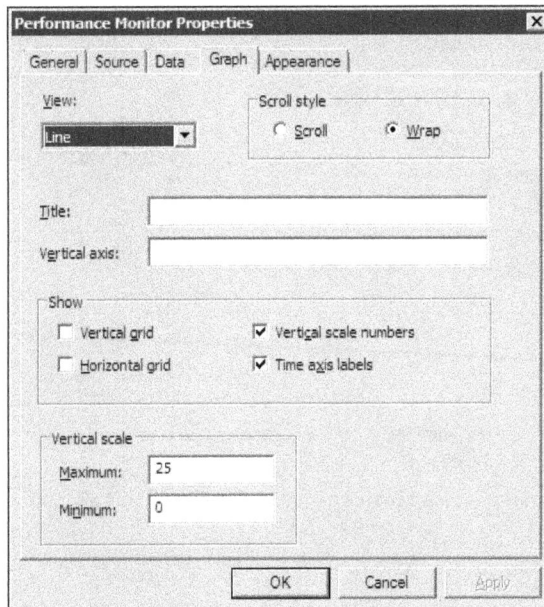

10. Now, open SQL Server Management Studio and establish a connection with the SQL server hosting the `AdventureWorks2012` database.

11. In the query window, type the following T-SQL script, and then execute the script twice against the `AdventureWorks2012` database:

```
USE AdventureWorks2012
GO


--Check if stored procedure exists
--or not. If it does, drop it.
IF OBJECT_ID('dbo.usp_GetSalesOrderDetail_ProductID') IS NOT NULL
    DROP PROCEDURE dbo.usp_GetSalesOrderDetail_ProductID
GO


--Creating stored procedure
CREATE PROCEDURE dbo.usp_GetSalesOrderDetail_ProductID
(
    @ProductID INT
)AS
BEGIN
    SELECT
        SalesOrderID
        ,SalesOrderDetailID
        ,CarrierTrackingNumber
        ,OrderQty
        ,ProductID
        ,SpecialOfferID
        ,UnitPrice
        ,UnitPriceDiscount
        ,LineTotal
        ,rowguid
        ,ModifiedDate
    FROM Sales.SalesOrderDetail
    WHERE ProductID > @ProductID
END

GO


--Execute Stored Procedure by passing it
--764 as the value of ProductID
EXECUTE usp_GetSalesOrderDetail_ProductID 764

GO

--Rebuilding an existing non-clustered
```

```
--index defined on ProductId column
ALTER INDEX IX_SalesOrderDetail_ProductID
ON Sales.SalesOrderDetail REBUILD

--Again execute Stored Procedure by passing it
--764 as the value of ProductID
EXECUTE usp_GetSalesOrderDetail_ProductID 764
GO
```

12. Now, switch to **Reliability and Performance Monitor** and note the statistics for compilations/recompilations. Also, note the spikes in the graph for compilations and recompilations:

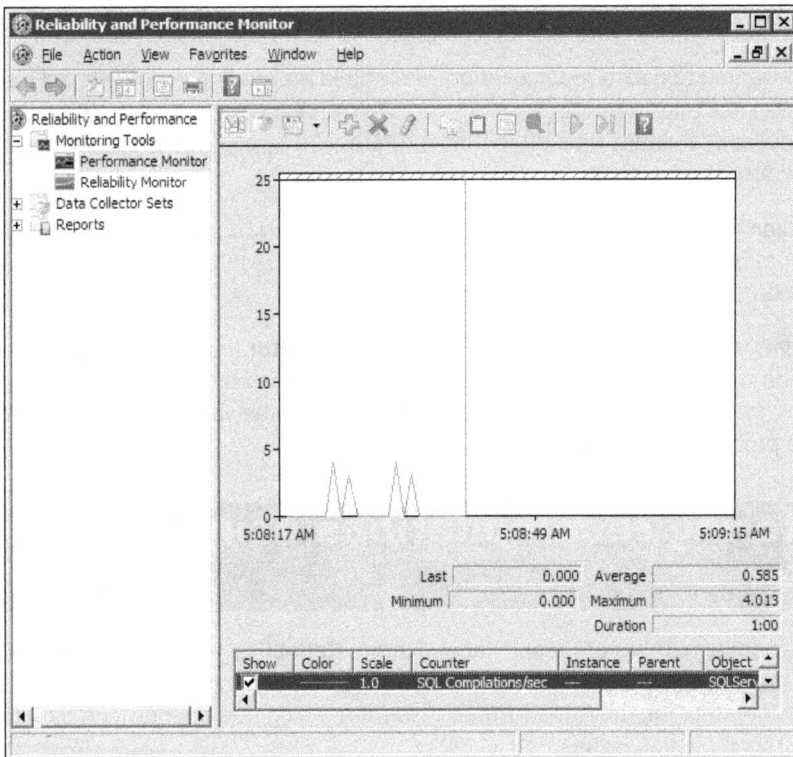

How it works...

In this recipe, we started by opening the **Reliability and Performance Monitor** tool. First, we deleted existing performance counters and added the following ones:

- ▸ **SQL Server:SQL Statistics:SQL Compilations/sec**
- ▸ **SQL Server:SQL Statistics:SQL Re-Compilations/sec**

We then reset the value of **Duration** to 60 and the value of **Maximum** to 25, so that the graph's maximum CPU usage value is 25 percent (on the vertical axis) and graph's maximum time length is 60 seconds (on the horizontal axis).

After setting up Reliability and Performance Monitor, we start SQL Server Management Studio and execute the T-SQL script that creates the stored procedure dbo.usp_GetSalesOrderDetail_ProductID. The script first checks whether the stored procedure already exists. If it exists, it is dropped before it is recreated. The stored procedure accepts a value for the @ProductID parameter, and based on the ProductID value, it retrieves data from the Sales.SalesOrderDetail table.

We executed the stored procedure dbo.usp_GetSalesOrderDetail_ProductID by passing 764 as ProductID. Because the stored procedure was executed for the first time, it was compiled and then executed.

Because we wanted to cause recompilation, we rebuild an existing non-clustered index, that is, IX_SalesOrderDetail_ProductID, which has been defined on the ProductID column. Rebuilding an index on a table that is referenced by a stored procedure causes that stored procedure to recompile.

After rebuilding the index, we executed dbo.usp_GetSalesOrderDetail_ProductID a second time. Because the index IX_SalesOrderDetail_ProductID was rebuilt, the stored procedure got recompiled and then executed.

Finally, we saw that the **Reliability and Performance Monitor** tool gathered statistics related to compilation and recompilation events for the performance counters that we had added. If the statistics/frequency of recompilation events is found to be very high, you can determine that you are probably facing a recompilation issue.

Monitoring recompilations using SQL Server Profiler

If you notice a large number of recompilations in the **Reliability and Performance Monitor** tool and suspect that your database server is facing a recompilation issue, you would want to confirm it by investigating the issue further, to identify which queries of which databases are causing the recompilation issues.

To investigate the root cause of the recompilation issue, we will use **SQL Server Profiler**. In this recipe, we will learn how we can trace recompilation events occurring on SQL server for individual SQL statements and stored procedures as well. With the help of SQL Server Profiler, we can identify the databases where recompilations occur and can identify queries and stored procedures that cause query recompilations. After identifying recompiling queries and stored procedures, you can look further into those queries and optimize them to minimize recompilation issues.

Getting ready

In this recipe, we will trace the following recompilation-related events through SQL Server Profiler:

- ▶ **SP:Recompile**: This event is raised when a stored procedure is recompiled
- ▶ **SQL:StmtRecompile**: This event is raised when an individual query in a batch or stored procedure is recompiled

In order to catch these events, we will set up a scenario to produce recompilations for stored procedures and queries. For this, we will execute a script that will create a stored procedure named `dbo.usp_GetOrderDetails_ByOrderYear`. This stored procedure will accept an integer value, representing a year value, as a parameter, and based on the year, it will return records from the `Sales.SalesOrderHeader` table by creating a filter on the `OrderDate` column.

We will call this stored procedure twice. However, before we call the stored procedure a second time, we will create a non-clustered index on the `OrderDate` column, which will cause stored procedure recompilation.

In another script, we will also execute two ad-hoc queries that we will run against the `Sales.SalesOrderHeader` table in the `AdventureWorks2012` database and retrieve records based on the `SalePersonID` value. We will see how the `OPTION (RECOMPILE)` query hint forces a query to recompile and raise a `SQL:StmtRecompile` event in SQL Trace.

Before you can continue with the recipe, here are the prerequisites that you should fulfill:

- ▶ An instance of SQL Server 2012 Developer or Enterprise Evaluation edition
- ▶ Sample `AdventureWorks2012` database on the instance of SQL Server

How to do it...

The following steps will enable you to capture recompilation events through SQL Server Profiler:

1. Start **SQL Server Profiler**.
2. Select **New Trace...** from the **File** menu. In the **Connect to Server** dialog box, provide connection details of the SQL server hosting the `AdventureWorks2012` database and click on **Connect**.
3. In the **General** tab for **Trace Properties**, select a **Blank** template from the **Use the template:** drop-down menu.
4. In the **Events Selection** tab, check the checkboxes for the event class, for the following events and event classes:
    - ❑ **Stored Procedures**
    - ❑ **SP:Completed**

         ❑ **SP:Recompile**

         ❑ **SP:Starting**

         ❑ **TSQL**

         ❑ **SQL:StmtCompleted**

         ❑ **SQL:StmtRecompile**

         ❑ **SQL:StmtStarting**

5. Select the following data columns and organize data columns by clicking on the **Organize Columns...** button in the **Events Selection** tab of the **Trace Properties** dialog box. The column should be organized in the order as shown here:

    1. **EventClass**

    2. **TextData**

    3. **EventSubClass**

    4. **DatabaseName**

    5. **DatabaseID**

    6. **ApplicationName**

    7. **Duration**

    8. **SPID**

6. Click on the **Run** button to run the trace in the **Trace Properties** dialog box.

7. Now, open SQL Server Management Studio and establish a connection to the SQL server hosting the `AdventureWorks2012` database.

8. In the query window, type the following T-SQL script, and then execute the script against the `AdventureWorks2012` database:

```
USE AdventureWorks2012
GO


--Check if stored procedure exists
--or not. If it does, drop it.
IF OBJECT_ID('dbo.usp_GetOrderDetails_ByOrderYear') IS NOT NULL
    DROP PROCEDURE dbo.usp_GetOrderDetails_ByOrderYear
GO


--Creating stored procedure
CREATE PROCEDURE dbo.usp_GetOrderDetails_ByOrderYear
(
    @OrderYear INT
) AS
```

```
BEGIN
    DECLARE @FromDate DATETIME
    DECLARE @ToDate DATETIME

    SET @FromDate = CAST(@OrderYear AS VARCHAR) + '0101'
    SET @ToDate = CAST(@OrderYear+1 AS VARCHAR) + '0101'

    IF ISDATE(@FromDate)=0 OR ISDATE(@ToDate)=0
        RETURN

    SELECT
        SalesOrderID
        ,OrderDate
        ,ShipDate
        ,SalesOrderNumber
        ,CustomerID
        ,SalesPersonID
        ,SubTotal
        ,TaxAmt
        ,Freight
        ,TotalDue
    FROM Sales.SalesOrderHeader
    WHERE OrderDate>= @FromDate AND OrderDate<@ToDate

END

GO

--Execute Stored Procedure by passing it
--2007 as the value of Order Year
EXECUTE usp_GetOrderDetails_ByOrderYear 2007

GO
```

9. Now, type and execute the following queries against the AdventureWorks2012 database, to create a non-clustered index and execute the stored procedure we have created in the previous step:

```
--Create nonclustered index on
--OrderDate column
CREATE INDEX idx_SalesOrderHeader_OrderDate
ON Sales.SalesOrderHeader(OrderDate)
```

```
GO

--Execute Stored Procedure by passing it
--2007 as the value of Order Year
EXECUTE usp_GetOrderDetails_ByOrderYear 2007
GO
```

10. Switch to **SQL Server Profiler**, and you should see the trace window with the trace events shown in following screenshot:

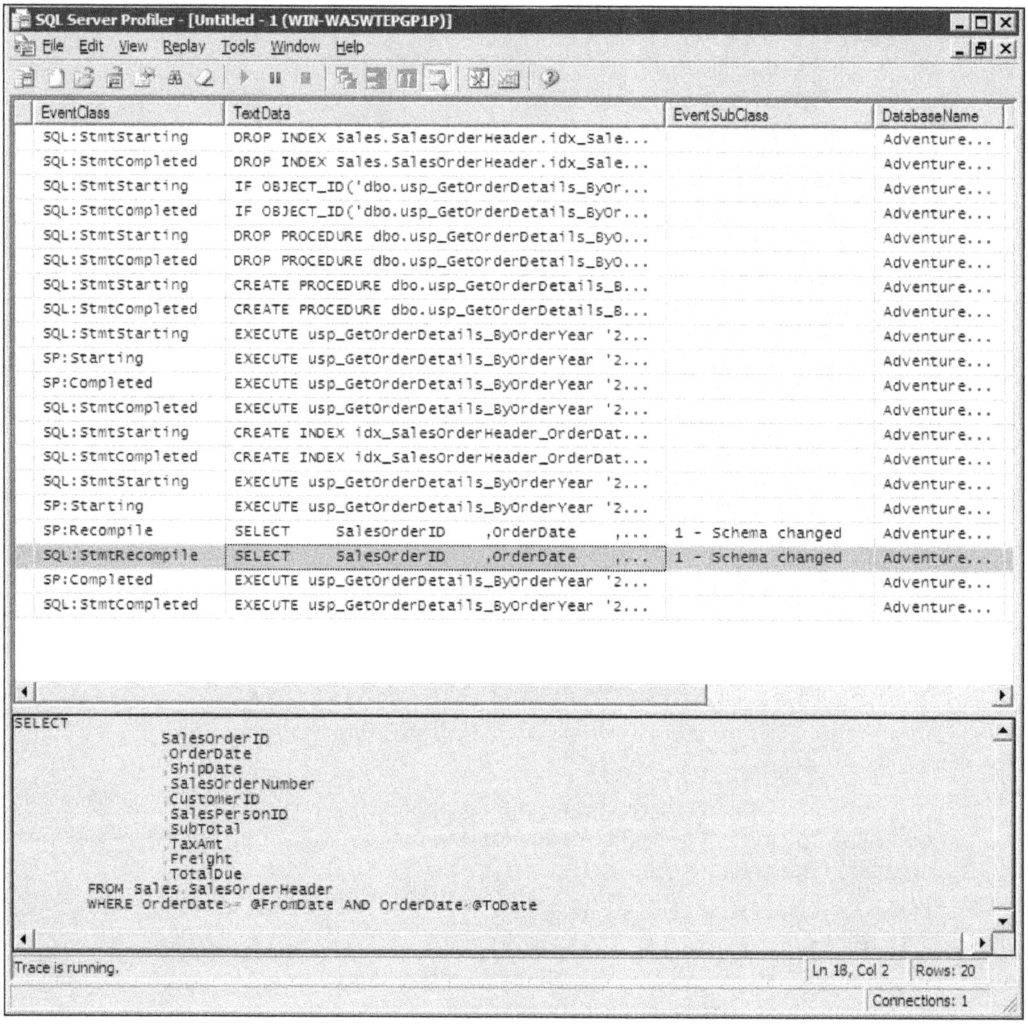

11. Now, in SQL Server Management Studio, type and execute the following queries in the query window, against the AdventureWorks2012 database:

```
--Select data from Sales.SalesOrderHeader
--for SalesPersionID = 279
SELECT
    SalesOrderID
    ,OrderDate
    ,ShipDate
    ,SalesOrderNumber
    ,CustomerID
    ,SalesPersonID
    ,SubTotal
    ,TaxAmt
    ,Freight
    ,TotalDue
FROM Sales.SalesOrderHeader
WHERE SalesPersonID = 279

GO


--Select data from Sales.SalesOrderHeader
--for SalesPersionID = 279 but with
-- RECOMPILE query hint.
SELECT
    SalesOrderID
    ,OrderDate
    ,ShipDate
    ,SalesOrderNumber
    ,CustomerID
    ,SalesPersonID
    ,SubTotal
    ,TaxAmt
    ,Freight
    ,TotalDue
FROM Sales.SalesOrderHeader
WHERE SalesPersonID = 279
OPTION (RECOMPILE)

GO
```

12. Now, switch to **SQL Server Profiler,** and you should see the trace window with the trace events shown in following screenshot:

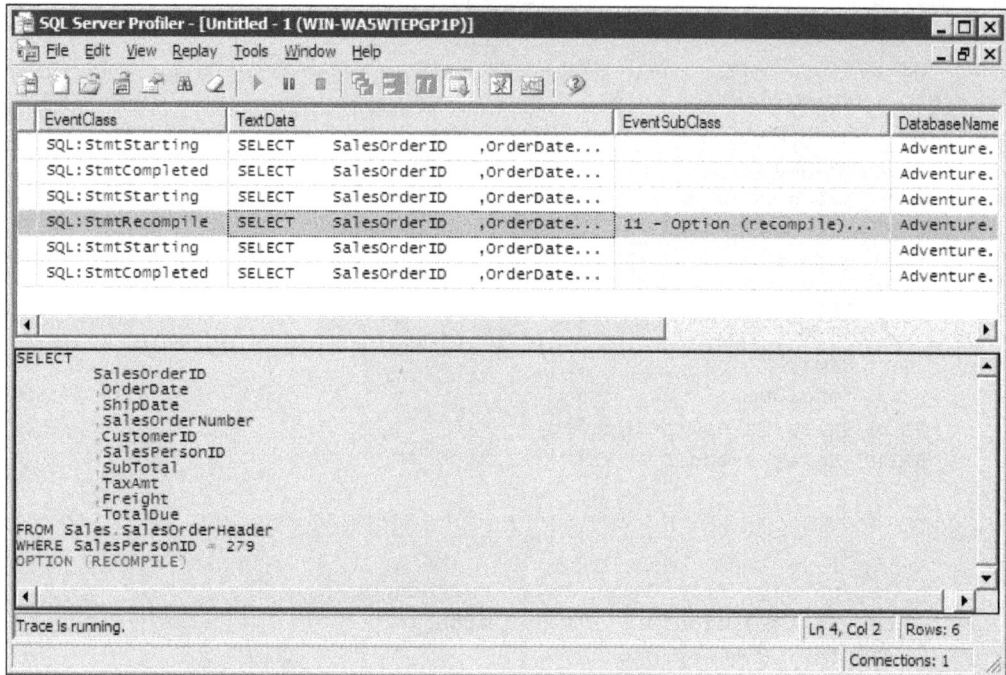

How it works...

We first started with an SQL Trace, with Blank template, and included the following events:

- ▸ **Stored Procedures**
    - ❑ **SP:Completed**
    - ❑ **SP:Recompile**
    - ❑ **SP:Starting**
- ▸ **TSQL**
    - ❑ **SQL:StmtCompleted**
    - ❑ **SQL:StmtRecompile**
    - ❑ **SQL:StmtStarting**

In this recipe, we have new events—SP:Recompile and SQL:StmtRecompile. The SP:Recompile trace event indicates the recompilation of whole stored procedure, whereas the SQL:StmtRecompile event indicates the recompilation of individual SQL statements.

In our trace definition, we included the **EventSubClass** data column. In the context of the
`SP:Recompile` and `SQL:StmtRecompile` events, the **EventSubClass** data column
indicates the type of recompilation that has occurred. It can be any of the following:

- 1 = Schema Changed
- 2 = Statistics Changed
- 3 = Recompile DNR
- 4 = Set Option Changed
- 5 = Temp Table Changed
- 6 = Remote Rowset Changed
- 7 = For Browse Perms Changed
- 8 = Query Notification Environment Changed
- 9 = MPI View Changed
- 10 = Cursor Options Changed
- 11 = With Recompile Option

> If you have declared your stored procedure with the `WITH`
> `RECOMPILE` option, do not expect that it will raise the
> `SP:Recompile` event in SQL Trace upon its execution. All that the
> `WITH RECOMPILE` option instructs is not to cache the query plan for
> the stored procedure and compile the stored procedure at runtime.
> So, technically it is not a recompilation, but a fresh compilation.

We started the trace and executed a script that created and executed the stored procedure
`dbo.usp_GetOrderDetails_ByOrderYear`. Before creating the stored procedure, we
checked whether it exists (if it does, we drop and then recreate it).

The store procedure accepts an integer value, which represents a year in the `OrderDate`
column for which the sales data from `Sales.SalesOrderHeader` is to be retrieved. Based
on the passed integer year, the stored procedure extracts `FromDate` and `ToDate` values to
be used in the `WHERE` clause to compare the `OrderDate` column.

We executed the `dbo.usp_GetOrderDetails_ByOrderYear` stored procedure by passing
`2007` as the order year, so it returns only the orders placed in the year 2007.

Because we used `OrderDate` in the `WHERE` clause of the query, in the stored procedure,
and because there is no index defined on the `OrderDate` column, we created an index
`idx_SalesOrderHeader_OrderDate` on the `OrderDate` column of the `Sales.`
`SalesOrderHeader` table, in next script. After creating the index, we executed the
same stored procedure again, by passing the same order year value, that is, `2007`.

We saw, in **SQL Server Profiler**, that the second execution of the stored procedure caused stored procedure recompilation. This resulted in raising `SP:Recompile` and `SQL:StmtRecompile` events, and can be seen in SQL Trace. This happened due to index creation just before executing the stored procedure for the second time.

In SQL Trace, you can even examine the cause of recompilation by looking at the **EventSubClass** column. The **EventSubClass** column shows **1 = Schema Changed**, which means that the recompilation has occurred due to change in schema. The **TextData** column indicates the SQL statement that caused the recompilation.

In the last script that we executed in this recipe, we executed two identical queries that retrieved data from the `Sales.SalesOrderHeader` table, based on the `SalePersonID` value as `279`. The only difference between the two queries in this script is that the second query uses the `OPTION (RECOMPILE)` query hint. The `OPTION (RECOMPILE)` query hint instructs SQL Server to remove the query plan from the procedure cache, after its execution, and forces recompilation the next time the query is executed. When we executed the script, we noticed that, in SQL Trace, the `SQL:StmtRecompile` event was fired.

Examine the value in the **EventSubClass** column, which happens to be **11 – Option (recompile)**. This suggests that the query hint `OPTION (RECOMPILE)` was used.

From the other columns, such as **DatabaseName** and **ApplicationName**, you can find out in exactly which database recompilations occurred, and from which application.

There's more...

For further recompilation analysis, you can use the following dynamic management views and functions:

- `sys.dm_exec_cached_plans`
- `sys.dm_exec_sql_text()`
- `sys.dm_exec_query_stats`

You can further analyze the causes of recompilations, based on the result of given DMVs and DMFs. By using these DMVs and DMFs in combination, you can identify the queries whose query plans are reused frequently.

For more information on query compilation and recompilation, you can refer to two good whitepapers that can be found at the following locations:

- `http://msdn.microsoft.com/en-us/library/ee343986%28v=sql.100%29.aspx`
- `http://technet.microsoft.com/library/Cc966425`

However, these whitepapers refer to older versions of SQL Server, though the information is applicable to SQL Server 2012 as well.

9
Implementing Indexes

In this chapter we will cover:

- ▶ Increasing performance by creating a clustered index
- ▶ Increasing performance by creating a non-clustered index
- ▶ Increasing performance by covering index
- ▶ Increasing performance by including columns in an index
- ▶ Improving performance by a filtered index
- ▶ Improving performance by a columnstore index

Introduction

Indexes are one of the most powerful objects in the RDBMS system, though the index itself is not a relational concept. It significantly reduces disk I/O and logical reads, to boost up the performance of the SELECT statement by locating proper data without even scanning the whole table. That is why it is mandatory to have a proper index on proper column(s) of the table. Missing indexes or Indexes on improper column(s) could start creating performance-related issues, such as implanting a wrong execution plan, which may create high I/O use and logical reads. Indexes are a double-edged sword, so use them with caution, otherwise it may be harmful for performance. This is because indexes come with a little overhead for DML statements, which requires storage space on the disk, and keeping your index up to date with changing data is also one of the overheads.

We could like to compare indexes to an English dictionary (this is really a widely used analogy for indexes). Suppose we are searching for the meaning of the word "Treasure", we are sure we have to search for it on the pages where all the words starting with "Tr" are listed. Once we come across words starting with "Tr", we don't need to search up to the end of the dictionary. For instance, if the words starting with "Tr" are listed from page number 725 to 729, we have to look at only those five pages. If we don't find "Treasure" within them, we will not find the meaning of that word in that dictionary.

Indexes are stored in the form of a B-Tree in SQL Server. Considering each index page as one node, the top-most node is called **root** and the bottom-most nodes in Index B-Tree are called **leaf** nodes. Any node between the root and a leaf node is called an **intermediate** node.

The leaf node contains the actual data pages of a database table. The root node and the intermediate node could have Key Value(s), and pointers to another intermediate node, downwards from the current node.

The following image shows the basic structure of an index:

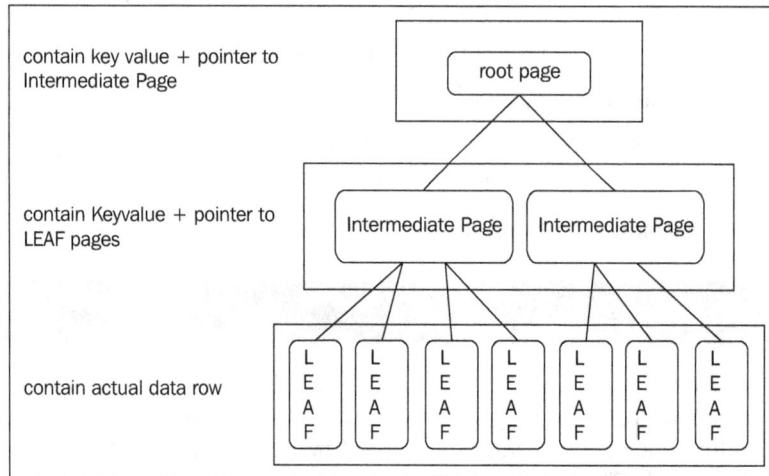

Increasing performance by creating a clustered index

Any RDBMS supports the functionality to perform the INSERT, UPDATE, and DELETE operations, and retrieve the data with the SELECT statement. As time passes by, data will increase in the database, and it will start creating an issue of slow retrieval of data whenever the SELECT statement is processed.

RDBMS is supposed to support a very large-scale database, especially when you are talking about SQL Server 2012. So, how can we eliminate this slow performance issue? Well, this is when index makes an entry into the life of a database administrator!

Prevention is always better than cure, so it is suggested that you implement proper indexes and keep changing the indexes over a period of time, if needed, even before performance issues start arising.

How to choose a proper field for the index defined in this recipe, and how to maintain the index properly and change it, will be covered in the next chapter—*Chapter 10, Maintaining Indexes*.

A **clustered index** is the base of all indexes; without it, the database table would be called a heap. The clustered index stores physically sorted data, and that is the reason we can have only one clustered index per table. Each clustered index has a row in the `sys.partitions` catalog view, with the value of `Index_ID` as 1.

Clustered indexes can be defined in one or more than one column (composite index). A clustered index should be on the column(s) that are going to be used the maximum amount of time in search ranges.

Getting ready

There are some prerequisites that need to be checked before starting to work with clustered indexes. We have to be prepared with some information, such as:

 ▶ Which table needs a clustered index

 ▶ Which column(s) is/are the prime candidate(s) for the index

A column should be chosen after considering the following facts:

 ▶ The column should contain a large number of distinct values. If you have a Gender column, which probably has two values—M for Male and F for Female—it shouldn't be selected as a clustered index. Instead, choose the Birth Date column or maybe a combination of First Name and Last Name columns, or maybe purchase order ID, sales order ID, and so on.

 ▶ Assigning of Primary Key to a column would create a clustered index on that column, by default. However, this is not mandatory; you can change it to a non-clustered index if you want to.

 ▶ The column or columns should have high selectivity. By high selectivity, it means that the column is being used frequently in the WHERE, JOIN, ORDER BY, or GROUP BY clauses.

 ▶ The columns should be widely used with search operators, such as >, <, >=, <=, BETWEEN, or IN, and return large result sets.

 ▶ The column should be short, like a wide key-value. This would increase the depth of the clustered index and reduce the performance a bit. Also, increase the size of a non-clustered index, as a Key Column value is present as a reference in all non-clustered indexes.

Best practices for selecting a column are:

▸ The column should be unique and **not NULL**

▸ Try to keep the index as short as possible by creating it on one column, or as few columns as possible, to keep your scan narrow and to get the best performance

▸ Create a clustered index on every table by selecting the column that is the best candidate for an index and that is being used very frequently in the WHERE clause

▸ If possible, try to avoid creating a clustered index on a varchar column

How to do it...

Well, after knowing about clustered index and finding out which table and column(s) (also known as Key Column or Key Columns, in case of composite index) require a clustered index, it is time to create the clustered index.

The following is the basic syntax for defining a clustered index:

```
CREATE CLUSTERED INDEX <Idx_Index_Name>
ON <table_Name> (column_name  [ASC | DESC] [,.......N])
```

You can use the template explorer to see the syntax, from **View | Template Browser**, or you can simply use the keyboard shortcut *Ctrl + Alt + T*. The index syntax is located in the **Template Browser**, as shown in the following screenshot:

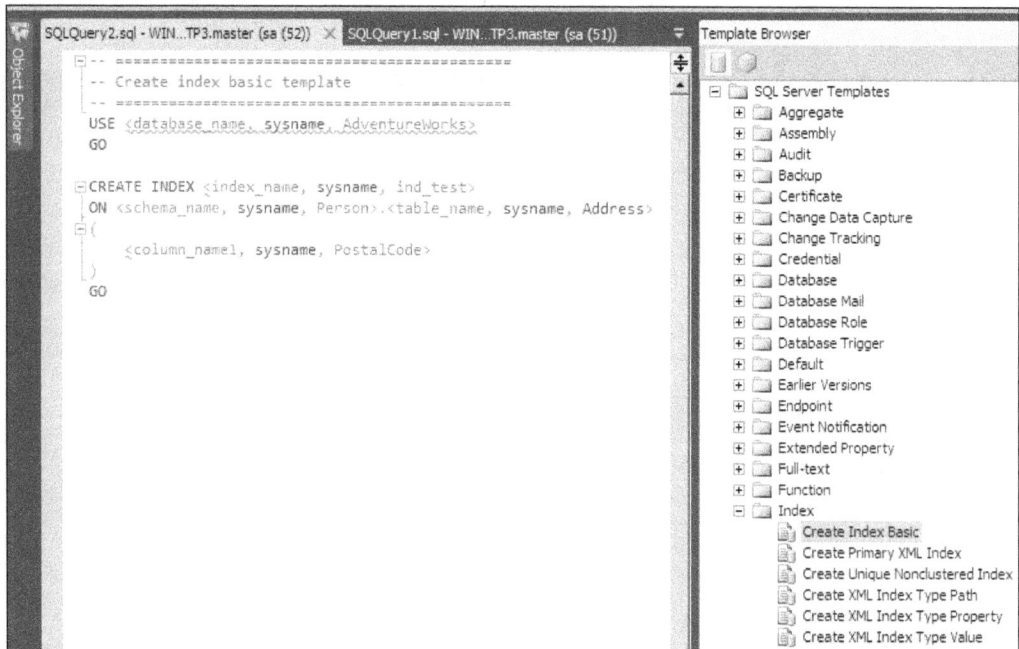

Here is an exercise to practically build a clustered index on one table, which will be created to observe the behavior of the index.

1. Run the following query:

```
--If the orders table is already present, you can delete it, and
then create new one with the name Orders
IF OBJECT_ID('ordDemo', 'U') IS NOT NULL BEGIN
        DROP TABLE ordDemo
END
GO


--creating table for demonstration
CREATE TABLE ordDemo (OrderID INT IDENTITY, OrderDate DATETIME,
Amount MONEY, Refno INT)
GO


--inserting 100000 fack rows into table
INSERT INTO ordDemo (OrderDate, Amount, Refno)
SELECT TOP 100000
        DATEADD(minute, ABS(a.object_id % 50000 ), CAST('2011-11-04'
AS DATETIME)),
        ABS(a.object_id % 10),
        CAST(ABS(a.object_id % 13) AS VARCHAR)
FROM sys.all_objects a
CROSS JOIN sys.all_objects b
GO
```

2. Now we are ready to see the effect of the index on the table ordDemo.

There are several ways to monitor performance-related stuff, already explained in the *Performance Monitoring* section (the first five chapters) of this book. Here is a list of some of the chapters in this book that will help to understand the concept of monitoring:

- ❑ The *Creating a trace or workload* recipe in *Chapter 1, SQL Server Profiler*

- ❑ The *Monitoring performance with Actual Execution Plan, Monitoring performance of query by SET SHOWPLAN_XML*, and *Monitoring Performance of query by SET STATISTICS XML* recipes in *Chapter 5, Monitoring with Execution Plans*

- ❑ The *Finding Table/Index Scans in execution plan and fixing them*, and *Introducing Key Lookups, finding them in execution plans, and resolving them* recipes in *Chapter 6, Tuning with Execution Plans*

3. We are going to use execution plan to see the effect of a clustered index. Execute the following T-SQL command by keeping your execution plan enabled:

```
SELECT OrderDate,Amount,Refno FROM ordDemo WHERE Refno<3
```

> In order to enable execution plan, select **QUERY | Include Actual Execution Plan**, from the Menu bar, or use the *Ctrl + M* keyboard shortcut.

4. As soon as this query finishes execution, thousands of rows will be displayed in the **Results** tab. Besides the **Results** tab, you will see two more tabs, as follows:

   - The **Messages** tab, which shows errors, warnings, and so on, that occurred during the execution

   - The **Execution Plan** tab, which is enabled before executing a query

   Here is a screenshot that shows a few of the rows in result set out of the query executed in step 1:

	OrderDate	Amount	Refno
1	2011-11-19 16:28:00.000	8.00	1
2	2011-11-19 16:28:00.000	8.00	1
3	2011-11-19 16:28:00.000	8.00	1
4	2011-11-19 16:28:00.000	8.00	1
5	2011-11-19 16:28:00.000	8.00	1
6	2011-11-19 16:28:00.000	8.00	1
7	2011-11-19 16:28:00.000	8.00	1
8	2011-11-19 16:28:00.000	8.00	1
9	2011-11-19 16:28:00.000	8.00	1
10	2011-11-19 16:28:00.000	8.00	1
11	2011-11-19 16:28:00.000	8.00	1
12	2011-11-19 16:28:00.000	8.00	1
13	2011-11-19 16:28:00.000	8.00	1
14	2011-11-19 16:28:00.000	8.00	1
15	2011-11-19 16:28:00.000	8.00	1
16	2011-11-19 16:28:00.000	8.00	1
17	2011-11-19 16:28:00.000	8.00	1
18	2011-11-19 16:28:00.000	8.00	1
19	2011-11-19 16:28:00.000	8.00	1
20	2011-11-19 16:28:00.000	8.00	1
21	2011-11-19 16:28:00.000	8.00	1
22	2011-11-19 16:28:00.000	8.00	1

Query executed successfully.

5. Move to the **Execution Plan** tab and see the graphical execution plan that the query has used. It will show **Table Scan**, which means it has to look into the whole table to find the rows we were searching. The following is a screenshot of the **Execution Plan** tab:

6. After a sneak preview of the query's execution plan, create a clustered index on the field `Refno` and execute the same `SELECT` statement given previously with the execution plan, to see the difference in the query when run before and after the clustered index is created. The main reasons for choosing the `Refno` field as the key column of the clustered index are:

   ❑ It is a numeric value (not a `varchar`), so the clustered index will be short

   ❑ `Refno` will be frequently used in searches and maybe in a `JOIN` clause.

> ❏ In the current scenario (table), it seems better than the other two (`Orderdate` and `amount`), in terms of selectivity.

```
--creating clustered index on column refno without discussing
--whether refno is right field to be a part of clustered index or
not
CREATE CLUSTERED INDEX idx_refno ON ordDemo(refno)
GO


--execute the same select statement again.
SELECT OrderDate,Amount,Refno
  FROM ordDemo WHERE Refno<3
GO
```

```
    --execute the same select statement again.
    SELECT OrderDate,Amount,Refno FROM ordDemo WHERE Refno<3
    |
100 %  ▼ ◄
```

Results | Messages | Execution plan

Query 1: Query cost (relative to the batch): 100%
SELECT [OrderDate],[Amount],[Refno] FROM [ordDemo] WHERE [Refno]<@1

```
SELECT            Clustered Index Seek (Clustered)
Cost: 0 %             [ordDemo].[idx_refno]
                          Cost: 100 %
```

Clustered Index Seek (Clustered)	
Scanning a particular range of rows from a clustered index.	
Physical Operation	Clustered Index Seek
Logical Operation	Clustered Index Seek
Actual Execution Mode	Row
Estimated Execution Mode	Row
Storage	RowStore
Actual Number of Rows	14448
Actual Number of Batches	0
Estimated Operator Cost	0.0732489 (100%)
Estimated I/O Cost	0.0571991
Estimated CPU Cost	0.0160498
Estimated Subtree Cost	0.0732489
Number of Executions	1
Estimated Number of Executions	1
Estimated Number of Rows	14448
Estimated Row Size	27 B
Actual Rebinds	0
Actual Rewinds	0
Ordered	True
Node ID	0

Object
[sqlhub].[dbo].[ordDemo].[idx_refno]
Output List
[sqlhub].[dbo].[ordDemo].OrderDate, [sqlhub].[dbo].
[ordDemo].Amount,[sqlhub].[dbo].[ordDemo].Refno
Seek Predicates
Seek Keys[1]: End: [sqlhub].[dbo].[ordDemo].Refno < Scalar
Operator(CONVERT_IMPLICIT(int,[@1],0))

Let us see how these tasks will work.

How it works...

In step 1, we created one purchase order table named ordDemo, by inserting a hundred thousand records. In step 3, we executed the SELECT query by filtering records based on the Refno field, with the execution plan enabled. We can see the execution plan with details, in step 5, which was simply to scan the whole table just to return a few records from the 100,000 records we inserted. This is a CPU- and I/O-centric operation, because to return a few thousand records, each and every record given in the table is scanned.

In step 6, we created the clustered index on the Refno column, based on the criteria we discussed in the *Getting Ready* section of this recipe. After creating an index, we executed the same SELECT query we ran in step 3, with execution plan enabled; you will see a big difference between the two execution plans given in steps 5 and 6.

I/O cost is 0.379421, in the first execution plan, and 0.0571991, in the second execution plan, even though both queries return the same number of rows. You might wonder why there is a difference in the same query that is run on the same table and returns the same number of rows.

The answer is really very simple if we know how an index works. When there was no index on the table ordDemo, SQL Server went through each and every row to check whether its Refno value is less than 3 or not. If it is less than 3, it was included in the results set. This process is called a Table Scan. However, if there is an index, SQL Server knows what values are contained in each data page. It directly moves to the particular pages, picks up all the qualified records, and displays them in a results set. This process is called an Index Seek.

There's more...

The following is an explanation of some of the technical vocabulary used in this recipe:

Heap

Any database table that doesn't have a clustered index on it is called heap. Heap has Index ID=0 in sys.partitions catalog view. Unlike the clustered index, which stores data sorted logically, heap is used to store data without any sorting order. Data pages in heap are linked to each other without any logical ordering, and one needs to scan the whole heap to search for any data, unlike the clustered index, resulting in slow performance.

Here is the T-SQL command that will show you catalog view sys.partitions:

```
Select OBJECT_NAME(object_id) AS TableName,
  * from sys.partitions
  WHERE index_id=0
```

Here is a screenshot of the results that came from this T-SQL command:

```
Select
    OBJECT_NAME(object_id) AS TableName
,
from
    sys.partitions
WHERE
    index_id=0
```

100 % ▼ ◄

☐ Results | ◌ Messages |

	TableName	partition_id	object_id	index_id	partition_number	hobt_id	rows	filestream_filegroup_id	data_compression	data_compression_desc
1	sysfiles1	524288	8	0	1	524288	2	0	0	NONE
2	DatabaseLog	72057594038976512	245575913	0	1	72057594038976512	1597	0	0	NONE
3	ProductProductPhoto	72057594041860096	562101043	0	1	72057594041860096	504	0	0	NONE
4	EmployeeDemo	72057594059816960	1287675635	0	1	72057594059816960	290	0	0	NONE
5	WorkOrderDemo	72057594060144640	1303675692	0	1	72057594060144640	72591	0	0	NONE
6	ProductModelDemo	72057594072530944	1668200993	0	1	72057594072530944	128	0	0	NONE
7	ProductDemo	72057594072596480	1684201050	0	1	72057594072596480	504	0	0	NONE

Table and Index Scan/Seek

Table/Index Scan means searching the whole table or index in sequential order, to locate rows that meet the criteria given in a search condition. Index Seek first scans the index root and intermediate node to find which leaf pages would have the data that meets search criteria, and after that, directly goes to those leaf pages and gets the data.

In most cases, a seek is good as it doesn't travel through each and every data page, but sometimes if a big chunk of data from the table is needed, for instance 30% or more, it is good to scan rather than travelling to each root and intermediate node to find the matching criteria, and then go to leaf pages to get the data. In an opposite situation, if only 5% to 10% data or even less is needed, and a scan is happening, it is a good idea to have a seek operation to boost up performance.

Increasing performance by creating a non-clustered index

It is now clear that indexes improve performance for most of the SELECT statements, if it is created wisely on a proper key field. There is one limitation on clustered indexes—only one clustered index is allowed per table, and in many cases, it may not be possible to cover all the required columns in one clustered index. There is another object provided by SQL Server, known as **non-clustered index**, which could be used on one or more than one column.

If you cover one highly selective column in the clustered index, it is not certain that you are going to use that column only, in all the WHERE and JOIN statements, especially when a table has many columns. In this scenario, we have to create a non-clustered index on the selective fields that are not covered inside a clustered index, so that we can get a performance benefit while using those fields as a predicate in the SELECT query.

[🖋️ Till SQL Server 2005, 249 non-clustered indexes were allowed, but after SQL Server 2008, including SQL Server 2012, 999 non-clustered indexes are allowed per table.]

Unlike the clustered index, the non-clustered index stores the key column value along with the row locator (pointer) to the actual data either in a clustered index, or in a heap if a clustered index is not available.

Generally, making a unique key on any column could, by default, generates a non-clustered index on that column. One row per non-clustered index is available in the `sys.partitions` table with `Index_ID>1`. The following is the T-SQL command that allows you to run a query on the `sys.partitions` catalog view, to get information regarding non-clustered indexes that exist in the database:

```
Select OBJECT_NAME(object_id)
    AS TableName,* from sys.partitions
    WHERE index_id>1
```

The following screenshot shows the result set generated by this query:

```
Select
    OBJECT_NAME(object_id) AS TableName
    ,*
from
    sys.partitions
WHERE
    index_id>1
```

	TableName	partition_id	object_id	Index_Id	partition_number	hobt_id	rows	filestream_filegroup_id	data_compression	data_compression_desc
73	Culture	72057594049724416	901578250	2	1	72057594049724416	8	0	0	NONE
74	Currency	72057594049789952	933578364	2	1	72057594049789952	105	0	0	NONE
75	CurrencyRate	72057594049855488	965578478	2	1	72057594049855488	13...	0	0	NONE
76	Customer	72057594049921024	997578592	2	1	72057594049921024	19...	0	0	NONE
77	Customer	72057594049986560	997578592	3	1	72057594049986560	19...	0	0	NONE
78	Customer	72057594050052096	997578592	5	1	72057594050052096	19...	0	0	NONE
79	Department	72057594050117632	1045578763	2	1	72057594050117632	16	0	0	NONE
80	Document	72057594050183168	1077578877	3	1	72057594050183168	13	0	0	NONE
81	Document	72057594050248704	1077578877	5	1	72057594050248704	13	0	0	NONE
82	Document	72057594050314240	1077578877	6	1	72057594050314240	13	0	0	NONE
83	EmailAddress	72057594050379776	1189578276	2	1	72057594050379776	19...	0	0	NONE
84	Employee	72057594050445312	1237579447	2	1	72057594050445312	290	0	0	NONE
85	Employee	72057594050510848	1237579447	3	1	72057594050510848	290	0	0	NONE
86	Employee	72057594050576384	1237579447	5	1	72057594050576384	290	0	0	NONE
87	Employee	72057594050641920	1237579447	6	1	72057594050641920	290	0	0	NONE
88	Employee	72057594050707456	1237579447	7	1	72057594050707456	290	0	0	NONE
89	EmployeeDepartmentHistory	72057594050772992	1445580188	2	1	72057594050772992	296	0	0	NONE
90	EmployeeDepartmentHistory	72057594050838528	1445580188	3	1	72057594050838528	296	0	0	NONE
91	JobCandidate	72057594050904064	1589580701	2	1	72057594050904064	13	0	0	NONE
92	Location	72057594050969600	1621580815	2	1	72057594050969600	14	0	0	NONE
93	Person	72057594051035136	1765581328	2	1	72057594051035136	19...	0	0	NONE
94	Person	72057594051100672	1765581328	3	1	72057594051100672	19...	0	0	NONE
95	PersonPhone	72057594051166208	1909581841	2	1	72057594051166208	19...	0	0	NONE
96	Product	72057594051231744	1973582069	2	1	72057594051231744	504	0	0	NONE
97	Product	72057594051297280	1973582069	3	1	72057594051297280	504	0	0	NONE
98	Product	72057594051362816	1973582069	4	1	72057594051362816	504	0	0	NONE
99	ProductCategory	72057594051428352	66099276	2	1	72057594051428352	4	0	0	NONE
100	ProductCategory	72057594051493888	66099276	3	1	72057594051493888	4	0	0	NONE
101	ProductDescription	72057594051559424	178099675	2	1	72057594051559424	762	0	0	NONE
102	ProductModel	72057594051624960	418100530	2	1	72057594051624960	128	0	0	NONE
103	ProductModel	72057594051690496	418100530	3	1	72057594051690496	128	0	0	NONE

Getting ready

Even before you start working with a non-clustered index, it is mandatory to find:

- A table that actually needs a non-clustered index
- A good candidate column for the non-clustered index

Without a proper candidate for the non-clustered key field, you will end up with an unused index that takes space to save itself, even though it is not going to be used anytime, and creates I/O overhead for DML statements.

The following points will help you decide which column(s) should have non-clustered indexes, so that you will be ready to process further, after obtaining the list of columns from a table:

- The column should contain a large number of distinct values. Flagging columns that might have only 0 or 1 as values, would be futile as they are not good candidates for an index. A scan is a good option in this case, instead of a non-clustered index seek.
- The column(s) should generally be used with an exact match conditional operator such as the = sign
- The columns should generally be used in an ON clause of JOIN, GROUP BY, and ORDER BY

How to do it...

Well, after learning about non-clustered indexes and finding out which table and column(s) (also known as Key Column or Key Columns, in case of the composite index) require a non-clustered index, it is time to create a non-clustered index.

The following is the basic syntax for defining a non-clustered index—it is a good idea to know its syntax before you actually deal with it:

```
CREATE [UNIQUE] NONCLUSTERED INDEX <Idx_Index_Name>
ON <table_Name> (column_name   [ASC | DESC] [,…….N])
```

Now follows an exercise to practically build a non-clustered index on a table that we have earlier used with a clustered index, and also to observe the behavior of the index.

1. Run the following query:

```
--checking the execution plan without having non-clustered Index
on the same table ordDemo that we had created in previous section.
--You might need to change the date based on the data in your
table.
SELECT OrderDate FROM ordDemo
  WHERE OrderDate='2011-11-28 20:29:00.000'
GO
```

Observe the following screenshot of the overhead query that we ran without a non-clustered index; especially look at the estimated I/O cost, operator cost, CPU cost, and the number of rows returned in the result set:

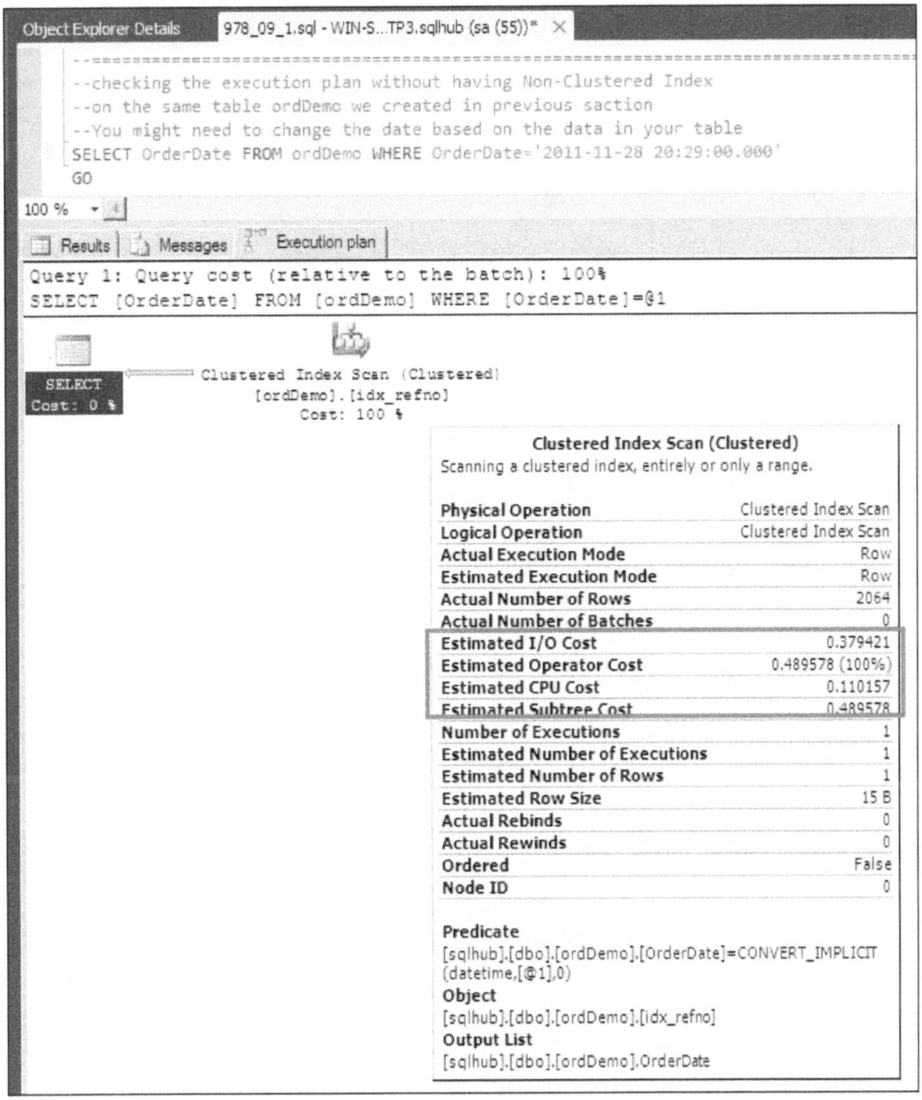

The overhead execution plan displays that the query has used a clustered index that is already available, but it has performed an index scan rather an than Index Seek.

2. Now, create a non-clustered index on the same table—`ordDemo`—and execute the `SELECT` statement used previously:

```
--creating Non-Clustered Index in Clustered Index example, one
column was used
CREATE NONCLUSTERED INDEX idx_orderdate
  on ordDemo(orderdate)
GO

--running the same query we ran earlier to see behavior after Non-
Clustered Index created
SELECT OrderDate FROM ordDemo
  WHERE OrderDate=
  '2011-11-28 20:29:00.000'
GO
```

The following is a screenshot of the execution plan of this `SELECT` query:

3. Now, it is time to compare both the execution plans, which will generate results in a screenshot. By comparing I/O Cost, CPU Cost, Operator Cost, and other parameters, a big difference will be seen in the cost figures, and that will prove that the second execution plan, which has been generated after creating a non-clustered index, is much better.

How it works...

In our case, all the data resides in a clustered index. So, any query you execute will get a clustered index scan, if it doesn't fall under the clustered or non-clustered index seek. The first query, which was run before the non-clustered index was created, had an OrderDate field in the WHERE clause, but there was no index for OrderDate, and hence SQL Server Query Optimizer decided to scan the complete clustered index.

After creating a non-clustered index on the OrderDate field, SQL Server Query Optimizer finds the row locator of the clustered index data page (leaf node) from the leaf node of the non-clustered index. This is because the non-clustered index's leaf node would have the OrderDate entry with a row locator to the clustered index's leaf node, where the actual data resides. So now, Optimizer doesn't need to scan all the leaf pages of the clustered index and only needs to perform the index seek operation on the non-clustered index, which reduces I/O, CPU, and other costs.

Here is the cost comparison before the non-clustered index's execution plan in (Step 1) and after the non-clustered index's execution plan in (step 2):

Operator	Cost before non-clustered index	Cost after non-clustered index
Estimated I/O Cost	0.379421	0.0073226
Estimated Operator Cost	0.489578 (100%)	0.00975 (100%)
Estimated CPU cost	0.110157	0.0024274
Estimated Subtree Cost	0.489578	0.00975

There's more...

While creating a non-clustered index, keep in mind that it will need additional space to store itself, along with the key column and row locator of the clustered index or heap. So, keep an eye on the hard drive for space, as a bigger table would need more space to accommodate the non-clustered index. We can define the non-clustered index on a separate database file or filegroup, which reduces the I/O hit on the same file.

Increasing performance by covering index

Before discussing covering index further, it should be understood that a covering index is not a separate type of index that has a different internal structure and algorithm. It is just a technique that is used to boost up the performance of data retrieval for the table.

You may wonder *If it is not a new type of index, why do we need to use it?*

Run the same SELECT query that we ran earlier in the *Increasing performance by creating non-clustered index* section, which was creating the non-clustered index seek operation. But now, run this query with some more fields in the SELECT clause, may be like this:

```
--running the same query we ran earlier to see behavior after
  --Non-Clustered Index was created with just one column extra
  --in the SELECT clause
SELECT OrderDate,OrderID FROM ordDemo
  WHERE OrderDate='2011-11-28 20:29:00.000'
GO
```

The ordDemo table already had a non-clustered index on the OrderDate field, so if you run this query, it should meet the non-clustered index seek, but it will actually go for the clustered index scan, in the execution plan. We can generate an execution plan and observe the same to confirm the difference.

SQL Server Query Optimizer is smart enough to choose the best plan for a query in most cases. However, what would happen if SQL Server were to have used the non-clustered index—idx_orderdate—we had created previously? Let us try by forcing Query Optimizer to use idx_orderdate forcefully with the WITH INDEX query hint.

```
--forcing the optimizer to use nonclustered index idx_orderdate
--rather than using Clustered Index scan
SELECT OrderDate,OrderID
  FROM ordDemo WITH (Index=idx_orderdate)
WHERE OrderDate='2011-11-28 20:29:00.000'
GO
```

Observe the given execution plan, which was generated by the SELECT query:

```
Object Explorer Details    978_09_1.sql - WIN-S...TP3.sqlhub (sa (55))*  ×
```

```
--forcing the optimizer to use nonclustered index idx_orderdate
--rather than using Clustered Index scan
SELECT OrderDate,OrderID FROM ordDemo WITH (Index=idx_orderdate)
WHERE OrderDate='2011-11-28 20:29:00.000'
GO
```

```
100 %   ▾ ◂
```

```
Results │ Messages │ Execution plan
```

```
Query 1: Query cost (relative to the batch): 100%
SELECT OrderDate,OrderID FROM ordDemo WITH (Index=idx_orderdate) WHERE OrderDate='2011-11
Missing Index (Impact 99.6032): CREATE NONCLUSTERED INDEX [<Name of Missing Index, sysnam
```

```
SELECT          Nested Loops         Index Seek (NonClustered)
Cost: 0 %       (Inner Join)         [ordDemo].[idx_orderdate]
                Cost: 0 %            Cost: 1 %

                                     Key Lookup (Clustered)
                                     [ordDemo].[idx_refno]
                                     Cost: 99 %
```

Key Lookup (Clustered)
Uses a supplied clustering key to lookup on a table that has a clustered index.

Physical Operation	Key Lookup
Logical Operation	Key Lookup
Actual Execution Mode	Row
Estimated Execution Mode	Row
Storage	RowStore
Actual Number of Rows	2064
Actual Number of Batches	0
Estimated I/O Cost	0.003125
Estimated Operator Cost	1.88943 (99%)
Estimated CPU Cost	0.0001581
Estimated Subtree Cost	1.88943
Number of Executions	2064
Estimated Number of Executions	2064
Estimated Number of Rows	1
Estimated Row Size	11 B
Actual Rebinds	0
Actual Rewinds	0
Ordered	True
Node ID	4

Object
[sqlhub].[dbo].[ordDemo].[idx_refno]
Output List
[sqlhub].[dbo].[ordDemo].OrderID
Seek Predicates
Seek Keys[1]: Prefix: [sqlhub].[dbo].[ordDemo].Refno,
Uniq1002 = Scalar Operator([sqlhub].[dbo].[ordDemo].
[Refno]), Scalar Operator([Uniq1002])

```
✓ Query executed successfully.
```

It has used a non-clustered index seek along with Key Lookup; key column's value (the orderDate column in our case) could come from the non-clustered index, but Optimizer has to go through one overhead of Key Lookup to get a non-key column's value (OrderID). To remove this Key Lookup overhead, covering the non-clustered index is required.

Getting ready

To perform a covering non-clustered index, it is necessary to find out which other columns need to be there in the non-clustered index. It is not rocket science to decide this; one has to go through with different options and check the execution plan for the best-suited match.

By looking at Key Lookup in an execution plan, we get to know that it is going to the clustered index, which is present on the RefNo column, to find out OrderID. So let us cover the OrderID field in the non-clustered index and see the difference.

How to do it...

Perform the following steps to see the usage of the covering index:

1. Drop the previously created non-clustered index:

   ```
   --Dropping the previously created non-clustered Index
   DROP INDEX idx_orderdate ON ordDemo
   GO
   ```

2. Create a non-clustered index by covering one more column, OrderID, within it:

   ```
   --recreating a non-clustered Index with OrderDate and OrderID
   --by sorting OrderDate in descending order in Index
   --and sorting OrderID in ascending order in Index
   CREATE NONCLUSTERED INDEX idx_orderdate_orderId
     on ordDemo(orderdate DESC,OrderId ASC)
   GO
   --running the same SELECT query we ran earlier to see
   --behavior after covering Non-Clustered Index created
   --with two fields
   SELECT OrderDate,OrderID FROM ordDemo
     WHERE OrderDate='2011-11-28 20:29:00.000'
   GO
   ```

Here is a screenshot of this SELECT query, which successfully removed the Key Lookup overhead, giving a better-looking execution plan:

How it works...

After observing the new execution plan for the SELECT query, it is now clear that the Key Lookup overhead is removed successfully by using a covering index. Actually, in this new situation, SQL Server Optimizer wouldn't need to go to a clustered index to get values of the non-key column, as the non-clustered index now covers both OrderID and OrderDate.

There's more...

While creating a non-clustered covering index, keep in mind that a maximum of 16 columns is allowed in one index, and the total size of index columns (key columns) should not exceed 900 bytes.

Increasing performance by including columns in an index

The concept of included columns in indexes was introduced in SQL Server 2005 and is also available in SQL Server 2008 and 2012. We can include non-key columns in a non-clustered index, as they are not counted in its index size.

There is a limitation wherein the maximum number of columns allowed is 16 and the maximum size of the index key column allowed is 900 bytes, so it is not a good idea to have an index with many unnecessary or non-key columns.

Only include the key column in the Index part, and to avoid the lookup of a non-key column, keep another non-key column in the INCLUDE part of a non-clustered Index. This is because any column given in the INCLUDE part of a non-clustered index doesn't fall under the limitations discussed previously.

Getting ready

In the *Increasing performance by a covering index* section, we had an OrderId column as a part of the main non-clustered index. However, OrderID is not the key column, as we have not used it in the search condition (WHERE). So, OrderId could be under the INCLUDE part of the non-clustered index instead of being a part of the main index. By doing so, we can reduce the size of the non-clustered index.

Apart from the limitations regarding the maximum number of columns (16) and maximum size of an index key column (900 bytes), there is one more limitation in creating a non-clustered index—SQL Server don't allow the use of certain data types as an index key. The following is a list of the data types that are not permitted to be a part of an index key column:

- `text`
- `ntext`
- `image`
- `nvarchar(max)`
- `varchar(max)`
- `varbinary(max)`

You can use any data type in the `INCLUDE` clause, except `text`, `ntext`, and `image`.

How to do it...

The following are the steps to create and include a column index:

1. Drop the previously created non-clustered index:

   ```
   --Dropping previously created non-clustered Index
   DROP INDEX idx_orderdate_orderId ON ordDemo
   GO
   ```

2. Create an index with the `INCLUDE` statement, which will have the `OrderID` column:

   ```
   --creating NONCLUSTERED index on OrderDate
   --have OrderID in Include section of Index
   CREATE NONCLUSTERED INDEX idx_orderdate_Included
     on ordDemo(orderdate DESC)
   INCLUDE(OrderID)
   GO
   ```

3. Run the same `SELECT` statement we ran earlier, by keeping the execution plan enabled:

   ```
   --running the same query we ran earlier to see behavior after
   --covering Non-Clustered Index created with two fields
   SELECT OrderDate,OrderID FROM ordDemo
     WHERE OrderDate='2011-11-28 20:29:00.000'
   GO
   ```

Observe the screenshot of this SELECT query:

```
Object Explorer Details    978_09_1.sql - WIN-S...TP3.sqlhub (sa (55))*  ×

⊟--running the same query we ran above to see behavior after
  --covering Non-Clustered Index created with two fields
  SELECT OrderDate,OrderID FROM ordDemo WHERE OrderDate='2011-11-28 20:29:00.000'
  GO

100 %  ▾ ◂
  Results |   Messages |   Execution plan
Query 1: Query cost (relative to the batch): 100%
SELECT [OrderDate],[OrderID] FROM [ordDemo] WHERE [OrderDate]=@1


   SELECT              Index Seek (NonClustered)
  Cost: 0 %         [ordDemo].[idx_orderdate_Included]
                            Cost: 100 %
```

Index Seek (NonClustered)	
Scan a particular range of rows from a nonclustered index.	
Physical Operation	Index Seek
Logical Operation	Index Seek
Actual Execution Mode	Row
Estimated Execution Mode	Row
Storage	RowStore
Actual Number of Rows	2064
Actual Number of Batches	0
Estimated Operator Cost	0.010545 (100%)
Estimated I/O Cost	0.0081176
Estimated CPU Cost	0.0024274
Estimated Subtree Cost	0.010545
Number of Executions	1
Estimated Number of Executions	1
Estimated Number of Rows	2064
Estimated Row Size	19 B
Actual Rebinds	0
Actual Rewinds	0
Ordered	True
Node ID	0

Object
[sqlhub].[dbo].[ordDemo].[idx_orderdate_Included]
Output List
[sqlhub].[dbo].[ordDemo].OrderID, [sqlhub].[dbo].
[ordDemo].OrderDate
Seek Predicates
Seek Keys[1]: Prefix: [sqlhub].[dbo].[ordDemo].OrderDate
= Scalar Operator(CONVERT_IMPLICIT(datetime,[@1],0))

How it works...

If you compare the execution plan we had for covering index and for the index with included column, you can see almost every cost is identical, but the INCLUDE column index will give you more freedom and get you out of the limitations. Apart from that, because of the INCLUDE column index, the index tree will be small in size as compared to covering index, which will result in fast searching.

Apart from the limitations discussed here, fewer columns in the index part would mean less space on disk and a lower maintenance cost for the index.

The following are the best practices you should follow:

 ► The columns that are going to be included in the WHERE, ORDER BY, GROUP BY, and ON clauses of JOIN, should be a part of index key columns and hence, it is supposed to be covered by a covering index.

 ► The columns that are going to be included in the SELECT or HAVING clauses, should be covered in the INCLUDE section of the include index. By doing this, we can reduce the size of the key columns and B-Tree (Index Tree) of an index, which gives you a faster search

Improving performance by a filtered index

The filtered column index is one of the enhancements of the non-clustered index provided in Microsoft SQL Server 2008, and it is still available in SQL Server 2012. We can consider a simple non-clustered index with the WHERE clause, as a filtered index. A well-defined filtered index reduces maintenance cost and index storage, and improves query performance.

Actually, a non-clustered index, whether it is a covering or include index, indexes all the rows available in a table, whereas a filtered index indexes only those rows that meet the criteria given in the WHERE clause of the CREATE INDEX command. This is the main reason that a filtered index needs low storage and displays improved performance.

Getting ready

It is time to be ready with some information that will be helpful in creating a filtered index. Let us now look into some cases where implementation of a filtered index could be beneficial:

 ► A big table with data of many years, but generally used to query data of only the current year or may be current year along with last year. We can consider filtered index based on date, in this case.

 ► A products table that has a complete list of: categories available in an inventory at the moment and all the past categories that may be deprecated or not in stock at the moment but that are still present in the database table.

- ▸ Suppose `Order StartDate` and `Order EndDate` are in an Orders table. If an order is completed, `OrderEndDate` is updated, otherwise it is `NULL` by default. Filtered index could be useful in this situation, too. If, most of the time, there is a need to query the table to find which orders are incomplete at the moment, have filtered index on the `OrderEndDate` column for `NULL` checking.

As an instance, we have only seen few situations to get an idea about when a filtered index is useful.

Some `SET` options should be set while creating a filtered index or while modifying data by `DML` commands. Here is a list of the same:

- ▸ `ARITHABORT`
- ▸ `CONCAT_NULL_YIELDS_NULL`
- ▸ `QUOTED_IDENTIFIER`
- ▸ `ANSI_WARNINGS`
- ▸ `ANSI_NULLS`
- ▸ `ANSI_PADDING`
- ▸ `NUMERIC_ROUNDABORT` – should be set to `OFF` and the rest of the specified options should be set to `ON`

How to do it...

To see the magic of filtered index, follow the steps given here:

1. Create one non-clustered index with an `INCLUDED` column (same as previous section), with an addition of the `WHERE` clause, which will make this index a filtered index:

```
--set environment variables.
SET ANSI_NULLS ON
SET ANSI_PADDING ON
SET ANSI_WARNINGS ON
SET ARITHABORT ON
SET CONCAT_NULL_YIELDS_NULL ON
SET QUOTED_IDENTIFIER ON
SET NUMERIC_ROUNDABORT OFF
GO

--create NONCLUSTERED index on OrderDate
--have OrderID in Include section of Index
--make a filter of date.
--you have to use the dates you have in your table, so if
necessary, change the date
CREATE NONCLUSTERED INDEX idx_orderdate_Filtered
   on ordDemo(orderdate DESC)
```

```
INCLUDE(OrderId)
WHERE OrderDate = '2011-11-28 20:29:00.000'
GO
```

2. After creating the filtered index, run the same `SELECT` query we ran earlier in the previous section:

```
--run the same query we ran earlier to see behavior after
--covering Non-Clustered Index created with two fields
--along with filter in WHERE clause on OrderDate Field
SELECT OrderDate,OrderID FROM ordDemo WHERE OrderDate='2011-11-28
20:29:00.000'
GO
```

Study the execution plan generated by this `SELECT` query, after creating a filtered index.

How it works...

After studying the execution plan that we created for the SELECT statement after creating the included index, and the recent execution plan, it is very clear that the current execution plan is much better.

The I/O cost in the recent execution plan is 0.003125 and it returns 1982 rows, whereas the I/O cost in the execution plan, which we created after the included index, is 0.0078751 and it returns the same amount of rows, that is, 1982. Isn't this a BIG difference?

All indexes are being created on a table, and the non-clustered index keeps all the rows within it (key column + pointer), whereas with the filtered index, the non-clustered index is used to keep only those rows that met the criteria. As a result, there are fewer leaf pages in the index, and the index will consume less disk space. Also, SQL Server doesn't need to go through all the pages during a search clause.

There's more...

A filtered index consumes less disk space, because it doesn't have information for all the rows. It has information for only those rows that satisfy the filter criteria of an index.

Filtered indexes have lower maintenance costs, because they will be maintained only when the data, which has qualified for a filtered index, gets changed.

Filtered indexes boost up performance because a filtered index is smaller in size compared to a full-table, non-clustered index. So, it will generate a good execution plan by using filtered statistics that are more accurate.

Improving performance by a columnstore index

All the indexes discussed here, so far, were **rowstore indexes**, which is a type available in SQL Server for long time. But, there is a new index called columnstore index, which was introduced in SQL Server 2012. So, now there are two types of indexes available in SQL Server 2012:

- ▶ Rowstore index
- ▶ Columnstore index

The rowstore index stores data row(s) in data pages, whereas the columnstore index stores each column in a different data page(s).

For example, if we had one table, tblEmployee, with columns empId, FirstName, and LastName, and an index on all three fields, the logical image of rowstore as well as columnstore, for illustration purposes, would be something like this:

Rowstore Index

data page example

Row 1	empId, FN, LN
Row 2	empId, FN, LN
Row 3	empId, FN, LN
Row 4	empId, FN, LN
Row 5	empId, FN, LN
Row 6	empId, FN, LN
Row 7	empId, FN, LN
Row 8	empId, FN, LN

Columnstore Index

data page example

empId	FN	LN
value of empID	value of FN	value of LN
value of empID	value of FN	value of LN
value of empID	value of FN	value of LN
value of empID	value of FN	value of LN
value of empID	value of FN	value of LN

FN = FirstName
LN = LastName

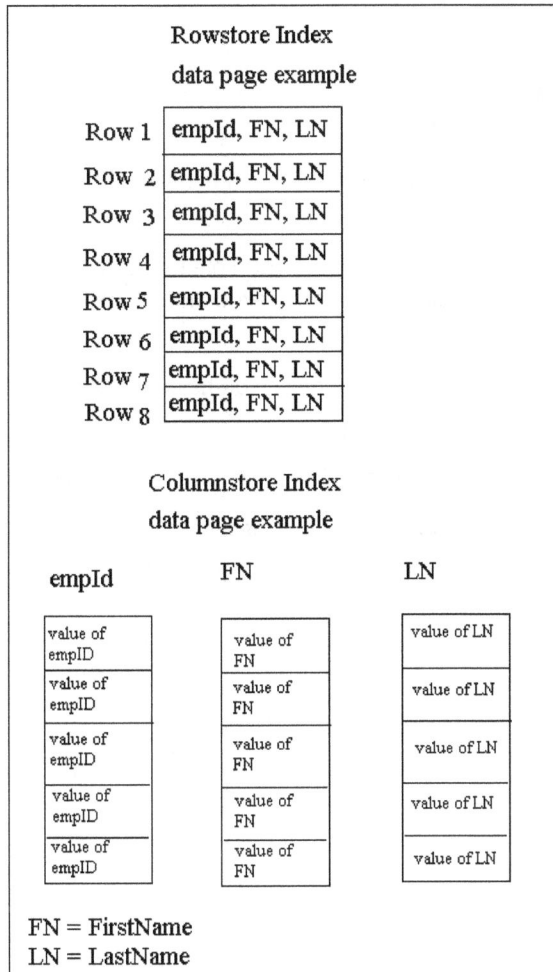

A data page is nothing but an 8-KB page that stores data. If you have 10 rows and the total size of those 10 rows is 16 KB, then each row should consume 2 data pages, in case of a rowstore index.

The columnstore index doesn't contain a whole row, but the data of one column only,. For example, the `empID` column has 100 values, and the size of those 100 values is 30 KB, therefore it would be contained in 4 columnstore data pages. The same thing will happen for the other two columns as well.

A columnstore index won't search all the data pages of all the columns, but it will search for only the required column, and this is one of the reasons that it gives output with good performance—due to less I/O. While storing data in a columnstore index, SQL Server compresses it heavily, so it occupies less size on disk, performs fast searches, and there's proper utilization of server resources.

Getting ready

Before you start working with the columnstore index, find out its requirements, by checking the following primary considerations:

▶ Whether it is feasible to make your table read-only by creating a columnstore index

▶ Is the table really very big with millions of rows?

▶ If your database is OLTP, find out if are you able to disable columnstore index while executing DML and enable it again after execution of DML to get the benefit of the SELECT statement

You may proceed to create a columnstore index if you have answered all the three questions with YES.

Keep the following points in mind while weighing the decision to use the columnstore index:

▶ You can't include more than 1024 columns

▶ Columns with the following data types can be a part of a columnstore index:

- ❑ int
- ❑ big int
- ❑ small int
- ❑ tiny int
- ❑ money
- ❑ smallmoney
- ❑ bit
- ❑ float
- ❑ real
- ❑ char(n)
- ❑ varchar(n)
- ❑ nchar(n)
- ❑ nvarchar(n)
- ❑ date
- ❑ datetime
- ❑ datetime2
- ❑ small datetime
- ❑ time
- ❑ datetimeoffset, with precision <=2
- ❑ decimal or numeric, with precision <=18

▶ Columns with the following data types should not be a part of a columnstore index:

- ❑ decimal or numeric with precision>18
- ❑ datetimeoffset with precision>2
- ❑ binary
- ❑ varbinary
- ❑ image
- ❑ text
- ❑ ntext
- ❑ varchar(max)
- ❑ nvarchar(max)
- ❑ cursor
- ❑ hierarchyid
- ❑ timestamp
- ❑ uniqueidentifier
- ❑ sqlvariant
- ❑ xml

How to do it...

Follow the steps given here to perform this recipe:

1. Execute the following query, which will seek the clustered index we had created earlier in this chapter:

```
--executing query before creating columnstore Index
--and observ execution plan
SELECT
        Refno
        ,sum(Amount) as SumAmt
        ,avg(Amount) as AvgAmt
FROM
        ordDemo
WHERE
        Refno>3
Group By
        Refno
Order By
        Refno
GO
```

Now, let us see the execution plan of this `SELECT` statement:

```
□--Columnstore Index Section
----------------------------------------------------------------------------------
--executing query before creating columnstore Index
--and observ execution plan
□SELECT
    Refno
    ,sum(Amount) as SumAmt
    ,avg(Amount) as AvgAmt
FROM
    ordDemo
WHERE
    Refno>3
Group By
    Refno
Order By
    Refno
```

Clustered Index Seek (Clustered)	
Scanning a particular range of rows from a clustered index.	
Physical Operation	Clustered Index Seek
Logical Operation	Clustered Index Seek
Actual Execution Mode	Row
Estimated Execution Mode	Row
Storage	RowStore
Actual Number of Rows	85552
Actual Number of Batches	0
Estimated Operator Cost	0.452945 (90%)
Estimated I/O Cost	0.358681
Estimated CPU Cost	0.0942642
Estimated Subtree Cost	0.452945
Number of Executions	1
Estimated Number of Executions	1
Estimated Number of Rows	85552
Estimated Row Size	19 B
Actual Rebinds	0
Actual Rewinds	0
Ordered	True
Node ID	2

Object
[sqlhub].[dbo].[ordDemo].[idx_refno]
Output List
[sqlhub].[dbo].[ordDemo].Amount, [sqlhub].[dbo].
[ordDemo].Refno
Seek Predicates
Seek Keys[1]: Start: [sqlhub].[dbo].[ordDemo].Refno > Scalar
Operator((3))

```
100 % ▾ ◄
□ Results | □ Messages | ⏚ Execution plan |
Query 1: Query cost (relative to the batch): 100%
SELECT Refno , sum(Amount) as SumAmt ,avg(Amount) as AvgAmt FROM ordDer

[SELECT]         [Compute Scalar]   [Stream Aggregate]  ⟸  [Clustered Index Seek]
Cost: 0 %        Cost: 0 %          (Aggregate)            [ordDemo].[idx_r
                                    Cost: 10 %             Cost: 90 %

⊘ Query executed successfully.
📇 Call Hierarchy
(s) Saved
```

2. After seeing the effect of the index in a previous query, it is time to create a columnstore index to see the magic. Remove the `idx_refno` clustered index, so that rowstore doesn't affect the columnstore index. By doing this, we are also ensuring that the columnstore index is not getting any performance help from the rowstore index.

```
--dropping clustered index idx_refno
DROP INDEX idx_refno ON ordDemo

--creating columnstore index
CREATE NONCLUSTERED COLUMNSTORE INDEX
    idx_columnstore_refno
ON ordDemo (Amount,refno)
```

3. As we now have a columnstore index, run the same query we ran earlier with the aggregate `SUM` and `AVG` functions, to see the effect of a columnstore index:

```
--executing same query after creating columnstore Index
--and observ execution plan
SELECT
```

```
      Refno
      ,sum(Amount) as SumAmt
      ,avg(Amount) as AvgAmt
FROM
      ordDemo
WHERE
      Refno>3
Group By
      Refno
Order By
      Refno
GO
```

4. As soon as the execution plan is generated, we can see the magical difference in operator cost, as shown in the following screenshot:

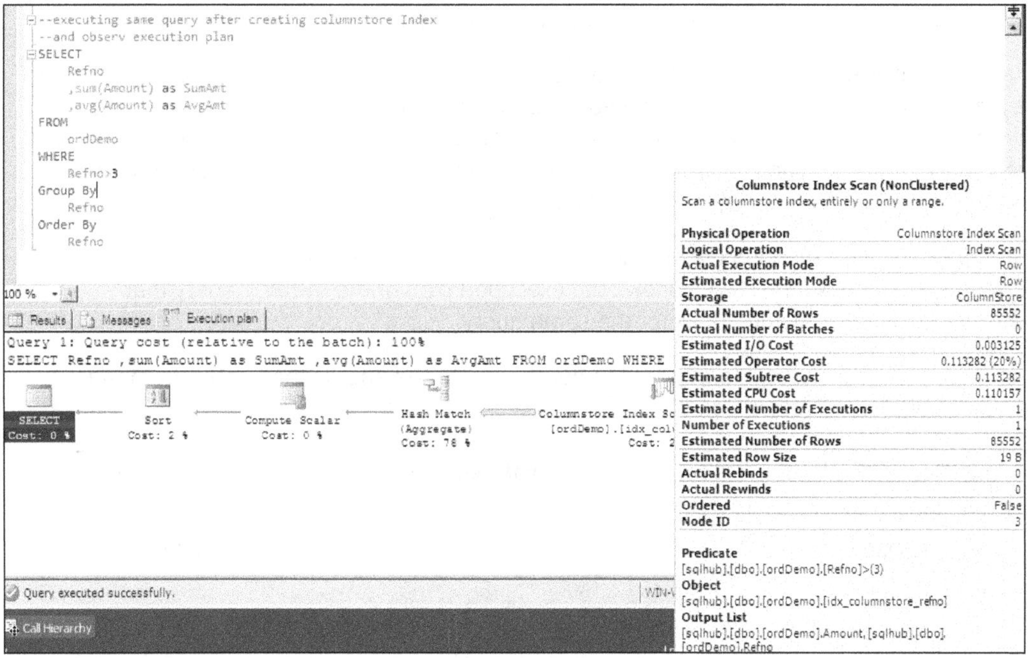

5. After comparing the result sets of both queries, it is clear that both queries return the same number of rows. But, if you see the I/O cost before the columnstore index, it is `0.358681`, and after the columnstore index, it is only `0.003125`. See how big difference is?

6. Create a clustered index again, for future use, and remove the columnstore index, so that the table will no longer be a read-only table:

```
--removing columnstore index
DROP INDEX idx_columnstore_refno ON ordDemo
GO
--creating clustered index again for
--future use
CREATE CLUSTERED INDEX idx_refno ON ordDemo(refno)
GO
```

How it works...

The columnstore index uses Microsoft's VertiPaq technology, which is why columnstore indexes don't have to fit in the main memory. However, they can effectively use as much memory as is available on the server. Portions of columns are moved in and out of memory on demand.

As per the image given in the introduction to this recipe, this technology stores column(s) in a single page, which results in faster searches than the rowstore index. Keep in mind that once you add a columnstore to a table, you cannot delete, insert, or update the data, as it is read-only. However, since the columnstore will be mainly (but not necessarily) used for data warehousing, this should not be a big problem.

Step 2 shows the execution plan of the SELECT query that was using the rowstore non-clustered index, and step 5 shows the execution plan of the SELECT query that was using the columnstore index for the same query.

Here are the differences in performance between both the approaches, taken from the screenshot given in steps 1 and 3:

Operator	Cost before non-custered index	Cost after non-clustered index
Estimated I/O Cost	0.358681	0.003125
Estimated Operator Cost	0.452945 (90%)	0.113282 (20%)
Estimated CPU cost	0.942642	0.110157
Estimated Subtree Cost	0.452945	0.113282

There's more...

Keep in mind that, by creating a columnstore index, you are going to keep your table read-only, and if partitioning is enabled on the table, data can still be loaded using the partition switch mechanism. It will not allow any DML statements such as INSERT, UPDATE, DELETE, and others. Apart from these limitations, the tables and columns cannot participate in a replication topology, and columns with large datatypes cannot participate in a columnstore index as well as in computed columns.

> To use DML statements, we have to disable columnstore indexes first, because the columnstore index is mainly designed for data warehousing purposes, where DML statements are not required.

10
Maintaining Indexes

In this chapter we will cover:

- ▶ Finding fragmentation
- ▶ Playing with Fill Factor
- ▶ Enhancing index efficiency by using the REBUILD index
- ▶ Enhancing index efficiency by using the REORGANIZE index
- ▶ How to find missing indexes
- ▶ How to find unused indexes
- ▶ Enhancing performance by creating indexed views
- ▶ Enhancing performance by creating an index on Computed Columns
- ▶ Determining disk space consumed by indexes

Introduction

The duty of a DBA is not finished by just creating an index on necessary fields. Actually, the DBA's duty of keeping database performance high *starts* at the point of creating a the necessary index.

From time to time, the DBA needs to keep an eye on some very important points, mentioned as follows, with regards to the index, because index maintenance is on-going task and needs the attention of the DBA.

- ▶ Fragmentation level of index
- ▶ Missing index
- ▶ Unused index

Finding fragmentation

Fragmentation is one of the common bottlenecks in performance, if indexes are not being maintained properly. Microsoft recommends going for a REORGANIZE index instead of the resource-consuming REBUILD index, if fragmentation percentage is between 5 and 30. If the fragmentation level is more than 30 percent, then go for the REBUILD index. It is recommended to treat these values as an approximation instead of considering them absolute. From the time of Microsoft SQL Server 2000, this recommended figure has not changed; at the same time, there are many things that have changed from Microsoft SQL Server 2000 to Microsoft SQL Server 2012.

"It depends!" is the favorite quote of all IT personnel, and it really depends on our environment. So, first check the server environment to decide what percentage level is good enough for us to go for REBUILD, because many other factors need to be considered while deciding to go for this resource-centric task. The following are a few of the tasks that need to be considered before making a decision. There are many other things to consider as well, but these are the major points:

- ▸ Backup schedules
- ▸ Workload on server
- ▸ Available disk space
- ▸ Recovery model

Though fragmentation makes a great impact on query performance, it also depends on the table, and how you use the table. In most cases, if you are returning only one record from the table by querying the Primary Key that has a clustered index, fragmentation doesn't play a role.

Getting ready

After learning what fragmentation is, it is obvious that our curiosity drives us to find an answer to the question *How can we determine the fragmentation of the Index?*.

Well, it is very simple: by using the query system function sys.dm_db_index_physical_stats and system catalog sys.Indexes.

How to do it...

Gathering information about fragmentation for your indexes is the first important task to perform, which could be done by using the following T-SQL query:

```
--for gathering information of all indexes/heap on specified table
SELECT
    sysin.name as IndexName
    ,sysIn.index_id
```

```
    ,func.avg_fragmentation_in_percent
    ,func.index_type_desc as IndexType
    ,func.page_count
FROM
    sys.dm_db_index_physical_stats (DB_ID(), OBJECT_ID(N'ordDemo'),
NULL, NULL, NULL) AS func
JOIN
    sys.indexes AS sysIn
ON
    func.object_id = sysIn.object_id AND func.index_id = sysIn.index_
id
--Clustered Index's Index_id MUST be 1
--nonclustered Index should have Index_id>1
--with following WHERE clause, we are eliminating HEAP tables
--uncomment following line if you don't want to see
--fragmentation of HEAP
--WHERE sysIn.index_id>0;

--for gathering information of all indexes available in
--database This query may take long time to execute
SELECT
    sysin.name as IndexName
    ,sysIn.index_id
    ,func.avg_fragmentation_in_percent
    ,func.index_type_desc as IndexType
    ,func.page_count
FROM
    sys.dm_db_index_physical_stats (DB_ID(), NULL, NULL, NULL, NULL)
AS func
JOIN
    sys.indexes AS sysIn
ON
    func.object_id = sysIn.object_id AND func.index_id = sysIn.index_
id
WHERE sysIn.index_id>0;
```

How it works...

Pass your database ID with the DB_ID() function in sys.dm_db_index_physical_stats,
along with the object ID (in our case, OBJECT_ID(N'ordDemo')) of the table name for which
fragmentation information is required. This system function provides very detailed information
regarding index. It will not have index name, but it displays index ID. For getting the exact
name of the index, one has to make a join with the sys.Indexes system catalog.

There's more...

Fragmentation comes into the picture when the logical sorting order of data in the leaf pages of an index doesn't match with the physical order of data in the actual data pages. When you create an index, it sorts everything, but when data gets manipulated by DML commands, there is no guarantee about which data pages will be used to accommodate the new records. When you delete records, they get deleted from the actual data page, and the free space in that data page might be used for any other records, which creates fragmentation.

Just keep in mind that when an index is first built up, there is no or very less fragmentation, but after having INSERT, UPDATE, and DELETE DMLs on the table, it starts creating fragmentation.

Playing with Fill Factor

It is already discussed in the previous chapter, *Chapter 9, Implementing Index*, that when an index is being created, it stores data in the B-Tree format that has a root page, intermediate level, and leaf level. Leaf level, which is the bottom-most level, contains the actual data in a clustered index. Each data page is 8 KB in size.

When insertion/updation/deletion of data to/from a table happens, it tries to insert in the proper data page according to the record being inserted. For example, we have clustered index on SSN number. We are inserting a new row with the SSN number. SQL Server tries to insert that record in an appropriate data page. Suppose our SSN number starts with "2", then it will find the last page that has SSN number starting with "2". SQL Server will insert our new row in that page only. If your 8 KB page is full or doesn't have enough room to accommodate the new row whose SSN starts with "2", it will split the page, and the data in that page will be shared between two or more pages of records, based on the size of the row whose SSN number starts with "2". Now we have two pages that are half filled, considering that the row is not too big; otherwise, we might have more than two pages as well. So our new row will be accommodated in that page. SQL Server tends to add new pages on the right-hand side of the current page in hierarchy of data pages.

If there is enough space in the data page that can accommodate the new row of SSN number starting with "2", the process doesn't need to wait till the page is getting split and then finish the I/O overhead. There is one more overhead; the page split task locks the page and prevents its usage until the process is finished.

This is the time when Fill Factor comes into the picture. Fill Factor decides how much of your page would be filled up initially. Suppose you give "10" as the Fill Factor, then your data page will consume only 10 percent of your 8 KB page size, and when you exceed this limit of 10 percent, it will keep 90 percent of the page empty and create a new page for other records.

Now, when you insert new records, you don't need to worry about I/O overhead of page split as you would have 90 percent free space and your record will be accommodated in that space easily. So, if we have a low Fill Factor, we can decrease the I/O overhead generated by a page split, which helps to write your data faster.

In short, I can say that Fill Factor is a double-edged sword—use it wisely or performance will be affected. Increasing the performance of write operations creates more pages, which decreases the performance of read operations.

> Fill Factor comes into the picture only while creating an index or rebuilding it; in regular DML operations, page will be filled up to 100 percent.

Getting ready

Before learning how to set the Fill Factor for an index, it is necessary to find the current Fill Factor value so that a decision can be made regarding the current Fill Factor and what the new value should be, based on the server environment. There are two places to look for the value of Fill Factor, given as follows:

- `sys.indexes`: This catalog view is used to know the Fill Factor value of a particular index, as given in the following query:

```
--find fill factor value in index
SELECT
    OBJECT_NAME(OBJECT_ID) AS TableName
    ,Name as IndexName
    ,Type_Desc
    ,Fill_Factor
FROM
    sys.indexes
WHERE
    --ommiting HEAP table by following condition therefore
    --it only displays clustered and nonclustered index details
    type_desc<>'HEAP'
```

- `sys.configurations`: This catalog view is used to find the default Fill Factor value of the server, as given in the following query:

```
--find default value of fill factor in database
SELECT
    Description
    ,Value_in_use
FROM
    sys.configurations
WHERE
    Name ='fill factor (%)'
```

The default Fill Factor value is 0 (zero), which means that it will not keep any free space on the page.

How to do it...

Once it is decided which table or index needs to set the Fill Factor, change it with the following T-SQL query:

```
--altering Index for FillFactor 80%
ALTER INDEX [idx_refno] ON [ordDemo]
REBUILD WITH (FILLFACTOR= 80)
GO
-- If there is a need to change the default value of Fill
-- Factor at server level, use the following T-SQL

--setting default value server-wide for Fill Factor

--turning on advanced configuration option
Sp_configure 'show advanced options', 1
GO
RECONFIGURE
GO

--setting up default value for fill factor
sp_configure 'fill factor', 90
GO
RECONFIGURE
GO
```

How it works...

As already defined in the discussion in the introduction of this recipe, Fill Factor is nothing but the value in percentage that is used while initial filling up of data pages. If the Fill Factor value is 90, the data page will be filled up to 90 percent initially, keeping 10 percent of data page blank for future use, so that while executing DML commands, it finds room for new records and can avoid page splits at the time of DML execution preventing I/O overheads.

> It is good that we can avoid page split by using Fill Factor, but again, use it wisely, because if we keep more space blank in data pages, it will increase the number of data pages, and while executing the SELECT statement, more data pages will need to be scanned.

There's more...

It is good to have a high Fill Factor value (greater than 90 percent and up to 100 percent) for static tables, for those tables that update once in a while, or for incrementally populated tables without UPDATE. If the table has a high frequency of updates, it is better to keep the Fill Factor value lower, maybe 70 percent to 80 percent.

If the table has a clustered index on the IDENTITY column, set Fill Factor at 100 percent without any issue, because each new record will be inserted after the last record available in the table. There is no chance to insert records in between, in the table, in most cases.

Enhance index efficiency by using the REBUILD index

Rebuilding an index will do nothing, but just drop the current index and recreate it internally, so that all fragmentations go away, statistics are updated, and physical sorting order in data pages are in co-ordination with each other. It compacts data pages, fills them up with a proper Fill Factor, and adds new data pages if needed. All these things will help in faster data retrieval, but at the same time this is a really very resource-centric job and takes a very long time to finish on large tables with millions of rows.

Getting ready

Decide first whether it is really necessary to rebuild an Index. If it is worth rebuilding an index, only then should one go for this option. Otherwise, use the REORGANIZE index, because the REBUILD index can use lots of server resources. If fragmentation is greater than 30 percent, it is good to use the REBUILD index.

Rebuilding an index can be done in two different modes and it is better to decide what mode to go for, before we actually start rebuilding indexes. The two modes are discussed as follows:

- ▶ **Offline**: Offline is the default mode for rebuilding indexes. It locks the table and, until rebuilding gets done, no one can access the table. If the table is big, it might take a few hours or more and the user won't be able to use that table. Offline mode works faster than Online mode and uses less time and space in the TempDB database, as compared to the Online mode.

- ▶ **Online**: If locking of tables is not possible in your environment and you must have the tables online, then there is the option of Online mode that will make index and table available even while creating or rebuilding the index. But it takes more time to finish and takes more server resources. It is worth noting that if the table has data types such as varchar (max), nvarchar (max), and text, it won't work if the Online mode is specified.

> Please note that the Online (ONLINE=ON) and Offline (ONLINE=OFF) options are available in development and enterprise editions only. All other editions will use OFFLINE, by default.

How to do it...

The following are ways to rebuild an index. In the previous chapter, *Chapter 9, Implementing Index*, we had one clustered index, idx_refno, and we are going to use that index for rebuild.

- To rebuild an index in Online mode, use the following query:

```
--rebulding index idx_refno with ONLINE=ON (online mode)
ALTER INDEX [idx_refno] ON [ordDemo]
REBUILD WITH (FILLFACTOR=80, ONLINE=ON)
GO
```

- To rebuild an index in Offline mode, use the following query:

```
--rebuilding index idx_refno with ONLINE=OFF (offline mode)
ALTER INDEX [idx_refno] ON [ordDemo]
REBUILD WITH (FILLFACTOR=80, ONLINE=OFF)
GO
```

- To rebuild all indexes of a table, use the following query:

```
--rebuilding all index on table ordDemo
ALTER INDEX ALL ON [ordDemo]
REBUILD WITH (FILLFACTOR=80, ONLINE=OFF)
GO
```

- To rebuild an index with DROP_EXISTING on, use the following query:

```
--rebuilding idx_reno index with DROP_EXISTING=ON
CREATE CLUSTERED INDEX [idx_refno] ON [ordDemo](refno)
WITH
(
    DROP_EXISTING = ON,
    FILLFACTOR = 70,
    ONLINE = ON
)
GO
```

- To rebuild all indexes of a table with DBCC DBREINDEX, use the following query:

```
--rebuilding all index of ordDemo table
DBCC DBREINDEX ('ordDemo')
GO
```

▶ To rebuild one index of a table with Fill Factor, use the following query:

```
--rebuilding idx_refno index of ordDemo table
--with Fill Factor 90
DBCC DBREINDEX ('ordDemo','idx_refno',90)
GO
```

> The DBCC DBREINDEX command will be deprecated from the future version of SQL Server, so it is best practice to avoid that command and use the alternate commands given in the previous list.

How it works...

Rebuilding an index is nothing more than dropping the existing index and creating a new one. While creating a new index, rebuilding locks your object (if the rebuild mode is not Online) and it will not be available for access until the process is finished. Rebuilding removes blank or unused pages, creates new ones, splits pages if they do not meet Fill Factor criteria, and sorts data pages to match up the logical sorting order in the index B-Tree.

There's more...

Based on personal experience, I recommend rebuilding an index of "large" tables with bulk-logged recovery mode or simple recovery mode rather than full recovery mode, to avoid excessive log file size. As soon as we finish with rebuilding an index in a large table, we can move to the simple recovery mode.

> A word of caution here: If you change your recovery mode from full to anything else, you will break your database backup chain, if there is any. So you will have to take a full backup again, after changing recovery mode back to full, which may not be possible in every production environment.

Because it is mentioned that a large table's index might take few hours or may be even a day, don't loose your patience and don't stop rebuilding the index in between. It could be dangerous and the database may fall into recovery mode.

The user should be the owner of the table or a member of the `sysadmin` fixed server role, the `db_owner` fixed database role, or the `db_ddladmin` fixed database role, in order to perform REBUILD or DBCC DBREINDEX.

Enhance index efficiency by using the REORGANIZE index

If the fragmentation level is less than 30 percent, one must use REORGANIZE on the index, instead of REBUILD. The REORGANIZE index doesn't produce locks on data pages or tables, leaving the object available for users to use, and takes less server resources and CPU utilization, as compared with REBUILD index.

In short, REORGANIZE is the process of cleaning up current B-Tree (especially leaf level of index), organizing data pages, and defragmenting it. Unlike REBUILD, REORGANIZE won't add any new pages; if this is needed, it just cleans up current pages and defragments them.

Getting ready

To decide whether to use a REORGANIZE index or not, have a look at the fragmentation level of the index first; if it is more than 10 percent and less than 30 percent, you require reorganization of your index. If it is less than 10 percent, you don't need to maintain that index.

How to do it...

Like rebuilding an index, there are several ways to reorganize your indexes. Have a look at the following queries:

- To reorganize an index of a table without specifying the Online or Fill Factor option, use the following query:

```
--reorganizing an index "idx_refno" on "ordDemo" table
--you can't specify ONLINE and FILLFACTOR option
ALTER INDEX [idx_refno] ON [ordDemo]
REORGANIZE
GO
```

- To reorganize all indexes of a table, use the following query:

```
--reorganizing all index on table ordDemo
ALTER INDEX ALL ON [ordDemo]
REORGANIZE
GO
```

- To reorganize all indexes of a table using DBCC INDEXDEFRAG, use the following query:

```
--reorganizing all index of ordDemo table
--in AdventureWorks2012 database
--give your database and table name in INDEXDEFRAG function
DBCC INDEXDEFRAG ('AdventureWorks2012','ordDemo')
GO
```

▶ To reorganize one index of a table using `DBCC INDEXDEFRAG`, use the following query:

```
--reorganizing idx_refno index of ordDemo table
--in AdventureWorks2012 database
DBCC INDEXDEFRAG ('AdventureWorks2012','ordDemo','idx_refno')
GO
```

> The `DBCC INDEXDEFRAG` command will be deprecated from the future version of SQL Server, so it is best practice to avoid that command and use the alternate commands given in the previous list.

How it works...

Index reorganization, also known as defragmentation, occurs serially. This means that the operation on a single index is performed using a single thread. No parallelism occurs. Also, operations on multiple indexes from the same `REORGANIZE` or `DBCC INDEXDEFRAG` statement are performed on one index at a time.

Reorganizing is simply rearranging data pages to match the physical sorting order of data pages with the logical sorting order in index leaf node. Unlike `REBUILD` index, `REORGANIZE` will not add new pages to match the Fill Factor defined, but it compacts the pages. If any page gets empty during the compacting process, it gets removed, so the Fill Factor option is not supported. `REORGANIZE` will not lock objects for a long time and hence the Online option is also not supported, as it is always in Online mode, by default.

There's more...

The user should be the owner of the table or a member of the `sysadmin` fixed server role, the `db_owner` fixed database role, or the `db_ddladmin` fixed database role, in order to perform `REORGANIZE` or `DBCC INDEXDEFRAG`.

How to find missing indexes

By now, we hope that you have understood the requirement of the index in performance. While developing a database table, initially it is not always possible for us to predict the right column as an index. So, as per our prediction, we used to generate an index that might be helpful; sometimes it would not even be used, and sometimes, we would need other indexes as well, apart from the initial index we had created. So, now the question arises as to how to find the indexes that are not even generated. How can we predict which indexes are missing and which we need to create?

Generally, whenever any query gets executed, SQL Server query optimizer finds the best index for the execution, and if it doesn't find it, the optimizer generates a suboptimal plan for your query, returns the result set, and stores that information about missing index in the DMVs.

As soon as SQL Server services restart or the whole server restarts, all information stored for this missing index would be lost. So it is a good idea to let the server keep running for one business cycle that may be a week, month, or any other time period. Then, you would have a proper list of all missing indexes.

Getting ready

For more details on index-related dynamic management views and functions, refer to the recipe *Monitoring index performance* in *Chapter 7, Dynamic Management Views and Dynamic Management Functions*. Along with the book, you can learn more from the Microsoft links given in the following list to get a detailed idea about the DMVs and DMFs we are going to use in this recipe:

- **sys.dm_db_missing_index_details**: This DMV returns details about the missing index you need to create. For more information, please visit:

  ```
  http://msdn.microsoft.com/en-us/library/ms345434%28SQL.110%29.
  aspx
  ```

- **sys.dm_db_missing_index_group_stats**: This DMV returns a summary of the benefit you would have gained if you had the particular index. For more information, please visit:

  ```
  http://msdn.microsoft.com/en-us/library/ms345421%28SQL.110%29.
  aspx
  ```

- **sys.dm_db_missing_index_groups**: This DMV returns information about which missing indexes are contained in which missing index group handle. For more information, please visit:

  ```
  http://technet.microsoft.com/en-us/library/
  ms345407%28SQL.110%29.aspx
  ```

- **sys.dm_db_missing_index_columns(Index_Handle)**: This DMV gives you an idea about what columns are missing in Index; it is based on the `Index_Handle` field of `sys.dm_db_missing_index_groups`. For more information, please visit:

  ```
  http://technet.microsoft.com/en-us/library/
  ms345364%28SQL.110%29.aspx
  ```

How to do it...

The following T-SQL query will give you information about missing indexes in your database:

```
--finding missing Index
SELECT
    avg_total_user_cost * avg_user_impact * (user_seeks + user_scans)
AS PossibleImprovement
    ,last_user_seek
    ,last_user_scan
    ,statement AS Object
    ,'CREATE INDEX [IDX_' + CONVERT(VARCHAR,GS.Group_Handle) + '_' +
CONVERT(VARCHAR,D.Index_Handle) + '_'
    + REPLACE(REPLACE(REPLACE([statement],']',''),'[',''),'.','') +
']'
    +' ON '
    + [statement]
    + ' (' + ISNULL (equality_columns,'')
    + CASE WHEN equality_columns IS NOT NULL AND inequality_columns IS
NOT NULL THEN ',' ELSE '' END
    + ISNULL (inequality_columns, '')
    + ')'
    + ISNULL (' INCLUDE (' + included_columns + ')', '')
    AS Create_Index_Syntax
FROM
    sys.dm_db_missing_index_groups AS G
INNER JOIN
    sys.dm_db_missing_index_group_stats AS GS
ON
    GS.group_handle = G.index_group_handle
INNER JOIN
    sys.dm_db_missing_index_details AS D
ON
    G.index_handle = D.index_handle
Order By PossibleImprovement DESC
```

How it works...

It is necessary to find out the possible improvement if a suggested index were created. The base logic to find this out is as follows:

▸ avg_total_user_cost * avg_user_impact * (user_seeks + user_scans)

This information resides in the `sys.dm_db_missing_index_group_stats` DMV. After finding out the possible improvement, it is better to see which table, which columns need which index. Therefore, even the suggested query has been given in the field `Create_Index_Syntax`, by using the following DMVs:

▸ `sys.dm_db_missing_index_group_stats`

▸ `sys.dm_db_missing_index_details`

These two DMVs contain all information regarding the column(s) of the table, that need an index, so a `CREATE INDEX` syntax would be created from these two DMVs. But, to get the relationship between these two DMVs, the `sys.dm_db_missing_index_groups` DMV is the only way, as it contains `Index_Group_Handle`, which makes join possible with `sys.dm_db_missing_index_group_stats`, and the `Index_Handle` field, which makes join possible with `sys.dm_db_missing_index_details`.

The list of indexes created by the preceding DMVs is just a piece of advice regarding which indexes are missing and need to be created. Finally it's up to you, based on your requirement, whether to create the index or not. You need to check whether the table name and column has any selectivity, and then decide whether or not to create it. More indexes on a table might improve the performance of your `SELECT` statement, but it will harm other DML statements. So, it is always advisable to make the decision manually rather than leaving everything to DMVs.

There's more...

These DMVs can keep information for a maximum of 500 indexes, and the information is lost whenever SQL Services restarts. Once again, this list of 500 missing indexes is a suggestion only; apply your expertise to find whether it is really worth creating the index or not.

How to find unused indexes

By this time, it is crystal clear that an index can boost up performance, but it comes at a price. Indexes need space in your desk to accommodate their own B-Tree and get updated each time a DML statement gets executed, so it is a good idea to check for any unused indexes in every business cycle.

Getting ready

Before executing the query to find the unused index, remember that we are going to use a `sys.dm_db_index_usage_stats` dynamic management view that removes all the data at every restart of a SQL Server instance and starts collecting data from scratch again.

If we just restart the server or SQL Server instance and look for the statistics, it will show that no index is used and will suggest dropping (DROP) all indexes; this is not right. So, keep your SQL Server running for at least one business cycle, and then check for the statistics.

> Business cycles differ from case tocase. Some tables and queries could be in use every day, but some queries for some reports may execute once in a month or year, may be by HR to see the performance of an employee, especially at the time of yearly appraisal. So, let everything run, and finish your business cycle, and then we will have an appropriate and correct picture.

How to do it...

There is one simple T-SQL query to execute for getting the information regarding unused indexes. The query is given as follows:

```
--following query will show you which index is never used
SELECT
    ind.Index_id,
    obj.Name as TableName,
    ind.Name as IndexName,
    ind.Type_Desc,
    indUsage.user_seeks,
    indUsage.user_scans,
    indUsage.user_lookups,
    indUsage.user_updates,
    indUsage.last_user_seek,
    indUsage.last_user_scan,
    'drop index [' + ind.name + '] ON [' + obj.name + ']' as
DropIndexCommand
FROM
    Sys.Indexes as ind
JOIN
    Sys.Objects as obj
ON
    ind.object_id=obj.Object_ID
LEFT JOIN
    sys.dm_db_index_usage_stats indUsage
ON
    ind.object_id = indUsage.object_id
AND
    ind.Index_id=indUsage.Index_id
```

```
WHERE
    ind.type_desc<>'HEAP' and obj.type<>'S'
AND
    objectproperty(obj.object_id,'isusertable') = 1
AND
    (isnull(indUsage.user_seeks,0) = 0
AND
    isnull(indUsage.user_scans,0) = 0
AND
    isnull(indUsage.user_lookups,0) = 0)
ORDER BY
    obj.name,ind.Name
GO
```

How it works...

Generally, we get all necessary information from the dynamic management view `sys.dm_db_index_usage_stats`, but to know index ID, index name, and index type, it is mandatory to join the `sys.Indexes` view, and to know the table name, it is mandatory to know the `Sys.Objects` view.

Generally, whenever an index is used, it fills up some value in the `sys.dm_db_index_usage_stats` dynamic management view in the `user_seek`, `user_scan`, or `user_lookup` columns. If the index has never performed seek, scan, and lookup, there is no need to keep that index (which utilizes disk space and increases overhead in DML statements). Instead, we can remove it and claim the disk space.

There's more...

Again, apply your expertise while deciding whether the index is actually used, and use the `DROP INDEX` command generated by the given query. The use of an index depends on the business cycle, and you might be running some HR or other report annually, so removing an index might reduce the performance of those reports that use the index we have removed. You might not see any scan/seek/lookup operator at the moment, because SQL Server might have restarted in a recent week or month, while the report is run annually. There are two more reasons given here that may change your decision about dropping the index:

▶ If the index is a Primary Key or a unique key, it can be there for the sake of data integrity even though it is not shown in any scan/seek/lookup

▶ A unique index assists the optimizer in building a more efficient execution plan, even though index itself isn't used, by providing information about data distribution

Enhancing performance by creating an indexed view

A view is a virtual table that consists of data columns from one or more tables. In simple terms, it is a stored query that works as an object of a database, such as a table. A view can be treated exactly like a table; it can be used in any stored procedure, JOIN, UDF, and so on.

A view provides the following two main benefits:

- A security mechanism that restricts users to a certain subset of data in one or more base tables
- A mechanism that allows developers to customize how users can logically view the data stored in base tables

When you query the view, the query optimizer complies a single execution plan for the query. The query optimizer searches through a set of possible execution plans for a query, and chooses the lowest cost plan.

In the absence of an indexed view, the portions of the view necessary to solve the query are materialized at execution time. All joins and/or aggregations are done at execution time. After creating an indexed view, the result set of view is materialized at the time of creating it and persisted in physical storage in the database. This operation saves the overhead of performing this costly operation at runtime for large tables in a complex query.

Getting ready

Before you start working with an indexed view, it is a prerequisite to find which column(s) needs to be indexed in the view, what point needs to be considered before selecting a candidate for indexed view, and whether the indexed view is worth creating or whether it just causes an overhead instead of providing any benefit. The following points will help you to make a decision:

- A view must not reference any other view
- A view can reference any required base tables
- Column name must be explicitly stated with appropriate alias

Index comes up with additional cost of overhead, as follows:

- Index consumes disk space to store itself
- Index creates overhead in DML statements, such as INSERT/UPDATE/DELETE, as whenever a DML statement is executed, the index needs to update itself
- Index maintenance cost

So, before making a decision to create an indexed view, it is better to identify the ratio of the approximate number of SELECT statements going to be executed on view to the approximate number of DML statements going to be run on base table of view. If a small number of SELECT statements is being executed and a higher number of DMLs are performed, or base tables are very volatile and have a very high update ratio, it is not a good idea to create an indexed view.

Before making any decision, it is advisable to gauge the workload of the database and apply your expertise to find the selectivity of the query. Generally, a query with aggregation and many joins, whose base tables are large (maybe millions of rows), and a query taking time to execute, are good candidates to be in indexed view.

> Based on my personal experience, I have observed that Online Analytical Processing (OLAP), Data Warehouse, Date Mart, and Data Mining get more benefit from indexed view over Online Transaction Processing (OLTP), because in most OLTP, there would be a chance of having more DML statements than SELECT statements in base tables, and hence each DML statement needs to update the index on the view along with the indexes on the base table.

Some SET options should be set while creating an indexed view. The following is a list of the same:

- ARITHABORT
- CONCAT_NULL_YIELDS_NULL
- QUOTED_IDENTIFIER
- ANSI_WARNINGS
- ANSI_NULLS
- ANSI_PADDING
- NUMERIC_ROUNDABORT

NUMERIC_ROUNDABORT should be set to OFF, and all the other options should be set to ON.

How to do it...

Follow the steps provided here to perform this recipe:

1. First, let us create a view with a table from the AdventureWorks2012 database, by using the following query:

   ```
   --Using AdventureWorks2008R2, renamed as AdventureWorks2012,
   --database which is compatible with SQL Server Denali and
   --freely downloadable, there is no AdventureWorks database
   --available for SQL Server 2012 at the moment.

   --creating view
   ```

```
CREATE VIEW POView
WITH SCHEMABINDING
AS
SELECT
    POH.PurchaseOrderID
    ,POH.OrderDate
    ,EMP.LoginID
    ,V.Name AS VendorName
    ,SUM(POD.OrderQty) AS OrderQty
    ,SUM(POD.OrderQty*POD.UnitPrice) AS Amount
    ,COUNT_BIG(*) AS Count
FROM
    [Purchasing].[PurchaseOrderHeader] AS POH
JOIN
    [Purchasing].[PurchaseOrderDetail] AS POD
ON
    POH.PurchaseOrderID = POD.PurchaseOrderID
JOIN
    [HumanResources].[Employee] AS EMP
ON
    POH.EmployeeID=EMP.BusinessEntityID
JOIN
    [Purchasing].[Vendor] AS V
ON
    POH.VendorID=V.BusinessEntityID
GROUP BY
    POH.PurchaseOrderID
    ,POH.OrderDate
    ,EMP.LoginID
    ,V.Name
GO

--creating clustered Index on View to make POView Indexed View
CREATE UNIQUE CLUSTERED INDEX IndexPOView ON POView
(PurchaseOrderID)
GO
```

2. After creating a view and then creating a clustered index on the view, it is time to check the effect of the index by running the query we have used in view definition and also by running the view.

```
--Executing both the following queries with keeping Execution
--plan on we can turn execution plan on by pressing ctrl+M
--short cut key
SELECT TOP 10
```

```
      POH.PurchaseOrderID
      ,POH.OrderDate
      ,EMP.LoginID
      ,V.Name AS VendorName
      ,SUM(POD.OrderQty) AS OrderQty
      ,SUM(POD.OrderQty*POD.UnitPrice) AS Amount
FROM
      [Purchasing].[PurchaseOrderHeader] AS POH
JOIN
      [Purchasing].[PurchaseOrderDetail] AS POD
ON
      POH.PurchaseOrderID = POD.PurchaseOrderID
JOIN
      [HumanResources].[Employee] AS EMP
ON
      POH.EmployeeID=EMP.BusinessEntityID
JOIN
      [Purchasing].[Vendor] AS V
ON
      POH.VendorID=V.BusinessEntityID
GROUP BY
      POH.PurchaseOrderID
      ,POH.OrderDate
      ,EMP.LoginID
      ,V.Name
GO

SELECT top 10 * FROM POView WITH (NOEXPAND)
GO
```

3. Now, if we review the execution plan, we can see that the execution plan of the **POView** view is much better, due to the clustered index we have created on the view. The first query searches records from the different indexes defined on the table that comes with the AdventureWorks2012 database, whereas the second query on the view searches records from the single clustered Index we have created on the view.

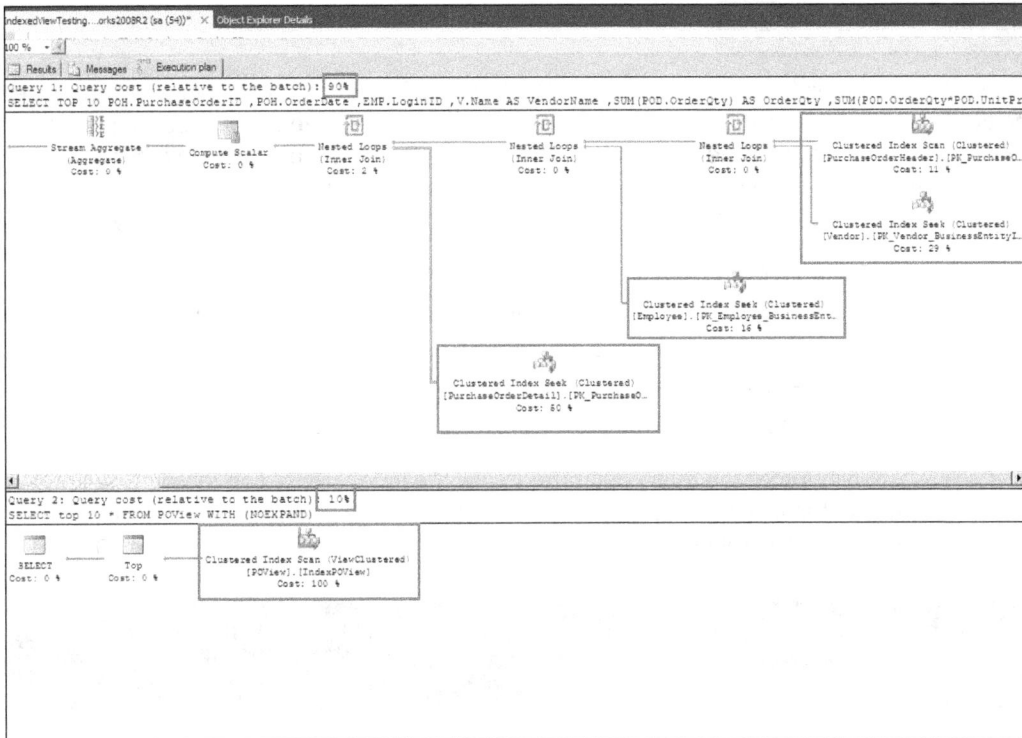

How it works...

As per BOL, the SQL Server query optimizer automatically determines when an indexed view can be used for a given query execution. The view does not need to be referenced directly in the query, for the optimizer to use it in the query execution plan. Therefore, existing applications may take advantage of the indexed views without any changes to the applications themselves; only the indexed views have to be created.

In fact, the optimizer always tries to find the best way to execute the query and it sometimes decides to use the index defined on the base table, rather than using the index created on view. In a development environment, we can test the execution of a query directly or in the indexed view. If the optimizer uses the base table's index for both executions, we can force it to use the index defined on the view while executing the view with the WITH NOEXPAND hint.

There's more...

Indexed view is available in every edition of SQL Server 2012. In the Developer and Enterprise editions of SQL Server 2012, the query processor can use an indexed view to solve queries that structurally match the view, even if they don't refer to the view by name. In other editions, we must reference the view by name and use the `NOEXPAND` hint on the view reference, to query the contents of an indexed view.

Indexed view must be created with the `WITH SCHEMABINDING` option, so that any object referenced in the view cannot be altered in a way that could make the view stop working.

If an indexed view has a `GROUP BY` clause in its definition, the `COUNT_BIG (*)` column must be included in the `SELECT` list of the view definition, and the view definition cannot specify `HAVING`, `CUBE`, and `ROLLUP`.

The `NOEXPAND` hint forces the query optimizer to use the index created on the view rather than searching for the index created in an underlying table. The `NOEXPAND` hint can only be applied if the indexed view is referenced directly in the `FROM` clause.

Enhancing performance with index on Computed Columns

Before trying to understand what "an index on a Computed Column" is, it is good to have a basic understanding of what a Computed Column is.

As per MSDN, a Computed Column is computed from an expression that can use other columns in the same table. The expression can be a non-computed column name, constant, function, or any combination of these, connected by one or more operators. The expression cannot be a subquery.

By default, a Computed Column is a virtual column and it is recalculated every time we call it, until we specify it as `PERSISTED` in the `CREATE TABLE` or `ALTER TABLE` commands.

If a Computed Column is defined as being `PERSISTED`, it stores the calculated value and those stored values are updated each time you change the value of the original column. Moreover, you can't use Computed Column names in `INSERT` and `UPDATE` statements.

As it is already proved that an index plays an important role in performance, in the previous chapter, *Chapter 9, Implementing Index*, it is good to know whether it plays any significant role in all re-calculative values.

Getting ready

First get yourself ready with some information to make sure whether it is possible to make an index on a Computed Column or not. A Computed Column should meet the following criteria in order to make an index on it:

- If a Computed Column is derived from Image, Text, and ntext datatypes, it could be a part of a non-key column of a non-clustered index only.

- Computed Column expressions shouldn't be of the REAL or FLOAT datatypes.

- A Computed Column should be precise.

- A Computed Column should be deterministic, meaning that it should return the same results for specific input. The IsDeterministic property of the COLUMNPROPERTY function is used to identify whether computed column is deterministic or not.

- If a Computed Column has used any function (user-defined function and/or built-in function), the owner of the table and function should be the same.

- Functions that depend on multiple rows, such as SUM or AVG, cannot be used in Computed Columns.

- INSERT, UPDATE, or DELETE statements executed on a table may change the value of the index on a Computed Column, so the table must have six SET options set to ON and one option set to OFF. SQL Server query optimizer won't use an index on a Computed Column for any SELECT statement executed by a connection that does not have the same option settings, as follows:

  - ARITHABORT
  - CONCAT_NULL_YIELDS_NULL
  - QUOTED_IDENTIFIER
  - ANSI_WARNINGS
  - ANSI_NULLS
  - ANSI_PADDING
  - NUMERIC_ROUNDABORT

NUMERIC_ROUNDABORT should be set to OFF, and all above options should be set to ON.

How to do it...

Follow the steps provided here to perform this recipe:

1. As said in the previous paragraph regarding the setting of the SET command, let us first set those options and then create one table for demonstration purposes. Accordingly, our demo table will be named SalesOrderDetailDemo and will be created from the AdventureWorks2012 database's SaleOrderDetail table, as in the following script:

```
--fix the value of SET environment variables.
SET ANSI_NULLS ON
SET ANSI_PADDING ON
SET ANSI_WARNINGS ON
SET ARITHABORT ON
SET CONCAT_NULL_YIELDS_NULL ON
SET QUOTED_IDENTIFIER ON
SET NUMERIC_ROUNDABORT OFF

--creating one table from the data of
--[Sales].[SalesOrderDetail] table
--from AdventureWorks2012 database for demonstration purpose.
SELECT
    [SalesOrderID]
    ,[SalesOrderDetailID]
    ,[CarrierTrackingNumber]
    ,[OrderQty]
    ,[ProductID]
    ,[SpecialOfferID]
    ,[UnitPrice]
INTO
    SalesOrderDetailDemo
FROM
    [AdventureWorks2012].[Sales].[SalesOrderDetail]
GO
```

2. Now, create one user-defined function that will be used in the Computed Column, and add the Computed Column NetPrice to the newly created table. This will get the calculated value from the user-defined function, UDFTotalAmount, as in the following script:

```
-- Creating User Defined Function to use in computed column
CREATE FUNCTION
[dbo].[UDFTotalAmount] (@TotalPrice numeric(10,3), @Freight
TINYINT)
RETURNS Numeric(10,3)
WITH SCHEMABINDING
AS
```

```
BEGIN
DECLARE @NetPrice Numeric(10,3)
SET @NetPrice = @TotalPrice + (@TotalPrice*@Freight/100)
RETURN @NetPrice
END
GO


--adding computed column SalesOrderDetailDemo table
ALTER TABLE SalesOrderDetailDemo
ADD [NetPrice] AS [dbo].[UDFTotalAmount] ( OrderQty*UnitPrice,5)
GO
```

3. Now, create one clustered index on the table, so that the table doesn't become a heap, as explained in the previous chapter, and set some SET options to measure performance for each SELECT query. After setting the STATISTICS option to ON, it will be time to execute one SELECT statement on the SalesOrderDetailDemo table. Keep in mind that we have not created any index on a Computed Column, yet.

```
--creating Clustered Index on table.
CREATE Clustered Index idx_SalesOrderID_SalesOrderDetailID_
SalesOrderDetailDemo
ON SalesOrderDetailDemo(SalesOrderID,SalesOrderDetailID)
GO


--checking SalesOrderDetailDemo with statistics option ON to
--measure performance

SET STATISTICS IO ON
SET STATISTICS TIME ON
GO


--checking SELECT statement without having Index on Computed
Column
SELECT * FROM SalesOrderDetailDemo WHERE NetPrice>5000
GO
```

In the **Messages** tab of the **Result** panel, you might receive results of our STATISTICS options, such as in the following text:

```
SQL Server parse and compile time:
    CPU time = 650 ms, elapsed time = 650 ms.
SQL Server parse and compile time:
    CPU time = 0 ms, elapsed time = 0 ms.


(3864 row(s) affected)
```

```
Table 'SalesOrderDetailDemo'. Scan count 1, logical reads 757,
physical reads 0, read-ahead reads 0, lob logical reads 0, lob
physical reads 0, lob read-ahead reads 0.

SQL Server Execution Times:
   CPU time = 562 ms, elapsed time = 678 ms.
```

> Please note that you might get different readings in the
> previous text, as it depends on many parameters, such as
> CPU of the server, memory, disk type, disk drive, server load,
> parallel processes running on server, and many more.

4. Now, before creating an index on a Computed Column, it is mandatory to meet certain requirements, as discussed in the *Getting Ready* section of this recipe. Let us check whether we meet all requirements or not, by executing the following simple T-SQL query:

```
--checking different property of column and table before making an
Index
--if 0 then answer is NO
--if 1 then answer is YES
SELECT
    COLUMNPROPERTY( OBJECT_ID('SalesOrderDetailDemo'),'NetPrice','
IsIndexable') AS 'Indexable?'
    ,COLUMNPROPERTY( OBJECT_ID('SalesOrderDetailDemo'),'NetPrice',
'IsDeterministic') AS 'Deterministic?'
    ,OBJECTPROPERTY(OBJECT_ID('UDFTotalAmount'),'IsDeterministic')
'UDFDeterministic?'
    ,COLUMNPROPERTY(OBJECT_ID('SalesOrderDetailDemo'),'NetPrice','
IsPrecise') AS 'Precise?'
```

5. Now, create an index on a Computed Column, if you have received all results as YES in the previous query and executed the same SELECT statement that was executed in the previous script. This can be done by executing the following script:

```
--creating an Index on Computed Column
CREATE INDEX idx_SalesOrderDetailDemo_NetPrice
ON SalesOrderDetailDemo
(
NetPrice
)
GO
```

```
--checking SalesOrderDetailDemo after an Index on Computed
--Column
SELECT * FROM SalesOrderDetailDemo WHERE NetPrice>5000
GO
```

6. Now, look at the results of our STATISTICS command in the **Messages** tab. Here is a copy from my server:

```
SQL Server parse and compile time:
   CPU time = 0 ms, elapsed time = 0 ms.
SQL Server parse and compile time:
   CPU time = 0 ms, elapsed time = 0 ms.

(3864 row(s) affected)
Table 'SalesOrderDetailDemo'. Scan count 1, logical reads 757,
physical reads 0, read-ahead reads 0, lob logical reads 0, lob
physical reads 0, lob read-ahead reads 0.

 SQL Server Execution Times:
   CPU time = 546 ms, elapsed time = 622 ms.
```

> Please note that you might get different readings in the previous text, in your installation of SQL Server 2012, as it depends on many parameters like CPU of server, memory, disk type, disk drive, server load, parallel processes running on the server, and many more.

How it works...

Creating an index on Computed Columns, stores key values in leaf-level pages and uses index statistics while executing the SELECT statement, and it works well most of the time. If, for any reason, the optimizer can't use a Computed Column Index, it will go for a regular index or table scan. There are many cases (that we have already discussed in the *Getting Ready* section of this recipe) where the optimizer won't use a Computed Column Index.

If you observe both copies of the STATISTICS figure, you will find differences in the SQL Server Parse and Compile time section and also in the SQL Server Execution Times section. The difference could be larger and better after creating an index on a Computed Column, if the table is very large (maybe millions of rows) and the calculation in the Computed Column is complicated.

Determining disk space consumed by indexes

Performance tuning is part of a DBA's job; at the same time, the DBA also has to take care of the SQL Server instance, the amount of disk space consumed by database(s), providing high availability to the database users, managing database backup/restore policy as a part of disaster management, and a lot more.

Out of these listed responsibilities, disk management is also one of the important tasks to manage. The DBA needs to keep a watch on it and claim any free space consumed by unused indexes, manage the size of log files and data files, and arrange for a larger-sized disk, if needed.

In *Chapter 9*, and in this chapter, we have discussed many times that an index comes with some overhead, and one of the overheads is that the index consumes disk space. So, this is the time to see how much space an index consumes, as either low space or no space on disk raises performance issues, and sometimes the query stops working due to the unavailability of disk space.

Getting ready

In order to perform this operation, the following two things are required:

- VIEW DATABASE STATE permission for the user
- Knowledge of the sys.dm_db_partition_stats dynamic management view

How to do it...

Follow the steps provided here to perform this recipe:

1. The following T-SQL query will display information about space consumed by the indexes:

```
SELECT
    CASE index_id
        WHEN 0 THEN 'HEAP'
        WHEN 1 THEN 'Clustered Index'
        ELSE 'Non-Clustered Index'
    END AS Index_Type,
    SUM(CASE
        WHEN FilledPage > PageToDeduct THEN (FilledPage-
PageToDeduct)
    ELSE
        0
    END )* 8 Index_Size
```

```
FROM
(
    SELECT
            partition_id,
            index_id,
            SUM (used_page_count) AS FilledPage,
            SUM (
                    CASE
                        WHEN (index_id < 2) THEN (in_row_data_
page_count + lob_used_page_count + row_overflow_used_page_count)
                        ELSE
                            lob_used_page_count + row_overflow_used_
page_count
                    END
                ) AS PageToDeduct

    FROM
        sys.dm_db_partition_stats
    GROUP BY
        partition_id
        ,index_id
) AS InnerTable
GROUP BY
    CASE index_id
        WHEN 0 THEN 'HEAP'
        WHEN 1 THEN 'Clusetered Index'
        ELSE 'Non-Clustered Index'
    END
GO
```

How it works...

sys.dm_db_partition_stats gives useful information to the DBA, such as the total row count in each table per partition, used pages, reserved pages for LOB, in-row, and overflow. Each page consumes 8 KB, so if the total number of pages found for any object is multiplied by 8, it would give us the total size in KB.

We can get the Used_Page_Count field, which displays information about total pages used by an object, and if it is a heap or clustered index (Index_id < 2), we remove in_row_data_page_count, lob_used_page_count, and row_overflow_used_page_count, otherwise only the last two fields are removed from total used pages. Multiply those pages with 8 to get the total used KB (Kilo Bytes).

The following table gives the meaning of an important column, `sys.dm_db_partition_stats`, along with those columns that we have used in our query:

Column Name	Description
`partition_id`	There is a database-wide unique ID available in the `sys.partitions` catalog view that is referenced here, in `sys.dm_db_partition_stats`
`index_id`	ID of the index; if ID is `0` then the index is a heap, if it is `1` then clustered index, and if it is greater than 1 then it always belongs to non-clustered index.
`used_page_count`	Total number of pages used for the partition; computed as `in_row_used_page_count` + `lob_used_page_count` + `row_overflow_used_page_count`.
`in_row_data_page_count`	Number of pages in use for storing in-row data in this partition. If the partition is part of a heap, the value is the number of data pages in the heap. If the partition is part of an index, the value is the number of pages in the leaf level. (Non-leaf pages in the B-Tree are not included in the count.) IAM (Index Allocation Map) pages are not included in either case.
`lob_used_page_count`	Number of pages in use for storing and managing out-of-row `text`, `ntext`, `image`, `varchar(max)`, `nvarchar(max)`, `varbinary(max)`, and XML columns within the partition. IAM pages are included.
`row_overflow_used_page_count`	Number of pages in use for storing and managing the row-overflow `varchar`, `nvarchar`, `varbinary`, and `sql_variant` columns within the partition. IAM pages are included.
`object_id`	Object ID of the table or indexed view that the partition is part of.
`row_count`	Total number of rows within partition.

11
Points to Consider While Writing Queries

In this chapter we will cover:

- ▶ Improving performance by limiting the number of columns and rows
- ▶ Improving performance by using sargable conditions
- ▶ Using arithmetic operators wisely in predicate, to improve performance
- ▶ Improving query performance by not using functions on predicate columns
- ▶ Improving performance by **Declarative Referential Integrity** (**DRI**)
- ▶ Trust your foreign key to gain performance

Introduction

Prevention is always better than cure is what I believe. It's a good idea to have a look at some safeguards so that common mistakes don't happen in the TSQL we write, which can cause performance issues later on. There are so many things to consider, to avoid common programming mistakes. Here, we are going to present few of them from the performance point of view.

Improving performance by limiting the number of columns and rows

It has been observed that many developers tend to use SELECT * in queries even if only a few columns of the tables are needed. It's also observed that, many a time, people execute the SELECT query without applying a proper filter clause, which returns more rows in the result set than actually required. After returning result sets to the application, filtering rows in the result sets in application logic as and when needed which is not really a good practice. Both of these cases create big result sets with unnecessary columns and rows, which has many drawbacks. The following are the few of them:

> ▸ A big result set creates I/O overhead by reading more columns/rows from the pages that can be ignored, which in fact is actually not needed.

> ▸ Creates unnecessary load on network traffic.

> ▸ The SELECT * query with JOIN may create some issues and throw an error while using the ORDER BY clause on columns, which are common in more than one table with the same name.

> ▸ If an application has used column number rather than column name from result sets, SELECT * changes the position of the column in the result set, if a new column is inserted in between any column in the table.

> ▸ The SELECT * query changes covering index into non-covering, thus requiring lookups. This is very important because lookup is an expensive iterator, so we can end up scanning the entire table (if optimizer decides that lookup is too expensive).

In SQL Server 2012, there is an intellisense facility, so it is not very difficult to mention the name of each and every column, which is really required in the result set. It is also a good practice to apply proper filters in the query and return only necessary columns/rows to the application.

Getting ready

Since this is a preventive action, there is no formulaic method to change your SELECT * with SELECT ColumnName automatically. Human skills are required to identify which column and which conditions are necessary to filter records in order to achieve the desired result set. Even one small script will help to identify which stored procedure, trigger, or view has used * or SELECT *:

```
SELECT DISTINCT
   so.name
   ,sc.definition
FROM
   sys.sql_modules sc
INNER JOIN
```

```
  sysobjects so
ON
  sc.object_id=so.id
WHERE
  so.xtype in ('P','TR','V')
  and
  sc.definition LIKE '%*%'
--or to make more precise filter, you can go for
--sc.definition LIKE '%SELECT *%'
ORDER BY
  Name
```

`Sys.sql_modules` contains the text that has been used to create objects such as functions, procedures, triggers, views, and so on, but it won't contain the name of the object. Hence `JOIN` is required with the `Sys.sql_modules` system view.

`Xtype` can filter out the type of object, for example, `P` represents stored procedure, `TR` represents trigger, and `V` stands for view.

This query displayed above will not give you 100 percent accurate results; it may bring any definition of an object that has used *, maybe for mathematical expression or comment. There is one free tool provided by Microsoft that helps you in identifying not only this issue but many other common mistakes, too. You can download this tool, Microsoft SQL Server 2012 Best Practices Analyzer, from the following URL:

`http://www.microsoft.com/download/en/details.aspx?id=29302`

How to do it...

Since we have now found how to find objects that have used `SELECT *`, we can manually update those objects by replacing * with the appropriate column name. It's always a good practice to give a column name while generating an object for the first time, so that we don't need to correct it repeatedly. Let us see how much it is affect if we do not provide a proper column name and/or filter.

1. Set two `STATISTICS` options to display the information about query execution:

   ```
   SET STATISTICS IO ON
   SET STATISTICS TIME ON
   ```

2. Execute a simple `SELECT` query on the `Sales.SalesOrderDetail` table with * to see the **Messages** tab displaying information about the execution time and IO load:

   ```
   SELECT
     *
   FROM
     Sales.SalesOrderDetail
   WHERE
     SalesOrderID>50000 and OrderQty>1
   ```

The **Messages** tab after executing this query is shown in the following screenshot:

```
Select * from Sales.SalesOrderDetail
where SalesOrderID>50000 and OrderQty>1
100 %  ▼
 Results  Messages  Execution plan
 SQL Server parse and compile time:
   CPU time = 0 ms, elapsed time = 0 ms.

 SQL Server Execution Times:
   CPU time = 0 ms,  elapsed time = 0 ms.
 SQL Server parse and compile time:
   CPU time = 0 ms, elapsed time = 0 ms.
 SQL Server parse and compile time:
   CPU time = 0 ms, elapsed time = 0 ms.

 (26558 row(s) affected)
 Table 'SalesOrderDetail'. Scan count 1, logical reads 891, physical reads 0, read-ahead reads 0, lob logical reads 0, lob physical reads 0, lob read-ahead reads 0.

 (1 row(s) affected)

 SQL Server Execution Times:
   CPU time = 47 ms,  elapsed time = 416 ms.
 SQL Server parse and compile time:
   CPU time = 0 ms, elapsed time = 0 ms.

 SQL Server Execution Times:
   CPU time = 0 ms,  elapsed time = 0 ms.
```

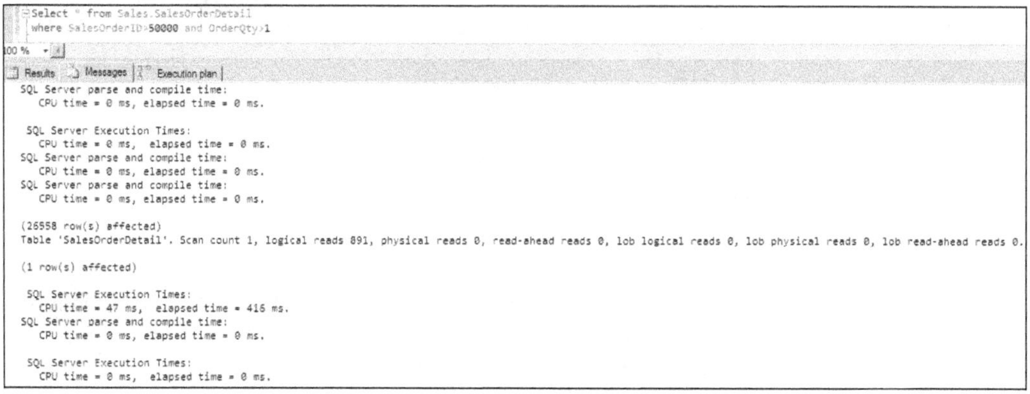

3. We may not need all columns of the `Sales.SalesOrderDetail` table in the result set. So we may like to control the number of columns in the `SELECT` query by specifying the proper column name with the query shown next:

```sql
SELECT
    CarrierTrackingNumber
    ,OrderQty
    ,ProductID
    ,SpecialOfferID
    ,UnitPrice
FROM
    Sales.SalesOrderDetail
WHERE
    SalesOrderID>50000 and OrderQty>1
```

The following screenshot shows the result of this query:

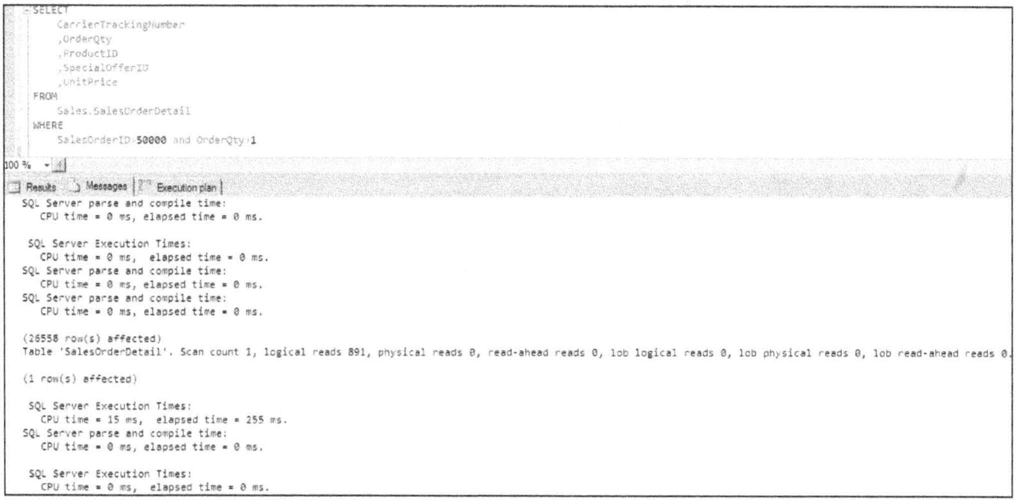

```
SELECT
    CarrierTrackingNumber
    ,OrderQty
    ,ProductID
    ,SpecialOfferID
    ,UnitPrice
FROM
    Sales.SalesOrderDetail
WHERE
    SalesOrderID>50000 and OrderQty>1
100 %  ▼
 Results  Messages  Execution plan
 SQL Server parse and compile time:
   CPU time = 0 ms, elapsed time = 0 ms.

 SQL Server Execution Times:
   CPU time = 0 ms,  elapsed time = 0 ms.
 SQL Server parse and compile time:
   CPU time = 0 ms, elapsed time = 0 ms.
 SQL Server parse and compile time:
   CPU time = 0 ms, elapsed time = 0 ms.

 (26558 row(s) affected)
 Table 'SalesOrderDetail'. Scan count 1, logical reads 891, physical reads 0, read-ahead reads 0, lob logical reads 0, lob physical reads 0, lob read-ahead reads 0.

 (1 row(s) affected)

 SQL Server Execution Times:
   CPU time = 15 ms,  elapsed time = 255 ms.
 SQL Server parse and compile time:
   CPU time = 0 ms, elapsed time = 0 ms.

 SQL Server Execution Times:
   CPU time = 0 ms,  elapsed time = 0 ms.
```

If you observe both the screenshots, you will get to know that **Scan count** and **logical reads** remain the same, as there is no change in filter of the query, but **CPU time** and **elapsed time** is better in the second query, because we have controlled the column.

1. Let's set the STATISTICS command as it was before so it doesn't get calculated for each query that we execute on the server:

    ```
    SET STATISTICS TIME OFF
    SET STATISTICS IO OFF
    ```

How it works...

A large number of unnecessary columns increases the I/O overheads and network traffic, and may make your index ineffective. The absence of an appropriate filter increases the number of rows, which again creates unnecessary network traffic, IO overhead, and forces the optimizer to scan more pages then necessary, which delays the execution of the query. All these details can be observed with the following two commands:

```
SET STATISTICS IO ON
SET STATISTICS TIME ON
```

See also

For more details on the SET command look at the *Enhancing performance with index on computed columns* recipe in *Chapter 10, Maintaining Indexes*.

Improving performance by using sargable conditions

Sargable stands for **S**earch **ARG**ument **Able**. Sargable conditions help query optimizers to use the index defined on column(s) effectively. Sargable conditions have a higher chance of meeting index seek than index or table scan.

Getting ready

Writing a sargable condition is also a preventive step. Consider this factor while writing the query or while working on performance tuning projects. There are some operators that make your query sargable or non-sargable. Here is the list:

Sargable operators:

► =

► >

- ▶ >=
- ▶ <
- ▶ <=
- ▶ BETWEEN
- ▶ LIKE (only those LIKE conditions that have a wildcard character as a suffix, for example, FirstName LIKE 'R%')

Non-sargable operators:

- ▶ !=
- ▶ !<
- ▶ !>
- ▶ <>
- ▶ NOT EXISTS
- ▶ IN
- ▶ NOT IN
- ▶ LIKE (LIKE conditions that have a wildcard character as a prefix in the filter, for example, FirstName LIKE '%R')
- ▶ NOT LIKE
- ▶ Functions on column name in predicate

The main intention for giving a list of operators for both situations is to help you, for as long as possible, try to avoid non-sargable operators to gain performance benefits from an index.

How to do it...

Follow the steps given here to perform this recipe:

1. Set two STATISTICS options to display information about the query execution:

```
SET STATISTICS IO ON
SET STATISTICS TIME ON
```

2. Now, execute a simple SELECT query on Sales.SalesOrderHeader with the IN operator, which is non-sargable:

```
SELECT * FROM Sales.SalesOrderHeader
WHERE SalesOrderID IN (75000,75001,75002)
```

3. The statistics received from the **Message** tab of the result panel is as follows:

```
Table 'SalesOrderHeader'. Scan count 3, logical reads 9, physical
reads 0, read-ahead reads 0, lob logical reads 0, lob physical
reads 0, lob read-ahead reads 0.
```

4. Now, execute the same query as above with the >= and <= operators, which are sargable operators:

```
SELECT * FROM Sales.SalesOrderHeader
WHERE SalesOrderID >=75000 AND SalesOrderID<=75002
```

5. The statistics received from the **Message** tab of the result panel is as follows:

```
Table 'SalesOrderHeader'. Scan count 1, logical reads 3, physical
reads 0, read-ahead reads 0, lob logical reads 0, lob physical
reads 0, lob read-ahead reads 0.
```

6. Execute the same SELECT statement with another sargable operator—BETWEEN:

```
SELECT * FROM Sales.SalesOrderHeader
WHERE SalesOrderID BETWEEN 75000 AND 75002
```

7. The statistics received from the **Message** table of the result panel is as follows:

```
Table 'SalesOrderHeader'. Scan count 1, logical reads 3, physical
reads 0, read-ahead reads 0, lob logical reads 0, lob physical
reads 0, lob read-ahead reads 0.
```

How it works...

Generally algebriser transforms the query in more suitable form for optimiser, for example, transforming the IN operator to multiple OR operators, and SQL Server Query optimiser performs a syntax-based tuning by its own before executing the query and tries to match up to your non-sargable , which is IN , operator with sargable operator, which is OR , in most case, so you might not see major difference.. I Personally recommend it is not good idea to leave choice of operator on optimiser.

Compare all three statistics we have received for three queries. The second and third statistics seem better than the first one the as second and third ones have Scan count as 1 and logical reads as 3, as compared to the first statistics, where Scan count is equal to 3 and logical reads is equal to 9.

Using arithmetic operator wisely in predicate to improve performance

Arithmetic operation directly on the column name in the WHERE condition makes your condition non-sargable and index defined on the column will not get performance benefits. As long as possible, try to avoid this situation by logical workarounds to gain performance boosts.

Getting ready

There is no automatic way to find this behavior; this is simply 'a manual process. You either keep this step in mind while developing the SQL script or while working on performance tuning projects.

Let us use two tables from the AdventureWorks2012 database to demonstrate this exercise.

- ▶ [AdventureWorks2012].[HumanResources].[Employee]
- ▶ [AdventureWorks2012].[HumanResources].[EmployeePayHistory]

How to do it...

Follow the steps given here to perform this recipe:

1. Select some basic details of an employee from the Employee table and get the latest the rate (considering rate as the hourly rate of an employee) from the EmployeePayHistory table. Suppose we want to select those employees whose latest hourly rate multiplied by eight is less than 152. A developer's obvious logic would be like this:

```
SELECT
  E.LoginID
  ,E.JobTitle
  ,E.BirthDate
  ,E.MaritalStatus
  ,E.Gender
  ,E.HireDate
  ,EP.HourlyRate
  ,EP.RateChangeDate
FROM [AdventureWorks2012].[HumanResources].[Employee] AS E
JOIN
(
  Select
    Max(BusinessEntityID) AS BusinessEntityID
    ,Max(RateChangeDate) AS RateChangeDate
    ,Rate AS HourlyRate
  FROM
    [AdventureWorks2012].[HumanResources].[EmployeePayHistory]
  GROUP BY
    Rate
) as EP
ON E.BusinessEntityID=EP.BusinessEntityID
WHERE EP.HourlyRate*8<=152
```

2. But, this is not an efficient method to make calculations on the column name in the `WHERE` clause. Instead, we should go for an alternate way, like this one:

```
SELECT
    E.LoginID
    ,E.JobTitle
    ,E.BirthDate
    ,E.MaritalStatus
    ,E.Gender
    ,E.HireDate
    ,EP.HourlyRate
    ,EP.RateChangeDate
FROM [AdventureWorks2012].[HumanResources].[Employee] AS E
JOIN
(
    Select
        Max(BusinessEntityID) AS BusinessEntityID
        ,Max(RateChangeDate) AS RateChangeDate
        ,Rate AS HourlyRate
    FROM
        [AdventureWorks2012].[HumanResources].[EmployeePayHistory]
    GROUP BY
        Rate
) as EP
ON E.BusinessEntityID=EP.BusinessEntityID
WHERE EP.HourlyRate<=152/8
```

3. If we had run both the queries with an execution plan, we would get 29 rows from each result set and the execution plan would look somewhat like the following screenshot:

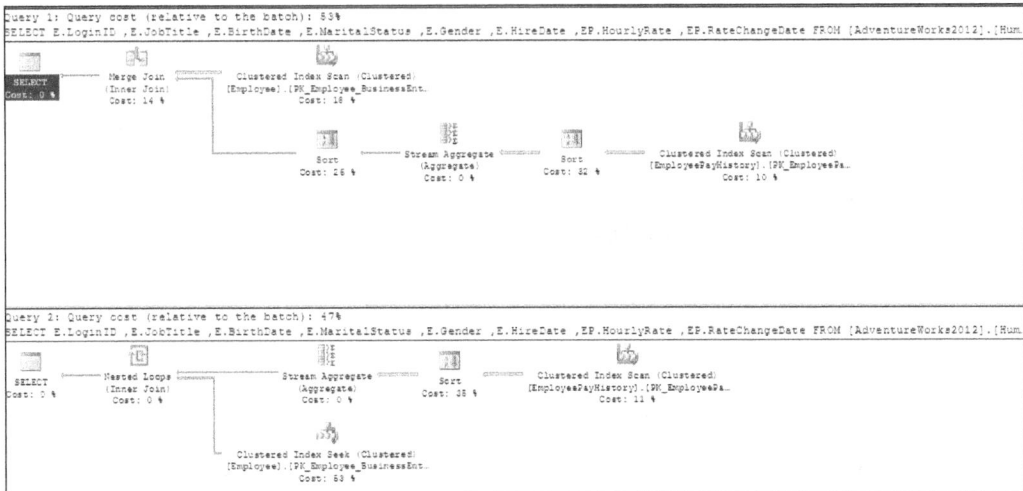

How it works...

The second execution plan seems much better, as it has used 47 percent of the total cost, as against 53 percent in the first query. Though the difference is not that large, the second execution plan has used Clustered Index Seek on the Employee table, as against "Clustered Index Scan" in the first execution plan. There are few more differences between both the plans, but overall the second query seems attractive from the performance point of view, because it calculates the whole column while executing the SELECT statement. Table data affects the result set; a big table shows you a large difference, and less data shows you a small difference. In short, any arithmetic operator on the column name in the WHERE clause affects the performance of the query, and the query optimizer will not be able to use the proper index.

Improving query performance by not using functions on predicate columns

Using a scalar function with column name in predicate would again make your condition non-sargable. It is really a heavy load on the query optimizer and consumes lot of resources. For as long as possible, try to use the alternate method and avoid using functions with column name in predicate, to achieve performance boosts from the indexes.

Getting ready

There is no automatic way to find this behavior; this is simply a manual process. You either keep this step in mind while developing the SQL script or while working on performance tuning projects.

How to do it...

There will be two different examples here, in this recipe. The first example will use the DATE function in predicate, and the second example will use string function in predicate.

1. For first example, let us first create one index on the Date column of the Person.Person table:

   ```
   CREATE INDEX IDX_Person_ModifiedDate ON Person.
   Person(ModifiedDate)
   GO
   ```

2. Now, if there is a need to list out all people from the `Person` table whose last modified date is in the year `2003`. A developer will be tempted to use the `DATEPART` function, as shown here:

```
SELECT
    BusinessEntityID
    ,ModifiedDate
FROM
    Person.Person
WHERE
    DATEPART(YYYY,ModifiedDate)='2003'
GO
```

3. This is really a bad way to draft the query; a shorter query is not always good. Let us twist the `WHERE` part a little bit to get a workaround to remove a function from the predicate in the `WHERE` clause, which will return the same logic:

```
SELECT
    BusinessEntityID
    ,ModifiedDate
FROM
    Person.Person
WHERE
    ModifiedDate >= '01/01/2003' AND ModifiedDate <= '12/31/2003'
GO
```

The following screenshot shows both the queries:

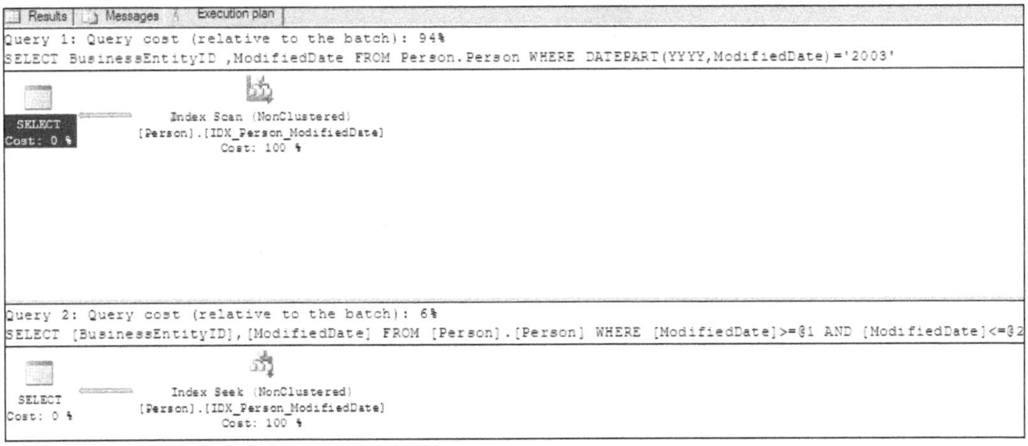

The first query has used scan on the non-clustered index, whereas the second query has used seek in the non-clustered index and used only 6 percent of total query execution cost. Isn't the second one better?

4. Now, dropping the non-clustered index created for this example and creates one "Non Clustered "on "First Name" column:

```
DROP INDEX IDX_Person_ModifiedDate ON  Person.Person
GO
CREATE INDEX IDX_Person_FirstName ON Person.Person(FirstName)
GO
```

5. Now, selecting all people from the `Person` table whose first name starts with `R`. In this kind of task, logical steps to use are string functions, such as `LEFT`, `RIGHT`, or `SUBSTRING`, which is again a bad idea:

```
SELECT
    BusinessEntityID
    ,FirstName
FROM
    Person.Person
WHERE
    Left(FirstName,1)='R'
GO
```

6. As already said, a shorter query is not always a smarter query, we can go for an alternative like this:

```
SELECT
    BusinessEntityID
    ,FirstName
FROM
    Person.Person
WHERE
    FirstName LIKE 'R%'
GO
```

7. By looking at the execution plan of both queries, the picture becomes clear. The second query seek on the non-clustered index `IDX_Person_FirstName` whereas first query makes scan on the non-clustered index `IDX_Person_FirstName`. The second query ran faster and used only 9 percent of the total query execution cost, which is faster.

Results | Messages | Execution plan

```
Query 1: Query cost (relative to the batch): 91%
SELECT BusinessEntityID ,FirstName FROM Person.Person WHERE Left(FirstName,1)='R'
```

```
SELECT              Index Scan (NonClustered)
Cost: 0 %           [Person].[IDX_Person_FirstName]
                              Cost: 100 %
```

```
Query 2: Query cost (relative to the batch): 9%
SELECT BusinessEntityID ,FirstName FROM Person.Person WHERE FirstName LIKE 'R%'
```

```
SELECT              Index Seek (NonClustered)
Cost: 0 %           [Person].[IDX_Person_FirstName]
                              Cost: 100 %
```

How it works...

In both the previous examples (first query of both examples), query optimizer was not able to use the proper non-clustered index that we had defined on the respective column due to the functions DATEPART and LEFT, used with column name in the WHERE clause. At the same time the second query, in both examples, has used an alternate way to achieve the same result set, which is why query optimizer has used the Index Seek operation on the indexes defined on predicate columns.

Improving performance by Declarative Referential Integrity (DRI)

Declarative Referential Integrity (DRI) ensures integrity of the database by a properly managed primary key and foreign key relationship. Correctly defined primary keys and foreign keys help query optimizer to select the best-suited execution plan for the query.

It has been observed many times that developers create a master table with a primary key and use that primary key field in the child table but don't define a foreign key in the table schema. This is not a good practice because by initiating a foreign key in the child table, you ensure that each record in the child table has a reference key in the parent table. This is a good thing, right? But, let us clarify that, by maintaining the parent and foreign key properly, we not only achieve integrity in the database but are also able to gain performance benefits. We have an example to prove it.

Getting ready

There is no automatic way to find this behavior; this is simply a manual process. You either keep this step in mind while developing the database schema or while working on performance tuning project.

In this recipe, we are going to see the magic of defining a proper primary key and foreign key relationship.

How to do it...

Follow the steps given here to perform this recipe:

1. First of all, we have to create two tables, for demonstration of this recipe, from the AdventureWorks2012 database:

```
IF OBJECT_ID('ProductDemo') IS NOT NULL
   DROP TABLE ProductDemo
GO


IF OBJECT_ID('ProductModelDemo') IS NOT NULL
   DROP TABLE ProductModelDemo
GO


select * into ProductModelDemo from Production.ProductModel
select * into ProductDemo from Production.Product WHERE
ProductModelID is not null
GO
```

2. After creating the child table, ProductDemo, and the parent table, ProductModelDemo, let us make sure that there is no the NULL value in the foreign key (ProductModelID) of the ProductDemo table:

```
ALTER TABLE ProductDemo
ALTER COLUMN ProductModelID INT NOT NULL
GO
```

3. Now is the time to create a primary key constraint for the child table, ProductDemo:

```
ALTER TABLE ProductDemo ADD  CONSTRAINT [PK_ProductDemo_ProductID]
PRIMARY KEY CLUSTERED
(
   [ProductID] ASC
)
GO
```

4. Now, create a primary key constraint in the parent table, `ProductModelDemo`:

```
ALTER TABLE ProductModelDemo ADD  CONSTRAINT [PK_ProductModelDemo_
ProductModelID] PRIMARY KEY CLUSTERED
(
   ProductModelID ASC
)
GO
```

5. It is observed that, after performing all of the given steps, people start executing TSQL statements on the parent and child tables without making proper foreign key constraints, such as the following SELECT query:

```
SELECT
   P.ProductID
   ,P.ProductModelID
FROM
   ProductDemo AS P
JOIN
   ProductModelDemo AS PM
ON
   P.ProductModelID=PM.ProductModelID
WHERE
   P.ProductID=680
GO
```

The following screenshot shows the execution plan generated by the given query:

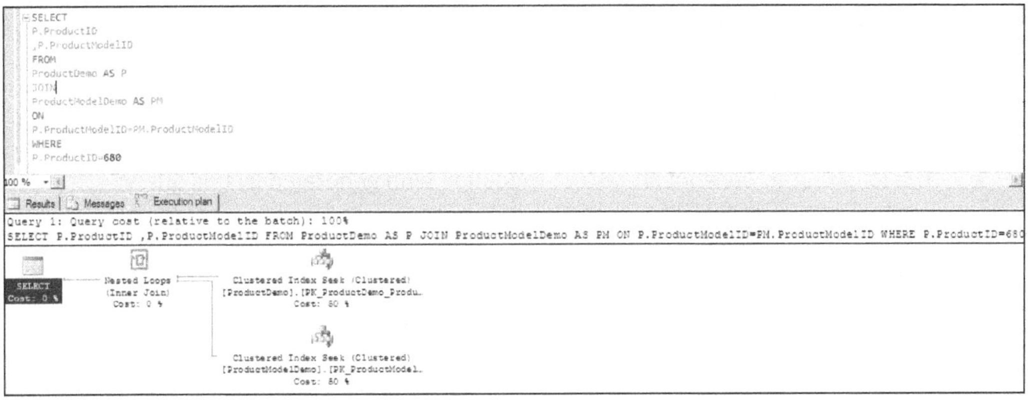

As we have already discussed (with respect to indexes)in *Chapter 9 Implementing Indexes*, and *Chapter 10, Maintaining Indexes*, seek is "good" and scan is "bad", in most cases. This query performs the seek operation on both tables' clustered indexes, which is good, isn't it? We'll decide later.

1. As of now, create a foreign key constraint on the child table:

```
ALTER TABLE ProductDemo
WITH CHECK
ADD CONSTRAINT
    FK_ProductDemo_ProductModelDemo_ProductModelID
FOREIGN KEY
    (ProductModelID)
REFERENCES
    ProductModelDemo(ProductModelID)
GO
```

2. After defining the foreign key constraint, let us execute the same SELECT query again:

```
SELECT
    P.ProductID
    ,P.ProductModelID
FROM
    ProductDemo AS P
JOIN
    ProductModelDemo AS PM
ON
    P.ProductModelID=PM.ProductModelID
WHERE
    P.ProductID=680
GO
```

The following screenshot shows the execution plan generated by this query:

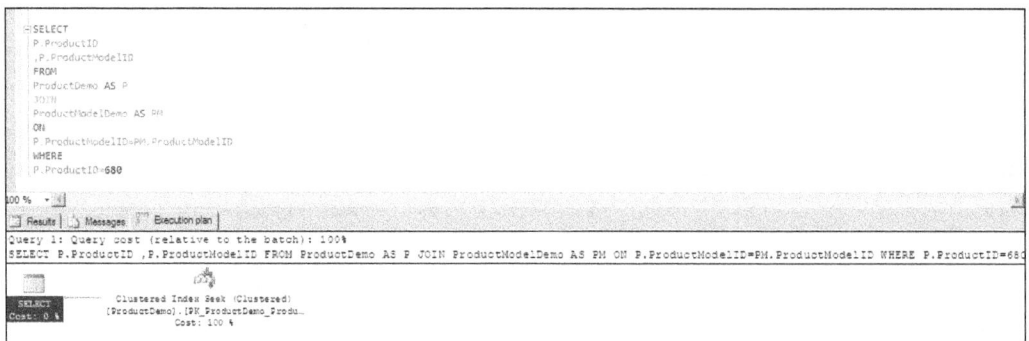

This time, query optimizer has performed the seek operation only on the `ProductDemo` table and didn't even get into checking anything in the parent table `ProductModelDemo`. Now judge which execution plan looks better: before the foreign key constraint or after the foreign key constraint.

How it works...

It is already said that DRI not only ensures the integrity of databases but also gains performance benefits, and this is proved by the previous screenshot. By defining foreign key field as `NOT NULL` in the child table, we are guiding the query optimizer that there is no value in child field without reference of parent field and hence optimizer keep trust on this foreign key and does not even go to look at the `ProductModelDemo` parent table to confirm this, if no other data is requested from the parent table. This is the reason, the second `SELECT` query performed seek operation on the child table only.

Apart from that, by defining the foreign key to the primary key field on the parent table, we also ensure that no `JOIN` operation of a single row from the child table would bring two or more rows from the parent table. Without it, optimizer would have to go to the parent table to check whether we possibly have more than one corresponding row for the same row in the child table.

"Trust" your foreign key to gain performance

We have already studied what DRI can do and by how much it can increase performance, in the previous recipe. This recipe is also related to DRI, which shows that even a single small option can play a big role as far as performance is concerned.

Getting ready

We are going to see the `sys.foreign_keys` system view to get information about the foreign key we defined in the table schema. Concentrate on the field `is_not_trusted`, in the view, which gives you information whether your foreign key is trusted or not.

How to do it...

Follow the steps given here to perform this recipe:

1. First of all, we have to create two tables for demonstration of this recipe from the `AdventureWorks2012` database:

```
IF OBJECT_ID('ProductDemo') IS NOT NULL
  DROP TABLE ProductDemo
GO

IF OBJECT_ID('ProductModelDemo') IS NOT NULL
  DROP TABLE ProductModelDemo
```

```
GO

select * into ProductModelDemo from Production.ProductModel
select * into ProductDemo from Production.Product WHERE
ProductModelID is not null
GO
```

2. After creating the child table, `ProductDemo`, and parent table, `ProductModelDemo`, let us make sure that there is no `NULL` value in the foreign key `ProductModelID` of the `ProductDemo` table:

```
ALTER TABLE ProductDemo
ALTER COLUMN ProductModelID INT NOT NULL
GO
```

3. Now is the time to create a primary key constraint for the child table, `ProductDemo`:

```
ALTER TABLE ProductDemo ADD  CONSTRAINT [PK_ProductDemo_ProductID]
PRIMARY KEY CLUSTERED
(
   [ProductID] ASC
)
GO
```

4. Now, create a primary key constraint in the parent table, `ProductModelDemo`:

```
ALTER TABLE ProductModelDemo ADD  CONSTRAINT [PK_ProductModelDemo_
ProductModelID] PRIMARY KEY CLUSTERED
(
   ProductModelID ASC
)
GO
```

5. Add a foreign key to the child table with the `WITH NOCHECK` option. The `WITH NOCHECK` option prevents the parser from checking the existence of existing data of child field with parent field data. By default, the `ALTER TABLE` command uses the `WITH CHECK` option if nothing is specified:

```
ALTER TABLE ProductDemo
WITH NOCHECK
ADD CONSTRAINT
   FK_ProductDemo_ProductModelDemo_ProductModelID
FOREIGN KEY
   (ProductModelID)
REFERENCES
   ProductModelDemo(ProductModelID)
GO
```

6. Now that we have created a foreign key, let us look at the system view for the `Is_Not_Trusted` field:

```
SELECT
    *
FROM
    sys.foreign_keys
WHERE
    name = 'FK_ProductDemo_ProductModelDemo_ProductModelID'
GO
```

7. The `Is_Not_Trusted` field will have value 1, which means that foreign key is not trusted. Though, it is not trusted; let us execute below given query by keeping the execution plan on to observe the way chosen by SQL Server while executing query on the foreign key which is not trusted :

```
SELECT
    P.ProductID
    ,P.ProductModelID
FROM
    ProductDemo AS P
WHERE
    EXISTS(SELECT 1 FROM ProductModelDemo AS PM WHERE
P.ProductModelID=PM.ProductModelID)
GO
```

8. Here is the screenshot of the execution plan of this query:

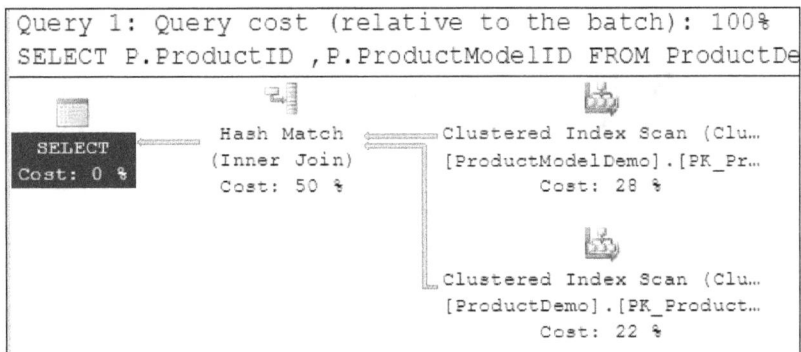

```
Query 1: Query cost (relative to the batch): 100%
SELECT P.ProductID ,P.ProductModelID FROM ProductDe

                          Hash Match  ⟸════  Clustered Index Scan (Clu...
  SELECT                  (Inner Join)        [ProductModelDemo].[PK_Pr...
  Cost: 0 %               Cost: 50 %                   Cost: 28 %

                                              Clustered Index Scan (Clu...
                                              [ProductDemo].[PK_Product...
                                                       Cost: 22 %
```

This screenshot shows clustered index scans for both the tables.

1. Now, let us alter the foreign key with the `WITH CHECK` option and see its effect on the `SELECT` query:

```
ALTER TABLE ProductDemo
WITH CHECK
CHECK CONSTRAINT
    FK_ProductDemo_ProductModelDemo_ProductModelID
GO
```

2. Before we execute our SELECT query in the parent/child table, it's good to check whether our foreign key becomes trusted or not. Confirm it with the following query:

```
SELECT *
FROM sys.foreign_keys
WHERE name = 'FK_ProductDemo_ProductModelDemo_ProductModelID'
GO
```

3. Now is the time to execute the query on the parent/child table with the actual execution plan:

```
SELECT
    P.ProductID
    ,P.ProductModelID
FROM
    ProductDemo AS P
WHERE
    EXISTS(SELECT * FROM ProductModelDemo AS PM WHERE
P.ProductModelID=PM.ProductModelID)
GO
```

4. Look at the following screenshot of the execution plan:

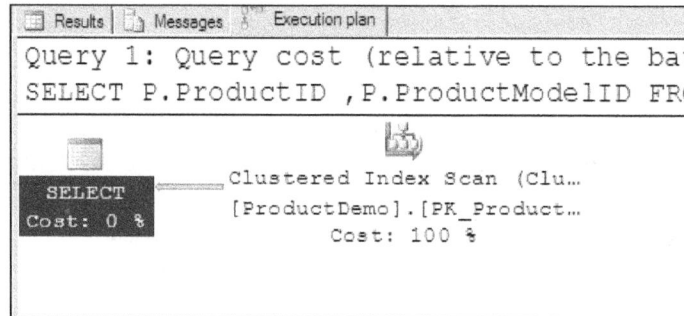

How it works...

A very small flag called Is_Not_Trusted, in the foreign key metadata, plays a big role in performance. In the absence of checked data, SQL Server can't assure query optimizer that every record of the ProductDemo table has a corresponding ProductModelID column in the ProductModelDemo table, and this is the reason for a different execution plan. In short, always use foreign key with the WITH CHECK option, so that it remains enabled and trusted as well. By doing this, the query performance will increase even without any extra efforts.

There's more...

Apart from the points we have discussed in the chapter, there are few more common points to keep in mind while writing the query, here is the list of the same which are helpful in performance gain.

- Specifying as many possible filters in the query, to all the tables participating in the query, even if the filter looks straightforward
- Avoid using the ORDER BY clause, if not needed
- Have smaller items in GROUP BY and make sure that they are from the same tables, if possible
- Have integer values in GROUP BY and not strings, if possible.
- Have columns from the same table in GROUP BY and in ORDER BY, if possible.

12

Statistics in SQL Server

In this chapter we will cover:

- ▸ Creating and updating statistics
- ▸ Effects of statistics on non-key columns
- ▸ Finding out-of-date statistics and correct them
- ▸ Effects of statistics on a filtered index

Introduction

Query Statistics:

By now, we have already learnt about the index in *Chapter 9*, *Implementing Indexes*, and *Chapter 10*, *Maintaining Indexes*. The optimizer chooses the index for a query if there are proper and updated statistics available for key columns of the index, because the SQL Server optimizer is a cost-based optimizer. An optimizer can decide the best way to execute the query, based on the data going to be displayed in result sets with the help of column(s) used in the WHERE and ON clauses. The optimizer can get all these details from statistics before executing the actual query.

While creating an index, SQL Server itself creates statistics on key columns of the index and if required, SQL Server 2012 creates statistics on non-key columns, too.

In short, statistics are nothing more than the description of the distribution of data residing in a column or in an index.

Query Selectivity:

Query Selectivity is represented by the number generated by:

Total number of distinct value in the column/Total number of value in the column

For example, one table with two fields, ID and Name, has a total of 1,000,000 records and has 900,000 unique names in the Name column. Thus, the selectivity of the column would be:

900,000 / 1,000,000 = 0.9

A higher selectivity always improves the performance of an index, and that is why the ideal selectivity is 1, which can be achieved by using Primary Key or a unique key.

Creating and updating statistics

Statistics is an integral part of performance as it helps the SQL Server optimizer choose the proper operation to be performed while executing the SELECT statement. There are two main ways to create and update statistics:

- ▶ Manually create/update statistics
- ▶ Automatically create/update statistics

We will see these options in this recipe.

Getting ready

Before we move further to generate statistics, let us see some commands to view the current settings of statistics for database and table.

The following script will let you know whether the Auto_Create_Statistics option is enabled for databases or not:

```
SELECT
    CASE
        WHEN
            DATABASEPROPERTYEX('Master','IsAutoCreateStatistics')=1
        THEN
            'Yes'
        ELSE
            'No'
    END as 'IsAutoCreateStatisticsOn?',
    CASE
        WHEN
            DATABASEPROPERTYEX('Master','IsAutoUpdateStatistics')=1
        THEN
```

```
                 'Yes'
         ELSE
                 'No'
     END as 'IsAutoUpdateStatisticsOn?',
     CASE
         WHEN
                 DATABASEPROPERTYEX('Master','is_auto_update_stats_async_
on')=1
         THEN
                 'Yes'
         ELSE
                 'No'
     END as 'isAutoUpdateStatsAsyncOn?'
GO
```

The following script will show you all the statistics available in a database or for a table based on the WHERE clause specified:

```
SELECT
     object_id
     ,OBJECT_NAME(object_id) AS TableName
     ,name AS StatisticsName
     ,auto_created
FROM
     sys.stats
--you can apply WHERE clause to filter records for
--particular table
--remove comment in below given line to see the fact.
--where object_id=OBJECT_ID('Sales.SalesOrderHeader')
Order by object_id desc
GO
```

Here is a very small and handy line of code to display the statistics name and statistics key column name generated by a user with the CREATE STATISTICS command, or it can be generated automatically:

```
sp_helpstats 'Sales.SalesOrderHeader'
```

How to do it...

Follow the steps provided here to perform this recipe:

1. After becoming aware of the current situation of statistics for database and table, it is now time to explore the different ways that help to create and update statistics. There is a way to enable Auto_Create_Statistics (ON and OFF) at database level; by default, Auto_Create_Statistics at database level is set to ON.

   ```
   ALTER DATABASE AdventureWorks2012 SET AUTO_CREATE_STATISTICS ON
   --OFF
   ```

2. Enabling `Auto_Create_Statistics` creates single column statistics synchronously, as and when needed by the predicate given in the `SELECT` query. The SQL Server query optimizer creates statistics on a single column only if a histogram (find more about histograms in the *There's more* section of this recipe) table is not available for that column while executing the query to get an exact estimation of the total number of rows and the pattern of data. Statistics created by SQL Server always start with the prefix _WA, so you can query your database to get a list of all statistics created by SQL Server.

```
SELECT
    st.name AS StatName
    , COL_NAME(stc.object_id, stc.column_id) AS ColumnName
    , OBJECT_NAME(st.object_id) AS TableName
FROM
    sys.stats AS st Join sys.stats_columns AS stc
ON
    st.stats_id = stc.stats_id AND st.object_id = stc.object_id
WHERE
    st.name like '_WA%'
```

3. The work does not end with switching your `Auto_Create_Statistics` option set to `ON`. It is mandatory to keep your statistics updated to gain proper performance benefits. Here is the setting for your statistics to auto-update synchronously, whenever needed. By default, this option is set to `ON`; you can change it as per your need. `Auto_Update_Statistics` generally works fine, but in some scenarios it may not cater to your needs, so there may be a need to manually update plans.

```
ALTER DATABASE AdventureWorks2012 SET AUTO_UPDATE_STATISTICS ON
--OFF
```

4. The `Auto_Update_Statistics` option will update statistics that are created by an index, auto-created by `Auto_Create_Statistics`, or manually created by a user, with the `CREATE STATISTICS` command. What follows is an interesting script for automatic updating of statistics.

```
ALTER DATABASE AdventureWorks2012 SET AUTO_UPDATE_STATISTICS_ASYNC
ON --OFF
```

5. Confirm all the three settings from the previous scripts, with the following query:

```
SELECT
    is_auto_update_stats_async_on
    , is_auto_create_stats_on
    , is_auto_update_stats_on
FROM
    sys.databases
WHERE
    name='AdventureWorks2012'
```

6. So, we have talked about automatically creating and updating statistics so far; now it is time to see how to manually create, update, and drop statistics:

```
--manually create stats
--CREATE STATISTICS <<Statastics name>> ON
--<<SCHEMA NAME>>.<<TABLE NAME>>(<<COLUMN NAME>>)
CREATE STATISTICS st_DueDate_SalesOrderHeader ON Sales.
SalesOrderHeader(DueDate)


--update statistics for Sales.SalesOrderHeader Table
UPDATE STATISTICS Sales.SalesOrderHeader;

--update statistics for st_DueDate_SalesOrderHeader stats
--of Sales.SalesOrderHeader Table
UPDATE STATISTICS Sales.SalesOrderHeader st_DueDate_
SalesOrderHeader

--update all statistics available in database
EXEC sp_updatestats

--manually deleting stats
--DROP STATISTICS
--<<SCHEMA NAME>>.<<TABLE NAME>>.<<Statastics name>>
DROP STATISTICS Sales.SalesOrderHeader.st_DueDate_SalesOrderHeader
```

How it works...

The optimizer creates statistics on key column(s) for an index created on a table or view, when the index is created. Apart from that, if you have the `Auto_Create_Statistics` option set to `ON`, the optimizer creates single column statistics, if it is not already present for the column(s) used as a predicate in your query. If you feel any query is under-performing, check all predicates; if you find any column has missing statistics, you will have to create it manually. Sometimes, DTA (Database Tuning Advisor) also suggests some columns for statistics, and you will have to manually create those statistics on column(s).

Generally, in a synchronous statistics update, before your query is compiled, SQL Server checks for the out-of-date statistics and if it finds any, it first causes the statistics to update, and then your query is executed with the up-to-date statistics that block the query, until the update statistics process is over. In the asynchronous update process, if the compiler finds any out-of-date statistics, it doesn't hold your query, instead it compiles the query with old statistics, executes the query, and then updates the statistics, so that the next query will benefit from newly updated statistics.

Step 4 enables an auto-update setting at database level that will check whether your current statistics, after having DML commands like `INSERT/UPDATE/DELETE` on your table, are out-of-date or not. If it is out-of-date or there is a schema modification, such as new index creation, the optimizer will first update your statistics, even before executing your query, so you may experience slow performance when the optimizer updates statistics while executing the query.

There's more...

By default, the members of the `sysadmin` fixed server role, the members of the `db_owner` fixed database role, or the owner of the object can create/update statistics.

Histogram:

A histogram is a kind of table generated by SQL Server for statistics. Consider it as a statistical report of the column with statistics that show the number of values in range within the minimum and maximum.

For example, consider there were 1500 children born in one maternity hospital in the year 2011, and it is now intended to find the highest and lowest birth weight of the new-born children in hospital, along with total number of children in each range. So the range would be like 0 KG to 1 KG, 1 KG to 2 KG, 2 KG to 3 KG, 3 KG to 4 KG, 4 KG to 5 KG, and 5 KG to 6 KG, where lower bound of the range is excluded and upper bound of the range is included.

By looking at the hospital chart, one can get an idea about the range with the highest number of children, and vice versa. A histogram works the same way; by looking at a histogram, we can understand the pattern of data in a table.

Let us look at one small example to confirm this. Execute the following T-SQL query:

```
--selecting AdventureWork2012 database
USE AdventureWorks2012
GO


--looking at statistics of SalesOrderHeader Table for index
--"PK_SalesOrderHeader_SalesOrderID
DBCC SHOW_STATISTICS ("Sales.SalesOrderHeader",PK_SalesOrderHeader_
SalesOrderID)

--counting total rows between two SalesOrderId to confirm the
--results of Histograme.
select Count(SalesOrderID) from Sales.SalesOrderHeader where
SalesOrderID between 43659 and 75123
```

The T-SQL query execution would give you a screen similar to the following screenshot:

```
USE AdventureWorks2012
GO

--seeing statistics of SalesOrderHeader Table for index "PK_SalesOrderHeader_SalesOrderID
DBCC SHOW_STATISTICS ("Sales.SalesOrderHeader",PK_SalesOrderHeader_SalesOrderID)

--counting total rows between two SalesOrderId to confirm the results of Histograme.
select Count(SalesOrderID) from Sales.SalesOrderHeader where SalesOrderID between 43659 and 75123
```

	Name	Updated	Rows	Rows Sampled	Steps	Density	Average key length	String Index	Filter Expression	Unfiltered Rows
1	PK_SalesOrderHeader_SalesOrderID	Aug 2 2010 5:26PM	31465	31465	2	1	4	NO	NULL	31465

	All density	Average Length	Columns
1	3.178134E-05	4	SalesOrderID

Result sets generated from DBCC command

	RANGE_HI_KEY	RANGE_ROWS	EQ_ROWS	DISTINCT_RANGE_ROWS	AVG_RANGE_ROWS
1	43659	0	1	0	1
2	75123	31463	1	31463	1

3rd result sets called Histogram

	(No column name)
1	31465

result set generated from SELECT statement

Now, let us understand what histogram tries to convey.

This histogram shows two steps (two rows), **RANGE_HI_KEY** in the first row shows the value **43659** with **1** matched row in **EQ_ROWS**. It means that if you query the Sales.SalesOrderHeader table with an exact search of 43659 for the SalesOrderID column, it will return one row only, which you can confirm by executing the SELECT statement on the said table.

The second row in the **RANGE_HI_KEY** column shows the **75123** column, which again shows **1** matched row in the **EQ_ROWS** column, and the **RANGE_ROWS** column shows **31463** rows between the range of **43659** and **75123**. The SELECT query given here shows a count of **31465**, which means:

31463 rows of range + 1 matched row of 43659 + 1 matched row of 75123 = 31465

The DISTINCT_RANGE_ROWS column in the second row shows that the total number of rows between the ranges are **31463**, and that all **31463** rows are unique (distinct). This is how the SQL Server query optimizer knows how many rows will be in a result set after matching the predicate given in the WHERE or ON clause of the SELECT statement, even before executing your SELECT query. This helps the optimizer to choose the proper execution plan in which it decides which index to use, whether to go for seek or scan, and so on.

> Here, in this example, histogram has shown two steps for the table `Sales.SalesOrderHeader`, in two rows. It can show you a maximum of 200 steps. Inserting more rows into the table increases the range of steps and the number of rows between two ranges. A histogram table gets updated as and when statistics get updated.

Density:

A histogram can show you the distribution of values for the first leading column, whereas **Density Vector** is used to measure cross-column correlation.

While making an execution plan, the query optimizer chooses the best-suited plan for a query by looking at query selectivity. A column with high selectivity returns a small number of rows, and one with low selectivity returns big result sets, which is why the query cost will be high in the second scenario.

The query optimizer finds selectivity by looking at the density of the column used in the WHERE and ON clauses of JOIN.

The relationship of selectivity with density is inverse; generally, a high-selectivity column would have low density and a low-selectivity column would have high density.

Density is calculated with the following formula:

Density=1.00/Number of distinct value in column

Let us look at the density table returned by statistics, and also manually calculate the density of columns, to tally it with the density returned by the statistics object:

```
--looking at the statistics of
--"PK_SalesOrderDetail_SalesOrderID_SalesOrderDetailID"
--this query will return 3 result sets
DBCC SHOW_STATISTICS ("Sales.SalesOrderDetail","PK_SalesOrderDetail_
SalesOrderID_SalesOrderDetailID")
GO


--manually confirming density of "SalesOrderID" column to
--match up with density of SalesOrderID column return by
--"DBCC SHOW_STATISTICS" (4th result set)
SELECT 1.000/ count (DISTINCT SalesOrderID) AS Manual_Density_
SalesOrderID FROM Sales.SalesOrderDetail
GO


--manually confirming density of "SalesOrderID" AND
--"SalesOrderDetailID" columns to match up with
```

```
--density of SalesOrderID,SalesOrderDetailID columns
--return by "DBCC SHOW_STATISTICS"(5th result set)
SELECT 1.000/count(*) AS Manual_Density_SalesOrderID_
SalesOrderDetailID FROM(
SELECT DISTINCT SalesOrderID,SalesOrderDetailID FROM Sales.
SalesOrderDetail
) AS t
GO
```

If all three queries given in the previous script are executed together, five result sets will be returned, as per the following screenshot:

Results | Messages

	Name	Updated	Rows	Rows Sampled	Steps	Density	Average key length	String Index	Filter Expression	Unfiltered Rows
1	PK_SalesOrderDetail_SalesOrderID_SalesOrderDeta...	Aug 2 2010 5:26PM	121317	121317	152	0.2695632	8	NO	NULL	121317

	All density	Average Length	Columns
1	3.178134E-05	4	SalesOrderID
2	8.242868E-06	8	SalesOrderID, SalesOrderDetailID

	RANGE_HI_KEY	RANGE_ROWS	EQ_ROWS	DISTINCT_RANGE_ROWS	AVG_RANGE_ROWS
1	43659	0	12	0	1
2	43692	282	28	32	8.8125
3	43898	716	28	205	3.492683
4	44079	403	27	180	2.238889
5	44288	766	34	208	3.682692
6	44488	570	27	199	2.864322
7	44538	614	35	49	12.53061
8	44570	370	32	31	11.93548
9	44758	409	27	187	2.187166
10	44801	504	26	42	12
11	45047	306	26	245	1.24898
12	45288	647	27	240	2.695833
13	45344	644	22	55	11.70909
14	45550	509	26	205	2.482927
15	45779	488	14	228	2.140351
16	46028	716	29	248	2.887097
17	46049	249	35	20	12.45
18	46105	715	35	55	13
19	46333	348	36	227	1.53304
20	46387	634	29	53	11.96226
21	46614	444	60	226	1.964602
22	46638	437	53	23	19
23	46662	505	57	23	21.95652
24	46930	641	21	267	2.400749
25	46957	446	56	26	17.15385
26	46988	683	59	30	22.76667
27	47018	620	57	29	21.37931
28	47042	489	53	23	21.26087

	Manual_Density_SalesOrderID
1	0.00003178134435

	Manual_Density_SalesOrderID_SalesOrderDetailID
1	0.00000824286785

Out of these five result set, the first three result sets come from the `DBCC SHOW_STATISTICS` command.

The second result sets out of these five, represents the density vector, the fourth result set is a manual calculation of density for `SalesOrderID`, and fifth result set is a manual calculation of density for `SalesOrderID` and `SalesOrderDetailID`.

Statistics density comes in the exponential value form, whereas the density we have calculated shows a real number. Let us confirm whether both are the same or not, by manual math calculations:

Statistics Density 3.178134E-05: 3.178134/100000=0.00003178134435

Statistics Density 8.242868E-06: 8.242868/1000000=0.00000824286785

So, this is all about the first column, **All density**, from the density vector result set from the statistics object. The second column is **Average Length**, which displays the length of the key. In first row, it shows **4**; SalesOrderID is an INT column, so it consumes 4 bytes. The second row shows **8**; 4 bytes for SalesOrderID (INT) and 4 bytes for SalesOrderDetailID (INT).

The last column, **Columns**, shows column names for those columns whose information is being displayed.

The density vector is used to display density for all columns, starting from leading column along with all other column(s). The PK_SalesOrderDetail_SalesOrderID_ SalesOrderDetailID statistics object has multi-column statistics on two columns, so you are able to see two rows in the density vector result sets.

Suppose we have table T1 with three columns: Col1, Col2, and Col3. If all three columns were to be included in the same statistics (multi-column statistics), then the first row would display details of density, average length, and column name for Col1, the second row would display the same details for both Col1 and Col2, and the third row for Col1, Col2, and Col3.

Effects of statistics on non-key column

The index always plays an important role, as far as the performance of the SELECT statement is concerned. Actually, the query optimizer first checks statistics of the predicate and then decides which index is supposed to be used. Generally, creating an index creates statistics on key columns of an index, by default, but it doesn't mean that statistics on non-key columns wouldn't get any benefit if it is available.

It is neither affordable nor desirable to have an index on each and every column of the table, or on all those columns that you use in predicate, because index comes with an overhead: it needs space to store itself as well as each DML statement update index.

Mostly, it is a good idea to have an index on a column you use in the WHERE or ON clauses, but if for any reason, it is not possible to create an index on the column you use in predicate (in other words, the non-key column), it is a good practice to at least create statistics on that column. If Auto_Create_Statistics is ON, the query optimizer will perform this task on behalf of you.

Getting ready

Generally, `Auto_Create_Statistics` is ON by default for databases, but let us make sure that it remains OFF (for this exercise only) to check the effect of statistics on a non-key column. Execute the following T-SQL script:

```
ALTER DATABASE AdventureWorks2012 SET AUTO_CREATE_STATISTICS OFF
GO


ALTER DATABASE AdventureWorks2012 SET AUTO_UPDATE_STATISTICS OFF
GO
```

After making the proper settings at database level, let us now create one table that will be used in demonstration of this recipe:

```
--creating one table "SaleOrdDemo" from
--Sales.SalesOrderHeader table of AdventureWorks2012
SELECT * into SalesOrdDemo FROM Sales.SalesOrderHeader
GO
```

How to do it...

Follow the steps provided here to perform this recipe:

1. Before we start anything, let us confirm that we have no statistics with us at the moment, for the `SalesOrdDemo` table, with the help of the following script:

```
SELECT
    object_id
    ,OBJECT_NAME(object_id) AS TableName
    ,name AS StatisticsName
    ,auto_created
FROM
    sys.stats
where object_id=OBJECT_ID('SalesOrdDemo')
Order by object_id desc
GO
```

2. Now, create one clustered index on the `SalesOrderID` column of the `SalesOrdDemo` table, which will create statistics for the `SalesOrderID` column:

```
CREATE Clustered Index idx_SalesOrdDemo_SalesOrderID
ON SalesOrdDemo(SalesOrderID)
GO
```

3. By running the previously given `SELECT` script, it can be confirmed that statistics is created automatically while creating a clustered index. Now, we are going to execute the `SELECT` statement by keeping the execution plan ON:

```
SELECT
    s.SalesOrderID,
    so.SalesOrderDetailID
FROM
    SalesOrdDemo AS s join Sales.SalesOrderDetail AS so
ON
    s.SalesOrderID = so.SalesOrderID
WHERE
    s.DueDate='2005-09-19 00:00:00.000'
```

4. Here is the screen capture of the execution plan of the previous query; please note that the `SalesOrdDemo` table has clustered index scan, which is expected because we have not used `SalesOrderID` in the `WHERE` clause. The `SalesOrderDetails` table has non-clustered index scan. The **Estimated Number of Rows** in the execution plan is **2362.49** and the **Actual Number of Rows** in execution plan is **5**.

5. Now is the time to create statistics on the `DueDate` column of the `SalesOrdDemo` table, since we have used the `DueDate` column in the `WHERE` clause but it is not part of the index.

```
CREATE STATISTICS st_SaledOrdDemo_DueDate ON SalesOrdDemo(DueDate)
```

6. After creating `STATISTICS` on the non-key column `DueDate`, let us again run the same `SELECT` query we ran in the previous script, without making any change to the execution plan.

```
SELECT
    s.SalesOrderID,
    so.SalesOrderDetailID
FROM
    SalesOrdDemo AS s join Sales.SalesOrderDetail AS so
ON
    s.SalesOrderID = so.SalesOrderID
wHERE
    s.DueDate='2005-09-19 00:00:00.000'
```

7. Here is a screenshot of the previous query we ran. If you observe, the `SalesOrdDemo` table has again used clustered index scan, as expected, but the `SalesOrderDetails` table has used clustered index seek rather than non-clustered index scan, which is a better situation as it uses only 2% of the cost during execution of the query. **Estimated Number of Rows** in the execution plan is **5.07** and **Actual Number of Rows** is **5**, which again is a better situation.

How it works...

If the query optimizer gets the statistics of each column used in predicate, it will have better a idea of the number of rows going to return, based on predicate, and will also know the pattern of data that helps the query optimizer in selecting the best route to execute your query. This will result in good execution, and we can see its effect via the execution plan generated.

Find out-of-date statistics and get it correct

The statistics object is the major source of information about data distribution for the predicate. Without knowing the exact data distribution, the query optimizer cannot have cardinality estimation, which is the process of calculating number of rows to return by applying the predicate.

After creating the statistics for the column, the column becomes out-of-date after executing DML commands, such as INSERT, UPDATE, and DELETE, because these commands change data, thereby affecting data distribution. In this scenario, a statistics update is needed.

In highly active tables, statistics become outdated in maybe a few hours; for static tables, statistics become outdated maybe in a few weeks. The decision about out-of-date statistics totally depends on the DML statements executed on the table

Before we move back to the core subject and start writing down the script, it is mandatory to draw attention to some facts and also to look at flashbacks.

Till SQL Server 2000, the query optimizer used to track each insert, update, and delete operation on the table and increment the value of the RowModCtr (Row Modification Counter) column in the SysIndexes system view. As soon as statistics get updated, RowModCtr reinitializes the value and starts count from zero again. So, by looking at the SysIndexes system view and the value of the RowModCtr column, we get to know whether statistics are out-of-date or not.

After SQL Server 2000, SQL Server Engine has changed the pattern of capturing the value of modification in tables. Rather than capturing each insert, update, and delete operation for every row, it now counts modifications made to each column and stores them. The query optimizer decides whether statistics are out-of-date or not, based on values stored for ColModCtr. Fortunately or unfortunately, ColModCtr is hidden for the user by all documented system views.

But the good news is, Sys.SysIndexes is still available in SQL Server 2012 so we can even use RowModCtr to decide whether statistics are out-of-date or not. Though RowModCtr is not as accurate as ColModCtr but it is better to have something rather than nothing.

Getting ready

In order to get the desired information, the following system view and compatibility view will be used.

Sys.SysIndexes: This compatibility view provides `RowModCtr` column, which is the heart of the script.

Sys.Indexes: Though we can get information about `RowModCtr` from the `Sys.SysIndexes` view, we have to join it with `Sys.Indexes`, using the table's ID, in order to get statistics name as well as the last update date.

Sys.Objects: The schema name will be received from the `Sys.Objects` view.

How to do it...

The following script will show you all statistics that have a greater `RowModCtr` value than zero, in descending order along with the `UPDATE STATISTICS` command:

```
SELECT DISTINCT
    OBJECT_NAME(SI.object_id) as Table_Name
    ,SI.[name] AS Statistics_Name
    ,STATS_DATE(SI.object_id, SI.index_id) AS Last_Stat_Update_Date
    ,SSI.rowmodctr AS RowModCTR
    ,SP.rows AS Total_Rows_In_Table
    ,'UPDATE STATISTICS ['+SCHEMA_NAME(SO.schema_id)+'].['
        + object_name(SI.object_id) + ']'
            + SPACE(2) + SI.[name] AS Update_Stats_Script
FROM
    sys.indexes AS SI (nolock) JOIN sys.objects AS SO (nolock)
ON
    SI.object_id=SO.object_id
JOIN
    sys.sysindexes SSI (nolock)
ON
    SI.object_id=SSI.id
AND
    SI.index_id=SSI.indid
JOIN
    sys.partitions AS SP
ON
    SI.object_id=SP.object_id
```

```
WHERE
    SSI.rowmodctr>0
AND
    STATS_DATE(SI.object_id, SI.index_id) IS NOT NULL
AND
    SO.type='U'
ORDER BY
    SSI.rowmodctr DESC
```

How it works...

As shown in the script, we are doing all these exercises to get the following information:

- How long since we have had the last statistics update

- How many transactions happen on the table after updating statistics

- What T-SQL script would be used to update statistics

- Whether it is feasible to update statistics or not; the decision should be made based on comparing the RowModCTR column with Total_Rows_In_table column.

Expertise is definitely required to read and understand the number in the RowModCtr column and find their criticalness before actually updating statistics.

Now, the question comes to mind about why we need to update statistics by ourselves, especially when we have set Auto_Update_Statistics to ON at the database level.

Well, even though you have set the Auto_Update_Statistics option, it will be triggered after the optimizer considers statistics as out-of-date; the RowModCtr and ColModCtr columns help the optimizer to decide whether statistics is out-of-date or not. As per Technet Library, the following are the criteria for deciding the same:

- The table size has gone from zero to more than zero rows

- The number of rows in the table, when the statistics were gathered, was 500 or less, and the ColModCtr of the leading column of the statistics object has changed by more than 500 since then

- The table had more than 500 rows when the statistics were gathered, and the ColModCtr of the leading column of the statistics object has changed by more than 500 + 20% of the number of rows in the table when the statistics were gathered

This means that if I have 1,000,000 (one million) rows in a table, then the optimizer considers it out-of-date after inserting 200,500 new rows. Until we insert 200,500 new rows, we have to work with old statistics. Is this desirable? The answer may be "yes" for some databases, but not for every database. This is the reason we have said that expertise is required for this operation, to decide criticalness.

There's more...

There is no direct and documented way of accessing the value of `ColModCtr`, as it is hidden and intend for use by the query optimizer itself. However, there is a way to look at this value in an undocumented way by looking at a system view (`Sys.SysRsCols.rcmodified`) via **Dedicated Administrator Connection** (**DAC**) in SQL Server 2008 R2. At the time of writing this chapter, SQL Server Denali CTP 3 is available, and DAC is not available in this version of SQL Server. For more information about how to connect as DAC in SQL Server, look at `http://www.sqlhub.com/2011/01/life-savior-dedicated-administrator.html`.

Effect of statistics on a filtered index

The filtered column index is one of the enhancements for non-clustered indexes, provided in Microsoft SQL Server 2008, and it is available in SQL Server 2012. We can consider a simple, non-clustered index with the `WHERE` clause as a filtered index. A well-defined, filtered index reduces maintenance costs, reduces index storage, and improves query performance. Since this chapter is about statistics, we are not going to see how a filtered index works, in this recipe. Look at the *Increasing performance by filtered index* recipe in *Chapter 9, Implementing Indexes*, to learn more about filtered indexes.

Getting ready

There is a table named `WorkOrder` in the `Production` schema in database `AdventureWorks2012`, and this is the table that we will use for our demonstration.

How to do it...

Follow the steps provided here to perform this recipe:

1. Create one non-clustered index on the `CurrencyRateID` column of the `SalesOrdDemo` table with following script:

   ```
   CREATE INDEX idx_WorkOrder_ScrapReasonID on [Production].
   [WorkOrder] (ScrapReasonID)
   GO
   ```

2. Creating a non-clustered index would create a statistics object automatically with the same name we have provided for the index.

   ```
   DBCC SHOW_STATISTICS ("[Production].[WorkOrder]",idx_WorkOrder_
   ScrapReasonID)
   ```

3. Here is the screenshot of the statistics window generated by the previous script:

	Name	Updated	Rows	Rows Sampled	Steps	Density	Average key length	String Index	Filter Expression	Unfiltered Rows
1	idx_WorkOrder_ScrapReasonID	Dec 28 2011 12:43PM	72591	72591	16	0.02380952	4.020085	NO	NULL	72591

	All density	Average Length	Columns
1	0.05882353	0.02008513	ScrapReasonID
2	1.377581E-05	4.020085	ScrapReasonID, WorkOrderID

	RANGE_HI_KEY	RANGE_ROWS	EQ_ROWS	DISTINCT_RANGE_ROWS	AVG_RANGE_ROWS
1	NULL	0	71862	0	1
2	1	0	44	0	1
3	2	0	44	0	1
4	3	0	54	0	1
5	4	0	45	0	1
6	6	42	44	1	42
7	7	0	32	0	1
8	8	0	37	0	1
9	9	0	47	0	1
10	10	0	37	0	1
11	11	0	52	0	1
12	12	0	37	0	1
13	13	0	63	0	1
14	14	0	52	0	1
15	15	0	48	0	1
16	16	0	51	0	1

4. After observing the **All density** column of the density vector result set, let us drop the index we created previously and recreate a non-clustered index with a filter:

```
DROP INDEX idx_WorkOrder_ScrapReasonID on [Production].[WorkOrder]
GO


CREATE INDEX idx_WorkOrder_ScrapReasonID on [Production].
[WorkOrder](ScrapReasonID)
WHERE ScrapReasonID IS NOT NULL
GO
```

5. Now, let us look at the **All density** column of the density vector result set, with the following script:

```
DBCC SHOW_STATISTICS ("[Production].[WorkOrder]",idx_WorkOrder_
ScrapReasonID)
GO


DROP INDEX idx_WorkOrder_ScrapReasonID on [Production].[WorkOrder]
GO
```

6. Now, look at the following screenshot of statistics, generated after creating a filtered index:

	Name	Updated	Rows	Rows Sampled	Steps	Density	Average key length	String Index	Filter Expression	Unfiltered Rows
1	idx_WorkOrder_ScrapReasonID	Dec 28 2011 12:50PM	729	729	15	0.02380952	6	NO	([ScrapReasonID] IS NOT NULL)	72591

	All density	Average Length	Columns
1	0.0625	2	ScrapReasonID
2	0.001371742	6	ScrapReasonID, WorkOrderID

	RANGE_HI_KEY	RANGE_ROWS	EQ_ROWS	DISTINCT_RANGE_ROWS	AVG_RANGE_ROWS
1	1	0	44	0	1
2	2	0	44	0	1
3	3	0	54	0	1
4	4	0	45	0	1
5	6	42	44	1	42
6	7	0	32	0	1
7	8	0	37	0	1
8	9	0	47	0	1
9	10	0	37	0	1
10	11	0	52	0	1
11	12	0	37	0	1
12	13	0	63	0	1
13	14	0	52	0	1
14	15	0	48	0	1
15	16	0	51	0	1

How it works...

Now, since we know that DBCC SHOW_STATISTICS returns three result sets. If you observe the first result sets, you get to know the difference in the **Row Sampled** column. In the first screenshot, it is **72591**, and the recent screenshot has only **729**, which is big difference. In the **Filter Expression** column, the filter we have used will be displayed rather than NULL.

In the **All density** column, the first row represents the ScriptReasonID column. There is no major difference between the two screenshots but the second row shows a major difference, because the ScriptReasonID column is a non-clustered index that points to the clustered index of the table WorkOrderID, and many WorkOrderID, are eliminated due to the filter we have applied.

13
Table and Index Partitioning

In this chapter we will cover:

- ▶ Partitioning a table with RANGE LEFT
- ▶ Partitioning a table with RANGE RIGHT
- ▶ Deleting and loading bulk data by splitting, merging, and switching partitions (sliding window)

Introduction

If data in a database table keeps growing and the number of records in a table reaches a count in billions or more, data retrieval and data manipulation operations on such a large table may become difficult. Due to very huge data, even simple `INSERT`, `UPDATE`, or `DELETE` operations can take a long time. Tasks such as deleting certain old data and rebuilding indexes become hard to perform. Managing and maintaining query performance becomes a challenge in this situation.

In the olden days of SQL Server, with versions prior to 2005, you might have worked with partitioned views to deal with huge amount of data. With SQL Server 2005, Microsoft introduced a great feature named Table Partitioning, which allows us to divide our data horizontally, into multiple partitions. SQL Server also allows us to put these multiple partitions on multiple disks by configuring them with multiple filegroups. This greatly improves the performance of queries when retrieving data in a certain fashion, because SQL Server needs to access only required partitions where the requested data is located, which eliminates the need for scanning or seeking other partitions.

With table partitioning, the following tasks can be performed in an efficient manner:

- ▸ Retrieving a certain range of data
- ▸ Deleting and archiving old data
- ▸ Loading new millions of data in bulk
- ▸ Rebuilding and reorganizing indexes

We can also partition an index on a large table and rebuild or reorganize a partitioned index on a particular partition. Because Table/Index partitioning is a very important feature that helps in managing a large amount of data in an efficient manner, this becomes the subject of this chapter.

> You can create as many as 15,000 partitions in SQL Server 2012. You cannot partition a column of the data type text, ntext, image, xml, timestamp, varchar (max), nvarchar (max), or varbinary (max).

Partitioning a table with RANGE LEFT

Let's suppose that you are required to design a database and there is one particular table that is expected to contain millions of rows. To improve the performance, you decide to partition this particular table based on ID column (identity column) in such a way that each partition contains a certain number of rows, rather than having all the millions of rows in one single table. Initially, you decide to start with four partitions, so that they contain rows as follows:

- ▸ Partition 1: Rows with ID values greater than or equal to 0
- ▸ Partition 2: Rows with ID values from 1 to 1,000,000
- ▸ Partition 3: Rows with ID values from 1,000,001 to 2,000,000
- ▸ Partition 4: Rows with ID values from 2,000,001 to 3,000,000

However, in our case, partition 1 is never going to contain any rows, because the value in the ID column will start from 1, increasing by 1, and partition 1 will always remain empty; it is still a good idea to have this partition range for scalability and the future requirement of archiving data.

Table partitioning has two configurations to set range values of partitions—RANGE LEFT and RANGE RIGHT. In this example, we will use RANGE LEFT to perform table partitioning.

To partition a table, there are two main objects that need to be created: **partition function** and **partition scheme**. First, a partition function is created to define the range values of the partitions, and then a partition scheme is created to defines the physical storage locations of defined partitions.

In this example, you will learn how to create a partition function, a partition scheme, and then a partition table on a partition scheme to partition data, based on an integer column value with the RANGE LEFT option.

Getting ready

To follow this recipe practically, all you have to do is create an instance of SQL Server 2012. Also, Sample_DB uses the path C:\SQLData. So, make sure that you have the specified path configured.

The following are the prerequisites for this recipe:

  ▸ An instance of SQL Server 2012 Developer or Enterprise Evaluation edition
  ▸ The path C:\SQLData should be available on your machine

How to do it...

Follow the given steps to implement table partitioning with the RANGE LEFT option:

1. Start SQL Server Management Studio and connect to SQL Server.
2. Execute the following T-SQL script to create the Sample_DB database.

```
USE master
GO

--Creating Sample_DB database
--Dropping the database if it exists.
--DROP DATABASE Sample_DB
IF DB_ID('Sample_DB') IS NOT NULL
    DROP DATABASE [Sample_DB]

CREATE DATABASE [Sample_DB]
ON PRIMARY
(
    NAME = N'Sample_DB'
    ,FILENAME = N'C:\SQLData\Sample_DB.mdf'
    ,SIZE = 3072KB , FILEGROWTH = 1024KB
)
,FILEGROUP [FG_1]
(
```

```
        NAME = N'FG_1_DataFile'
        ,FILENAME = N'C:\SQLData\FG_1_DataFile.ndf'
        ,SIZE = 3072KB , FILEGROWTH = 1024KB
    )
    ,FILEGROUP [FG_2]
    (
        NAME = N'FG_2_DataFile'
        ,FILENAME = N'C:\SQLData\FG_2_DataFile.ndf'
        ,SIZE = 3072KB , FILEGROWTH = 1024KB
    )
    ,FILEGROUP [FG_3]
    (
        NAME = N'FG_3_DataFile'
        ,FILENAME = N'C:\SQLData\FG_3_DataFile.ndf'
        ,SIZE = 3072KB , FILEGROWTH = 1024KB
    )
    ,FILEGROUP [FG_N]
    (
        NAME = N'FG_N_DataFile'
        ,FILENAME = N'C:\SQLData\FG_N_DataFile.ndf'
        ,SIZE = 3072KB , FILEGROWTH = 1024KB
    )
    LOG ON
    (
        NAME = N'Sample_DB_log'
        ,FILENAME = N'C:\SQLData\Sample_DB_log.ldf'
        ,SIZE = 1024KB , FILEGROWTH = 10%
    )

    GO
```

3. Create the partition function `pf_OneMillion_LeftRange` with RANGE LEFT, by running the following T-SQL script:

```
USE Sample_DB
GO

--Creating Partition Function with RANGE LEFT
CREATE PARTITION FUNCTION pf_OneMillion_LeftRange(INT)
AS RANGE LEFT FOR VALUES(0,1000000,2000000,3000000)

GO
```

4. Verify that the partition function `pf_OneMillion_LeftRange` has been created with the specified partition ranges:

```
USE Sample_DB
GO

--Verify that the Partition Function
--and Range Values
SELECT
    name
    ,function_id
    ,type
    ,type_desc
    ,fanout
    ,boundary_value_on_right
    ,create_date
FROM sys.partition_functions

SELECT
    function_id
    ,boundary_id
    ,parameter_id
    ,value
FROM sys.partition_range_values

GO
```

5. After executing the preceding query, you should see a result similar to the one shown in the following screenshot:

	name	function_id	type	type_desc	fanout	boundary_value_on_right	create_date
1	pf_OneMillion_LeftRange	65536	R	RANGE	5	0	2012-02-12 12:30:14.657

	function_id	boundary_id	parameter_id	value
1	65536	1	1	0
2	65536	2	1	1000000
3	65536	3	1	2000000
4	65536	4	1	3000000

6. Now, run the following script, which will create and verify the partition scheme `ps_OneMillion_LeftRange` based on the partition function `pf_OneMillion_LeftRange` that we just created:

```
USE Sample_DB
GO

--Creating Partition Scheme
```

```
CREATE PARTITION SCHEME ps_OneMillion_LeftRange
AS PARTITION pf_OneMillion_LeftRange
TO ([PRIMARY],[FG_1],[FG_2],[FG_3],[FG_N])

--Verify that the Partition Scheme
--has been created
SELECT
    name
    ,data_space_id
    ,type
    ,type_desc
    ,function_id
FROM sys.partition_schemes
GO
```

7. The preceding query should give you output similar to that shown in the following screenshot:

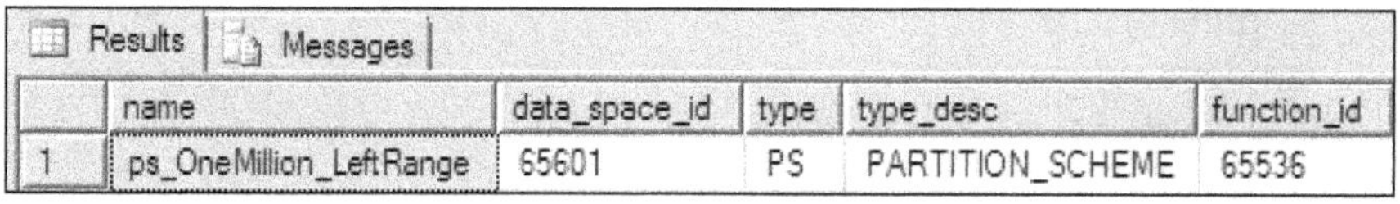

	name	data_space_id	type	type_desc	function_id
1	ps_OneMillion_LeftRange	65601	PS	PARTITION_SCHEME	65536

8. Now, let us create our table `tbl_SampleRecords` on the partition scheme `ps_OneMillion_LeftRange`, that we defined, and insert 5 million sample rows:

```
USE Sample_DB
GO

--Create Sample Table
IF OBJECT_ID('tbl_SampleRecords') IS NOT NULL
    DROP TABLE tbl_SampleRecords

CREATE TABLE tbl_SampleRecords
(
    ID INT
    ,SomeData sysname
    ,CONSTRAINT pk_tbl_SampleRecords_id PRIMARY KEY CLUSTERED(ID)
) ON ps_OneMillion_LeftRange (ID)
GO

--Inserting Sample Records
INSERT INTO tbl_SampleRecords
SELECT TOP 5000000
    ID = ROW_NUMBER() OVER(ORDER BY C1.name)
```

```
    ,SomeData = C1.name
FROM sys.columns AS C1
CROSS JOIN sys.columns AS C2
CROSS JOIN sys.columns AS C3
GO
```

> The preceding script may take a few seconds as it inserts 5 million records.

9. Now, verify the number of partitions and number of rows in each partition by using the following query:

```
USE Sample_DB
GO


--Verifying Partitions and Number of Records
SELECT
    partition_id
    ,object_id
    ,index_id
    ,partition_number
    ,rows
FROM sys.partitions
WHERE object_id = OBJECT_ID('tbl_SampleRecords')
GO
```

10. The preceding query should return a result similar to the one shown in the following screenshot:

	partition_id	object_id	index_id	partition_number	rows
1	72057594039042048	245575913	1	1	0
2	72057594039107584	245575913	1	2	1000000
3	72057594039173120	245575913	1	3	1000000
4	72057594039238656	245575913	1	4	1000000
5	72057594039304192	245575913	1	5	2000000

11. You can now fetch only those records that belong to a particular partition, with the following query:

```
USE Sample_DB
GO


--Fetching only records belonging to
--Partition 4
```

```
SELECT
     ID
     ,SomeData
FROM tbl_SampleRecords
WHERE $PARTITION.pf_OneMillion_LeftRange(ID)=4
```

How it works...

In this recipe, we first create a sample database named `Sample_DB`. If the database already exists, we first drop it and recreate it. The following filegroups along with their respective secondary data files are created when the `Sample_DB` database is created:

▶ FG_1

▶ FG_2

▶ FG_3

▶ FG_N

After creating our sample database using the `CREATE PARTITION FUNCTION` command, we create a partition function named `pf_oneMillion_LeftRange` by specifying the datatype of the partitioning column (`ID INT`) based on the table that will be partitioned. The partition function specifies `RANGE LEFT` values 0, 1000000, 2000000, and 3000000. These `RANGE LEFT` values specify the boundary values for each partition, designating each range value as the last highest value in its corresponding partition. In other words, the boundary value will belong to the partition on the *left* when a partition function is defined with `RANGE LEFT`. Thus, for this partitioned function, we will have a total of 5 partitions, as follows:

▶ Partition 1: Rows with ID values less than or equal to 0

▶ Partition 2: Rows with ID values from 1 to 1,000,000

▶ Partition 3: Rows with ID values from 1,000,001 to 2,000,000

▶ Partition 4: Rows with ID values from 2,000,001 to 3,000,000

▶ Partition 5: Rows with ID values greater than 3,000,000

A partition function defines the number of partitions in a partitioned table and range values for partitions. After creating the partition function, we verify it by querying the `sys.partition_functions` and `sys.partition_range_values` system catalog views. `sys.partition_functions` returns the list of all partition functions available in the database and `sys.partition_range_values` returns all boundary values (range values) specified in each partition function.

We then create a partition scheme using the `CREATE PARTITION SCHEME` command and map each partition specified by a partition function to a filegroup defined by a partition scheme. A partition scheme defines the storage scheme for each partition in a partitioned table. By querying `sys.partition_schemes`, we verify that the partition scheme has been created.

We then create our sample table called `tbl_SampleRecords`, with `ID` as the clustered primary key. Note that the syntax of `CREATE TABLE` is followed by the `ON ps_OneMillion_LeftRange(ID)` clause. This clause specifies the name of the partition scheme and the partitioning column, which happen to be `ps_OneMillion_LeftRange` and `ID`, respectively. Remember that the data type specified in the partition function and the data type of the partitioning column ID must match.

Once the table is created, we insert 5 million sample records. In order to generate 5 million sample rows, we cross join the system catalog view `sys.columns` twice and retrieve the top 5000000 rows of resulting cross joins. We generate the serial value of ID with the help of the `ROW_NUMBER()` function. The resulting rows will be inserted into our partitioned table `tbl_SampleRecords`.

By querying the `sys.partitions` catalog view, we examine the state of partitions and the number of rows in each partition. Note how the first partition remains empty because there is no record whose `ID` value is less than 1. Also notice that after the first 3 million rows are inserted into partitions 2, 3, and 4, each having 1 million rows, the remaining rows are inserted into partition 5, because partition 5 is the last partition and an open-ended partition.

Finally, we use the `$PARTITION.pf_OneMillion_LeftRange()` function to retrieve only rows of partition 4. This function accepts the value of the partitioning column (value of the `ID` column) and returns the partition number to which that particular value belongs. This is the most obvious benefit of table partitioning; once our table is partitioned, we can retrieve data only from a specific partition of the table and the remaining partitions are eliminated from being queried, which greatly improves the performance of queries.

Partitioning a table with RANGE RIGHT

As we saw previously, there are two ways to apply partition ranges while performing table partitioning. In this recipe, we will do the same table partitioning that we did in the previous recipe, *Partitioning table with RANGE LEFT*. However, this time we use the `RANGE RIGHT` option for our table partitioning.

Getting ready

The following are the prerequisites for this recipe:

▸ An instance of SQL Server 2012 Developer or Enterprise Evaluation edition

▸ Path `C:\SQLData` should be available on your machine

How to do it...

Follow the given steps to implement table partitioning with the RANGE RIGHT option:

1. Start SQL Server Management Studio and connect to SQL Server.

2. Execute the following T-SQL script to create the Sample_DB database.

```
USE master
GO
--Creating Sample_DB database
--if it does not exist.
--DROP DATABASE Sample_DB
IF DB_ID('Sample_DB') IS NOT NULL
    DROP DATABASE [Sample_DB]

CREATE DATABASE [Sample_DB]
ON  PRIMARY
(
    NAME = N'Sample_DB'
    ,FILENAME = N'C:\SQLData\Sample_DB.mdf'
    ,SIZE = 3072KB , FILEGROWTH = 1024KB
)
,FILEGROUP [FG_1]
(
    NAME = N'FG_1_DataFile'
    ,FILENAME = N'C:\SQLData\FG_1_DataFile.ndf'
    ,SIZE = 3072KB , FILEGROWTH = 1024KB
)
,FILEGROUP [FG_2]
(
    NAME = N'FG_2_DataFile'
    ,FILENAME = N'C:\SQLData\FG_2_DataFile.ndf'
    ,SIZE = 3072KB , FILEGROWTH = 1024KB
)
,FILEGROUP [FG_3]
(
    NAME = N'FG_3_DataFile'
    ,FILENAME = N'C:\SQLData\FG_3_DataFile.ndf'
    ,SIZE = 3072KB , FILEGROWTH = 1024KB
)
,FILEGROUP [FG_N]
(
    NAME = N'FG_N_DataFile'
    ,FILENAME = N'C:\SQLData\FG_N_DataFile.ndf'
```

```
    ,SIZE = 3072KB , FILEGROWTH = 1024KB
)
LOG ON
(
    NAME = N'Sample_DB_log'
    ,FILENAME = N'C:\SQLData\Sample_DB_log.ldf'
    ,SIZE = 1024KB , FILEGROWTH = 10%
)

GO
```

3. Create the partition function `pf_OneMillion_RightRange` with `RANGE RIGHT`, by running the following T-SQL script:

```
USE Sample_DB
GO

--Creating Partition Function with RANGE RIGHT
CREATE PARTITION FUNCTION pf_OneMillion_RightRange(INT)
AS RANGE RIGHT FOR VALUES(1,1000001,2000001,3000001)

GO
```

4. Verify that the partition function has been created along with its specified partition ranges:

```
USE Sample_DB
GO

--Verify that the Partition Function
--and Range Values.
SELECT
    name
    ,function_id
    ,type
    ,type_desc
    ,fanout
    ,boundary_value_on_right
    ,create_date
FROM sys.partition_functions

SELECT
    function_id
    ,boundary_id
    ,parameter_id
    ,value
FROM sys.partition_range_values

GO
```

> If you have performed the previous recipe, *Partitioning a table with RANGE LEFT*, you will find that the given script will also return the details, as shown in following output screenshot, for the partition function and its range values, as in the previous recipe.

5. After executing the previous query, you should see a result similar to the one shown in the following screenshot:

	name	function_id	type	type_desc	fanout	boundary_value_on_right	create_date
1	pf_OneMillion_RightRange	65536	R	RANGE	5	1	2012-02-12 12:55:11.660

	function_id	boundary_id	parameter_id	value
1	65536	1	1	1
2	65536	2	1	1000001
3	65536	3	1	2000001
4	65536	4	1	3000001

6. Now, run the following script, which will create and verify the partition scheme ps_OneMillion_RightRange based on the partition function pf_OneMillion_RightRange that we just created:

```
USE Sample_DB
GO


--Creating Partition Scheme
CREATE PARTITION SCHEME ps_OneMillion_RightRange
AS PARTITION pf_OneMillion_RightRange
TO ([PRIMARY],[FG_1],[FG_2],[FG_3],[FG_N])

--Verify that the Partition Scheme
--has been created
SELECT
    name
    ,data_space_id
    ,type
    ,type_desc
    ,function_id
FROM sys.partition_schemes
GO
```

> If you have performed the previous recipe, *Partitioning a table with RANGE LEFT*, the given script will also return the details, as shown in following output screenshot, for the partition function and its range values, as in the previous recipe.

7. The preceding query should give you a result similar to the one shown in the following screenshot:

	name	data_space_id	type	type_desc	function_id
1	ps_OneMillion_RightRange	65601	PS	PARTITION_SCHEME	65536

8. Now, let us create our table `tbl_SampleRecords` on the partition scheme `ps_OneMillion_RightRange`, that we defined, and insert 5 million sample rows:

```
USE Sample_DB
GO

--Create Sample Table
IF OBJECT_ID('tbl_SampleRecords') IS NOT NULL
    DROP TABLE tbl_SampleRecords

CREATE TABLE tbl_SampleRecords
(
    ID INT
    ,SomeData sysname
    ,CONSTRAINT pk_tbl_SampleRecords_id PRIMARY KEY CLUSTERED(ID)
) ON ps_OneMillion_RightRange (ID)
GO

--Insertinng Sample Records
INSERT INTO tbl_SampleRecords
SELECT TOP  5000000
    ID = ROW_NUMBER() OVER(ORDER BY C1.name)
    ,SomeData = C1.name
FROM sys.columns AS C1
CROSS JOIN sys.columns AS C2
CROSS JOIN sys.columns AS C3
GO
```

9. Verify the number of partitions and number of rows in each partition, by executing the following query:

```
USE Sample_DB
GO

--Verifying Partitions and Number of Records
SELECT
    partition_id
    ,object_id
    ,index_id
    ,partition_number
    ,rows
FROM sys.partitions
WHERE object_id = OBJECT_ID('tbl_SampleRecords')
GO
```

10. The preceding query will return a result that should be similar to the one shown in the following screenshot:

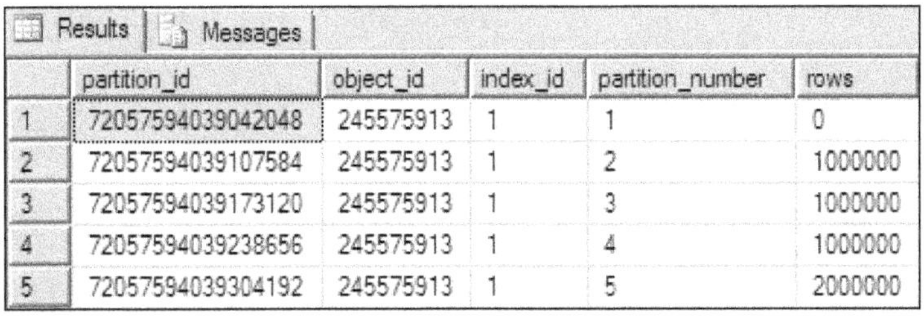

	partition_id	object_id	index_id	partition_number	rows
1	72057594039042048	245575913	1	1	0
2	72057594039107584	245575913	1	2	1000000
3	72057594039173120	245575913	1	3	1000000
4	72057594039238656	245575913	1	4	1000000
5	72057594039304192	245575913	1	5	2000000

11. Click on the **Include Actual Execution Plan** button in the SSMS query window. Now, execute the following query to fetch the row by creating a filter on the partitioning column, and observe the execution plan of the query:

```
USE Sample_DB
GO

--Following query will access only one
--partition to which the 499999 belongs
SELECT
    ID
    ,SomeData
FROM tbl_SampleRecords
WHERE ID = 4999999
```

12. After execution of the preceding query, look at the execution plan in the **Execution Plan** tab and hover the mouse over the **Clustered Index Seek** operator. You should see the following tool-tip window:

Clustered Index Seek (Clustered)

Scanning a particular range of rows from a clustered index.

Physical Operation	Clustered Index Seek
Logical Operation	Clustered Index Seek
Actual Execution Mode	Row
Estimated Execution Mode	Row
Storage	RowStore
Actual Number of Rows	1
Actual Number of Batches	0
Estimated I/O Cost	0.003125
Estimated Operator Cost	0.0032831 (100%)
Estimated CPU Cost	0.0001581
Estimated Subtree Cost	0.0032831
Number of Executions	1
Estimated Number of Executions	1
Estimated Number of Rows	1
Estimated Row Size	143 B
Actual Rebinds	0
Actual Rewinds	0
Partitioned	True
Actual Partition Count	1
Ordered	True
Node ID	0

Object
[Sample_DB].[dbo].[tbl_SampleRecords].
[pk_tbl_SampleRecords_id]
Output List
[Sample_DB].[dbo].[tbl_SampleRecords].ID, [Sample_DB].
[dbo].[tbl_SampleRecords].SomeData
Seek Predicates
Seek Keys[1]: Prefix: PtnId1000, [Sample_DB].[dbo].
[tbl_SampleRecords].ID = Scalar Operator(RangePartitionNew
([@1],(1),(1),(1000001),(2000001),(3000001))), Scalar
Operator([@1])

> Always try to keep your indexes aligned with your partitions. This means that if the table is partitioned, the values in indexes should also be aligned and partitioned according to the partitions. You can align an index by specifying the name of a partition scheme in the ON clause in the CREATE INDEX command. For more information on how to create a partitioned index, look at the syntax of the CREATE INDEX command at http://msdn.microsoft.com/en-us/library/ms188783.aspx.
>
> If you do not specify the ON clause in CREATE INDEX, the index is created on the same partition as the underlying table. By aligning your indexes with your table partitions, you can avoid and eliminate unnecessary partitions from being scanned/sought in queries, and this improves query performance.

How it works...

In this recipe, we first create a sample database named Sample_DB. If the database already exists, we first drop it and recreate it. The following filegroups, along with their respective secondary data files, are created when the Sample_DB database is created:

- FG_1
- FG_2
- FG_3
- FG_N

After creating our sample database using the CREATE PARTITION FUNCTION command, we create a partition function named pf_OneMillion_RightRange by specifying the datatype of the partitioning column (ID INT), based upon which the table will be partitioned. The partition function specifies RANGE RIGHT values 1, 1000001, 2000001, and 3000001. These RANGE RIGHT values specify the boundary values for each partition, designating each range value as the lowest starting value in the partitioning column for its corresponding partition. In other words, the boundary value will belong to the partition on the *right* when the partition function is defined with RANGE RIGHT. Thus, for the preceding partitioned function, we will have a total of five partitions, given as follows:

- Partition 1: Rows with ID values less than or equal to 0
- Partition 2: Rows with ID values from 1 to 1,000,000
- Partition 3: Rows with ID values from 1,000,001 to 2,000,000
- Partition 4: Rows with ID values from 2,000,001 to 3,000,000
- Partition 5: Rows with ID values greater than 3,000,000

After creating the partition function, we verify it by querying the sys.partition_functions and sys.partition_range_values system catalog views.

We created a partition scheme named `ps_OneMillion_RightRange`, using the `CREATE PARTITION SCHEME` command, mapped each partition specified by a partition function to a file group defined by a partition scheme, and verified that the partition scheme has been created by querying `sys.partition_schemes`.

We then created our sample table called `tbl_SampleRecords`, with `ID` as the clustered primary key. Note that the syntax of `CREATE TABLE` is followed by the `ON ps_OneMillion_ RightRange (ID)` clause. This clause specifies the name of the partition scheme and the partitioning column, which happen to be `ps_OneMillion_RightRange` and `ID`, respectively.

Once the table is created, we insert 5 million sample records. In order to generate 5 million sample rows, we cross join the system catalog view `sys.columns` twice and retrieve the top 5,000,000 rows of resulting cross joins. We generate the serial value of `ID` with the help of the `ROW_NUMBER()` function. The resulting rows will be inserted into our partitioned table `tbl_SampleRecords`.

By querying the `sys.partitions` catalog view, we examine the number of partitions and the number of rows in each partition. Note how the first partition remains empty because there is no record whose `ID` value is less than 1. Also note that, after the first 3 million rows are inserted into partitions 2, 3, and 4, each having 1 million rows, the remaining rows are inserted into partition 5, because partition 5 is the last partition and is an open-ended partition.

Finally, the data for `ID = 4999999` is retrieved from the `tbl_SampleRecords` table, and the execution plan of the query is examined. By observing the execution plan, you can see that **Seek Predicates** indicates the partition qualifier; also note the value of **Actual Partition Count**, which is **1**. This suggests that only one partition was accessed while performing the query and other partitions were eliminated from being accessed. This is the one of the advantages of implementing table partitioning.

Deleting and loading bulk data by splitting, merging, and switching partitions (sliding window)

Many times there is a requirement to archive or delete a large amount of data and load a large amount of new data into a large table periodically, based on the date and time column. Let's say for example, you regularly need to delete a large amount of data that belongs to the oldest quarter. At the same time, you want to load a large amount of data into an existing table. With billions of rows in a table, this operation is not trivial and can take hours. However, if you implement table partitioning based on the date and time column, you can perform this task very efficiently.

In this recipe, we will learn how to efficiently delete a large amount of data belonging to one quarter of the year, and load a large amount of data for a whole quarter into an existing table by splitting, merging, and switching partitions.

Assume that we need to store data on a quarterly basis and that data belonging to each quarter is stored in a partition. On a quarterly basis, we need to purge data for the oldest quarter and load new data for the latest quarter. For example, in our partitioned table we have partitions to contain data for the following quarters:

- Quarter 1: January 2011 to March 2011
- Quarter 2: April 2011 to Jun 2011
- Quarter 3: July 2011 to September 2011
- Quarter 4: October 2011 to December 2011

We want to delete data for quarter 1(January 2011 to March 2011) and load new data into a new partition for quarter 1 (January 2012 to March 2012). For this, we can use the date and time column in the table to implement table partitioning in such a way that the partition contains data for one quarter. We can merge two partitions or split an existing partition by introducing a new boundary range value in the partition function. We will delete the data and partition for an older quarter by merging the partition, and will introduce a new partition by splitting the last partition. For this, initially we will have the following partitions:

PARTITION-1	PARTITION-2	PARTITION-3	PARTITION-4	PARTITION-5	PARTITION-6
(EMPTY)	(DATA)	(DATA)	(DATA)	(DATA)	(EMPTY)
< JAN-11	JAN-11 TO MAR-11	APR-11 TO JUN-11	JUL-11 TO SEP-11	OCT-11 TO DEC-11	JAN-12 TO MAR-12

This example will give you a foundation to implement a **sliding window** scenario. In a sliding window, we purge the oldest data from a partition by switching it to a staging table and truncating the staging table. In our case, partition 2 (the oldest quarter) will be switched to a staging table and truncated. After deleting data, partition 2 will also be empty, and we will merge it with partition 1. So, the total number of partitions will become five from six. The following figure shows how partition switching and merging will occur:

Before Merging Partition					
PARTITION-1	PARTITION-2	PARTITION-3	PARTITION-4	PARTITION-5	PARTITION-6
(EMPTY)	(DATA)	(DATA)	(DATA)	(DATA)	(EMPTY)
< JAN-11	JAN-11 TO MAR-11	APR-11 TO JUN-11	JUL-11 TO SEP-11	OCT-11 TO DEC-11	JAN-12 TO MAR-12

Staging Table

After Merging Partition				
PARTITION-1	PARTITION-2	PARTITION-3	PARTITION-4	PARTITION-5
(EMPTY)	(DATA)	(DATA)	(DATA)	(EMPTY)
< APR-11	APR-11 TO JUN-11	JUL-11 TO SEP-11	OCT-11 TO DEC-11	JAN-12 TO MAR-12

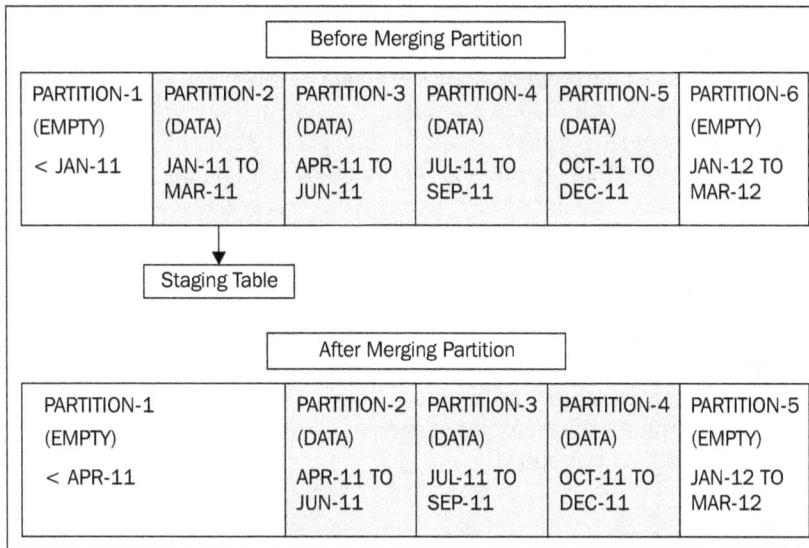

To load new bulk data (for the quarter spanning Jan 12 to Mar 12), we split the last partition by introducing a new boundary value (which will be 1st, Apr 12) and loading data for the quarter spanning Jan 12 to Mar 12 to its respective partition. The following figure shows how partition splitting and switching will occur:

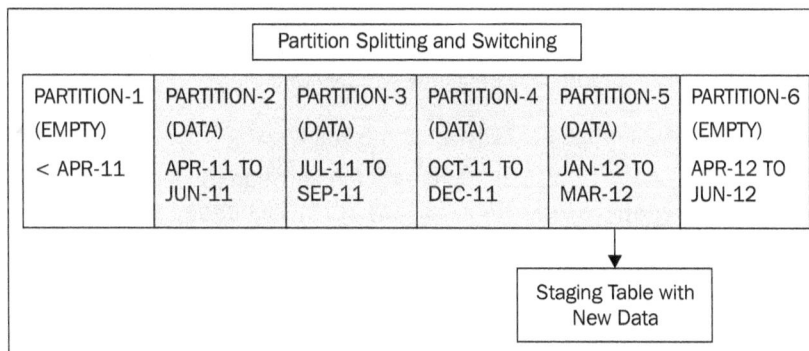

Partition Splitting and Switching					
PARTITION-1	PARTITION-2	PARTITION-3	PARTITION-4	PARTITION-5	PARTITION-6
(EMPTY)	(DATA)	(DATA)	(DATA)	(DATA)	(EMPTY)
< APR-11	APR-11 TO JUN-11	JUL-11 TO SEP-11	OCT-11 TO DEC-11	JAN-12 TO MAR-12	APR-12 TO JUN-12

Staging Table with New Data

Note that, during the whole cycle, partition 1 and partition 6 always remain empty and will not contain any data at any given point in time. They are required to provide the sliding window mechanism. Therefore, they have deliberately been kept empty here. This is necessary when you are implementing the sliding window scenario, because in this scenario, we need to purge/archive the oldest data (partition 2) by truncating the partition and merging it with partition 1, at the same time making room for new data by splitting the last existing empty partition into two! The reason behind always keeping the first and last partition empty is the data movement that SQL Server may have to perform across these partitions while merging or splitting partitions. If two non-empty partitions are merged or split, it can cause data movement across the partitions, based on new range values from one partition to the other, which is quite an expensive operation in terms of I/O and may take a long time depending upon the volume of data. On the other hand, merging or splitting two empty partitions does not cause any data movement and is thus a very fast operation. So, to avoid any data movement across the partitions for a faster sliding window operation, we always keep partition 1 and partition 6 empty.

Getting ready

The following is the prerequisite for this recipe:

▶ An instance of SQL Server 2012 Developer or Enterprise Evaluation edition

How to do it...

Follow the given steps to implement table partitioning on the DATETIME column for deleting data and loading bulk data periodically in sliding window fashion:

1. Start SQL Server Management Studio and connect to SQL Server.

2. Execute the following T-SQL script to create the partition function pf_Quaterly_RangeRight with RANGE RIGHT boundaries and the partition scheme ps_Quaterly_RangeRight.

```
USE master
GO

--Creating Sample_DB database
--if it does not exist.
--DROP DATABASE Sample_DB
IF DB_ID('Sample_DB') IS NOT NULL
    DROP DATABASE [Sample_DB]

CREATE DATABASE [Sample_DB]
ON PRIMARY
(
    NAME = N'Sample_DB'
```

```
    ,FILENAME = N'C:\SQLData\Sample_DB.mdf'
    ,SIZE = 3072KB , FILEGROWTH = 1024KB
)
LOG ON
(
    NAME = N'Sample_DB_log'
    ,FILENAME = N'ON'C:\SQLData\Sample_DB_log.ldf'
    ,SIZE = 1024KB , FILEGROWTH = 10%
)

GO


USE Sample_DB
GO


--Creating Partition Function pf_Quaterly_RangeRight
CREATE PARTITION FUNCTION pf_Quaterly_RangeRight(DATETIME)
AS RANGE RIGHT FOR VALUES
('20110101','20110401','20110701','20111001','20120101')
GO


--Creating Partition Scheme ps_Quaterly_RangeRight
CREATE PARTITION SCHEME ps_Quaterly_RangeRight
AS PARTITION pf_Quaterly_RangeRight ALL TO ([PRIMARY])
GO
```

When partitioning a table on the DATETIME column, always try to apply RANGE RIGHT values. This makes it easier for you to partition tables perfectly with less effort. If you apply RANGE LEFT values, you have to consider and specify the "time" part, including milliseconds, to accurately specify range values while partitioning a table. For example, if we partition the DATETIME column with RANGE LEFT values, then you have to consider the last possible date and time value for a given month, such as 20110331 23:59:59.997 (the last and highest possible value for the first quarter that should appear as boundary value in the _left_ partition). Partitioning a table on the DATETIME column with RANGE RIGHT automatically takes care of the "time" part while specifying range values in table partitioning.

3. Now, let's create our partitioned table `tbl_MyData` and insert 275000 sample records by executing the following T-SQL script:

```sql
USE Sample_DB
GO

--Creating Partitioned table tbl_MyData
CREATE TABLE tbl_MyData
(
    RecordDateTime DATETIME NOT NULL
    ,RecordID INT NOT NULL
    ,RecordData varchar(40) NOT NULL
)
GO

--Creating clustered index of tbl_MyData
--on partition scheme ps_Quaterly_RangeRight
CREATE CLUSTERED INDEX idx_tbl_MyData_RecordDateTime
ON tbl_MyData(RecordDateTime,RecordID) ON ps_Quaterly_RangeRight
(RecordDateTime)

--Inserting Sample Data
INSERT INTO tbl_MyData
SELECT
    '2011'
    + RIGHT('0' + CAST((CASE WHEN ID%12=0 THEN 12 ELSE ID%12 END)
AS VARCHAR),2)
    + RIGHT('0' + CAST((CASE WHEN ID%28=0 THEN 28 ELSE ID%28 END)
AS VARCHAR),2)
    AS RecordDateTime
    ,ID
    ,RecordData
FROM
(
    SELECT TOP  275000
        ID = ROW_NUMBER() OVER(ORDER BY C1.name)
        ,RecordData = NEWID()
    FROM sys.columns AS C1
    CROSS JOIN sys.columns AS C2
    CROSS JOIN sys.columns AS C3
) AS T
GO
```

4. Examine the number of partitions and total number of rows in each partition by running the following query:

```
USE Sample_DB
GO


--Examining Partitions and row count
SELECT
    partition_number
    ,rows
FROM sys.partitions
WHERE object_id = OBJECT_ID('tbl_MyData')
ORDER BY partition_number
```

5. The preceding query should give you a result similar to the one shown in the following screenshot:

	partition_number	rows
1	1	0
2	2	68751
3	3	68751
4	4	68750
5	5	68748
6	6	0

6. Now, we will remove data for the first quarter of 2011 (partition 1). For that, let's create a staging table `tbl_MyStagingData` by executing the following script:

```
USE Sample_DB
GO


IF OBJECT_ID('tbl_MyStagingData') IS NOT NULL
    DROP TABLE tbl_MyStagingData


--Creating Staging table
CREATE TABLE tbl_MyStagingData
(
    RecordDateTime DATETIME NOT NULL
    ,RecordID INT NOT NULL
    ,RecordData varchar(40) NOT NULL
)
GO
```

```
--Creating clustered index
--on tbl_MyStagingData
CREATE CLUSTERED INDEX idx_tbl_MyStagingData_RecordDateTime
ON tbl_MyStagingData(RecordDateTime,RecordID)
GO
```

7. Now, switch partition 2 of `tbl_MyData` to staging table `tbl_MyStagingData` and truncate the staging table. After truncating the table, examine the number of partitions and total rows in partitions. For this, execute the following script:

```
USE Sample_DB
GO

--Switching Partition 2 of tbl_MyData
--to tbl_MyStagingData and truncating table
ALTER TABLE tbl_MyData
SWITCH PARTITION 2 TO tbl_MyStagingData PARTITION 1
GO
TRUNCATE TABLE tbl_MyStagingData
GO

--Examining Partitions and row count
SELECT
    partition_number
    ,rows
FROM sys.partitions
WHERE object_id = OBJECT_ID('tbl_MyData')
ORDER BY partition_number
```

8. The preceding query should return the following partition details:

partition_number	rows
1	0
2	0
3	68751
4	68750
5	68748
6	0

9. Now, merge partition 2 with partition 1, set the next used filegroup for partition scheme `ps_Quaterly_RangeRight` to `PRIMARY` and examine the number of partitions, using the following script:

```
USE Sample_DB
GO

--Merging Partition 2 to Partitin 1
ALTER PARTITION FUNCTION pf_Quaterly_RangeRight()
```

```
MERGE RANGE ('20110101')
GO
--Setting Next Used Filegroup
--for next partition
ALTER PARTITION SCHEME ps_Quaterly_RangeRight
NEXT USED [PRIMARY]

--Examining Partitions and row count
SELECT
    partition_number
    ,rows
FROM sys.partitions
WHERE object_id = OBJECT_ID('tbl_MyData')
ORDER BY partition_number
```

10. Examine the output returned by the preceding query, as shown in the following screenshot:

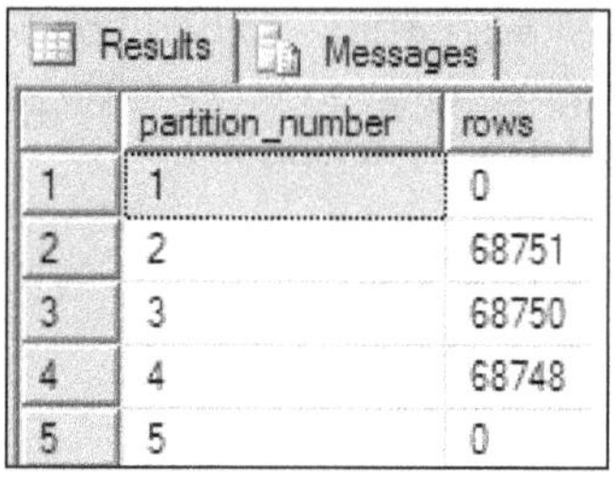

	partition_number	rows
1	1	0
2	2	68751
3	3	68750
4	4	68748
5	5	0

11. Now, we will bulk load data into our table `tbl_MyData`. To do this, we first generate some sample data and insert it into our staging table `tbl_MyStagingData`, which we have just created.

```
USE Sample_DB
GO

--Adding Check constraint to tbl_MyStagingData
ALTER TABLE tbl_MyStagingData
ADD CONSTRAINT ck_tbl_MyStagingData_RecordDateTime
CHECK (RecordDateTime >='20120101' AND RecordDateTime <
'20120401')

--Inserting data into tbl_MyStagingData
--for first quarter of 2012
INSERT INTO tbl_MyStagingData
SELECT
    '2012'
```

```
        + RIGHT('0' + CAST((CASE WHEN ID%3=0 THEN 3 ELSE ID%3 END) AS
VARCHAR),2)
        + RIGHT('0' + CAST((CASE WHEN ID%28=0 THEN 28 ELSE ID%28 END)
AS VARCHAR),2)
    AS RecordDateTime
    ,ID
    ,RecordData
FROM
(
    SELECT TOP  100000
        ID = 275000 + ROW_NUMBER() OVER(ORDER BY C1.name)
        ,RecordData = NEWID()
    FROM sys.columns AS C1
    CROSS JOIN sys.columns AS C2
    CROSS JOIN sys.columns AS C3
) AS T
```

12. Now, add a new partition by splitting the last blank partition. After splitting the partition, switch `tbl_MyStagingData` to partition 5 of `tbl_MyData` and set the next used filegroup for the partition scheme `ps_Quaterly_RangeRight` to `PRIMARY`, by running the following script:

```
USE Sample_DB
GO

--Add a new partition by splitting
--last empty partition.
ALTER PARTITION FUNCTION pf_Quaterly_RangeRight()
SPLIT RANGE ('20120401')
GO

--Switch table tbl_MyStagingData
--to partition 5 of tbl_MyData
--to load data
ALTER TABLE tbl_MyStagingData
SWITCH PARTITION 1 TO tbl_MyData PARTITION 5

--Setting Next Used Filegroup
--for next partition
ALTER PARTITION SCHEME ps_Quaterly_RangeRight
NEXT USED [PRIMARY]
GO
```

13. Now, verify that the new rows are inserted into proper partitions by executing the following query:

```
USE Sample_DB
GO

--Examining Partitions and row count
SELECT
    partition_number
    ,rows
FROM sys.partitions
WHERE object_id = OBJECT_ID('tbl_MyData')
ORDER BY partition_number
```

14. Observe the result returned by executing the preceding query, as shown in the following screenshot:

	partition_number	rows
1	1	0
2	2	68751
3	3	68750
4	4	68748
5	5	100000
6	6	0

How it works...

In this recipe, by using the CREATE PARTITION FUNCTION command, we first create a partition function named pf_Quaterly_RangeRight, by specifying the datatype of the partitioning column (RecordDateTime DATETIME), based upon which the table will be partitioned. The partition function specifies RANGE RIGHT values 20110101, 20110401, 20110701, 20111001, and 20120101. These RANGE RIGHT values specify the boundary values for each partition, designating each range value as the lowest starting value in the partitioning column for a partition. By using the CREATE PARTITION SCHEME command, we create partition scheme ps_Quaterly_RangeRight, to map all partitions to the PRIMARY filegroup.

For the sake of simplicity in this example, we used the PRIMARY filegroup for all partitions. However, in production environments, it is recommended to place your partitions in different locations by specifying different filegroups.

We then create our sample table called `tbl_MyData` with `RecordDateTime` and `RecordID` as clustered composite primary keys. Note that the syntax of `CREATE INDEX` is followed by the `ON ps_Quaterly_RangeRight (RecordDateTime)` clause. This clause specifies the name of the partition scheme and the partitioning column, which happen to be `ps_Quaterly_RangeRight` and `RecordDateTime`, respectively. By specifying the partition scheme, the index is partitioned and aligned with the partitions as specified in the partition scheme.

Once the table is created, we insert sample records. We generate rows by cross joining the system catalog view `sys.columns` twice and then retrieve the top 275000 rows of the resulting cross joins. We generate the serial value of `ID` with help of the `ROW_NUMBER()` function in the subquery. Observe how we generate date values for the year 2011 by doing some math and string manipulation. The resulting rows will be inserted into our partitioned table `tbl_MyData`.

By querying the `sys.partitions` catalog view, we examine the number of partitions and the number of rows in each partition. Note how we have kept first and last partitions empty. For the whole year 2011, we get rows for each quarter in its respective partition—partition 2, partition 3, partition 4, and partition 5.

We then created a staging table named `tbl_MyStagingData`, with the same schema as `tbl_MyData`.

After creating the staging table, using the `ALTER TABLE...SWITCH PARTITION` statement, we switch partition 2 of `tbl_MyData` (the partition that contains data for the first quarter of 2011) to our staging table `tbl_MyStagingData`. When we do this, SQL Server just changes the reference of data pages, so that `tbl_MyStagingData` points to the data pages of partition 2 of `tbl_MyData`. All the data from partition 2 is now in our staging table `tbl_MyStagingData`. We truncate the table `tbl_MyStagingData` and delete all data. The switching operation does not move any data but just changes the references of data pages. In this way, it is much faster and only takes a few milliseconds. After truncating the table, we merge the emptied partition, partition 2, with partition 1.

> Always try to merge two empty partitions. If you merge partitions that contain data, then SQL Server may have to move actual data pages from one filegroup to another filegroup, which is very expensive in terms of I/O operations.

After truncating the table `tbl_MyStagingData`, we verify the number of partitions and number of rows in partitions by querying the `sys.partitions` system catalog view. Observe that the data from partition 2 is removed.

We then merge partition 2 with partition 1 by specifying the range value of partition 2 in the ALTER PARTITION ...MERGE statement. We alter the partition scheme ps_Quaterly_RangeRight to set the next used filegroup. As long as we have all partitions on the PRIMARY filegroup, this is not necessary. However, if we have multiple partitions on multiple filegroups, we have to specify the name of the filegroup to be used for the next partition. After merging the partition, we examine the partitions again, to verify that the partition has indeed been removed. You should now see a total of five partitions, rather than six partitions.

Next, we remove the data for oldest quarter and remove its corresponding partition as well. Next, we need to load new bulk data and create new partitions. The process is exactly the reverse of what we do to purge old data.

We load data for the new quarter, January 2012 to March 2012, into our staging table tbl_MyStagingData, by generating 100,000 records. Note that we create a check constraint on the table, which checks that the date falls between January 2012 and March 2012. This check constraint is a mandatory part, without which it is not possible to load data from the staging table into the partition.

We then add a new partition by altering the partition function by splitting the last empty partition (January 12 to March 12) by specifying a new range value, 20120401. This creates one new partition, to the "right", whose lowest range value happens to be 20120401.

Once the partition is created, we switch tbl_MyStagingData to partition 5 of the tbl_MyData table. Again, for this switching, SQL Server just updates the page references, and partition 5 will contain new loaded data in just a few milliseconds. As before, we set the next used filegroup for ps_Quaterly_RangeRight.

Finally, we again verify the number of partitions, and the number of rows in partitions, by querying the sys.partitions system catalog view. Note that partition 5 now contains the 100000 records that we just loaded from the staging table.

> While switching between tables with the ALTER TABLE...SWITCH command, the schema of the corresponding table and partition must be identical.

There's more...

This recipe is an example of a basic sliding window and provides a solution for archiving/deleting old data, removing old partitions, and loading new data in new partitions, periodically.

Based on this, you can implement a solution in your production environment to perform the same task at regular intervals. This can be weekly, monthly, quarterly, yearly, or at any time interval that you choose. The important thing is your script should be intelligent and dynamic enough to create and remove partitions on the fly, appropriately, by setting range values dynamically. This way you can delete a large amount of data from your data store in small amount of time and load new bulk data in very large tables without locking the table for long time.

14
Implementing Physical Database Structure

In this chapter we will cover:

- ▶ Configuring a data file and log file on multiple physical disks
- ▶ Using files and filegroups
- ▶ Moving an existing large table to a separate physical disk
- ▶ Moving non-clustered indexes to a separate physical disk
- ▶ Configuring the tempdb database on separate physical disk

Introduction

Your database performance heavily depends on how you have physically placed your database objects and how you have configured your disk subsystem. Designing the physical layout of your database correctly is the key factor to improve the performance of your database queries and thus the performance of your database. However, the correct decision on a physical design structure of the database depends on the available hardware resources that you might have. This includes the number of processors, RAM, and storage resources, such as how many ,disks or RAID controllers you might have in your database environment. The best thing while designing physical layout of the database is to have multiple physical disks for your database. If you configure your database in such a way that it spreads across multiple disks, it can benefit from parallel I/O operations.

The following are some of the decisions that influence your database performance:

 ▸ Where do you place data files?

 ▸ Where do you place log files?

 ▸ Where do you place large objects?

 ▸ Where do you place indexes?

 ▸ Where do you place the `tempdb` database?

You can control the physical location of database objects within the database by using files and filegroups.

In this chapter, we will learn how to best design the physical structure of the database on your disk subsystem when you have enough available hardware resources, such as multiple processors and multiple physical disks.

Configuring data file and log file on multiple physical disks

If you know the exact difference between the ways in which data files and log files of a database are accessed, you can understand why you should place data files and log files on separate physical disks for better performance.

The data file of a database, which is normally a file with a `.mdf` or `.ndf` extension, is used to store the actual data in the database. The data is stored in pages that are 8 KB in size. When particular data is queried by the user, SQL Server reads the required data pages from the disk into memory containing the requested data from the data file. In case SQL Server needs to make any modification in the existing data, it reads the required data pages into the buffer cache, updates those cached data pages in memory, writes modifications to the log file, when the transaction is committed, and then writes the updated data pages back to the disk, when the checkpoint operation is performed. SQL Server performs configurable checkpoint operations at regular intervals. In-memory modified data pages are called **dirty pages**. When a checkpoint is performed, it permanently writes these dirty pages on disk.

The log file is used to record any change that is made to the database. It's intended for recovery of the database in case of disaster or failure. Because a log file is intended to record the changes, it is not designed to be read randomly, as compared to a data file. Rather, it is designed to be written and accessed in a sequential manner.

SQL Server is designed to handle and process multiple I/O requests simultaneously, if we have enough hardware resources. Even if SQL Server is capable of handling simultaneous I/O requests in parallel, it may face the issue of disk contention while reading large amounts of data from data files and writing large a number of transaction logs to log files in parallel with two different requests if data files and log files reside on the same physical disk. However, if data file and log file are located on separate physical disks, SQL Server gracefully handles and processes such requests in parallel.

When simultaneous requests for reading data and writing transaction logs are commonly expected in the OLTP database environment, placing data files and log files on separate physical drives greatly improves the performance of the database.

Let's suppose that you are a DBA and, in your organization, you maintain and administer a production database called AdventureWorks2012 database. The database was created/ installed by an inexperienced team and has been residing in the default location for SQL Server. You are required to separate the data files and log files for this database and place them on different physical disks to achieve maximum I/O performance. How would you perform this task?

The goal of this recipe is to teach you how to separate the data files and log files for an existing database to improve the I/O response time and database performance.

Getting ready

This recipe refers to the following physical disk volumes:

 ▶ E drive—to store the data file
 ▶ L drive—to store the log file

> In this chapter, wherever it is said "separate disk volume"or "separate drive", consider it a separate physical drive and not logical partitioned drive.

The following are the prerequisites for completing this recipe:

 ▶ An instance of SQL Server 2012 Developer or Enterprise Evaluation edition
 ▶ Sample AdventureWorks2012 database on the instance of SQL server. For more details on how to install the AdventureWorks2012 database, please refer to the *Preface* of this book
 ▶ E drive should be available on your machine
 ▶ L drive should be available on your machine

How to do it...

The following are the steps you need to perform for this recipe:

1. Start SQL Server Management Studio and connect to SQL Server.

2. In the query window, type and execute the following script to verify the existing path for data files and log files for the AdventureWorks2012 database:

```
--Switch the current database
--context to AdventureWorks2012
USE AdventureWorks2012
GO

--Examine the current
--location of the database.
SELECT physical_name
FROM sys.database_files
GO
```

3. Assuming that the AdventureWorks2012 database resides in its default location, depending upon your SQL Server installation path, you may see a result in the output of the previous query, similar to the one given here:

Results	Messages

	physical_name
1	C:\Program Files\Microsoft SQL Server\MSSQL11.MSSQLSERVER\MSSQL\DATA\AdventureWorks2012_Data.mdf
2	C:\Program Files\Microsoft SQL Server\MSSQL11.MSSQLSERVER\MSSQL\DATA\AdventureWorks2012_log.ldf

4. Now, execute the following query to bring the database offline:

```
USE master
GO

--Bring database offline
ALTER DATABASE AdventureWorks2012
SET OFFLINE WITH ROLLBACK IMMEDIATE
GO
```

5. Once the database is offline, you can detach it without any problem. Right-click on **AdventureWorks2012**, in **Object Explorer**, and select **Tasks** and then **Detach…**, as shown in following screenshot:

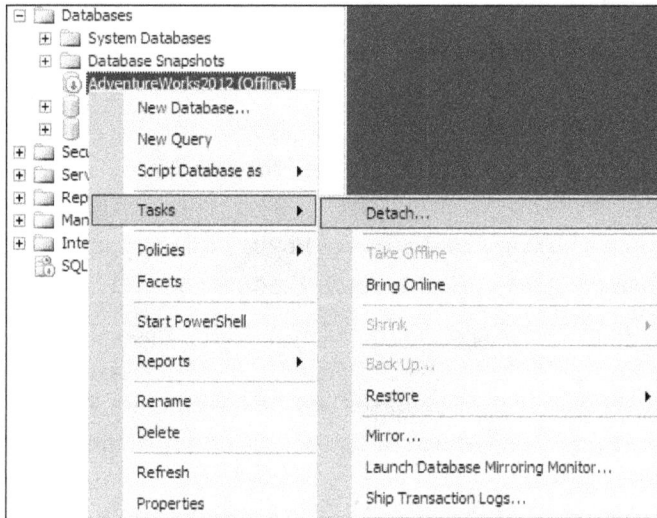

6. This step brings up the **Detach Database** dialog box, as shown in following screenshot. Press the **OK** button on this dialog box. This will detach the AdventureWorks2012 database from the SQL Server instance and it will no longer appear in **Object Explorer**:

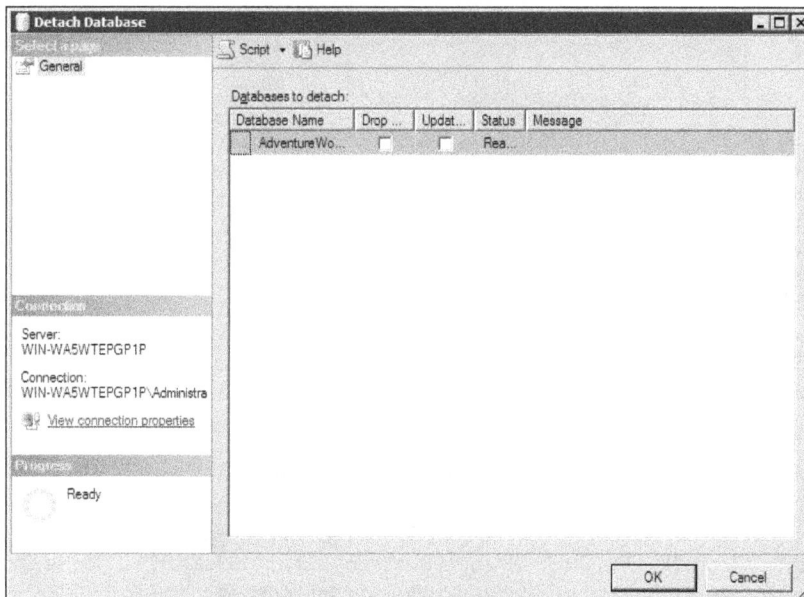

7. Create the two following directories to place data files (`.mdf` files) and log files (`.ldf` files), respectively, for the `AdventureWorks2012` database, on different physical disks:

   - ❏ `E:\SQL_Data\`
   - ❏ `L:\SQL_Log\`

8. Now, using Windows Explorer, move the `AdventureWorks2012_data.mdf` and `AdventureWorks2012_log.ldf` database files manually from their original location to their respective new directories. The following paths should be the respective destinations

   - ❏ `E:\SQL_Data\AdventureWorks2012_Data.mdf`
   - ❏ `L:\SQL_Log\ AdventureWorks2012_Log.ldf`

9. After the data and log files are copied to their new locations, we will attach them and bring our `AdventureWorks2012` database back online. To do this, in **Object Explorer**, right-click on the **Databases** node and select **Attach...**

10. You will see the following **Attach Databases** dialog box. In this dialog box, click on the **Add...** button:

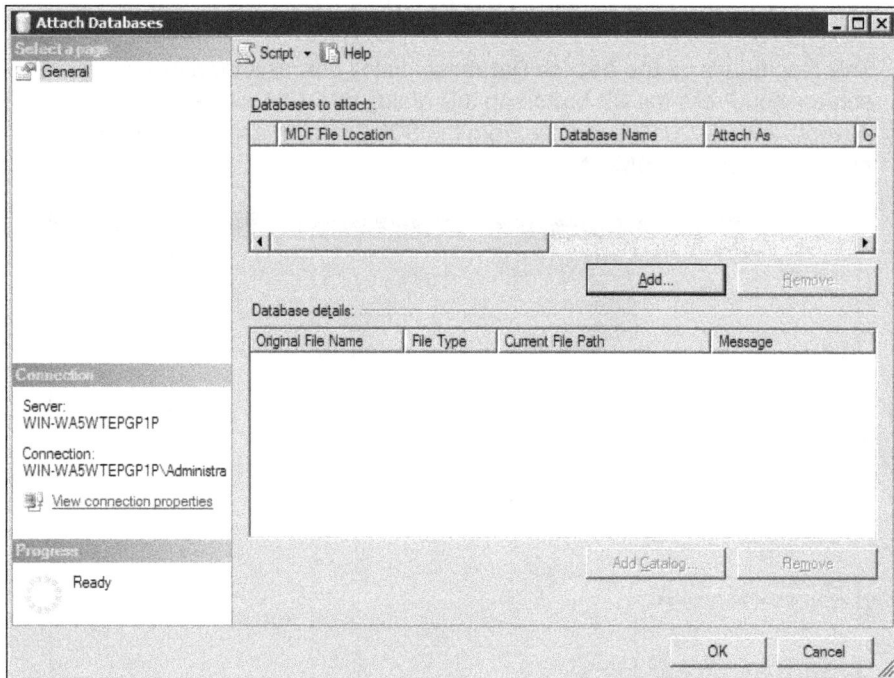

11. The previous step opens the **Locate Database Files** dialog box. In this dialog box, locate the `.mdf` data file `E:\SQL_Data\AdventureWorks2012_Data.mdf` and click on the **OK** button, as shown in following screenshot:

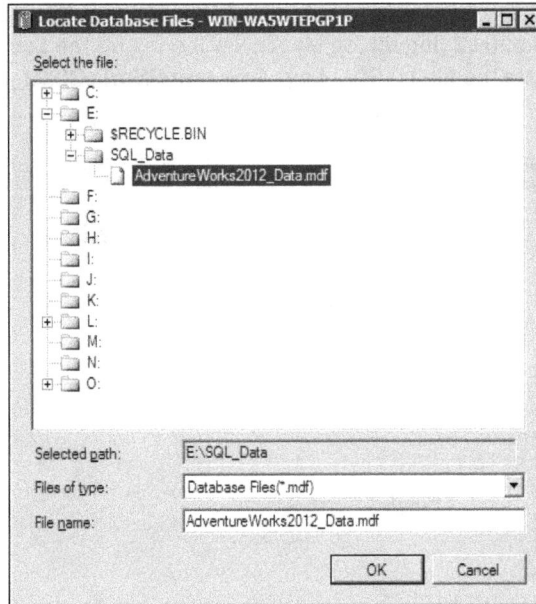

12. After locating the `.mdf` data file, the **Attach Databases** dialog box should look similar to the following screenshot. Note that the log file (`.ldf` file) could not be located at this stage and there is a **Not Found** message against **AdventureWorks2012_log.ldf**, under the **AdventureWorks2012 database details:** section. This happens because we have moved the log file to our new location, `L:\SQL_Log\`, and SQL Server tries to find it in its default location:

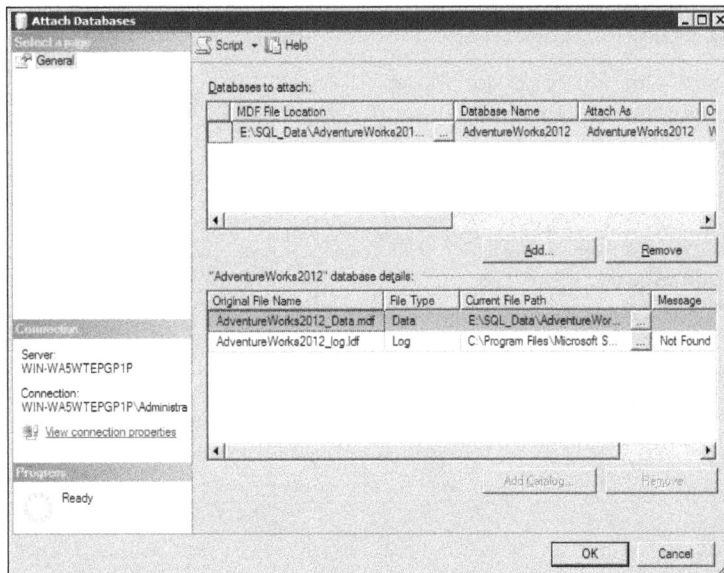

13. To locate the log file, click on the **...** button in the **Current File Path** column for the **AdventureWorks2012_log.ldf** log file. This will bring up the **Locate Database Files** dialog box. Locate the file **L:\SQL_Log\AdventureWorks2012_log.ldf** and click on the **OK** button. Refer to the following screenshot:

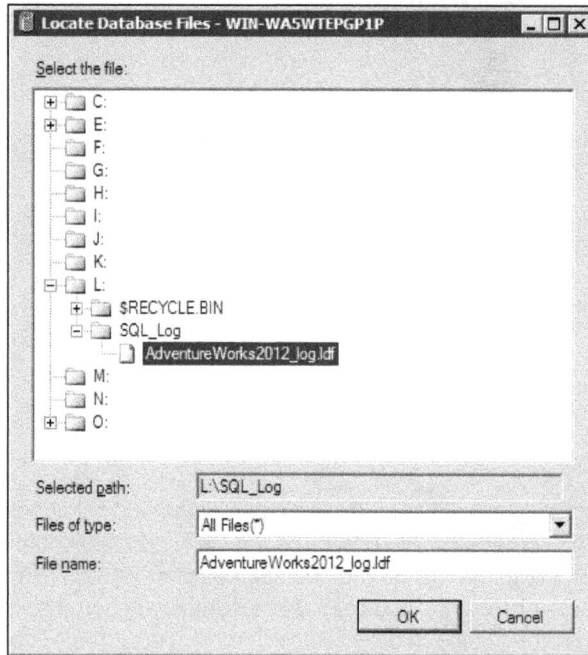

14. To verify the new location of the AdventureWorks2012 database, run the following query in SSMS:

```
--Switch the current database
--context to AdventureWorks2012
USE AdventureWorks2012
GO

--Verify the new location of
--the database.
SELECT
  physical_name
  ,name
FROM sys.database_files
GO
```

15. In the query result, examine the new locations of the data files and log files for the `AdventureWorks2012` database; see the following screenshot:

	physical_name	name
1	E:\SQL_Data\AdventureWorks2012_Data.mdf	AdventureWorks2012_Data
2	L:\SQL_Log\AdventureWorks2012_log.ldf	AdventureWorks2012_Log

How it works...

In this recipe, we first queried the `sys.database_files` system catalog view to verify the current location of the AdventureWorks2012 database. Because we wanted to move the `.mdf` and `.ldf` files to new locations, we had to bring the database offline.

We brought the database offline with the `ALTER DATABASE` command. Note that, in the `ALTER DATABASE` command, we included the `ROLLBACK IMMEDIATE` option. This rolls back the transactions that are not completed, and current connections to AdventureWorks2012 database are closed. After bringing the database offline, we detached the AdventureWorks2012 database from the instance of SQL server.

> You cannot move a database file to a new location if the database is online. If a database is to be moved, it must not be in use by SQL Server. In order to move a database, you can either stop the SQL Server service or bring the database offline. Bringing the database offline is a preferable option because stopping SQL Server service stops the functioning of the whole SQL Server instance. Alternatively, you can also select the checkbox **Drop Connections** in the **Detach Database** dialog box, which does not require bringing a database offline.

We then created two new directories—`E:\SQL_Data\` and `L:\SQL_Log\`—to place the data and log files for AdventureWorks2012 and moved `AdventureWorks2012_Data.mdf` and `AdventureWorks2012_Log.ldf` over there. We then attached the AdventureWorks2012 database by attaching the `.mdf` and `.ldf` files from their new locations. Finally, we verified the new location of the database by querying `sys.database_files`.

> You can script your **Attach Database** and **Detach Database** actions by clicking on the **Script** button in the wizard. This allows you to save and re-use the script for future purposes.

Using files and filegroups

By placing certain database objects on different physical disks, you can improve the performance of your databases. But, how do we control the placement of certain database objects on particular physical disks?

Well, files and filegroups are used in SQL Server to physically organize your database files and database objects. By organizing data files with the help of filegroups, you can place specific database objects, such as tables and indexes, on particular physical disks.

Let's say that you are responsible for creating and designing a new production database, which will be accessed by many applications. You expect one particular table to grow very large with time. You are lucky enough to have enough hardware resources in the form of multiple physical disks that you can use to distribute your database physically. You decide to place the table that you estimate will become very large and expect will be accessed heavily by many requests, so that you can achieve the maximum disk I/O performance on the requests made on this table. How would you configure this implementation? Well, to find out, follow this recipe!

Getting ready

In this recipe, you will learn how to configure databases for large objects. To do this, we will create a sample database that we will configure with multiple data files and filegroups. This recipe requires that you have at least three physical drives available, as this example references following physical disk volumes:

- E drive—for primary data file (primary filegroup)
- G drive—for secondary data file (fg_LargeData filegroup)
- L drive—for log file

The following are the prerequisites to completing this recipe:

- An instance of SQL Server 2012 Developer or Enterprise Evaluation edition
- E—drive should be available on your machine
- G—drive should be available on your machine
- L—drive should be available on your machine

How to do it...

The following steps will describe how to work with files and filegroups, to distribute your database across multiple physical disk drives:

1. Start SQL Server Management Studio and connect to SQL Server.

2. In the query window, type and execute the following query to create a new sample database named `SampleDB`:

```
--Creating Sample Database
CREATE DATABASE SampleDB
ON PRIMARY
(
  Name = SampleDB_Data
  ,FileName = 'E:\SQL_Data\SampleDB_Data.mdf'
  ,SIZE = 256MB
  ,FILEGROWTH = 128MB
  ,MAXSIZE = 1024GB
)
,FILEGROUP fg_LargeData
(
  Name = SampleDB_fg_LargeData_Data
  ,FileName = 'G:\SQL_LargeData\SampleDB_fg_LargeData_Data.ndf'
  ,SIZE = 256MB
  ,FILEGROWTH = 128MB
  ,MAXSIZE = 1024GB
)
LOG ON
(
  Name = SampleDB_Log
  ,FileName = 'L:\SQL_Log\SampleDB_Log.ldf'
  ,SIZE = 128MB
  ,FILEGROWTH = 64MB
  ,MAXSIZE = 128GB
)
GO
```

3. Run the following script to create a new sample table named `tbl_SmallTable`, on the default filegroup, which happens to be a primary filegroup in our case:

```
USE SampleDB
GO

--Creating table tbl_SmallTable
CREATE TABLE tbl_SmallTable
(
  ID INT IDENTITY(1,1) PRIMARY KEY
  ,ObjectID INT
  ,ColumnID INT
  ,ColumnName sysname
)
GO
```

```
--Inserting sample data into tbl_SmallTable
INSERT INTO tbl_SmallTable
SELECT
   object_id
   ,column_id
   ,name
FROM sys.all_columns AS AC1
GO
```

4. Execute the following script to create another sample table named `tbl_LargeTable`, on filegroup `fg_LargeTable`, which we anticipate will become very large:

```
USE SampleDB
GO

--Creating table tbl_LargeTable
CREATE TABLE tbl_LargeTable
(
   ID INT IDENTITY(1,1) PRIMARY KEY
   ,ObjectID INT
   ,ColumnID INT
   ,ColumnName sysname
) ON [fg_LargeData]
GO

--Inserting sample data into tbl_LargeTable
INSERT INTO tbl_LargeTable
SELECT
   AC1.object_id
   ,AC1.column_id
   ,AC1.name
FROM sys.all_columns AS AC1
CROSS JOIN sys.all_columns AS AC2
GO
```

5. Now, to verify the location of both the tables created with the previous script, execute the following query:

```
USE SampleDB
GO

--Verifying the location of the tables.
SELECT
   OBJECT_NAME(I.object_id) AS TableName
   ,FG.name AS FileGroupName
```

```
        ,DF.physical_name AS DataFilePath
FROM sys.indexes AS I
INNER JOIN sys.tables AS T
   ON I.object_id = T.object_id
INNER JOIN sys.filegroups AS FG
   ON I.data_space_id = FG.data_space_id
INNER JOIN sys.database_files AS DF
   ON I.data_space_id = DF.data_space_id
WHERE I.index_id <= 1
GO
```

6. You will observe that, as specified in our database definition, two tables are created on different disks. Note the filegroup and physical path of database files where the table data for both the tables will be stored in the following output of the previous query:

	TableName	FileGroupName	DataFilePath
1	tbl_SmallTable	PRIMARY	E:\SQL_Data\SampleDB_Data.mdf
2	tbl_LargeTable	fg_LargeData	G:\SQL_LargeData\SampleDB_fg_LargeData_Data.ndf

How it works...

We created a `SampleDB` database with a `CREATE DATABASE` statement. We created the database definition such that its primary data file is stored in `E:\SQL_Data\` and log file is stored in `L:\SQL_Log`. In the database definition, we also specified a new filegroup called `fg_Largedata` and added a secondary data file named `SampleDB_fg_LargeData_Data.ndf` to this filegroup.

> Remember that a log file is never associated with a filegroup. In other words, you cannot specify a filegroup name in a log file definition.

In the provided script, we created two tables. Table `tbl_SmallTable` will be created on the primary filegroup, because we did not specify any filegroup in the table definition and primary filegroup is the default filegroup in our case. We specified the `fg_LargeTable` filegroup with the `ON` clause in the table definition of `tbl_LargeTable`, so that it gets stored on its separate physical drive at `G:\SQL_LargeData`.

> If we do not specify the target filegroup name while creating an object, it is always created in the default filegroup. By default, primary filegroup is the default filegroup. A user-defined filegroup can be set as the default filegroup with the `ALTER DATABASE ...MODIFY FILEGROUP` statement.

We then verify the location of our tables by executing a query that makes use of several joins. We fetch details from `sys.indexes`, `sys.tables`, `sys.filegroups`, `sys.database_files`. We join `sys.indexes` and `sys.tables` on the `object_id` column. `data_space_id` is the ID of the filegroup in `sys.indexes`, `sys.filegroups`, and `sys.database_files`; then we join these system views, based on `data_space_id`. We retrieve table name by using the `OBJECT_NAME()` function, name of the filegroup from the `sys.filegroups` system view, and path of the data files from the `sys.database_files` system view. Remember that for a table that is on heap, the value of `index_id` is always 0. `index_id` for a clustered index is always 1. Clustered index means that the data of the table itself is attached to it. This is the reason why we have specified the condition `I.index_id <= 1`, so that we get details only for a clustered table or a heap table. Any non-clustered index entries are filtered. Note that as we have not partitioned the table, we have not included the `sys.partitions` system catalog view in our query. In case the table was partitioned and you had wanted to return a list of locations for each partition on the table, you would also have needed to join `sys.partitions` in the query, to retrieve the partition-specific location information.

Moving the existing large table to separate physical disk

In the previous recipe, *Using Files and Filegroups*, we saw that we can create a filegroup and create a table that is expected to become large and place it on different physical disks using filegroup.

But what if there is already an existing large table in an existing database that is extensively used by queries? Let's say that you are responsible for the AdventureWorks2012 database in your production environment, and there is one large table named `Sales.SalesOrderDetail`, which is located on the primary filegroup. You observe that the table is very large, I/O operations with a large volume of data made on this table are taking more time to be completed causing blocking issues, and other transactions have to wait for I/O operations on the same resources, resulting in bad I/O response time. You realise that there is a need to move this large table (`Sales.SalesOrderDetail`) containing billions of rows onto a dedicated physical disk to improve the I/O response time. How would you achieve this task of moving a large table to another disk?

In this recipe, you will learn how to move an existing large table to a different physical disk.

> Placing two large tables used frequently in join queries on two different physical disks can also help in improving performance by allowing SQL Server to perform parallel read operations on two tables specified join queries.

Getting ready

This recipe refers to the F: drive to place SalesOrderDetails data.

The following are the prerequisites to completing this recipe:

- ▸ An instance of SQL Server 2012 Developer or Enterprise Evaluation edition.
- ▸ A sample AdventureWorks2012 database on the instance of SQL server. For more details on how to install AdventureWorks2012 database, please refer to the *Preface* of this book.
- ▸ F drive should be available on your machine.

How to do it...

The following are the steps that will describe how to move a large table to a different physical disk:

1. Start SQL Server Management Studio and connect to SQL Server.
2. In the query window, type and execute the following T-SQL commands to add a new filegroup and data file to the AdventureWorks2012 database:

```
--Adding new filegroup
--named fg_SalesOrderDetails
ALTER DATABASE AdventureWorks2012
ADD FILEGROUP fg_SalesOrderDetails
GO


--Adding new data file to new
--filegroup fg_SalesOrderDetails
ALTER DATABASE AdventureWorks2012
ADD FILE
(
  Name = fg_SalesOrderDetails_Data
  ,FileName = 'F:\SalesOrderDetails_Data\fg_SalesOrderDetails_
Data.ndf'
  ,SIZE = 512MB
  ,FILEGROWTH = 128MB
  ,MAXSIZE = 512GB
) TO FILEGROUP [fg_SalesOrderDetails]
GO
```

3. Verify the current location of the table `Sales.SalesOrderDetail`, by executing the following query:

```
USE AdventureWorks2012
GO


--Verifying the current physical location
--of table Sales.SalesOrderDetail
SELECT
  OBJECT_NAME(I.object_id) AS TableName
  ,FG.name AS FileGroupName
  ,DF.physical_name AS DataFilePath
FROM sys.indexes AS I
INNER JOIN sys.tables AS T
  ON I.object_id = T.object_id
INNER JOIN sys.filegroups AS FG
  ON I.data_space_id = FG.data_space_id
INNER JOIN sys.database_files AS DF
  ON I.data_space_id = DF.data_space_id
WHERE I.index_id <= 1 AND I.object_id = OBJECT_ID('Sales.
SalesOrderDetail')
GO
```

If `AdventureWorks2012` is created at its default location; depending upon your SQL Server installation path, you should get output similar to that shown in the following screenshot:

	TableName	FileGroupName	DataFilePath
1	SalesOrderDetail	PRIMARY	E:\SQL_Data\AdventureWorks2012_Data.mdf

4. Run the following script, which will drop the existing clustered index (clustered primary key) and create it on a new filegroup, `fg_SalesOrderDetails`:

```
USE AdventureWorks2012
GO


--Dropping existing clustered primary key
--constraint (Clustered Index) from the table.
ALTER TABLE [Sales].[SalesOrderDetail]
DROP CONSTRAINT [PK_SalesOrderDetail_SalesOrderID_
SalesOrderDetailID]
GO


--Adding clustered primary key constraint
--(Clustered Index) on filegroup fg_SalesOrderDetails
```

```
ALTER TABLE [Sales].[SalesOrderDetail]
ADD CONSTRAINT [PK_SalesOrderDetail_SalesOrderID_
SalesOrderDetailID]
PRIMARY KEY CLUSTERED
(
    [SalesOrderID] ASC,
    [SalesOrderDetailID] ASC
) ON [fg_SalesOrderDetails]
GO
```

5. Now, verify the new location of the table Sales.SalesOrderDetail, by running the following query:

```
USE AdventureWorks2012
GO

--Verifying new physical location
--of table Sales.SalesOrderDetail
SELECT
    OBJECT_NAME(I.object_id) AS TableName
    ,FG.name AS FileGroupName
    ,DF.physical_name AS DataFilePath
FROM sys.indexes AS I
INNER JOIN sys.tables AS T
    ON I.object_id = T.object_id
INNER JOIN sys.filegroups AS FG
    ON I.data_space_id = FG.data_space_id
INNER JOIN sys.database_files AS DF
    ON I.data_space_id = DF.data_space_id
WHERE I.index_id <= 1 AND I.object_id = OBJECT_ID('Sales.
SalesOrderDetail')
GO
```

The following screenshot is the output of the previous query after moving the Sales.SalesOrderDetail table to a new location:

	TableName	FileGroupName	DataFilePath
1	SalesOrderDetail	fg_SalesOrderDetails	F:\SalesOrderDetails_Data\fg_SalesOrderDetails_Data.ndf

How it works...

In order to place Sales.SalesOrderDetail on separate physical disk, we created a new filegroup, fg_SalesOrderDetails, in the AdventureWorks2012 database and added a new data file, fg_SalesOrderDetails_Data.ndf, to this filegroup. After creating a new filegroup and data file, we observed the current location of the Sales.SalesOrderDetail table with a query similar to what we had used in the previous recipe.

We then executed a script that drops the existing clustered index from the `Sales.SalesOrderDetail` table with an `ALTER TABLE` statement. Because it's a clustered primary key, we needed to drop the clustered primary key constraint instead of dropping the index, as dropping the clustered primary key constraint automatically drops its associated clustered index. After dropping the clustered primary key constraint, we recreated it with the `ON [fg_SalesOrderDetails]` filegroup option, by using `ALTER TABLE`. Creating the clustered index on the `fg_SalesOrderDetails` filegroup moves all data pages of the `Sales.SalesOrderDetail` table to `F` drive.

Finally, we executed the query to verify the new location of `Sales.SalesOrderDetail`.

Moving non-clustered indexes on separate physical disk

If you have few large tables and some non-clustered indexes on these tables, which are frequently used in queries, you can consider placing the non-clustered indexes on a separate physical drive. By having non-clustered indexes on a separate physical disk, SQL Server can perform bookmark lookups in parallel and can simultaneously read data pages and index pages. This parallelism improves the performance of queries.

In this recipe, we will move all non-clustered indexes of table `Sales.SalesOrderDetail` to a separate physical disk (the table `Sales.SalesOrderDetail` that we moved to `F`: drive in the previous recipe, *Moving Existing Large Table to Separate Physical Disk*).

Getting ready

This example refers the `I` drive to place non-clustered indexes.

The following are the pre-requisites to completing this recipe:

 ▸ An instance of SQL Server 2012 Developer or Enterprise Evaluation edition.

 ▸ Sample `AdventureWorks2012` database on the instance of SQL server. For more details on how to install `AdventureWorks2012`, please refer to the *Preface* of this book

 ▸ `I` drive should be available on your machine

How to do it...

The following are the steps that will describe how to move non-clustered indexes to a separate physical disk:

1. Start SQL Server Management Studio and connect to SQL Server.

2. In the query window, type and execute the following T-SQL commands to add a new filegroup `fg_Indexes`, and data file `fg_Indexes_Data.ndf`, to the `AdventureWorks2012` database:

```
--Adding new filegroup
--named fg_Indexes
ALTER DATABASE AdventureWorks2012
ADD FILEGROUP fg_Indexes
GO


--Adding new data file to new
--filegroup fg_Indexes
ALTER DATABASE AdventureWorks2012
ADD FILE
(
  Name = fg_Indexes_Data
  ,FileName = 'I:\SQLIndex_Data\fg_Indexes_Data.ndf'
  ,SIZE = 512MB
  ,FILEGROWTH = 128MB
  ,MAXSIZE = 256GB
) TO FILEGROUP [fg_Indexes]
GO
```

3. Execute the following query to examine the current location of non-clustered indexes:

```
USE AdventureWorks2012
GO


--Verifying the current physical location of
--nonclustered indexes on table Sales.SalesOrderDetail
SELECT
  OBJECT_NAME(I.object_id) AS TableName
  ,I.name AS IndexName
  ,FG.name AS FileGroupName
  ,DF.physical_name AS DataFilePath
FROM sys.indexes AS I
INNER JOIN sys.tables AS T
  ON I.object_id = T.object_id
INNER JOIN sys.filegroups AS FG
  ON I.data_space_id = FG.data_space_id
INNER JOIN sys.database_files AS DF
  ON I.data_space_id = DF.data_space_id
WHERE I.object_id = OBJECT_ID('Sales.SalesOrderDetail')
GO
```

4. If the AdventureWorks2012 database is installed at its current location, depending upon your **SQL Server** installation path, you will see a result set similar to the one shown in the following screenshot:

	TableName	IndexName	FileGroupName	DataFilePath
1	SalesOrderDetail	AK_SalesOrderDetail_rowguid	PRIMARY	E:\SQL_Data\AdventureWorks2012_Data.mdf
2	SalesOrderDetail	IX_SalesOrderDetail_ProductID	PRIMARY	E:\SQL_Data\AdventureWorks2012_Data.mdf
3	SalesOrderDetail	PK_SalesOrderDetail_SalesOrde...	fg_SalesOrderDetails	F:\SalesOrderDetails_Data\fg_SalesOrderDetails_Data.ndf

5. Now, the following query will drop and recreate the non-clustered indexes on a new filegroup, `fg_indexes`:

```
USE AdventureWorks2012
GO


--Dropping and re-creating nonclustered
--index on filegroup fg_Indexes
CREATE NONCLUSTERED INDEX [IX_SalesOrderDetail_ProductID] ON
[Sales].[SalesOrderDetail]
(
   [ProductID] ASC
) WITH (DROP_EXISTING = ON)
ON [fg_Indexes]
GO


--Dropping and re-creating nonclustered
--index on filegroup fg_Indexes
CREATE UNIQUE NONCLUSTERED INDEX [AK_SalesOrderDetail_rowguid] ON
[Sales].[SalesOrderDetail]
(
   [rowguid] ASC
) WITH (DROP_EXISTING = ON)
ON [fg_Indexes]
GO
```

6. To verify the new location of indexes, run the following query:

```
USE AdventureWorks2012
GO


--Verifying the new physical location of
--nonclustered indexes on table Sales.SalesOrderDetail
SELECT
   OBJECT_NAME(I.object_id) AS TableName
   ,I.name AS IndexName
```

```
       ,FG.name AS FileGroupName
       ,DF.physical_name AS DataFilePath
    FROM sys.indexes AS I
    INNER JOIN sys.tables AS T
       ON I.object_id = T.object_id
    INNER JOIN sys.filegroups AS FG
       ON I.data_space_id = FG.data_space_id
    INNER JOIN sys.database_files AS DF
       ON I.data_space_id = DF.data_space_id
    WHERE I.object_id = OBJECT_ID('Sales.SalesOrderDetail')
    GO
```

The following is the screenshot of the result after moving the non-clustered index onto table
`Sales.SalesOrderDetail`:

	TableName	IndexName	FileGroupName	DataFilePath
1	SalesOrderDetail	PK_SalesOrderDetail_SalesOrd...	fg_SalesOrderDetails	F:\SalesOrderDetails_Data\fg_SalesOrderDetails_Data.ndf
2	SalesOrderDetail	AK_SalesOrderDetail_rowguid	fg_Indexes	I:\SQLIndex_Data\fg_Indexes_Data.ndf
3	SalesOrderDetail	IX_SalesOrderDetail_ProductID	fg_Indexes	I:\SQLIndex_Data\fg_Indexes_Data.ndf

How it works...

In order to place non-clustered indexes on a separate physical disk, we created a new
filegroup `fg_Indexes` in the `AdventureWorks2012` database and added a new data file,
`fg_Indexes_Data.ndf`, to this filegroup. After creating a new filegroup and data file, we
observed the current location of all indexes specified on the `Sales.SalesOrderDetail`
table with a query similar to what we had used in the previous recipe. However, we did not
put any filter on `index_id` this time, as we wanted to return rows for every index.

We then executed a script that drops the existing non-clustered indexes, `IX_
SalesOrderDetail_ProductID` and `AK_SalesOrderDetail_rowguid`, and recreated
them on the `Sales.SalesOrderDetail` table with the `CREATE INDEX` statement. Note the
inclusion of the index option `DROP_EXISTING = ON`. This drops the existing index with the
same name before it creates a new one. Also note that we created two non-clustered indexes,
`IX_SalesOrderDetail_ProductID` and `AK_SalesOrderDetail_rowguid`, with the `ON`
`[fg_Indexes]` filegroup option. This places index data in our new location.

Finally, we executed the query to verify the new location of all indexes specified on the
`Sales.SalesOrderDetail` table.

Configuring the tempdb database on separate physical disk

The `tempdb` database is one of the system databases of SQL Server that is essential for its normal functioning. SQL Server relies on the `tempdb` database to perform many of its operations and stores internal objects in this database. The following are some of the operations for which the `tempdb` database is used by SQL Server:

- Performing grouping or sorting operations in queries
- Cursor operations
- Version store operation
- Online index creation
- Storing intermediate results in worktables
- Storing user objects, such as local or global temporary tables and table variable data

The `tempdb` database is the central database for all the databases and applications per the SQL Server instance. Therefore, if many database applications are using `tempdb` extensively, the performance of the `tempdb` database is very crucial for the overall performance of the SQL Server instance. If `tempdb` resides on the same disk, which is also used by the other application databases, it is possible to have poor I/O response time depending upon the number of read/write operations being performed on other databases and the usage of the `tempdb` database by various applications.

This is the reason why, the `tempdb` database is configured on a separate physical disk, on production database servers where the `tempdb` database is used extensively, to get the best I/O performance. It is also advisable to add more data files to the `tempdb` database.

The goal of this recipe is to teach you how you can configure and move your `tempdb` database, so that its database files reside on their dedicated physical drives. Configuring the `tempdb` database on its separate physical drives reduces the I/O load on the disk where the application database resides. Placing the `tempdb` database on different disks also increases the chances of the SQL Server's performing parallel read/write operations. This improves the performance of the database server.

Getting ready

This example refers following two physical disk volumes as new file locations to place the `tempdb` database files:

- `M` drive—for data files (`.mdf` files) of the `tempdb` database
- `N` drive—for log files (`.ldf` files) of the `tempdb` database

The following are the prerequisites to completing this recipe:

- An instance of SQL Server 2012 Developer or Enterprise Evaluation edition
- Sample AdventureWorks2012 database on the instance of SQL server. For more details on how to install the AdventureWorks2012 database, please refer to the *Preface* of this book.
- M drive should be available on your machine.
- N drive should be available on your machine.

How to do it...

The following are the steps that will describe how to move a tempdb database to a new location.

1. Start SQL Server Management Studio and connect to SQL Server.

2. In the query window, type and execute the following query to verify the current physical location of the tempdb database:

```
--Switching database context to tempdb
USE tempdb
GO

--Examining curent physical location
--of tempdb database
SELECT
  name AS LogicalFileName
  ,physical_name AS PhysicalFilePath
FROM sys.database_files
GO
```

3. If the tempdb database has been created at its default location and you have not changed it yet, you will see the physical location of database files of the tempdb database; depending on your SQL Server installation path, it will be similar to the one shown in following screenshot:

	LogicalFileName	PhysicalFilePath
1	tempdev	C:\Program Files\Microsoft SQL Server\MSSQL11.MSSQLSERVER\MSSQL\DATA\tempdb.mdf
2	templog	C:\Program Files\Microsoft SQL Server\MSSQL11.MSSQLSERVER\MSSQL\DATA\templog.ldf

4. Create the following directories on the specified disks to place data files and log files of tempdb on separate physical drives:

- M:\TempDB_Data\
- N:\TempDB_Log\

5. Once the these directories are created, execute the following script to modify the location of the `tempdb` database for your SQL Server instance:

```
USE master
GO

--Changing the location of data file
--(.mdf file) of tempdb database.
ALTER DATABASE tempdb
MODIFY FILE
(
  Name = tempdev
  ,FileName = 'M:\TempDB_Data\tempdb.mdf'
)
GO

--Changing the location of log file
--(.ldf file) of tempdb database.
ALTER DATABASE tempdb
MODIFY FILE
(
  Name = templog
  ,FileName = 'N:\TempDB_Log\templog.ldf'
)
GO
```

6. After executing the previous commands, you will need to restart SQL Server service. For this, select **SQL Server Configuration Manager** from the **Configuration Tools** option in the **Microsoft SQL Server 2012** program group in the **Start** menu.

7. In **SQL Server Configuration Manager**, select **SQL Server Services** from the left pane. Right-click on the name of a SQL Server service for your SQL Server instance, and then select **Restart** to restart the service. Refer to the following screenshot for more details:

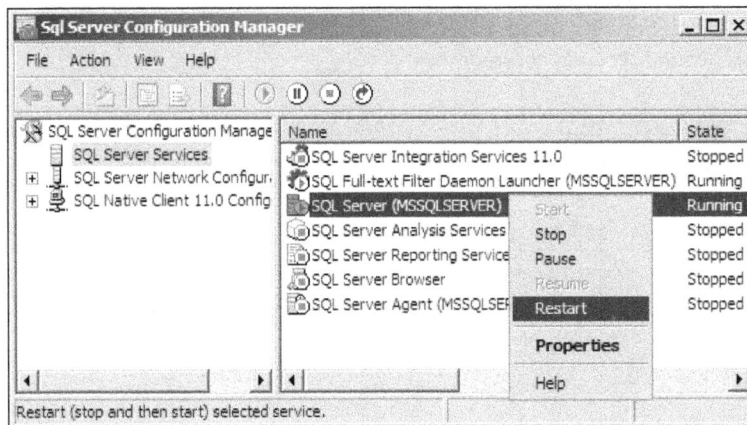

> Always use SQL Server Configuration Manager to restart the **SQL Server Service**. Do not restart SQL Server service directly from the Windows Services MMC.

8. Once the SQL Server service is restarted, the `tempdb` database can be located at a new specified location. To verify that the `tempdb` database is now at its new location, run the following query:

```
--Switching database context to tempdb
USE tempdb
GO


--Examining new physical location
--of tempdb database
SELECT
  name AS LogicalFileName
  ,physical_name AS PhysicalFilePath
FROM sys.database_files
GO
```

9. After executing the previous query, you should see a result similar to the one shown in following screenshot:

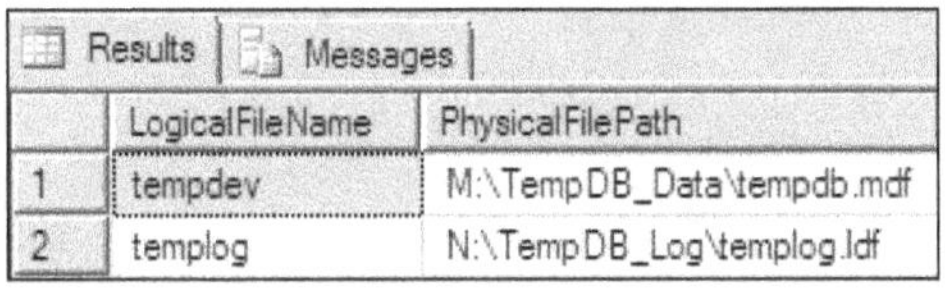

	LogicalFileName	PhysicalFilePath
1	tempdev	M:\TempDB_Data\tempdb.mdf
2	templog	N:\TempDB_Log\templog.ldf

How it works...

We first retrieved the current location of the `tempdb` database by querying the `sys.database_files` system catalog view. We then altered the locations of the data file and log file of the `tempdb` database using the `ALTER DATABASE` command, so that the data file and log file are stored on different physical drives, `M:\TempDB_Data\tempdb.mdf` and `N:\TempDB_Log\templog.ldf`, respectively, after SQL Server restarts. We then restarted SQL Server service through **SQL Server Configuration Manager**. Finally, we queried the `sys.database_files` system catalog view again, to verify the changes in location of the `tempdb` database.

15
Advanced Query Tuning Hints and Plan Guides

In this chapter we will cover:

- ▸ Using the NOLOCK table query hint
- ▸ Using the FORCESEEK and INDEX table hints
- ▸ Optimizing a query using an object plan guide
- ▸ Implementing a fixed execution plan using a SQL plan guide

Introduction

When you submit a SQL query to the SQL Server, SQL Server first parses the query to check whether it's syntactically correct or not. Once the query is parsed, a parse tree is generated. The parse tree becomes the input of the next process, which is known as **algebraization**. The algebrizer resolves all the names, data types, and aliases of columns of various objects and creates a query tree, which the query optimizer can understand. Query optimizer optimizes queries, depending on various factors, such as available indexes and statistics, and produces the execution plan. A query can be executed in a number of different ways to retrieve the same result set. However, it's the job of a query optimizer to select the best possible execution plan for a query so that it can be executed faster and will require fewer hardware resources. In most cases, the query optimizer selects the optimum execution plan, provided that statistics are up to date. However, sometimes it's possible that the execution plan picked up by the query optimizer is sub-optimal, and you may not be happy with the execution plan of the query.

To address this issue, SQL Server comes with a feature called **hints**. Hints can be specified within DML statements, so that you can give the SQL Server a hint as to how a particular query should be executed and can thus control the way a query executes. This affects the query execution plan. So, by using query hints, you instruct the query optimizer to execute a query in a certain way.

SQL server has the following three types of hints that you can use in queries, to force the query execution plan:

- ▶ Query hint
- ▶ Table hint
- ▶ Join hint

In this chapter, we will see how to use these different hints while writing our queries.

In addition to hints, SQL server also offers another unique feature called a **plan guide**. A plan guide is a kind of object that is created in the database. A plan guide can be helpful in tuning and optimizing queries that are developed by a third party and that you are not allowed or don't have access to modify. But by using plan guides, you can attach query hints and force execution plans to those queries, whenever those queries execute.

In this chapter, we will also learn how we can use these different types of plan guides and tune the performance of queries without touching their source code.

Using NOLOCK table query hint

As you may know, SQL Server uses different kinds of locks on resources belonging to the requested data and objects, to manage and maintain data consistency and data concurrency. By default, SQL Server acquires a shared lock on the resources when a SELECT query is executed. The resources can be anything from a table, to a range of keys, or single row. So, when we execute a SELECT query, the SQL Server tries to acquire a shared lock on the requested resources. However, if another transaction is updating the same data and has acquired the UPDATE locks on the same resource, the SELECT query that tries to acquire a SHARED lock on the resources may have to wait until another transaction is completed, based on the transaction isolation level.

The SQL Server allows us to specify query hints in the queries that we execute against the database engine. To avoid the query waiting time caused by lock conflicts, as we just discussed, we can use one of the table hints, WITH (NOLOCK), in our queries.

The NOLOCK hint instructs the SQL Server to retrieve the requested data without acquiring any locks on the resources. The power of NOLOCK is that it ignores other locks. This ensures that the query will not cause any shared locks on the resources and will always return data without waiting. Note that using the NOLOCK query hint is equivalent to using the READ UNCOMMITTED concurrency level.

So, data read with the NOLOCK query hint also includes dirty data that other transactions have not committed. However in some cases, using a NOLOCK query hint is usually safe and offers performance benefit, based on architecture and requirements of the application. The NOLOCK query hint can be used, if the data concurrency scenarios are well-known in advance.

In this recipe, we will see how we can use the NOLOCK table hint while writing our queries, to make sure that in most of the cases queries do not need to wait and always return the result set immediately, without acquiring any locks on the resources.

Getting ready

The following are the prerequisites for this recipe:

▸ An instance of SQL Server 2012 Developer or Enterprise Evaluation edition.

▸ A sample AdventureWorks2012 database on the SQL Server instance. For more details on how to install AdventureWorks2012 database, please refer to the *Preface* of this book.

How to do it...

The following are the steps to be performed in this recipe:

1. Open SQL Server Management Studio and connect to the SQL Server hosting the instance of AdventureWorks2012 database.

2. In a new query window (Connection-1), execute following script. The script will begin a new transaction and acquire an update lock (UPDLOCK) on the rows and hold it (HOLDLOCK) until the transaction is completed:

```
USE AdventureWorks2012
GO

--Beginning Transaction (From Connection-1)
BEGIN TRANSACTION
  --Fetching Order Details for
  --which LineTotal>10000.00 with
  --UPDATE and HOLD lock query hint
  SELECT
    SalesOrderID
    ,SalesOrderDetailID
    ,ProductID
    ,OrderQty
    ,UnitPrice
    ,UnitPriceDiscount
    ,LineTotal
  FROM Sales.SalesOrderDetail WITH (UPDLOCK,HOLDLOCK)
  WHERE LineTotal>10000.00
```

3. Open a new query window and try to run the following SELECT query. You will notice that the query will not execute and it will have to wait:

```
--Fetching Order Details for
--which LineTotal>10000.00 (From Connection-2)
SELECT
   SalesOrderID
   ,SalesOrderDetailID
   ,ProductID
   ,OrderQty
   ,UnitPrice
   ,UnitPriceDiscount
   ,LineTotal
FROM Sales.SalesOrderDetail
WHERE LineTotal>10000.00
```

4. Now, open one more query window (Connection-3). In this query window, type and execute the following query, which is the same as the preceding one, except the fact that the following query is using a NOLOCK query hint:

```
--Fetching Order Details for
--which LineTotal>10000.00
--with NOLOCK query hint (From Connection-3)
SELECT
   SalesOrderID
   ,SalesOrderDetailID
   ,ProductID
   ,OrderQty
   ,UnitPrice
   ,UnitPriceDiscount
   ,LineTotal
FROM Sales.SalesOrderDetail WITH (NOLOCK)
WHERE LineTotal>10000.00
```

5. Note that this query will succeed and return the result set immediately. Now, go back to the first query window (Connection-1) where the transaction was started, and in this query window, run the following command to end the transaction:

```
--Rolling back the transaction
--(From Connection-1)
ROLLBACK TRANSACTION
```

6. Now, go to the second query window (Connection-2) where you can observe that the query was able to retrieve data as the transaction which was started from Connection-1 was completed.

How it works...

In this recipe, we first executed a query from Connection-1, which retrieved records from the `Sales.SalesOrderDetail` table where `LineTotal > 10000`. Note that we have used the `UPDLOCK` and `HOLDLOCK` query hints here. The `UPDLOCK` query hint acquires the `UPDATE` lock on rows, as if the rows are going to be updated and `HOLDLOCK` holds that lock until the transaction is completed. In a real-life scenario, you can think of these rows as if they are going to be updated by the `UPDATE` statement.

> We could have used the `UPDATE` statement instead of using the `UPDLOCK` and the `HOLDLOCK` hints here. However, this has been done purposefully, just to show you how incorrectly used query hints can block other queries.

We then executed the same query without any query hint from Connection-2. The `SELECT` statement in the second query tried to acquire the `SHARED` locks (default behavior of the `SELECT` statement) to access the same set of records but the request was blocked, because there are `UPDATE` locks on the same rows held by Connection-1.

Finally, we executed the same query from Connection-3, to retrieve the same set of rows, but this time with the query hint `NOLOCK`. This hint instructed SQL Server to simply retrieve the data without acquiring any shared lock on the data. Because SQL Server did not need to acquire any lock, it could run the query to return the same rows, which are locked by Connection-1.

> Considering the database application architecture and requirements, try to use the `NOLOCK` query hint when it is safe to use. It reduces the overhead on SQL Server caused by acquiring and releasing locks. Using the `NOLOCK` hint reduces the blocking issues, as queries with a `NOLOCK` hint do not have to wait for the result. This improves the overall performance of queries.

Using FORCESEEK and INDEX table hint

A major role of a query optimizer is to choose the best execution plan among the different available plans for query execution. In most of the cases, query optimizer always chooses the right execution plan, and we generally don't need to specify query hints to force the query optimizer to execute a query in a desired way. However, in rare cases, it can happen that query optimizer may fail to choose the right query plan.

SQL Server allows us to specify query hints while writing queries, which forces the query optimizer to execute the query in a specific way only.

In this recipe, we will see how we can force a query to perform an index seek operation by using the `FORCESEEK` and `INDEX` table query hints when the query optimizer performs an index scan operation.

Getting ready

In this recipe, we first see that certain ProductIDs cause an index scan operation while retrieving data from the `Sales.SalesOrderDetail` table. Then we will use the query hints `INDEX` and `FORCESEEK`, so that an index seek operation can be used.

Before starting this recipe, make sure that you fulfil the following prerequisites:

▸ An instance of SQL Server 2012 Developer or Enterprise Evaluation edition

▸ Sample `AdventureWorks2012` database on the instance of SQL Server

How to do it...

Follow the ensuing steps to perform this recipe:

1. Start SQL Server Management Studio and connect to SQL Server.

2. In a new query window, execute the following T-SQL script against the AdventureWorks2012 database. Make sure that, before executing a query, you click on **Include Actual Execution Plan** to view the execution plan once query execution is completed:

```
USE AdventureWorks2012
GO

--Retrieving Data from Sales.SalesOrderDetail table
-- for ProductID 800,801,802,803,804,805
SELECT
  SalesOrderID
 ,SalesOrderDetailID
 ,ProductID
 ,OrderQty
 ,UnitPrice
 ,UnitPriceDiscount
 ,LineTotal
FROM Sales.SalesOrderDetail
WHERE ProductID >= 800 AND ProductID <=805

GO
```

3. Click on the **Execution plan** tab at the bottom of the result pane and observe the execution plan. As it can been seen from the following screenshot, the query optimizer has chosen an index scan operation to retrieve records:

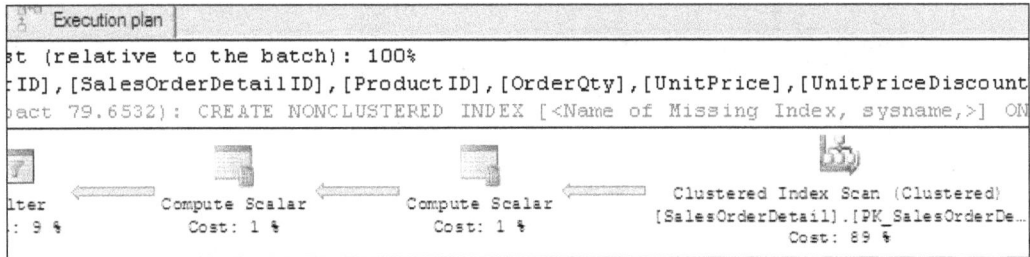

```
Execution plan

st (relative to the batch): 100%
 ID],[SalesOrderDetail ID],[Product ID],[OrderQty],[UnitPrice],[UnitPriceDiscount
bact 79.6532): CREATE NONCLUSTERED INDEX [<Name of Missing Index, sysname,>] ON
```

4. Now, execute the following query to retrieve the same set of records, but this time using the FORCESEEK and INDEX table hints along with the index name, as shown next:

```
USE AdventureWorks2012
GO

--Retrieving Data from Sales.SalesOrderDetail
--table for ProductID 800,801,802,803,804,805
--using FORCESEEK and INDEX query hints
SELECT
    SalesOrderID
    ,SalesOrderDetailID
    ,ProductID
    ,OrderQty
    ,UnitPrice
    ,UnitPriceDiscount
    ,LineTotal
FROM Sales.SalesOrderDetail WITH (INDEX(IX_SalesOrderDetail_
ProductID), FORCESEEK)
WHERE ProductID >= 800 AND ProductID <=805

GO
```

5. Now click on the **Execution Plan** table in the result pane and observe the execution plan that the preceding query has used. You will notice that the previous query has used the index seek operation and used index on the ProductID column, as shown next:

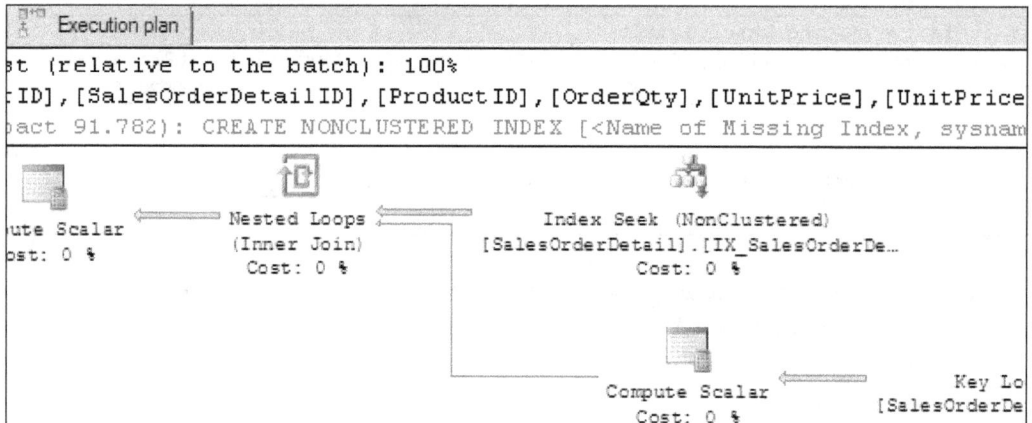

```
⌐̵ Execution plan

t (relative to the batch): 100%
ID],[SalesOrderDetailID],[ProductID],[OrderQty],[UnitPrice],[UnitPrice
act 91.782): CREATE NONCLUSTERED INDEX [<Name of Missing Index, sysnam

ute Scalar          Nested Loops             Index Seek (NonClustered)
st: 0 %            (Inner Join)              [SalesOrderDetail].[IX_SalesOrderDe...
                    Cost: 0 %                        Cost: 0 %

                                              Compute Scalar              Key Lo
                                                Cost: 0 %              [SalesOrderDe
```

How it works...

In this recipe, we retrieved records from Sales.SalesOrderDetail, for which the ProductID is any from 800, 801, 802, 803, 804, 805, and hence we specified the condition WHERE ProductID >= 800 AND ProductID <=805. However, the returned rows are not "most of the rows" and though they are few in number, the query optimizer has still elected to perform a clustered index scan operation, which can be seen in the execution plan.

The second query uses the table hints INDEX and FORCESEEK. The FORCESEEK table hint forces a query to perform an index seek operation. By specifying INDEX along with the index name IX_SalesOrderDetail_ProductID, we suggest that the query optimizer use the index IX_SalesOrderDetail_ProductID, so that it performs an index seek operation.

Remember that using table/query hints does not guarantee that there will always be a performance gain. You should use table/query hints as the last option. Before applying query hints, first confirm that there will be a gain in query performance. This is because, in most cases, the query optimizer is intelligent enough to find out cheap execution plan among the other execution plans. If you observe that the query optimizer uses an index scan operation instead of an index seek operation in a specific scenario, it does not always mean that the query optimizer has failed at choosing the right query plan. It also means that the query optimizer has estimated that an index scan operation is less costly than an index seek operation. That usually happens when the query optimizer estimates a clustered index scan operation to be cheaper than an index seek and a key lookup operation. Therefore before using query hints, always check and compare the query execution statistics.

Optimizing a query using an object plan guide

Plan guide is a feature in SQL Server that you can use to tune queries, which are developed/ deployed by third parties and for which you are not allowed to modify the code. With a plan guide, it's possible to attach query hints to the queries that are executed against the database server. A SQL Server attaches the query hints, as specified by the plan guide, to the query before executing it. In this way, an ad-hoc query or a query in the stored procedure can be tuned without changing it in the source code.

There are three types of plan guides, as follows:

▸ **Object plan guide**: Used with stored procedures and user-defined functions

▸ **SQL plan guide**: Used with ad-hoc SQL queries

▸ **Template plan guide**: Used with ad-hoc SQL queries

We will learn how to use an object plan guide to optimize a query for a particular value. An object plan guide is created upon a stored procedure or user defined functions. A SQL query statement specified in the plan guide is matched against the query found within the stored procedure for optimization, and if it is matched, the query is optimized before it gets executed.

In this recipe, we will create a stored procedure named `Sales.GetSalesOrderByCountry_TestPlanGuide`, which retrieves the data from the `Sales.SalesOrderHeader` table, based on parameter `@Country_region`, representing a specific country region by joining it with `Sales.Customer` and `Sales.SalesTerritory`. Knowing in advance that most of the orders are from the US country region, we will apply a plan guide to the stored procedure, so that the query that retrieves sales data in the stored procedure is optimized for the US country region, with the `OPTIMIZE FOR` query hint.

Getting ready

The following are the prerequisites for this recipe:

▸ An instance of SQL Server 2012 Developer or Enterprise Evaluation edition.

▸ A sample `AdventureWorks2012` database on the SQL Server instance. For more details on how to install the `AdventureWorks2012` database, please refer to the *Preface* of this book.

Also, you need to know how a plan guide is created. We will be creating plan guides with a system stored procedure named `sp_create_plan_guide`. The following are the parameters that are passed to `sp_create_plan_guide`:

- `@name`: Name of the plan guide
- `@stmt`: Query text, which is to be optimized
- `@type`: Type of the plan guide—this can be `OBJECT`, `SQL`, or `TEMPLATE`
- `@module_or_batch`: Name of the stored procedure, if the plan guide is an object plan guide
- `@params`: Parameter definition for SQL statements
- `@hints`: Can be a table/query hint or a forced execution plan XML

Creating a plan guide using SSMS

A plan guide can also be created using SQL Server Management Studio by right-clicking on the **Databases|AdventureWorks2012|Programmability|Plan Guides** node and then selecting **New Plan Guide...** in **Object Explorer**.

How to do it...

For this recipe, follow the given steps:

1. Start SQL Server Management Studio and connect to SQL Server.
2. In a new query window, execute the following T-SQL script against the AdventureWorks2012 database to create the stored procedure Sales.GetSalesOrderByCountry_TestPlanGuide:

```
USE AdventureWorks2012
GO

CREATE PROCEDURE Sales.GetSalesOrderByCountry_TestPlanGuide
(
  @Country_region NVARCHAR(60)
) AS
BEGIN
    SELECT *
    FROM Sales.SalesOrderHeader AS SOH
    INNER JOIN Sales.Customer AS C
    ON SOH.CustomerID = C.CustomerID
    INNER JOIN Sales.SalesTerritory AS ST
        ON C.TerritoryID = ST.TerritoryID
    WHERE ST.CountryRegionCode = @Country_region;
END
GO
```

3. Now let us create a plan guide, `MyObjectPlanGuide`, for the stored procedure `Sales.GetSalesOrderByCountry_TestPlanGuide`, with the following script:

```
USE AdventureWorks2012
GO

--Creating plan guide for
--stored procedure MyObjectPlanGuide
EXEC sp_create_plan_guide
    @name =  N'MyObjectPlanGuide',
    @stmt = N'SELECT *
    FROM Sales.SalesOrderHeader AS SOH
    INNER JOIN Sales.Customer AS C ON SOH.CustomerID =
C.CustomerID
    INNER JOIN Sales.SalesTerritory AS ST
        ON C.TerritoryID = ST.TerritoryID
    WHERE ST.CountryRegionCode = @Country_region;',
    @type = N'OBJECT',
    @module_or_batch = N'Sales.GetSalesOrderByCountry_
TestPlanGuide',
    @params = NULL,
    @hints = N'OPTION (OPTIMIZE FOR (@Country_region = N''US''))';
GO
```

4. In **Object Explorer**, expand **Databases|AdventureWorks2012|Programmability|P
lan Guides** node, make sure that the new plan guide has been created, as shown in the following screenshot:

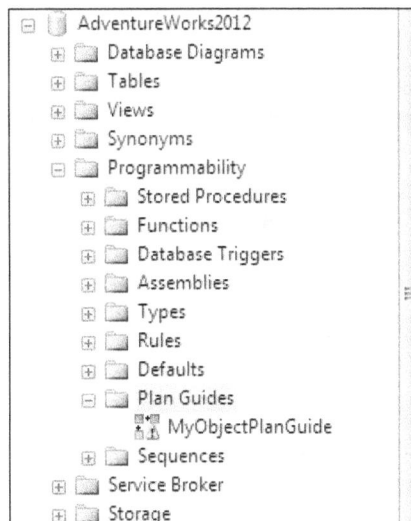

5. Now, execute the stored procedure as shown in following script. Make sure that before executing the following script, you click on **Include Actual Execution Plan**, to view the execution plan once the stored procedure execution is completed:

```
USE AdventureWorks2012
GO


EXECUTE Sales.GetSalesOrderByCountry_TestPlanGuide 'US'
GO
```

6. Press *F4* to display the **Properties** window, if it is not shown. Click on the **Execution Plan** tab in the result pane and click on the icon for the SELECT statement in the execution plan. In the **Properties** window, examine the value for the property **PlanGuideName**, which is used by the execution plan. The following screenshot shows a plan guide name in the **Properties** window:

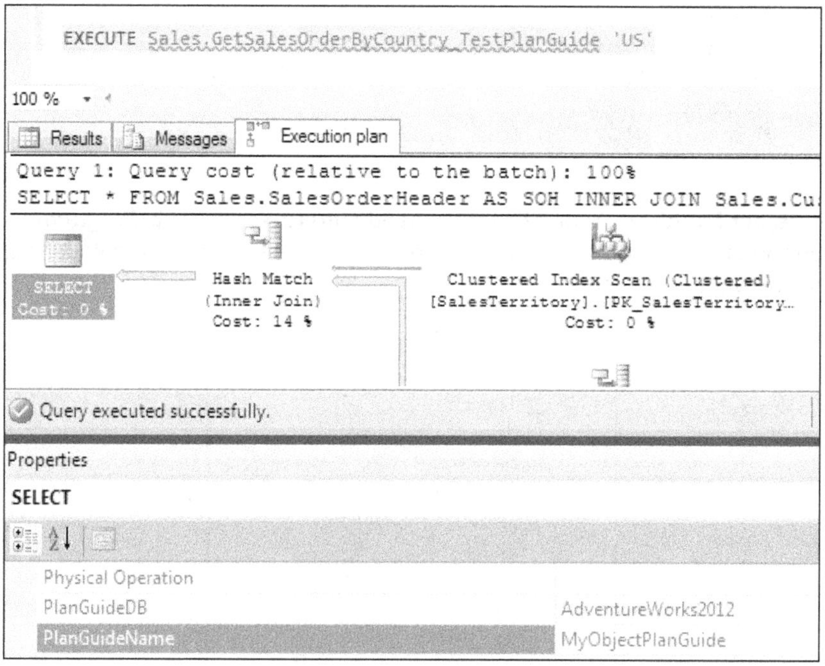

> **Plan Guide and SQL Server Profiler**
>
> When a plan guide is used successfully in an execution plan for a query or stored procedure, you will also see the `Plan Guide Successful` event captured in SQL Server Profiler, if you include this event in your trace.

How it works...

In this recipe, we first created a stored procedure `Sales.GetSalesOrderByCountry_ TestPlanGuide`. In a real-life example, this stored procedure can be compared to a database object developed by a third party and which you don't have access to modify. The procedure accepts a country region as parameter and retrieves sales data by joining tables `Sales.SalesOrderHeader`, `Sales.Customer`, and `Sales.SalesTerritory`. The data is filtered by the `@Country_region` parameter.

We then created a plan guide named `MyObjectPlanGuide`, by calling the system stored procedure `sp_create_plan_guide`. The `@stmt` parameter in `sp_create_plan_guide` represents the exact query text in the stored procedure, which is to be optimized. The `@type` parameter is set to `OBJECT`, as we wanted to create an object plan guide. The `@module_or_ batch` parameter specifies the name of the stored procedure for which the plan guide is to be created, which happens to be `Sales.GetSalesOrderByCountry_TestPlanGuide` in this example. The `@params` parameter was set to null in our example, as this parameter is not relevant to our case. Finally, we specified the query hint `OPTIMIZE FOR` with the `OPTION` clause and with the value `US` to be optimized for the `@Country_region` parameter. This option instructs the SQL server to optimize the query for the US country region. Because majority of the orders are from the US country region, the overall performance of the query will be optimized whenever the sales data for the US country region is requested.

We verified the newly created plan guide in **Object Explorer** in SQL Server Management Studio.

Finally, we executed the stored procedure `Sales.GetSalesOrderByCountry_ TestPlanGuide` and examined the execution plan of the query to verify that the execution plan used the plan guide we created.

Implementing a fixed execution plan using SQL plan guide

As plan guides can be used to specify query hints for SQL statements, they can also specify an execution plan instead of query hints to force an execution plan.

In this recipe, we first observe that even though there is a non-clustered index on ProductID column, some of the values of `ProductID` cause an index scan operation when data is retrieved. We will create an SQL plan guide so that all the queries as specified by the plan guide performs the index seek operation for every `ProductID` by forcing a previously saved execution plan.

Getting ready

We will see that `ProductID 806` causes an index seek operation while `ProductID 800` causes an index scan operation. We will generate an execution plan with an index seek operation and force that plan for the same type of queries so that for every `ProductID` an index seek is performed.

The following are the prerequisites for this recipe:

▸ An instance of SQL Server 2012 Developer or Enterprise Evaluation edition.

▸ A sample `AdventureWorks2012` database on the SQL Server instance. For more details on how to install the `AdventureWorks2012` database, please refer to the *Preface* of this book.

How to do it...

For this recipe, follow the given steps:

1. Start SQL Server Management Studio and connect to SQL Server.

2. In the query window, execute the following T-SQL script against the `AdventureWorks2012` database, to retrieve sales order details from the `Sales.SalesOrderDetail from Sales.SalesOrderDetail` table for `ProductID` equal to `806`. Just make sure that before executing the following script, you click on **Include Actual Execution Plan**, to view the execution plan of the query:

```
USE AdventureWorks2012
GO

DECLARE @ProductID INT = 806
DECLARE @Param NVARCHAR(100)= '@ProductID int'
DECLARE @SQL NVARCHAR(MAX) = 'SELECT
   SalesOrderID
   ,SalesOrderDetailID
   ,ProductID
   ,OrderQty
   ,UnitPrice
   ,UnitPriceDiscount
   ,LineTotal
FROM Sales.SalesOrderDetail
WHERE ProductID = @ProductID
OPTION (RECOMPILE)'

--Retrieving Sales Order Details for
--Product = 806
EXECUTE sp_executesql @SQL,@Param,@ProductID
GO
```

3. Click on the **Execution Plan** tab in the result pane and observe the execution plan for the preceding query. Note that for `ProductID 806`, the query optimizer has performed the index seek operation. The execution plan of the preceding query should look like the following screenshot:

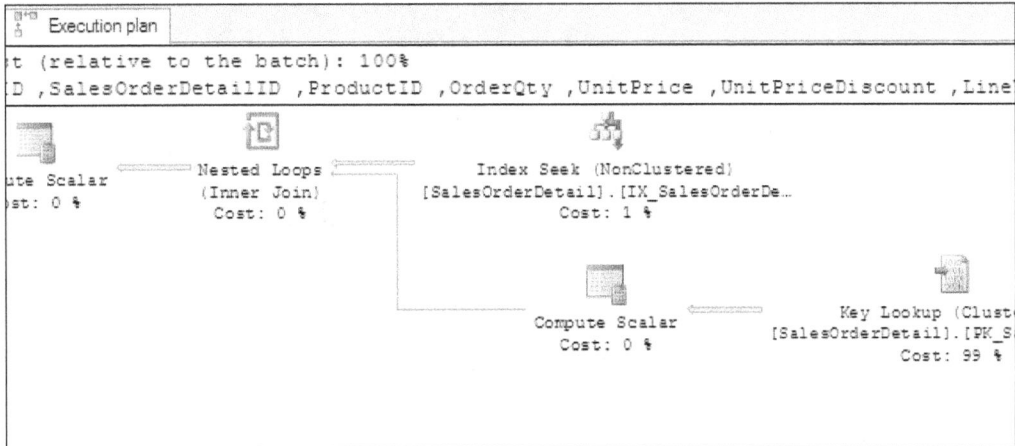

4. Now, execute the following query to retrieve data for `ProductID` equal to `800` from the `Sales.SalesOrderDetail` table:

```
USE AdventureWorks2012
GO

DECLARE @ProductID INT = 800
DECLARE @Param NVARCHAR(100)= '@ProductID int'
DECLARE @SQL NVARCHAR(MAX) = 'SELECT
    SalesOrderID
    ,SalesOrderDetailID
    ,ProductID
    ,OrderQty
    ,UnitPrice
    ,UnitPriceDiscount
    ,LineTotal
FROM Sales.SalesOrderDetail
WHERE ProductID = @ProductID
OPTION (RECOMPILE)'

--Retrieving Sales Order Details for
--Product = 800
EXECUTE sp_executesql @SQL,@Param,@ProductID
GO
```

5. Click on the **Execution Plan** tab in the result pane and observe the execution plan for the preceding query. Note that for `ProductID 800`, the query optimizer has performed an index scan operation. The execution plan should look like the following screenshot:

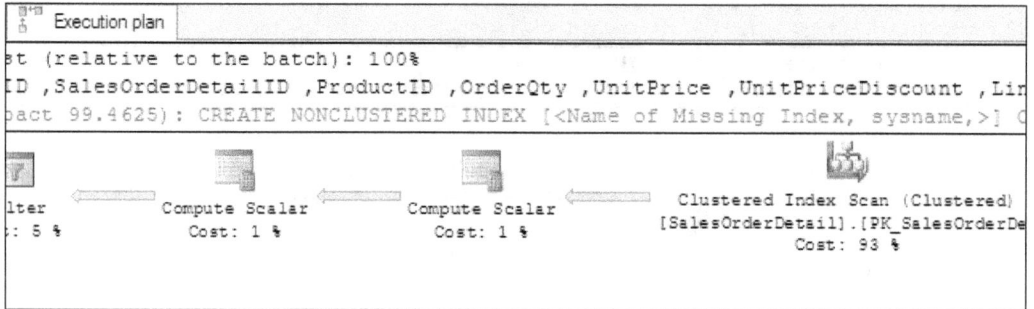

6. We want an execution plan to be generated, which performs an index seek operation. Let's execute the following query, which retrieves the sales order details for `ProductID` equal to `806`:

```
USE AdventureWorks2012
GO

--Retrieving Sales Order Details for
--Product = 806 to in order to generate
--optimum Execution Plan with Index Seek
--operation.
SELECT
  SalesOrderID
  ,SalesOrderDetailID
  ,ProductID
  ,OrderQty
  ,UnitPrice
  ,UnitPriceDiscount
  ,LineTotal
FROM Sales.SalesOrderDetail
WHERE ProductID = 806
GO
```

7. The following script will retrieve an execution plan for the preceding query in XML format by querying **Dynamic Management Views** (**DMVs**) and store it in a variable. It also creates a SQL plan guide named `MySQLFixedPlanGuide`, by using the execution plan. Run the following script:

```
USE AdventureWorks2012
GO
```

```sql
--Retrieving Execution Plan of above
--query in XML Format from DMVs and
--Saving in Variable @Execution_Plan_XML
DECLARE @Execution_Plan_XML nvarchar(max);
SET @Execution_Plan_XML = (SELECT TOP 1 query_plan
    FROM sys.dm_exec_query_stats AS QS
    CROSS APPLY sys.dm_exec_sql_text(QS.sql_handle) AS ST
    CROSS APPLY sys.dm_exec_text_query_plan(QS.plan_handle,
DEFAULT, DEFAULT) AS QP
    WHERE ST.text LIKE
  N'SELECT
  SalesOrderID
  ,SalesOrderDetailID
  ,ProductID
  ,OrderQty
  ,UnitPrice
  ,UnitPriceDiscount
  ,LineTotal
FROM Sales.SalesOrderDetail
WHERE ProductID = 806%');

--Creating SQL Plan Guide using
--the generated execution plan
EXEC sp_create_plan_guide
@name = N'MySQLFixedPlanGuide',
@stmt = 'SELECT
  SalesOrderID
  ,SalesOrderDetailID
  ,ProductID
  ,OrderQty
  ,UnitPrice
  ,UnitPriceDiscount
  ,LineTotal
FROM Sales.SalesOrderDetail
WHERE ProductID = @ProductID',
@type = N'SQL',
@module_or_batch = NULL,
@params = '@ProductID int',
@hints =  @Execution_Plan_XML;

GO
```

8. Verify that the plan guide has been created with appropriate values as expected. To do this, right-click on the plan guide named **MySQLFixedPlanGuide**, located at **Databases | AdventureWorks2012 | Programmability | Plan Guides** , and then select **Properties** in **Object Explorer**. You should see a dialog box that is similar to the following screenshot. Verify the details of all parameters:

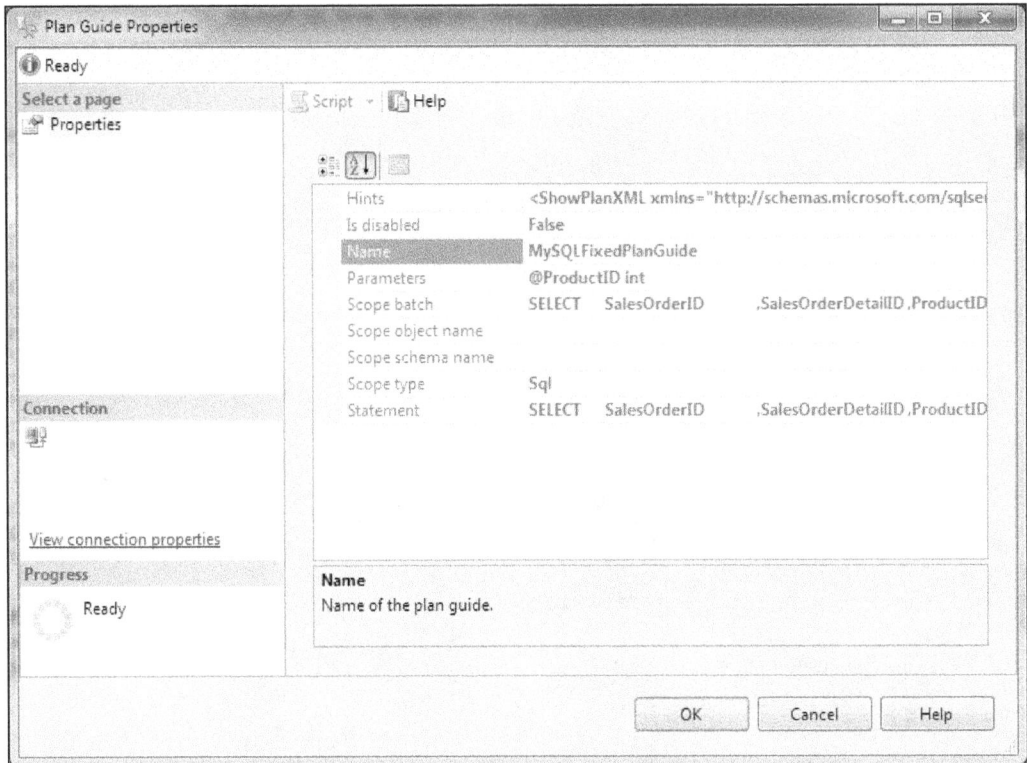

9. After a plan guide is created, run the following query to retrieve the sales order details for when `ProductID` is `800`, once again:

```
USE AdventureWorks2012
GO

DECLARE @ProductID INT = 800
DECLARE @Param NVARCHAR(100) = '@ProductID int'
DECLARE @SQL NVARCHAR(MAX) = 'SELECT
  SalesOrderID
  ,SalesOrderDetailID
  ,ProductID
  ,OrderQty
  ,UnitPrice
  ,UnitPriceDiscount
  ,LineTotal
```

```
FROM Sales.SalesOrderDetail
WHERE ProductID = @ProductID'

--Retrieving Sales Order Details for
--Product = 800
EXECUTE sp_executesql @SQL,@Param,@ProductID
```

10. Now, go to the **Execution Plan** tab and look at the execution plan for the preceding query. Your execution plan should be similar to the one shown as follows:

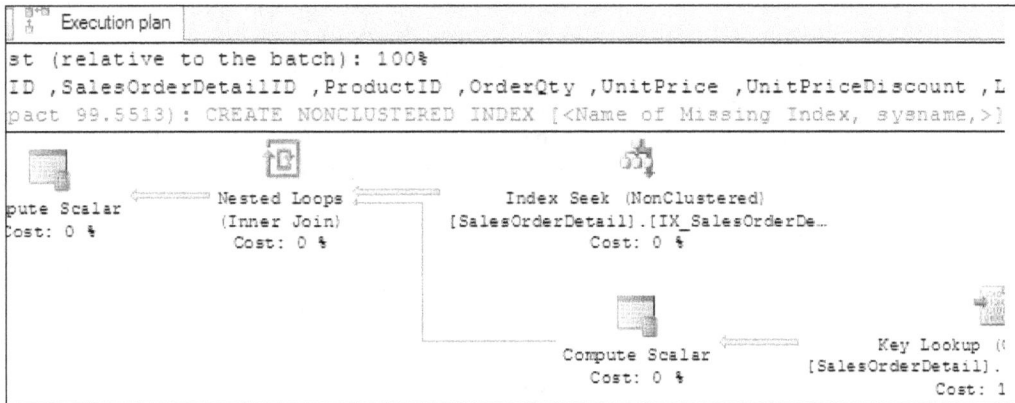

11. Note, in the preceding execution plan, that the query now performs an index seek operation. To make sure that the plan guide was applied indeed and used, press *F4* to display the **Properties** window, if it is not shown. In the execution plan, click on the icon for SELECT statement in execution plan. In the properties window, examine the value for the property PlanGuideName, which is used by the execution plan. The following screenshot shows a plan guide name in the **Properties** window:

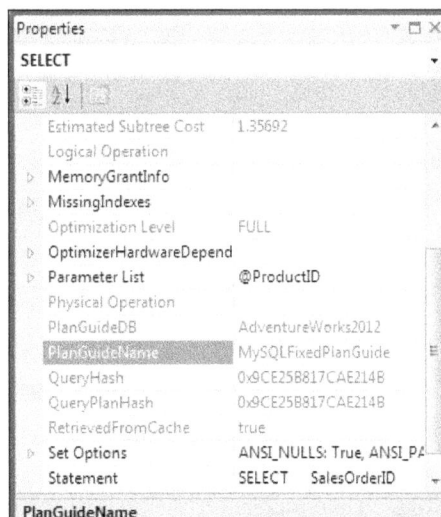

How it works...

In this recipe, we first executed a parameterized query to retrieve data from the `Sales.SalesOrderDetail` table for when `ProductID` is `806` with a `sp_executesql` system stored procedure, and then we observed that the execution plan uses an index seek operation to retrieve data.

Next, we executed the same query for when `ProductID` is `806`, and we noticed in the execution plan that, for `ProductID 800`, the query optimizer used an index scan operation. Note that in both the queries we have used the `OPTION (RECOMPILE)` query hint, so that both the queries produce their own execution plan and do not use any previously generated execution plan. This guarantees that we get the exact execution plan for a particular `ProductID` that a query optimizer generates for a specific `ProductID`. If we had not used the `WITH (RECOMPILE)` query hint, the second query might have used the same execution plan with an index seek operation that was generated by the first query. Also note that if we had run the query with `Product ID` equal to `800` first and then executed the same query for when `ProductID` is `806`, without the `OPTION (RECOMPILE)` query hint, we might have ended up getting an index scan operation for both the queries, as the second query also should have used the execution plan residing in the cache.

We knew that for when `ProductID` is `806`, the query optimizer performs an index seek operation. Therefore, we once again executed the query for when `ProductID` is `806`. After this query is executed, we retrieved its XML execution plan by joining DMVs and functions—`sys.dm_exec_query_stats`, `sys.dm_exec_sql_text()` and `sys.dm_exec_text_query_plan()`. To do this, we cross-apply the result of `sys.dm_exec_query_stats` with `sys.dm_exec_sql_text()`, passing it `sql_handle`, filtering the query text by our actual query text; then we cross applied result with `sys.dm_exec_text_query_plan()` by passing `plan_handle` to it and accessing the XML execution plan from there. We stored XML execution in the `@Execution_Plan_XML` variable. This XML was then passed in the stored procedure `sp_create_plan_guide` to `@hints parameter` to create our plan guide named `MySQLFixedPlanGuide`.

Because we had an XML execution plan for when `ProductID` is `806`, the plan was generated having an index seek operation performed on the index defined in the `ProductID` column. We wanted to force the index seek operation by forcing the same execution plan for every product. Hence, we have specified a parameter `@ProductID` in our query text that we passed to the `@stmt` variable and defined parameter `@ProductID int` for `@params` variable in the `sp_create_plan_guide` stored procedure call. Because we wanted to create a SQL plan guide, we passed a literal value `SQL` to the `@type` parameter and `NULL` value to the `@module_or_batch` parameter.

We then verified that our plan guide was created by opening **Databases | AdventureWorks2012 | Programmability | Plan Guides** and then selecting **Properties** in **Object Explorer**.

Once the plan guide was created, we executed the same parameterized query for `ProductID` equal to `800` with a `sp_executesql` system stored procedure and observed it execution plan. When we executed our query, the plan guide's query template was matched against the executed query and the plan guide was used for query optimization, which forced the execution plan that we had specified. We could see that the execution plan of the query resulted in an index seek operation and not in an index scan, this time.

Finally, we verified that the plan guide `MySQLFixedPlanGuide` was indeed used by looking at the execution plan property and by examining the value of the **PlanGuideName** property in the **Properties** window.

16
Dealing with Locking, Blocking, and Deadlocking

In this chapter we will cover:

- ▶ Determining long-running transactions
- ▶ Detecting blocked and blocking queries
- ▶ Detecting deadlocks with SQL Server Profiler
- ▶ Detecting deadlocks with Trace Flag 1204

Introduction

Transactions are an integral part of any OLTP database system. They manage data consistency and data concurrency issues, to make sure that data always remains in a valid state in the database, when multiple sources read or update the same data at the same time. In SQL Server, this is achieved through a locking mechanism that SQL Server applies while reading and writing data from and to the database. The lock manager in SQL Server is responsible for applying this locking mechanism. SQL Server issues different types of locks on different types of resources, such as database, file, object, table, extent, page, and key.

While working with transactions, there is always a chance that you will face the issues caused by transactions. These issues are generally related to locking, blocking, and deadlocking. We often need to troubleshoot such issues and fix them, so that we can avoid them.

This chapter will discuss such challenges and provide you with insight on how to cope with these types of situations.

Determining long-running transactions

Long-running transactions block the other transactions and in turn introduce new long-running transactions! This affects the performance of the database server.

As a DBA, you should regularly monitor your database transactions and should take necessary remedial steps whenever you identify such long-running transactions, as they can degrade the performance of the application drastically.

In this recipe, you will see how you can monitor the transactions by looking at their time duration. If you frequently find some transactions running for a long time, you may probably want to find if they are blocked by other transactions. You may also probably look into the query to investigate which statements of the transaction are taking more time and why, so that you can know which part of the T-SQL code should be modified accordingly.

Getting ready

This will be a very simple recipe that will show you how to track the transaction time. With the script that has been provided in this example, you can see all the current running transactions along with the time duration for which they have been executing.

The following are the prerequisites for this recipe:

▶ An instance of SQL Server 2012 Developer or Enterprise Evaluation edition.

▶ A sample `AdventureWorks2012` database on the SQL Server instance. For more details on how to install the `AdventureWorks2012` database, please refer to the *Preface* of this book.

How to do it...

Follow the ensuing steps to perform this recipe:

1. Start SQL Server Management Studio and establish a connection to the SQL Server hosting the `AdventureWorks2012` database.

2. In the query window (Connection-1), type the following T-SQL statements and then execute them to begin a sample transaction from Connection-1:

```
--Beginning a sample transaction
USE AdventureWorks2012
GO

BEGIN TRANSACTION

SELECT * FROM Sales.SalesOrderHeader
```

3. Now, to monitor currently running transactions, type and execute the following T-SQL script in a new query window (Connection-2):

```sql
--Detecting Long-Running Transaction
SELECT
      ST.transaction_id AS TransactionID
      ,DB_NAME(DT.database_id) AS DatabaseName
      ,AT.transaction_begin_time AS TransactionStartTime
      ,DATEDIFF (SECOND, AT.transaction_begin_time, GETDATE()) AS
TransactionDuration
      ,CASE AT.transaction_type
            WHEN 1 THEN 'Read/Write Transaction'
            WHEN 2 THEN 'Read-Only Transaction'
            WHEN 3 THEN 'System Transaction'
            WHEN 4 THEN 'Distributed Transaction'
      END AS TransactionType
      ,CASE AT.transaction_state
            WHEN 0 THEN 'Transaction Not Initialized'
            WHEN 1 THEN 'Transaction Initialized & Not Started'
            WHEN 2 THEN 'Active Transaction'
            WHEN 3 THEN 'Transaction Ended'
            WHEN 4 THEN 'Distributed Transaction Initiated Commit
Process'
            WHEN 5 THEN 'Transaction in Prepared State & Waiting
Resolution'
            WHEN 6 THEN 'Transaction Committed'
            WHEN 7 THEN 'Transaction Rolling Back'
            WHEN 8 THEN 'Transaction Rolled Back'
      END AS TransactionState
FROM sys.dm_tran_session_transactions AS ST
INNER JOIN sys.dm_tran_active_transactions AS AT
ON ST.transaction_id = AT.transaction_id
INNER JOIN sys.dm_tran_database_transactions AS DT
ON ST.transaction_id = DT.transaction_id
ORDER BY TransactionStartTime
GO
```

4. You should get an output similar to the one shown in following screenshot:

	TransactionID	DatabaseName	TransactionStartTime	TransactionDuration	TransactionType	TransactionState
1	66812	AdventureWorks2012	2012-01-29 08:04:01.420	123	Read/Write Transaction	Active Transaction

5. Execute the following statement in the first query window(Connection-1), to roll back the transaction initiated previously:

```
--Rolling Back sample transaction

ROLLBACK TRANSACTION
GO
```

How it works...

We first connected to the SQL Server instance that is hosting the `AdventureWorks2012` database. In a query window (Connection-1), we started a new transaction in which we queried data from the table `Sales.SalesOrderHeader`.

In another query window (Connection-2), we executed a query to see all currently running transactions. In this query we used the following transaction-related dynamic management views:

- **sys.dm_tran_session_transactions**, which provides transaction-related information along with some session specific information
- **sys.dm_tran_active_transactions**, which provides information on all transactions currently active at instance level
- **sys.dm_tran_database_transactions**,which provides information on transactions that are database-specific

All these DMVs are joined to the `transaction_id` column. To know with which database a particular transaction is associated, we used the `DB_NAME()` function by passing the `database_id` column.

The `transaction_begin_time` column specifies the time when the transaction was started. By using `DATEDIFF()` function on this column, we calculated the number of seconds for which a particular transaction has been running.

The other columns denote the types and states of the transaction.

Finally, we sorted the output of the query based on `TransactionStartTime`, so that we get the oldest and longest-running transactions at the top of the list.

Detecting blocked and blocking queries

If a transaction is waiting for some resources because the same resources are locked by other transactions, that transaction is considered a **blocked transaction**. On the contrary, a transaction that has locked the resources and caused other transactions to wait is considered a **blocking transaction**.

Long-running transactions can block other transactions and queries for a long time. In a heavily transacted database, many times we face the "blocking" problem. If a transaction is not completed because it is blocked, it can take time to complete, which in turn blocks the other transactions.

In this recipe, we will learn how to find which queries are blocked by which queries, and how to kill those blocking queries, as part of the immediate solution!

Getting ready

As we are going to see how to find blocked and blocking queries, we will first create a scenario so that we can create a blocking query.

The following are the prerequisites for this recipe:

▶ An instance of SQL Server 2012 Developer or Enterprise Evaluation edition.

▶ A sample AdventureWorks2012 database on the SQL Server instance. For more details on how to install the AdventureWorks2012 database, please refer to the *Preface* of this book.

How to do it...

The following are the steps for detecting blocked and blocking queries:

1. Start SQL Server Management Studio and establish a connection to the SQL Server hosting the AdventureWorks2012 database.

2. In the query window (Connection-1), type the following T-SQL statements and then execute them, to begin a transaction from Connection-1:

```
--Execute this script from Connection-1
USE AdventureWorks2012
GO

SET TRANSACTION ISOLATION LEVEL REPEATABLE READ
GO

--Beginning a transaction.
BEGIN TRANSACTION

--Fetching SessionID
SELECT @@SPID AS Connection1_SessionID

SELECT * FROM Sales.SalesOrderDetail
WHERE SalesOrderDetailID = 121316
```

3. After executing the previous statements, you should see output similar to that shown in the following screenshot. Note that the session ID that you get in your output is likely to be different.

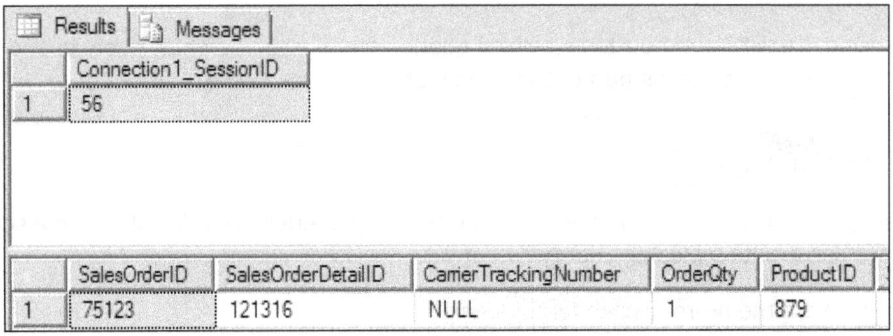

4. Now, open another query window (Connection-2). Type the following T-SQL script, and then execute the script to begin a transaction from Connection-2. Note that the UPDATE statement in this script will not complete and will be waiting because the same row is blocked by Connection-1.

```
--Execute this script from Connection-2
USE AdventureWorks2012
GO

--Begin transaction and try
--to update row that is blocked
--by Connection-1
BEGIN TRANSACTION

UPDATE Sales.SalesOrderDetail
SET OrderQty = 10
WHERE SalesOrderDetailID = 121316

COMMIT TRANSACTION
```

5. In another new query window (Connection-3), type and execute the following query, to find out the blocked and blocking queries:

```
--Finding Blocking Information
SELECT
    R.session_id AS BlockedSessionID
    ,S.session_id AS BlockingSessionID
    ,Q1.text AS BlockedSession_TSQL
    ,Q2.text AS BlockingSession_TSQL
    ,C1.most_recent_sql_handle AS BlockedSession_SQLHandle
```

```
        ,C2.most_recent_sql_handle AS BlockingSession_SQLHandle
        ,S.original_login_name AS BlockingSession_LoginName
        ,S.program_name AS BlockingSession_ApplicationName
        ,S.host_name AS BlockingSession_HostName
FROM sys.dm_exec_requests AS R
INNER JOIN sys.dm_exec_sessions AS S
ON R.blocking_session_id = S.session_id
INNER JOIN sys.dm_exec_connections AS C1
ON R.session_id = C1.most_recent_session_id
INNER JOIN sys.dm_exec_connections AS C2
ON S.session_id = C2.most_recent_session_id
CROSS APPLY sys.dm_exec_sql_text (C1.most_recent_sql_handle) AS Q1
CROSS APPLY sys.dm_exec_sql_text (C2.most_recent_sql_handle) AS Q2
```

6. Considering that the query we executed from Connection-1 has been blocking other queries for a long time, we need to terminate its process by killing its session, with the following T-SQL command:

```
KILL 56
GO
```

7. Switch to the second query window (Connection-2) and observe that, as soon as we kill the blocking session (56), the UPDATE statement is successfully executed and the transaction in Connection-2 gets committed.

How it works...

We first created a connection through SSMS and started a transaction in AdventureWorks2012 database. Note that we have set the transaction isolation level to REPEATABLE READ. Why have we used the **REPEATABLE READ** transaction isolation level? Well, on this isolation level, shared locks issued on resources are held until the transaction is complete. So, when we fetched data from the table Sales.SalesOrderDetail, when the value of SalesOrderDetailID was specified as 121316, it issued a shared lock on that particular row and held it. The lock will not be released until the transaction is committed or rolled back.

When we executed the UPDATE statement from Connection-2, it could not complete the request, as this transaction was blocked by Connection-1, because the transaction in Connection-1 was running on the REPEATABLE READ isolation level and was not still committed and rolled back. Therefore, the transaction in Connection-2 became a blocked transaction and the transaction in Connection-1 became a blocking transaction that actually locked the resources.

To identify the blocked and blocking requests, we executed a query that joined the following dynamic management views and dynamic management functions:

- ▸ `dm_exec_requests`
- ▸ `dm_exec_sessions`
- ▸ `dm_exec_connections`
- ▸ `dm_exec_sql_text`

The DMVs in the query are joined using `session_id`. By using CROSS APPLY on the dynamic management function by passing the `sql_handle` value of the most recent request of a session, we retrieved the T-SQL queries for both blocked query and blocking query as well. The resulting columns are very helpful in detecting the source of blocking queries.

We then fictitiously assumed that the transaction that was started from Connection-1 was blocking the other transactions and we killed the process of that transaction by passing its `session_id` value(56) to the KILL command.

As soon as the transaction with `session_id` value 56 was killed, the update was successful and the transaction in Connection-2 was committed.

Detecting deadlocks with SQL Server Profiler

Let's suppose you are a database administrator. One of your colleagues reports to you about frequent deadlocks occurring in the database due to inefficient application code and asks you to investigate such deadlocks and to analyze when they occur. As a DBA you are required to detect such situations and find out the queries that are the culprits behind these deadlocks.

Deadlock is a state of blockage that occurs when two or more transactions are blocked by one another in such a way that, in order to complete its transaction, each transaction waits to acquire a lock on the resource that the other one has locked. In this state, each transaction waits for the other one to be finished, in order to be able to complete its own transaction. This results in endless blocking and neither transaction can be completed. The following sample diagram represents the deadlock in action:

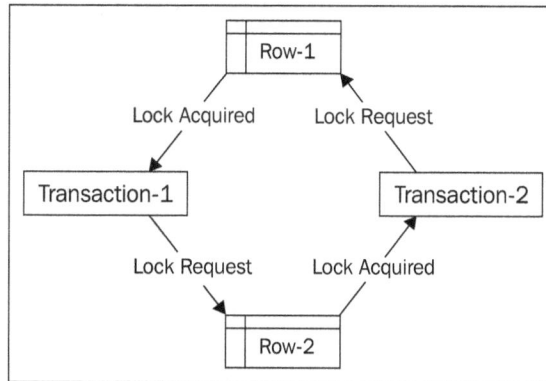

In this recipe, we will learn how to detect such deadlocks occurring in the database by using SQL Server Profiler. Once the part of code that causes the deadlock to occur is identified, necessary corrections can be made to modify the code to prevent any possible deadlocks from occurring.

Getting ready

To detect deadlocks with SQL Server Profiler, we first need to create a scenario such that we can produce a deadlock condition.

In this recipe, we will run two transactions from two different sessions and produce a deadlock. We will then see how this deadlock can be detected using SQL Server Profiler and how we can save a deadlock graph in a file for later analysis.

The following are the prerequisites for this recipe:

- An instance of SQL Server 2012 Developer or Enterprise Evaluation edition.
- A sample AdventureWorks2012 database on the SQL Server instance. For more details on how to install the AdventureWorks2012 database, please refer to the _Preface_ of this book.

How to do it...

The following steps enable you to detect deadlocks with SQL Server Profiler:

1. Start SQL Server Profiler.
2. Select **New Trace...** from the **File** menu. In the **Connect to Server** dialog box, provide the connection details for the SQL Server hosting the AdventureWorks2012 database and click on **Connect**.
3. In the **General** tab of **Trace Properties**, select the **Blank** template in the **Use the template:** dropdown list.

4. Click on the **Events Selection** tab. On this screen, expand the **Locks** event category and select the following events:

   - **Deadlock graph**
   - **Lock:Deadlock**
   - **Lock:Deadlock Chain**

5. Expand the **TSQL** event category and select the following events:

   - **SQL:StmtCompleted**
   - **SQL:StmtStarting**

6. Click on the **Column Filters...** button in the **Events Selection** tab of the **Trace Properties** dialog box. In the **Edit Filter** dialog box, select the **DatabaseName** data column from the list of available data columns on the left-hand side. Expand the **Like** option, enter the string value `AdventureWorks2012`, and click on the **OK** button.

7. Click the **Organize Columns...** button in the **Events Selection** tab of the **Trace Properties** dialog box and organize the data columns in the order shown in following screenshot. Click on the **Ok** button in the **Organize Columns** dialog box.

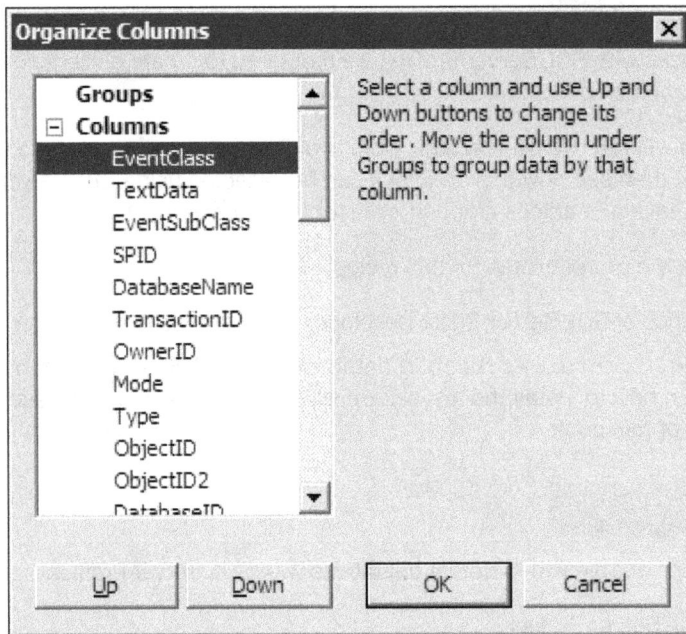

8. Click on the **Run** button to start the trace.

9. Now, open SQL Server Management Studio and establish a connection to the SQL server.

10. In the query window (Connection-1), type the following T-SQL statements and then execute them, to begin a transaction from Connection-1:

```
USE AdventureWorks2012
GO
--Execute this script from Connection-1
SET TRANSACTION ISOLATION LEVEL REPEATABLE READ
GO


BEGIN TRANSACTION


SELECT * FROM Sales.SalesOrderDetail
WHERE SalesOrderDetailID = 121316
```

11. Now, open another query window (Connection-2). Type the following T-SQL script, and then execute the script to begin a transaction from Connection-2:

```
USE AdventureWorks2012
GO


--Execute this script from Connection-2
SET TRANSACTION ISOLATION LEVEL REPEATABLE READ


BEGIN TRANSACTION


SELECT * FROM Sales.SalesOrderDetail
WHERE SalesOrderDetailID = 121317
```

12. Now, in the first query window (Connection-1), type the following query underneath previously entered T-SQL statements. Select and highlight the following query and execute this query only, to try to update the record:

```
--Execute this script from Connection-1
UPDATE Sales.SalesOrderDetail
SET OrderQty = 2
WHERE SalesOrderDetailID = 121317
```

13. Next, in the second query window (Connection-2), type the following query underneath previously entered T-SQL statements. Select and highlight the following query, and execute this query only, to try to update the record:

```
--Execute this script from Connection-2
UPDATE Sales.SalesOrderDetail
SET OrderQty = 2
WHERE SalesOrderDetailID = 121316
```

14. You will notice that both the updates will not occur as each transaction will be waiting for the locked row that the other one has locked to be released. This creates a deadlock between these two transactions, and you will see following error message:

```
Msg 1205, Level 13, State 51, Line 1
Transaction (Process ID 55) was deadlocked on lock resources with
another process and has been chosen as the deadlock victim. Rerun
the transaction.
```

15. Switch to the **SQL Server Profiler** window and stop the trace. Your trace window along with captured trace events should look as shown in following screenshot:

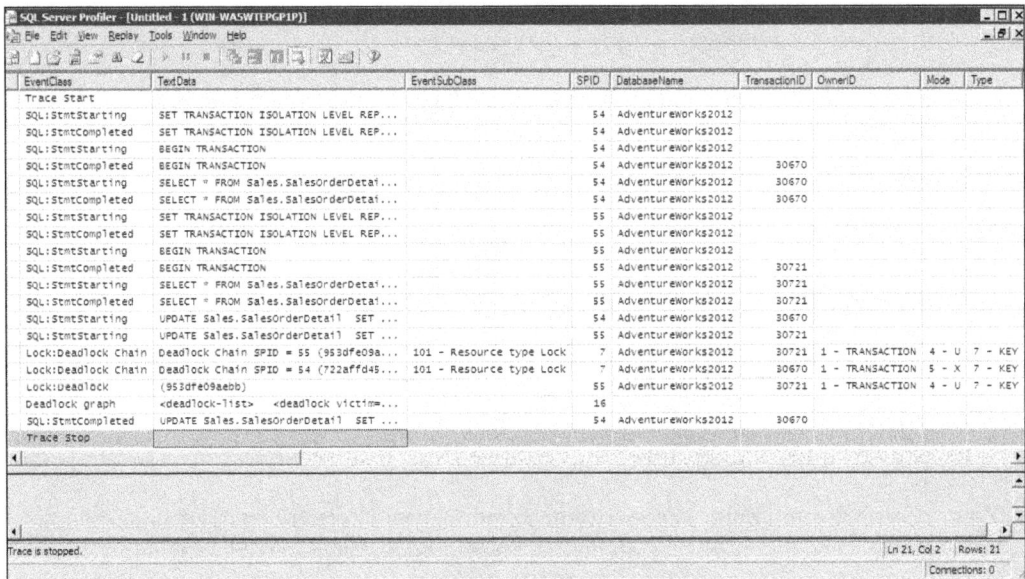

16. Examine the deadlock-related events that SQL Server Profiler has captured. Locate the **Deadlock graph** event in the **EventClass** data column and click its associated row. SQL Server Profiler will display the deadlock graph in the bottom pane of the trace window, as shown in following screenshot:

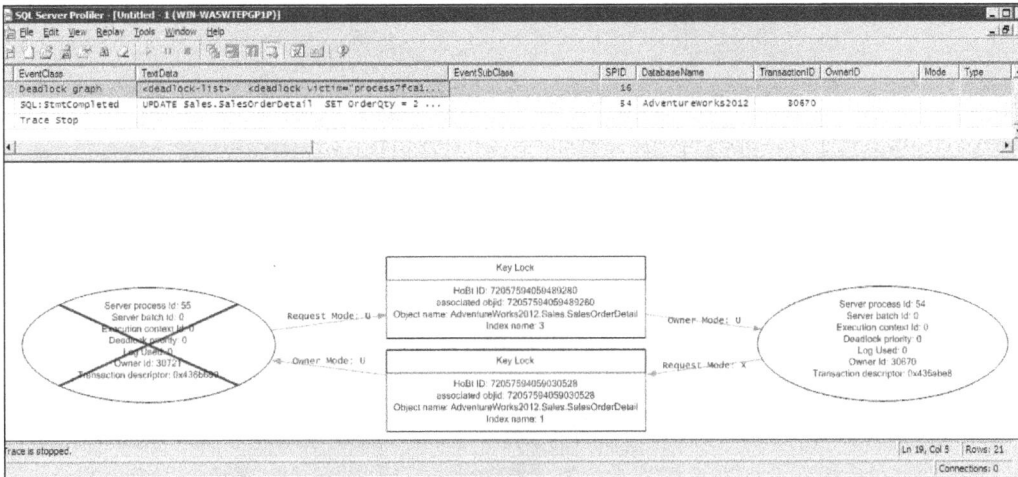

17. To save the deadlock graph, right-click the row with the event **Deadlock graph** and then select **Extract Event Data....** In the **Save As** dialog box, specify a file name and click on **Save**. This will save the deadlock file with the extension .xdl, which is an XML file. The following screenshot shows the partial XML of the deadlock that occurred:

```
<deadlock-list>
  <deadlock victim="process7fca188">
    <process-list>
      <process id="process7fca188" taskpriority="0" logused="0" wai
        <executionStack>
          <frame procname="adhoc" line="2" stmtstart="30" sqlhandle
            UPDATE [Sales].[SalesOrderDetail] set [OrderQty] = @1
          </frame>
          <frame procname="adhoc" line="2" stmtstart="4" sqlhandle=
            UPDATE Sales.SalesOrderDetail
            SET OrderQty = 2
            WHERE SalesOrderDetailID = 121316
          </frame>
        </executionStack>
        <inputbuf>

          UPDATE Sales.SalesOrderDetail
          SET OrderQty = 2
          WHERE SalesOrderDetailID = 121316
        </inputbuf>
      </process>
      <process id="process4341e20" taskpriority="0" logused="0" wai
        <executionStack>
          <frame procname="adhoc" line="1" stmtstart="30" sqlhandle
            UPDATE [Sales].[SalesOrderDetail] set [OrderQty] = @1
          </frame>
          <frame procname="adhoc" line="1" sqlhandle="0x0200000005f
            UPDATE Sales.SalesOrderDetail
            SET OrderQty = 2
            WHERE SalesOrderDetailID = 121317
```

How it works...

In this recipe, we first created a trace by using the Blank trace template. To capture the T-SQL statements that are executed and the deadlock events that occurred, we selected the following events for our trace:

- **Deadlock graph**
- **Lock:Deadlock**
- **Lock:Deadlock Chain**
- **SQL:StmtCompleted**
- **SQL:StmtStarting**

We configured the trace by specifying a filter on **DatabaseName**, so that it only captured events raised against the database AdventureWorks2012. We also organized columns, so that we can view the necessary columns relevant to deadlocks, on screen.

After configuring and starting the trace, we ran two separate transactions from two different query sessions from SSMS. In both transactions, we selected a row from the table Sales. SalesOrderDetail, on the basis of the value of SalesOrderDetailID, and tried to update the same row with the other transaction. Note that in both the transactions, we set the transaction isolation level to REPEATABLE READ. This isolation level holds the shared locks issued on SELECT statements until the transaction is completed. This is the reason why Connection-1 had to wait while updating the same row (SalesOrderDetailID = 121317) on which Connection-2 had held the lock, because Connection-2 had not completed its transaction. We ran the same type of query from Connection-2 and tried to update the same row (SalesOrderDetailID = 121316) that the Connection-1 had held the lock on. This creates permanent blocking from both sides and creates a deadlock situation.

SQL Server automatically handles and detects such types of deadlocks. It then selects one of the processes involved in the deadlock as the deadlock victim and kills that process. That's why we received the error (1205) in Connection-2 after executing the UPDATE query.

In SQL Server Profiler, we examined how the trace captured the deadlock events. In the trace result, you can see that two transactions tried to issue an EXCLUSIVE lock on the KEY for the UPDATE operation that the other had a SHARED lock on. The lock was requested on a single row in an index, and this can be confirmed by looking at the value in the **Type** data column. In our case, this happens to be KEY, which indicates a single key value in an index.

By clicking the row associated with the **Deadlock graph** event, we could see the deadlock graph in the bottom pane of the trace window. This graph gives the details of the deadlock that occurred. As you can see, it also shows which process was chosen as the deadlock victim and killed. We then saved the deadlock graph by right-clicking the **Deadlock graph** row in the trace window. This is an XML file that consists of deadlock details. A part of this XML file is shown in the last step of this recipe, in the form of a screenshot.

To prevent/minimize deadlock issues as much as possible, here are some precautions that you can take while developing your code:

- Make sure that your transactions are as small as possible.

- Try to use lower-level isolation, as a lower level of isolation increases the data concurrency.

- When possible, you can use the NOLOCK query hint to minimize blocking.

- Normalize your database design properly, so that appropriate related data is distributed between multiple tables through relationships.

- Create an index on the required columns, so that tables don't have to be scanned. Whole table scans can also increase the locking issues.

- Access database objects in your transaction in the same order as everywhere else in your application.

Detecting deadlocks with Trace Flag 1204

In the previous recipe, *Detecting deadlocks with SQL Server Profiler*, we learned to detect deadlocks using SQL Server Profiler. This can be useful when deadlocks occur regularly in a specific pattern and you are able to reproduce them by executing certain part of application code that you know produces the deadlock. For this type of investigation, you simply start an SQL Trace session, reproduce the deadlock condition, and analyze the queries.

However, when deadlocks occur irregularly, without any specific pattern, it becomes hard for you to investigate them because you do not know in which case they occur. Thus, it also becomes difficult for you to reproduce them. To troubleshoot such irregular deadlocks, you might prefer not to keep a trace session running and wait for deadlocks to occur for hours.

This recipe will show you how you can configure SQL Server so that whenever deadlocks occur, SQL Server logs the deadlock-related information into the SQL Server error log. Once the server is configured in this way and someone comes to you and complains about any deadlock occurrence, you can simply analyze the error log to investigate whether any deadlock occurred in the database and if so, where.

Getting ready

In this example, we will learn how to configure SQL Server by setting **TRACE Flag 1204** at instance level.

We will be using the same code that was used in the previous recipe, *Detecting deadlocks with SQL Server Profiler*, to produce a deadlock condition. So, the prerequisites are the same as those for the previous recipe.

How to do it...

Follow the ensuing steps to configure Trace Flag 1204 at instance level, to log the deadlock information into SQL Server error log:

1. Start **SQL Server Configuration Manager** from **Configuration Tools**, in the **Microsoft SQL Server 2012 Program** group in the Start menu.

2. Select the **SQL Server Services** node in the left-hand side pane, right-click the instance of SQL Server Service in the right-hand side pane, and select **Properties** from the context menu, as shown in following screenshot:

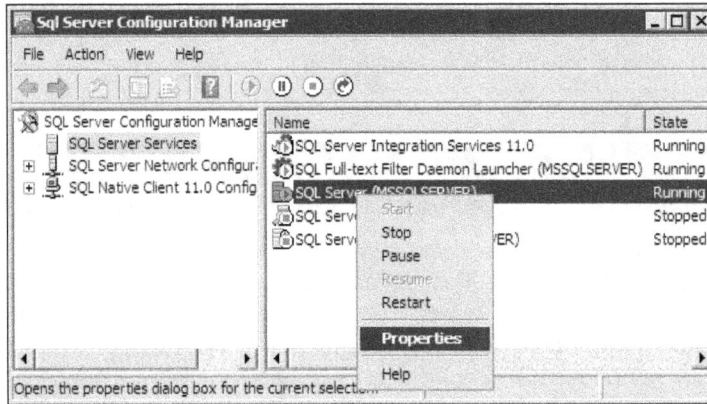

3. In the **SQL Server (MSSQLSERVER) Properties** window, select the **Startup Parameters** tab. Type -t1204 in the textbox provided under **Specify a startup parameter:**. Click on the **Add** button to add this new parameter to the list of **Existing parameters**. The following screenshot shows the **Startup Parameters** tab with the added trace flag:

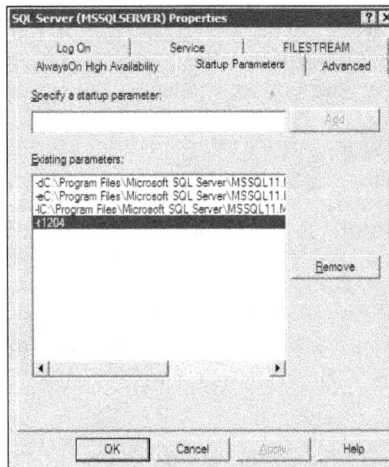

4. Click on the **Ok** button in the **Properties** window.

5. Again, right-click the instance of SQL Server Service that you just configured and select **Restart** from the context menu, as shown in following screenshot. This will restart the SQL Server Service.

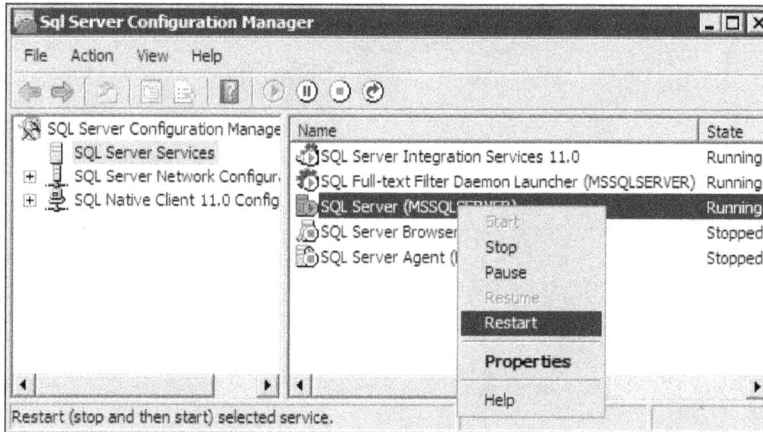

> Always use SQL Server Configuration Manager to restart SQL Server Service. Do not restart SQL Server service directly from the Windows Services MMC.

6. Now, perform the same steps to produce the deadlock condition as in the preceding recipe. Execute the queries from step 9 through step 14, provided in the previous recipe.

7. Performing the previous step generates a deadlock and you will receive the same error (**1205**) as in the previous recipe.

8. Now, based on the name of SQL Server instance and your SQL Server installation directory, navigate to the directory that contains the ERRORLOG file located in the Log directory. The following is the default installation path for a default instance of SQL Server 2012 by which the ERRORLOG file can be located:

```
C:\Program Files\Microsoft SQL Server\MSSQL11.MSSQLServer\
MSSQL\Log
```

9. The following screenshot shows the deadlock information that you can find in the
   ERRORLOG file:

```
2012-01-28 23:52:28.52 spid7s    Deadlock encountered .... Printing deadlock information
2012-01-28 23:52:28.52 spid7s    wait-for graph
2012-01-28 23:52:28.52 spid7s
2012-01-28 23:52:28.52 spid7s    Node:1

2012-01-28 23:52:28.52 spid7s    KEY: 5:72057594059489280 (953dfe09aebb) CleanCnt:2 Mode:U Flags: 0x1
2012-01-28 23:52:28.53 spid7s     Grant List 0:
2012-01-28 23:52:28.53 spid7s       Owner:0x078A2240 Mode: U        Flg:0x40 Ref:1 Life:02000000 SPID:51
2012-01-28 23:52:28.53 spid7s       SPID: 51 ECID: 0 Statement Type: UPDATE Line #: 1
2012-01-28 23:52:28.53 spid7s       Input Buf: Language Event: UPDATE Sales.SalesOrderDetail
SET OrderQty = 2
WHERE SalesOrderDetailID = 121317

2012-01-28 23:52:28.53 spid7s    Requested by:
2012-01-28 23:52:28.53 spid7s      ResType:LockOwner Stype:'OR'Xdes:0x08A6C9F0 Mode: U SPID:52 BatchID:0
2012-01-28 23:52:28.53 spid7s
2012-01-28 23:52:28.53 spid7s    Node:2

2012-01-28 23:52:28.53 spid7s    KEY: 5:72057594059030528 (722affd45fb5) CleanCnt:2 Mode:U Flags: 0x1
2012-01-28 23:52:28.53 spid7s     Grant List 0:
2012-01-28 23:52:28.53 spid7s       Owner:0x078A1EE0 Mode: S        Flg:0x40 Ref:0 Life:02000000 SPID:52
2012-01-28 23:52:28.53 spid7s       SPID: 52 ECID: 0 Statement Type: UPDATE Line #: 2
2012-01-28 23:52:28.53 spid7s       Input Buf: Language Event: --Execute this scirpt from Connection-2
UPDATE Sales.SalesOrderDetail
SET OrderQty = 2
WHERE SalesOrderDetailID = 121316

2012-01-28 23:52:28.53 spid7s    Requested by:
2012-01-28 23:52:28.53 spid7s      ResType:LockOwner Stype:'OR'Xdes:0x0447ABE8 Mode: X SPID:51 BatchID:0
2012-01-28 23:52:28.56 spid7s
2012-01-28 23:52:28.56 spid7s    Victim Resource Owner:
2012-01-28 23:52:28.56 spid7s      ResType:LockOwner Stype:'OR'Xdes:0x08A6C9F0 Mode: U SPID:52 BatchID:0
```

How it works...

In SQL Server, Trace Flag 1204 is used to redirect deadlock-related information to ERRORLOG.
The SQL Server service can use some parameters while starting up; these are called startup
parameters. We can add, modify, or delete these startup parameters from within SQL Server
Configuration Manager.

We started this recipe by adding a new parameter, specified by –t1204, to the list of startup
parameters for the SQL Server Service instance. The parameter added comes into effect only
when SQL Server Service is restarted. This is the reason we restarted the SQL Server Service.
Once the SQL Server Service restarts, the new parameter, Trace Flag 1204, comes into effect
and starts logging deadlock-related information into SQL Server's ERRORLOG file.

We then produced a deadlock to test how the SQL Server logs deadlock information in
ERRORLOG file. We used the same sequence to execute the scripts (to generate the deadlock)
that was used in previous recipe. Finally, we examined the ERRORLOG file in which SQL Server
logged the deadlock-related information.

17
Configuring SQL Server for Optimization

In this chapter we will cover:

- ▸ Configuring SQL Server to use more processing power
- ▸ Configuring memory in 32 bit versus 64 bit
- ▸ Configuring "Optimize for Ad hoc Workloads"
- ▸ Optimizing SQL Server instance configuration

Introduction

SQL Server provides one system stored procedure, named SP_Configure, which helps you to manage the SQL Server instance-level configuration. A configuration comes with a default value, but based on the server, load on the server, and your own usage, you can change its default value to something else that can give you benefits from the performance point of view. Apart from the settings given in the SP_Configure stored procedure, the type of instance (32 bit/64 bit) also affects a bit.

It has been often observed that people use a SQL Server machine along with IIS, as a file server, or as a domain controller. Performance will be affected if you are using the same server for SQL Server Services along with other services, such as, IIS, domain controller, and so on.

Configuring SQL Server to use more processing power

In today's age, databases keep getting bigger and bigger, so in order to get information quickly from a database, it is not enough to manage your database wisely; you will also need a CPU with faster processing power.

No matter how efficiently you maintain indexes and statistics, you will not receive a prompt response from your SQL Server if you are running with low processing power. Choosing a proper CPU for your database need, is a part of "capacity planning", which is out of the scope of this chapter, as it itself requires few chapters to describe it in-depth. However, here we will learn how to utilize your current processing power efficiently.

Have you ever wondered how many CPUs are used by a SQL Server while processing a query? Users used to buy increasingly powerful computers, with many processors and cores, but it is interesting to know how many of them are used while executing a query in SQL server.

Getting ready

Before we move forward, it is important to know how many CPUs there are in the server. I will be using the `sys.dm_os_sys_info` DMV to retrieve that information, as it tends to provide miscellaneous useful information about the computer and about the resources available to—and consumed by—the SQL Server:

```
SELECT
    cpu_count AS 'Cores'
    ,hyperthread_ratio
FROM
    sys.dm_os_sys_info
```

The `hyperthread_ratio` column given in this query does not distinguish between actual hyper-threaded cores and true physical cores. This makes it even more difficult to guess which processor is being used in the server. It would nice if Microsoft includes more information about cores in this DMV, in its next release of SQL Server 2012.

How to do it...

Follow the steps given here to perform this recipe:

1. To set the number of CPUs that can be used while executing a query on an instance level, execute the following query:

```
--0 is the default value
sp_configure 'max degree of parallelism', 0
RECONFIGURE WITH OVERRIDE
GO
```

2. To set the value of parallelism at the query level, execute the two following SELECT queries, using SET STATISTICS TIME along with the MAXDOP option a few times, and observe the value of SET STATISTICS TIME in the **Message** tab:

```
set statistics time on
SELECT
    *
FROM
    Sales.SalesOrderDetail
OPTION (MAXDOP 1)
set statistics time off
GO

set statistics time oN
SELECT
    *
FROM
    Sales.SalesOrderDetail
OPTION (MAXDOP 0)
set statistics time ofF
```

Here is the one of the screenshots of the preceding query, after running it a few times:

How it works...

SQL Server has a smart algorithm to decide whether to generate parallelism (the use of more than one processor to execute the query) for a query or not. Overriding SQLServer's decisionabout the number of processors to use needs expertise as well as experience. There is no predefined number available for this setting, as deciding on a number depends completely on the type of server you are using, the type of use you are having, the workload on the server, and many other factors. There is only one sure way of deciding upon the number of CPUs—by experimenting on the server.

In Step 1, we had executed the `SP_Configure` stored procedure for "max degree of parallelism" with value 0 (zero), which is the default value. The zero indicates that SQL Server has the power to decide whether to generate parallelism or not, and if yes, how many CPUs should be used. If you set the value as 4 rather than 0, SQL Server will use up to four cores to process the query. If you set the value as 1, it means that parallelism will not occur and the query will be processed by one processor only.

In Step 2, `OPTION (MAXDOP` *numeric value*`)` sets the parallelism value for that particular query as against the instance-level settings given in Step 1.

There are two `SELECT` queries executed in Step 2, out of which the first query uses (`MAXDOP` 1). It means that no parallelism will occur and the process will be processed by one processor only. In the second `SELECT` query, (`MAXDOP` 0) is used, which means that SQL Server decides whether to use parallelism or not.

Because of the `SET STATISTICS TIME` option with a `SELECT` query, we can see how much CPU time is consumed by each query, in the **Messages** tab, beside the **Results** panel. You might get a different CPU time in your instance, as it depends on the number of servers, available memory, and many more things. You might also get a different CPU time and elapsed time each time you execute the query.

There's more...

Change the default settings for "max degree of parallelism", as they can be dangerous on a live server. So, keep the current value handy, in case you are making a change, and also consult a senior or colleague before doing this on a live server. Based on my experience, I'm not comfortable assigning all the available processors to process a single query in SQL Server. Apart from that, I wouldn't touch this setting on an OLTP database, as changing this setting in a big OLTP database creates uncertainty in performance that users won't like. But, it is good to assign as many processors as possible in the database warehouse system.

If you have 16 cores and change the **Max Degree of Parallelism** setting to **8**, it doesn't mean that only eight cores will work with SQL Server. It only means that any single query optimizer can't use more than eight cores, even when it runs using a parallel plan. But, SQL Server will continue to use all the available 16 cores.

Configuring memory in 32 bit versus. 64 bit

I have observed quite a few times that in SQL Server 2005/2008, DBAs tend to use the **AWE Enabled** option to limit memory. However, from SQL Server 2012 onwards, this option has been deprecated so we cannot use more memory than what the virtual address space limits in 32-bit instances of SQL Server. If you have more memory for this instance of SQL Server, you have to migrate to a 64-bit instance of SQL Server. Here is the memory limit given by Microsoft:

SQL Server and operating system settings	Maximum amount of memory used by SQL Server
32-bit SQL Server on 32-bit OS	2 GB
32-bit SQL Server on 32-bit OS with /3G boot option	3 GB
32-bit SQL Server on 64-bit OS	4 GB

Though the **AWE Enabled** option is deprecated in SQL Server 2012, it would be helpful to understand its usage in the previous version to understand other memory-related options. **Address Windowing Extensions** (**AWE**) allows 32-bit operating systems to access large amounts of memory. AWE is exposed by the operating system.

If the available physical memory is greater than the value of the **Maximum server memory** option, the SQL Server instance locks the amount of memory specified in **Maximum server memory**.

If the available physical memory is less than the value of the **Maximum server memory** option, or if the **Maximum server memory** option has not been set, the SQL Server instance locks all the available memory except 256 megabytes (MB).

The main intention to expose facts about AWE here is to emphasize that even though it is deprecated by Microsoft, the role of the **Maximum server memory** option when there was AWE working.

Getting ready

Keep the current list of values for **Minimum server memory (MB)** and **Maximum Server Memory (MB)** by querying `sys.configurations`, which contains a row for each server-wide configuration option value in the system. So, if you wish, you can set the current value in these parameters after completing the exercise given in this recipe.

How to do it...

Follow the steps given here to perform this recipe:

1. Set the minimum memory for SQL Server and execute the following query:

    ```
    --setting 1024 MB as a minimum memory for SQL Server
    EXEC  sp_configure 'min server memory (MB)',1024
    GO
    RECONFIGURE WITH OVERRIDE;
    GO
    ```

2. Set the maximum memory for SQL Server and execute the following query:

    ```
    --setting 3000 MB as a maximum memory for SQL Server
    EXEC  sp_configure 'max server memory (MB)',3000
    GO
    RECONFIGURE WITH OVERRIDE;
    GO
    ```

How it works...

Step 1 configures minimum memory allocation for the SQL Server. The default value of `min server memory` is 0 (zero). You can set any value to `min server memory` that is less than or equal to the value of `max server memory`.

Step 2 configures maximum memory allocation for the SQL Server. The default value of `max server memory` is `2147483647`, which is 2 TB. You cannot configure `max server memory` value as less than `64`.

Both of the memory settings reserve the memory for the SQL Server buffer pool. By ensuring this, if you are dealing with 32-bit systems, you can't use more than 3 GB for your SQL Server instance, no matter how much available memory you have on the server; this is possible if enabling AWE and PAE, in older versions of SQL Server. But these features are deprecated in SQL Server 2012, so if possible, go in for the 64-bit version of SQL Server 2012, which allows you to utilize as much memory as supported by your OS or by the SQL Server edition you are using.

If the SQL Server service is the only server service running on your system, it is fine to have the default value for max server memory. However, if multiple services are running on the server, and if the domain controller uses maximum memory, SQL Server will be starved of memory; on the other hand, if SQL Server uses maximum memory, the domain controller will be starved of memory. Therefore, it is good to assign proper memory to SQL Server, so it doesn't run out of memory, but it also doesn't consume memory unnecessarily.

Configuring "Optimize for Ad hoc Workloads"

Execution of any query or stored procedure for the first time creates an execution plan, which is stored in SQL Server 's procedure cache memory. It happens many times that we execute a simple query once, which is not even going to be used again anytime soon and it may never run again in future too even execution plan generated for that query will consume space in procedure cache. You may run out of cache sometimes, due to lack of memory, which affects performance. This was really a big issue till SQL Server 2005. In order to remedy this, Microsoft introduced "Optimize for Ad hoc Workloads" in SQL Server 2008, and it is still available in SQL Server 2012. This setting is instance-wide in SQL Server.

> In one of my performance tuning consultation projects, I had observed the company's SQL developer making and testing a query directly on the production server. If they didn't get the required results, they'd change the query and re-test it on the production server, which was creating immense pressure on the procedure cache. I pointed out and explained the side effects of their testing on the production server; they then cleared the procedure cache and changed their habits. I hope that none of the readers of this book finds themselves in this situation.

Getting ready

Before moving further, let us clean up the procedure cache and buffer on the testing server that we are using.

1. Before cleaning up the cache and buffer, let's look at how many rows come from our saved plan DMV:

```
SELECT
   CP.usecounts AS CountOfQueryExecution
   ,CP.cacheobjtype AS CacheObjectType
   ,CP.objtype AS ObjectType
   ,ST.text AS QueryText
FROM
sys.dm_exec_cached_plans AS CP
CROSS APPLY
```

```
sys.dm_exec_sql_text(plan_handle) AS ST
WHERE
CP.usecounts > 0
GO
```

Here is the result I received on my development server; you will get a different result in your environment:

	CountOfQueryExecution	CacheObjectType	ObjectType	QueryText
1	1	Compiled Plan	Proc	------------------ sp_configure ------------------ create procedure sys.sp_configure @configname varchar(35) = null -- option name ...
2	1	Compiled Plan Stub	Adhoc	SELECT CP.usecounts AS CountOfQueryExecution ,CP.cacheobjtype AS CacheObjectType ,CP.objtype AS ObjectType ,ST.text AS Qu...
3	4	Compiled Plan	Prepared	(@_msparam_0 nvarchar(4000),@_msparam_1 nvarchar(4000),@_msparam_2 nvarchar(4000))SELECT clmns.name AS [Name], clmns.colum...
4	1	Compiled Plan	Prepared	(@_msparam_0 nvarchar(4000),@_msparam_1 nvarchar(4000))SELECT clmns.column_id AS [ID], clmns.name AS [Name], clmns.is_nullable ...
5	1	Compiled Plan Stub	Adhoc	select * from sqlhub.dbo.ordDemo
6	1	Compiled Plan Stub	Adhoc	SELECT satypes.name AS [Schema], atypes.name AS [Name] FROM sys.assembly_types AS atypes INNER JOIN sys.assemblies AS asmbl O...
7	1	Compiled Plan Stub	Adhoc	SELECT SCHEMA_NAME(tt.schema_id) AS [Schema], tt.name AS [Name] FROM sys.table_types AS tt INNER JOIN sys.schemas AS stt ON ...
8	1	Compiled Plan Stub	Adhoc	SELECT sst.name AS [Schema], st.name AS [Name] FROM sys.types AS st INNER JOIN sys.schemas AS sst ON sst.schema_id = st.schema...
9	1	Compiled Plan Stub	Adhoc	SELECT SCHEMA_NAME(xproc.schema_id) AS [Schema], xproc.name AS [Name], xproc.object_id AS [ID], CAST(xproc.is_ms_sh...
10	1	Compiled Plan Stub	Adhoc	SELECT SCHEMA_NAME(s.schema_id) AS [Schema], s.name AS [Name] FROM sys.synonyms AS s ORDER BY [Schema] ASC,[Name] ASC
11	1	Compiled Plan	Prepared	(@_msparam_0 nvarchar(4000),@_msparam_1 nvarchar(4000),@_msparam_2 nvarchar(4000))SELECT SCHEMA_NAME(sp.schema_id) AS [...
12	1	Compiled Plan	Prepared	(@_msparam_0 nvarchar(4000))SELECT SCHEMA_NAME(udf.schema_id) AS [Schema], udf.name AS [Name], udf.object_id AS [ID], (case w...
13	1	Compiled Plan Stub	Adhoc	SELECT SCHEMA_NAME(obj.schema_id) AS [Schema], obj.name AS [Name], obj.object_id AS [ID], usrt.name AS [DataType], ISNULL(baset...
14	1	Compiled Plan	Prepared	(@_msparam_0 nvarchar(4000))SELECT SCHEMA_NAME(v.schema_id) AS [Schema], v.name AS [Name], v.object_id AS [ID] FROM sys.all_...
15	1	Compiled Plan Stub	Adhoc	SELECT SCHEMA_NAME(tbl.schema_id) AS [Schema], tbl.name AS [Name], tbl.object_id AS [ID] FROM sys.tables AS tbl ORDER BY [Sche...
16	1	Compiled Plan	Prepared	(@_msparam_0 nvarchar(4000),@_msparam_1 nvarchar(4000))SELECT u.name AS [Name], u.principal_id AS [ID], CAST(CASE WHEN u.prin...
17	1	Compiled Plan Stub	Adhoc	SELECT u.name AS [Name], u.principal_id AS [ID], ISNULL(ak.name.N') AS [AsymmetricKey], ISNULL(cert.name.N') AS [Certificate], ISNULL...
18	1	Compiled Plan Stub	Adhoc	SELECT tr.name AS [Name], tr.object_id AS [ID], CASE WHEN tr.type = N'TR' THEN 1 WHEN tr.type = N'TA' THEN 2 ELSE 1 END AS [Impl...
19	1	Compiled Plan Stub	Adhoc	SELECT s.name AS [Name] FROM sys.schemas AS s ORDER BY [Name] ASC
20	1	Compiled Plan Stub	Adhoc	SELECT rl.name AS [Name] FROM sys.database_principals AS rl WHERE (rl.type = 'R') ORDER BY [Name] ASC
21	1	Compiled Plan Stub	Adhoc	SELECT rl.name AS [Name] FROM sys.database_principals AS rl WHERE (rl.type = 'A') ORDER BY [Name] ASC
22	1	Compiled Plan	Adhoc	select case when cfg.configuration_id = 124 -- configuration id for default language then (select lcid from sys.syslanguages as sl where sl.l...
23	1	Compiled Plan	Prepared	(@_msparam_0 nvarchar(4000),@_msparam_1 nvarchar(4000),@_msparam_2 nvarchar(4000))SELECT param.is_readonly AS [IsReadOnly], ...
24	1	Compiled Plan	Prepared	(@_msparam_0 nvarchar(4000),@_msparam_1 nvarchar(4000))SELECT param.parameter_id AS [ID], param.name AS [Name], usrt.name AS [...
25	1	Compiled Plan	Prepared	(@_msparam_0 nvarchar(4000),@_msparam_1 nvarchar(4000),@_msparam_2 nvarchar(4000))SELECT udf.name AS [Name], udf.object_id A...
26	1	Compiled Plan	Prepared	(@_msparam_0 nvarchar(4000),@_msparam_1 nvarchar(4000))SELECT NULL AS [Text], ISNULL(smudf.definition, semudf.definition) AS [Defi...
27	6	Compiled Plan	Prepared	(@_msparam_0 nvarchar(4000),@_msparam_1 nvarchar(4000),@_msparam_2 nvarchar(4000),@_msparam_3 nvarchar(4000))SELECT clmns...

2. Now, clear the cache and buffer:

```
--don't execute these two commands on production server
--this is just to prove the case given in this recipe...
--this should run on testing or development servers only
DBCC FREEPROCCACHE
GO
```

3. If you want to check whether our saved plan is cleaned up so far, execute the query we ran in step 1, again:

```
SELECT
   CP.usecounts AS CountOfQueryExecution
  ,CP.cacheobjtype AS CacheObjectType
  ,CP.objtype AS ObjectType
  ,ST.text AS QueryText
FROM
sys.dm_exec_cached_plans AS CP
CROSS APPLY
```

```
sys.dm_exec_sql_text(plan_handle) AS ST
WHERE
CP.usecounts > 0
GO
```

After clearing the cache in step 2, here is the result of the query we ran in step 3:

	CountOfQueryExecution	CacheObjectType	ObjectType	QueryText
1	1	Compiled Plan Stub	Adhoc	SELECT CP.usecounts AS CountOfQueryExecution ,...
2	2	Parse Tree	View	CREATE FUNCTION sys.dm_exec_sql_text(@handle var...
3	2	Parse Tree	View	create view sys.dm_exec_cached_plans as select * fro...

How to do it...

Follow the steps given here to perform this recipe:

1. Execute the following query.

    ```
    SELECT * FROM Sales.SalesOrderDetail WHERE SalesOrderID=43659
    GO
    ```

2. Check whether anything come in plan cache for query run above or not. After clearing the cache, it was the first time we executed the preceding query:

    ```
    SELECT
        CP.usecounts AS CountOfQueryExecution
        ,CP.cacheobjtype AS CacheObjectType
        ,CP.objtype AS ObjectType
        ,ST.text AS QueryText
    FROM
    sys.dm_exec_cached_plans AS CP
    CROSS APPLY
    sys.dm_exec_sql_text(plan_handle) AS ST
    WHERE
    CP.usecounts > 0
    AND CP.cacheobjtype='Compiled Plan'
    AND ST.text LIKE 'SELECT * FROM Sales.SalesOrderDetail WHERE
    SalesOrderID=43659%'
    GO
    ```

> You can find a long running query in the **Activity Monitor** tool. Use the *Ctrl + Alt + A* keyboard shortcut or the standard toolbar from SSMS to open **Activity Monitor**.

3. By running the `SELECT` query in step 1, it made and entry in plan cache in the very first time. Confirm the same with the following screenshot.

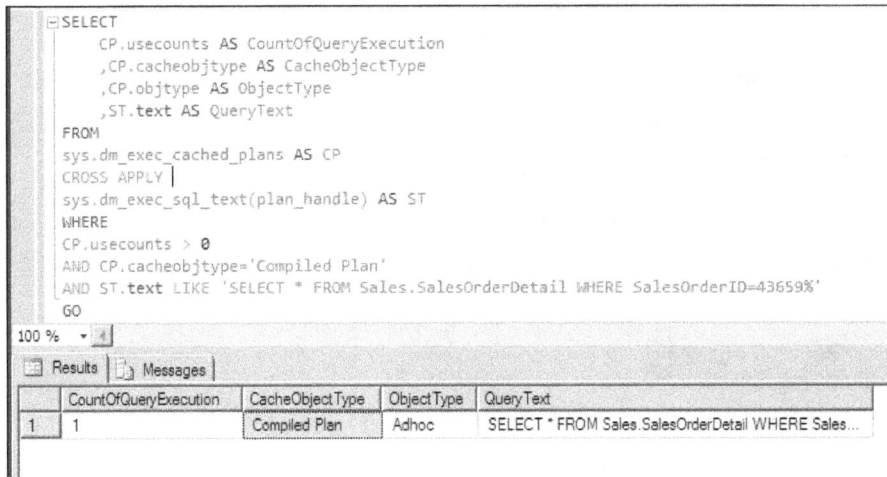

```
SELECT
        CP.usecounts AS CountOfQueryExecution
        ,CP.cacheobjtype AS CacheObjectType
        ,CP.objtype AS ObjectType
        ,ST.text AS QueryText
    FROM
    sys.dm_exec_cached_plans AS CP
    CROSS APPLY |
    sys.dm_exec_sql_text(plan_handle) AS ST
    WHERE
    CP.usecounts > 0
    AND CP.cacheobjtype='Compiled Plan'
    AND ST.text LIKE 'SELECT * FROM Sales.SalesOrderDetail WHERE SalesOrderID=43659%'
    GO
100 %    ▾ ◂
```

	CountOfQueryExecution	CacheObjectType	ObjectType	QueryText
1	1	Compiled Plan	Adhoc	SELECT * FROM Sales.SalesOrderDetail WHERE Sales...

4. Now, set the value of **Optimize for Ad hoc Workloads** to **1**, by executing the following query:

```
EXEC  sp_configure 'optimize for ad hoc workloads',1
RECONFIGURE
GO
```

5. Again, clear the cache:

```
DBCC FREEPROCCACHE
GO
```

6. Execute the `SELECT` query again:

```
SELECT * FROM Sales.SalesOrderDetail WHERE SalesOrderID=43659
GO
```

7. You can confirm whether anything was inserted in plan cache or not by executing the following query:

```
SELECT
    CP.usecounts AS CountOfQueryExecution
    ,CP.cacheobjtype AS CacheObjectType
    ,CP.objtype AS ObjectType
    ,ST.text AS QueryText
FROM
sys.dm_exec_cached_plans AS CP
CROSS APPLY
sys.dm_exec_sql_text(plan_handle) AS ST
```

```
WHERE
CP.usecounts > 0
AND CP.cacheobjtype='Compiled Plan'
AND ST.text LIKE 'SELECT * FROM Sales.SalesOrderDetail WHERE
SalesOrderID=43659%'
GO
```

8. You will not get anything in the plan cache, so execute the SELECT query from step 6, again:

```
SELECT * FROM Sales.SalesOrderDetail WHERE SalesOrderID=43659
GO
```

9. Confirm again whether anything came in the plan cache after executing the preceding query for the second time after clearing the cache:

```
SELECT
   CP.usecounts AS CountOfQueryExecution
   ,CP.cacheobjtype AS CacheObjectType
   ,CP.objtype AS ObjectType
   ,ST.text AS QueryText
FROM
sys.dm_exec_cached_plans AS CP
CROSS APPLY
sys.dm_exec_sql_text(plan_handle) AS ST
WHERE
CP.usecounts > 0
AND CP.cacheobjtype='Compiled Plan'
AND ST.text LIKE 'SELECT * FROM Sales.SalesOrderDetail WHERE
SalesOrderID=43659%'
GO
```

10. This time you will get one entry in the plan cache:

How it works...

When the new query arrives for the first time, only the `query_hash` value is kept in memory, instead of the entire plan. When the same query arrives for the second time, SQL Server identifies that it already has a `query_hash` for this query, for example, it is not the first time this query runs. From this point, query plan will be stored in cache. This way, plans for all the queries that run only once won't be kept in cache. That is why it is recommended to keep this setting on; this will not cause any harm, but will save space in the plan cache.

Generally, whenever you run the query, it generates an execution plan and saves it in the procedure cache. So, when we run the `SELECT` query in step 1, we get an entry in the cached plan DMV, but when we run the same `SELECT` query in step 6, after enabling **Optimize for Ad hoc Workloads** in step 4 and clearing up the buffer in step 5, we don't receive any row in the cached plan DMV. After executing the same `SELECT` query in step 8, we get an entry in the cached plan DMV. This is a useful feature, if we have ad hoc queries, which are supposed to be used only once or rarely executed then why do we need to save the plan for that and consume the "Procedure Cache"?

I have observed many databases that have saved plans of a few gigabytes; they can simply reduce it to half, as most of the ad-hoc queries in those saved plans run only once and there is no chance that they run again.

By the way, if you are curious to know how much space is consumed by ad hoc queries in a procedure cache that has been run only once, you can run following query:

```
SELECT
    SUM(size_in_bytes) as TotalByteConsumedByAdHoc
FROM
    sys.dm_exec_cached_plans
WHERE
    objtype = 'Adhoc'
    AND usecounts = 1
```

It is worth repeating the warning to not use the "DBCC" command on your live server. It was just to prove the recipe in this example so you can test these commands in your testing or development server.

Optimizing SQL Server instance configuration

MSDN introduced the concept of `SP_Configure` with the following understanding. You can manage and optimize SQL Server resources through configuration options by using SQL Server Management Studio or the `sp_configure` system stored procedure. The most commonly used server configuration options are available through SQL Server Management Studio; all configuration options are accessible through `sp_configure`. Consider the effects on your system carefully before setting these options.

Getting ready

To perform this recipe, you will need a developer or an enterprise edition of SQL Server Denali CTP 3 or a greater edition. In order to see the current instance level configuration settings in SQL Server, execute the following query:

```
SELECT
  *
FROM
  sys.configurations
ORDER BY
  name
GO
```

The result of this query will show you the list of settings out of which we are going to see few of the most important performance-related settings. All configurations are given in the following two screenshots:

First screen:

	configuration_id	name	value	minimum	maximum	value_in_use	description	is_dynamic	is_advanced
1	1582	access check cache bucket count	0	0	16384	0	Default hash bucket count for the access check re...	1	1
2	1583	access check cache quota	0	0	2147483647	0	Default quota for the access check result security c...	1	1
3	16391	Ad Hoc Distributed Queries	0	0	1	0	Enable or disable Ad Hoc Distributed Queries	1	1
4	1550	affinity I/O mask	0	-2147483648	2147483647	0	affinity I/O mask	0	1
5	1535	affinity mask	0	-2147483648	2147483647	0	affinity mask	1	1
6	16384	Agent XPs	0	0	1	0	Enable or disable Agent XPs	1	1
7	102	allow updates	0	0	1	0	Allow updates to system tables	1	0
8	1579	backup compression default	0	0	1	0	Enable compression of backups by default	1	0
9	1569	blocked process threshold (s)	0	0	86400	0	Blocked process reporting threshold	1	1
10	544	c2 audit mode	0	0	1	0	c2 audit mode	0	1
11	1562	clr enabled	0	0	1	0	CLR user code execution enabled in the server	1	0
12	1577	common criteria compliance enabled	0	0	1	0	Common Criteria compliance mode enabled	0	1
13	16393	contained database authentication	0	0	1	0	Enables contained databases and contained authe...	1	0
14	1538	cost threshold for parallelism	5	0	32767	5	cost threshold for parallelism	1	1
15	400	cross db ownership chaining	0	0	1	0	Allow cross db ownership chaining	1	0
16	1531	cursor threshold	-1	-1	2147483647	-1	cursor threshold	1	1
17	16386	Database Mail XPs	0	0	1	0	Enable or disable Database Mail XPs	1	1
18	1126	default full-text language	1033	0	2147483647	1033	default full-text language	1	1
19	124	default language	0	0	9999	0	default language	1	0
20	1568	default trace enabled	1	0	1	1	Enable or disable the default trace	1	1
21	114	disallow results from triggers	0	0	1	0	Disallow returning results from triggers	1	1
22	1578	EKM provider enabled	0	0	1	0	Enable or disable EKM provider	1	1
23	1580	filestream access level	0	0	2	0	Sets the FILESTREAM access level	1	0
24	109	fill factor (%)	0	0	100	0	Default fill factor percentage	0	1
25	1567	ft crawl bandwidth (max)	100	0	32767	100	Max number of full-text crawl buffers	1	1
26	1566	ft crawl bandwidth (min)	0	0	32767	0	Number of reserved full-text crawl buffers	1	1
27	1565	ft notify bandwidth (max)	100	0	32767	100	Max number of full-text notifications buffers	1	1
28	1564	ft notify bandwidth (min)	0	0	32767	0	Number of reserved full-text notifications buffers	1	1
29	1505	index create memory (KB)	0	704	2147483647	0	Memory for index create sorts (kBytes)	1	1

Second screen:

Results	Messages

	configuration_id	name	value	minimum	maximum	value_in_use	description	is_dynamic	is_advanced
30	1570	in-doubt xact resolution	0	0	2	0	Recovery policy for DTC transactions with unknow...	1	1
31	1546	lightweight pooling	0	0	1	0	User mode scheduler uses lightweight pooling	0	1
32	106	locks	0	5000	2147483647	0	Number of locks for all users	0	1
33	1539	max degree of parallelism	0	0	32767	0	maximum degree of parallelism	1	1
34	1563	max full-text crawl range	4	0	256	4	Maximum crawl ranges allowed in full-text indexing	1	1
35	1544	max server memory (MB)	2147483647	64	2147483647	2147483647	Maximum size of server memory (MB)	1	1
36	1536	max text repl size (B)	65536	-1	2147483647	65536	Maximum size of a text field in replication.	1	0
37	503	max worker threads	0	128	32767	0	Maximum worker threads	0	1
38	1537	media retention	0	0	365	0	Tape retention period in days	1	1
39	1540	min memory per query (KB)	1024	512	2147483647	1024	minimum memory per query (kBytes)	1	1
40	1543	min server memory (MB)	0	0	2147483647	8	Minimum size of server memory (MB)	1	1
41	115	nested triggers	1	0	1	1	Allow triggers to be invoked within triggers	1	0
42	505	network packet size (B)	4096	512	32767	4096	Network packet size	1	1
43	16388	Ole Automation Procedures	0	0	1	0	Enable or disable Ole Automation Procedures	1	1
44	107	open objects	0	0	2147483647	0	Number of open database objects	0	1
45	1581	optimize for ad hoc workloads	0	0	1	0	When this option is set, plan cache size is further re...	1	1
46	1557	PH timeout (s)	60	1	3600	60	DB connection timeout for full-text protocol handler (s)	1	1
47	1556	precompute rank	0	0	1	0	Use precomputed rank for full-text query	1	1
48	1517	priority boost	0	0	1	0	Priority boost	0	1
49	1545	query governor cost limit	0	0	2147483647	0	Maximum estimated cost allowed by query governor	1	1
50	1541	query wait (s)	-1	-1	2147483647	-1	maximum time to wait for query memory (s)	1	1
51	101	recovery interval (min)	0	0	32767	0	Maximum recovery interval in minutes	1	1
52	117	remote access	1	0	1	1	Allow remote access	0	0
53	1576	remote admin connections	0	0	1	0	Dedicated Admin Connections are allowed from rem...	1	0
54	1519	remote login timeout (s)	10	0	2147483647	10	remote login timeout	1	0
55	542	remote proc trans	0	0	1	0	Create DTC transaction for remote procedures	1	0
56	1520	remote query timeout (s)	600	0	2147483647	600	remote query timeout	1	0
57	16392	Replication XPs	0	0	1	0	Enable or disable Replication XPs	1	1
58	1547	scan for startup procs	0	0	1	0	scan for startup stored procedures	0	1
59	116	server trigger recursion	1	0	1	1	Allow recursion for server level triggers	1	0
60	1532	set working set size	0	0	1	0	set working set size	0	1
61	518	show advanced options	0	0	1	0	show advanced options	1	0
62	16387	SMO and DMO XPs	1	0	1	1	Enable or disable SMO and DMO XPs	1	1
63	1555	transform noise words	0	0	1	0	Transform noise words for full-text query	1	1
64	1127	two digit year cutoff	2049	1753	9999	2049	two digit year cutoff	1	1
65	103	user connections	0	0	32767	0	Number of user connections allowed	0	1
66	1534	user options	0	0	32767	0	user options	1	0
67	16390	xp_cmdshell	0	0	1	0	Enable or disable command shell	1	1

How to do it...

Follow the steps given here to perform this recipe:

1. Execute the following query to show you some of the instance-level configuration options:

```
sp_configure
GO
```

2. To see the full list of all configuration options available with the SP_Configure stored procedure, execute the following query:

```
sp_configure 'show advanced options', 1;
GO
RECONFIGURE WITH OVERRIDE;
GO
```

3. Execute again the same query that we ran in step 1, and see the difference in the result set:

```
sp_configure
GO
```

4. Execute the following query to set a recovery time in minutes, for the server:

```
EXEC sp_configure 'recovery interval', 5
RECONFIGURE WITH OVERRIDE
GO
```

5. To set the memory for the index creation task, execute the following query.

```
EXEC sp_configure 'index create memory (KB)',1024
RECONFIGURE WITH OVERRIDE
GO
```

> Please note that the value I have provided here is just an example; it may vary from environment to environment.

How it works...

Before we move further, we would like to clarify one statement given from step 2 onwards; we have used the statement RECONFIGURE WITH OVERRIDE. This statement asks SQL Server to accept the value; if it is in the correct data type format, given in the sp_configure stored procedure and forces it to reconfigure the option with the provided value.

In step 1, we executed the sp_configure stored procedure, which shows a list of instance-level configuration along with its value. The list consists of basic options. If you want to display the advanced options list, provide **Show Advanced Option** with the value **1** (by default, it is **0**), which is executed in step 2.

We executed the same SQL statement in step 3 that we executed in step 1, but this time, it will show all options, as we set the **Show Advanced Option** value to 1 in step 2.

Step 4 sets the value for recovery interval to five minutes. It means that recovery should take up to five minutes. SQL Server issues CHECKPOINT so that it can maintain a recovery interval time. At the time CHECKPOINT runs, it transfers all data from data pages to the disk, writes all committed transactions to disk from the log file, and rolls back all the uncommitted transactions, so the question of data integrity doesn't arise.

The index creation operation is one of the heaviest operations, especially when the table is large, with millions of rows, though SQL Server manages memory dynamically and efficiently by itself This nature of SQL Server may affect the performance of the server adversely sometimes, when we have some other services running on the server simultaneously, such as those for file server, domain controller, IIS server, and so on. At that time, we may need to control the memory consumed by the index creation operation, which you can perform by the query given in step 5.

There's more...

I witnessed an incident a while ago wherein a junior DBA had executed T-SQL that created one non-clustered index on a table, which had approximately 22 million rows and 79 columns (don't you think that normalization rules should be followed?). It was peak hour for the server, which had been catering to requests for SQL Server as well as the web server. As soon as the index operation started it made the log files increasingly bigger and after few hours, the database went into recovery mode and nobody was able to access it, either directly or from the website. I had to be called in to bring the situation under control. I hope you now understand the importance of the memory management concept. In this kind of situation, the DBA had to plan out so many more things apart from memory management. I can't list the complete procedure to follow before executing these kinds of commands, as it is out of the scope of this book, but here are a few considerations:

▶ Check the recovery model, and if possible, make it bulk logged or simple from full, if you can afford to take a full database backup after the index operation, so that your backup chain won't break

▶ Try to schedule in off-hours or over the weekend, if possible.

▶ If possible, perform the index operation offline.

▶ Set the `index create memory` option so it won't be used beyond a limit.

18
Policy-based Management

In this chapter we will cover:

- ▶ Evaluating database properties
- ▶ Restricting database objects

Introduction

Microsoft made database administrators very happy by introducing a feature called **Policy-based Management** (**PBM**). PBM helps administrators to manage one or more instances of SQL Server and manage database entities and/or other SQL Server objects, based on the policy defined in PBM. It helps DBAs to apply/enforce policies for server objects and databases, or to manage different tasks effortlessly and effectively.

The following terms will be needed in the recipes coming up in this chapter, so keep them in mind to ensure that you can understand all the recipes properly:

- ▶ **Policies**: Defined rules for the database or server objects under Policy-Based Management
- ▶ **Conditions**: A condition is a Boolean value that shows the status of facets

▶ **Facets**: A set of properties that models the behavior of a target in Policy-Based Management

> A few years ago, when I visited a small company, I observed that there were no rules defined for naming conventions. All the user stored procedures in that company had the prefix sp_. The sp_ prefix is being used by SQL Server 2012 for the system stored procedure. By defining the prefix sp_ along with the user stored procedure, we are not only creating confusion between the user object and the system object, but it also has a small overhead on the performance. This is because whenever SQL Server finds a stored procedure with the prefix sp_, it checks the list of system stored procedures first. I suggested using PBM to forcefully implement a naming convention policy along with some other policies required for their setup.

Evaluating database properties

I still remember the days when a DBA's life was not as easy as it is today. Some of the database configurations are very important, and changes in those properties can cause big issues. So, we had to write a customized script to check those database properties, schedule them in SQL Server Agent, and get a report by e-mail every day, so that if any change were found in an important property of the database, we could take action immediately, before it started creating an issue. Life is not that difficult now; we can use PBM to keep an eye on those properties.

Getting ready

The following are the prerequisites for the recipe:

▶ SQL Server Denali (2012) CTP 3 or higher

▶ Login credentials that have the sysadmin role in SQL Server, may be SA or an administrator login for windows, if we connect through windows authentication

How to do it...

Follow the steps given here to perform this recipe:

1. Connect to the server, using **Object Explorer**, and move to **Management | Policy Management | Policies**. Right-click on **Policies** and click on the **New Policy...** option from the pop-up menu, as shown in the following screenshot:

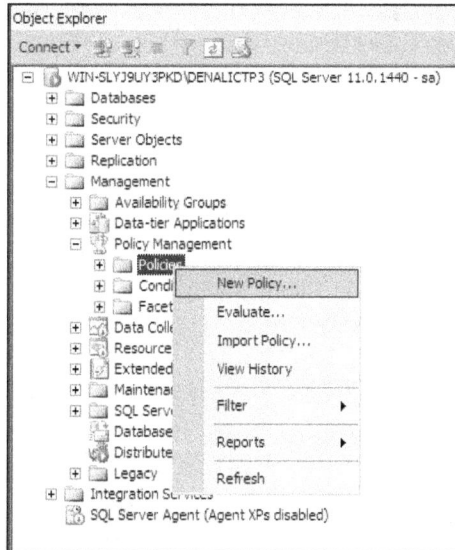

2. Type the name `Property Monitor` in the textbox besides **Name**, in the pop-up window, and then click on the **New Condition...** option in the drop-down box beside **Check Condition**.

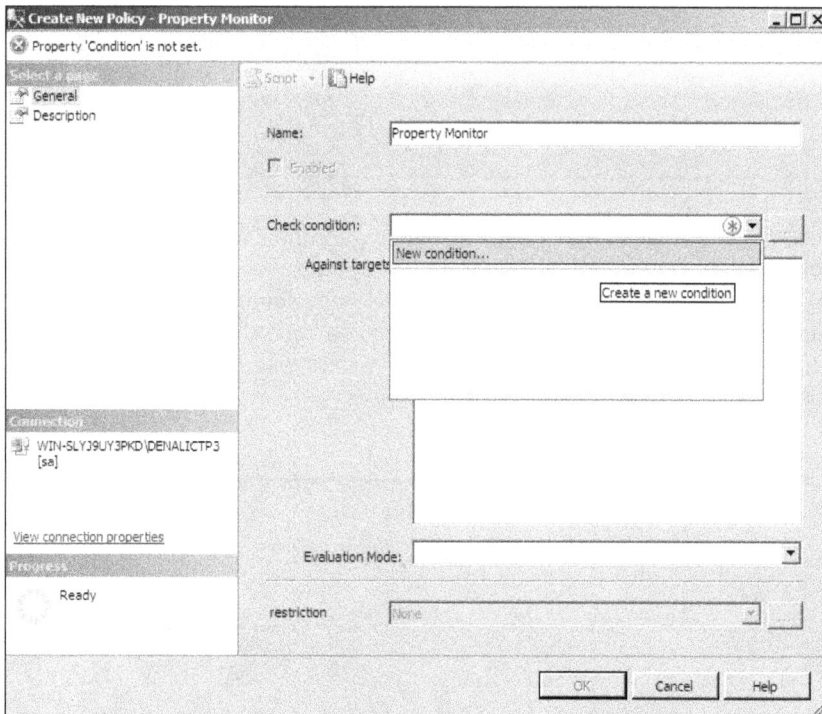

3. In the **Create New Condition** dialog box, give the name **Database Property Monitor** to the new condition. Select **Database** from the **Facet** drop-down menu. Set the property **@AutoShrink** to **False**, the **@Status** property to **Offline**, and the **@Status** property to **EmergencyMode**, and finally click on the **OK** button, as shown in the following screenshot:

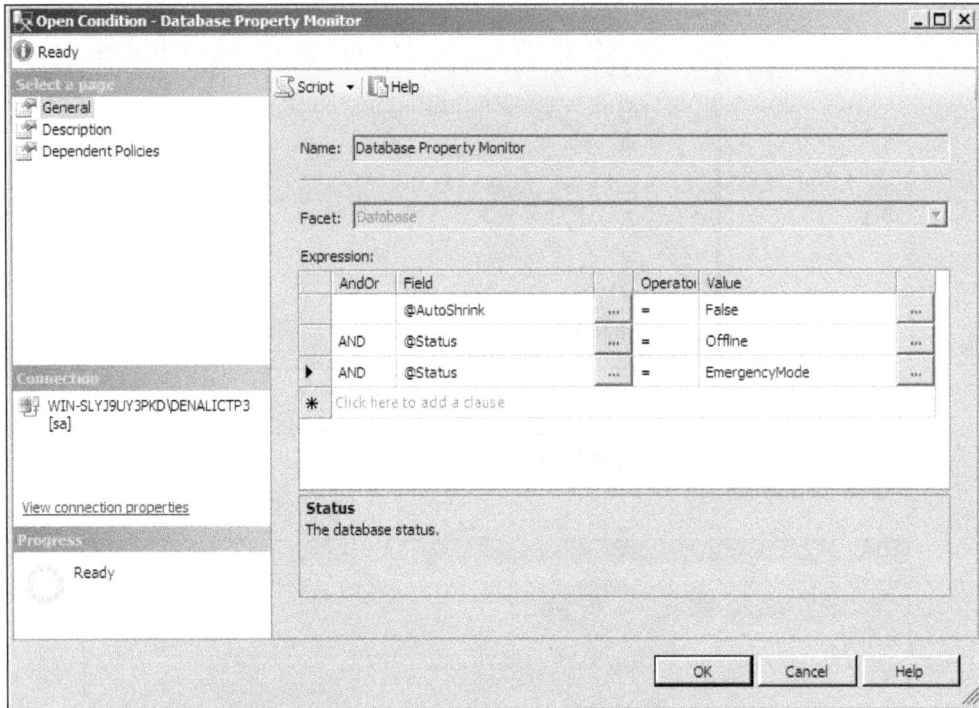

4. Now, from the **Create new Policy** dialog box, set the **Evaluation Mode** to **On Schedule**. By clicking on the **New** button, set the schedule for when you want to run this condition, and click on the **OK** button in both the dialog boxes that are open at the moment. Generally, the schedule should be set at the end of the day or at the start of the working day. If you have set up a database mail in your server, you can get the report by e-mail too.

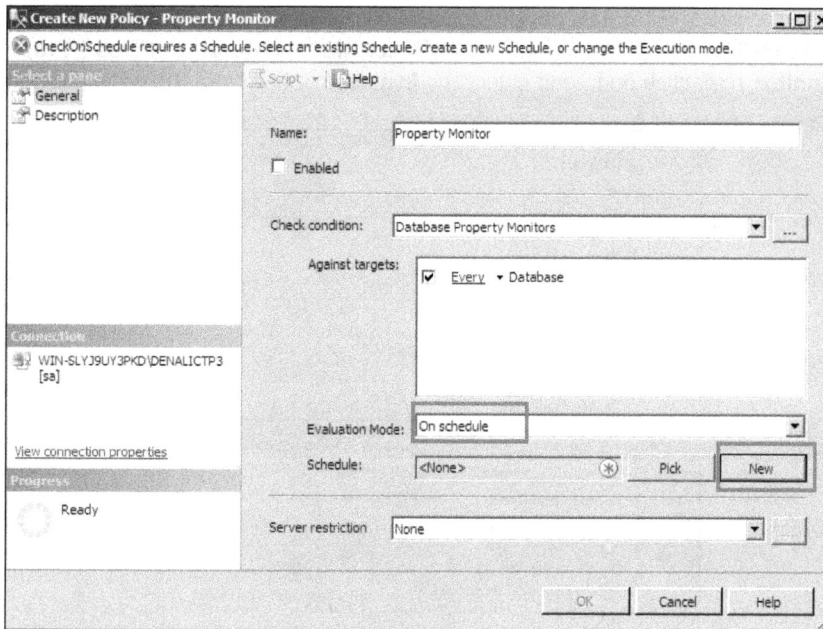

5. Click on the **New** button and open following dialog box:

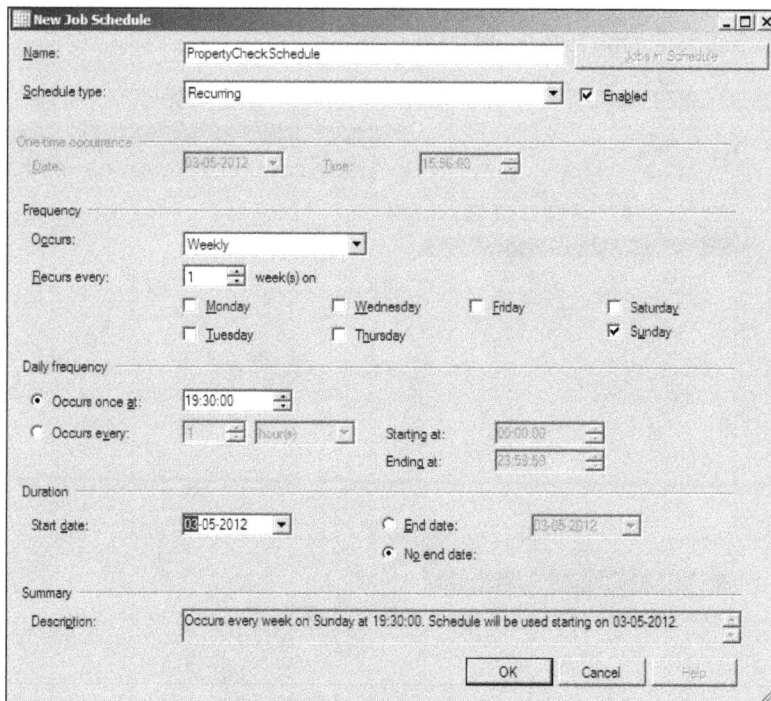

6. Now, the policy will run as per the schedule, but at the moment, we are going to execute it manually to see what it shows. Go to **Policy Management | Policies | Property Monitor**, right-click on it, and select the **Evaluate** option from the pop-up menu:

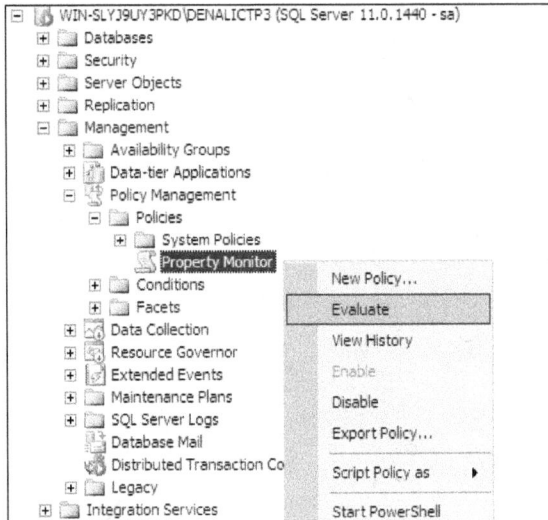

7. The **Evaluate** option will execute the policy and display the result; for more information, click on the link named **View...** under the **Details** column in the grid, as shown in the following screenshot:

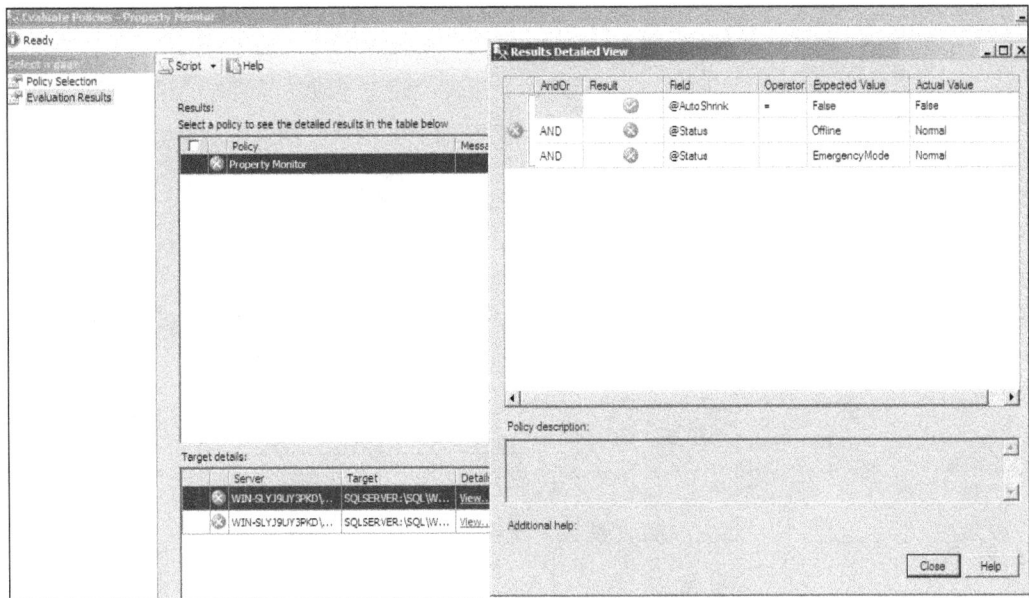

How it works...

There are many different database properties available to check in the **Create New Condition** dialog box, but we have checked only two of them for demonstration. **Auto Shrink** is a dangerous property; leaving it as **True** has very few pros but so many cons that we strongly advise you to leave it set to **False**. Whenever a condition is evaluated, it will give us a result as to whether the **AutoShrink** property of the database is **True** or **False**.

The **Status** property of a database is also one of the important properties; it should be **Normal**. So we are supposed to check the condition **!=Normal** while also showing the use of the two conditions we used earlier—**=offline** and **=EmergencyMode**. If any of these two properties shows **TRUE**, we can take immediate action, but in our case it will show False as our database condition is **Normal**.

The red-cross symbol you observed in the **Result** field conveys that the policy doesn't meet the required value. For example, we set the value **Offline** for **@Status**, but at the moment the value is **Normal**, and hence it shows the red-cross mark.

> **AutoShrink** should generally be off, so if it becomes **TRUE**, PBM should notify the concerned person. That was the reason we selected **FALSE** for the **AutoShrink** property.

There's more...

Administering PBM requires membership in the PolicyAdministratorRole role in the `msdb` database, as policies are stored in this database. This role has complete control over all policies on the system. This control includes creating and editing policies and conditions, and enabling and disabling policies.

You can find the available policy in the SQL Server instance by using the following T-SQL script:

```
Select name,date_created ,facet,obj_name  from msdb.dbo.syspolicy_
conditions order by date_created desc
```

Here is a screenshot of the results I have received in my instance; you may get more or fewer rows:

	name	date_created	facet	obj_name
1	Database Property Monitors	2012-05-03 15:55:18.900	Database	
2	Stored Procedure Naming Rule	2012-03-19 17:42:36.330	IMultipartNameFacet	sp_%
3	Stored Procedure Name Rules	2012-03-19 17:38:20.383	IMultipartNameFacet	usp_%
4	Database Property Monitor	2012-03-15 11:55:09.687	Database	

Restricting database objects

In an organization, you might have more than one developer creating a SQL script for the project. It is mandatory to maintain some kind of naming convention rules to maintain consistency and readability. There is a chance that a mistake or lack of co-ordination among developers may occur, so it would be great if we could handle the rules for this kind of naming convention forcefully, by some policy.

Naming the object in the right way is not only necessary for maintaining consistency and readability but also impacts performance, sometimes. So, to avoid performance penalties, restrict the naming convention for database objects. Generally, SP_ is the prefix used for stored procedures in SQL Server (system stored procedure), but it has been observed that many developers tend to use it for their own customized stored procedure, too. It has little overhead in terms of performance.

We are going to learn how to restrict certain names for the database objects. You can see the difference in SQL Profiler by your own by making one stored procedure with the SP_ prefix and same stored procedure code without using the SP_ prefix.".

Getting ready

The following are the prerequisites for the recipe:

- SQL Server Denali (2012) CTP 3 or higher
- Login credentials with the sysadmin role in SQL Server, may be SA or Administrator login of Windows, if we connect through Windows authentication

How to do it...

Follow the steps given here to perform this recipe:

1. Connect to the server, using **Object Explorer**, and move to **Management | Policy Management | Policies**. Right-click on **Policies** and click on the **New Policy** option from the pop-up menu, as shown in the following screenshot:

2. Enter `Stored Procedure Naming Convention` as **Name** for your policy and click on the **New Condition...** option from the drop-down list for **Check condition**:

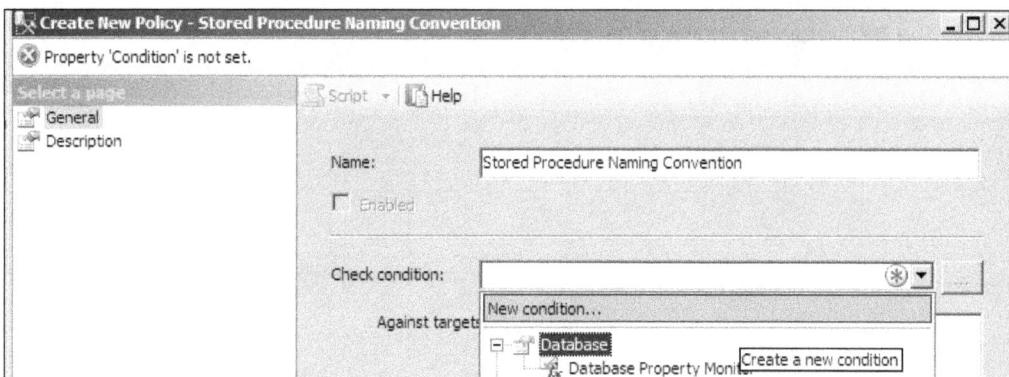

3. On the **Open Condition** dialog box, enter `Stored Procedure Naming` as the **Name**, select **Multipart Name** from the **Facet** drop-down menu, and in the **Expression** grid, select **@Name** as the **Field**, **Not LIKE** as the **Operator**, and **sp_%** as the **Value,** and click on the **OK** button:

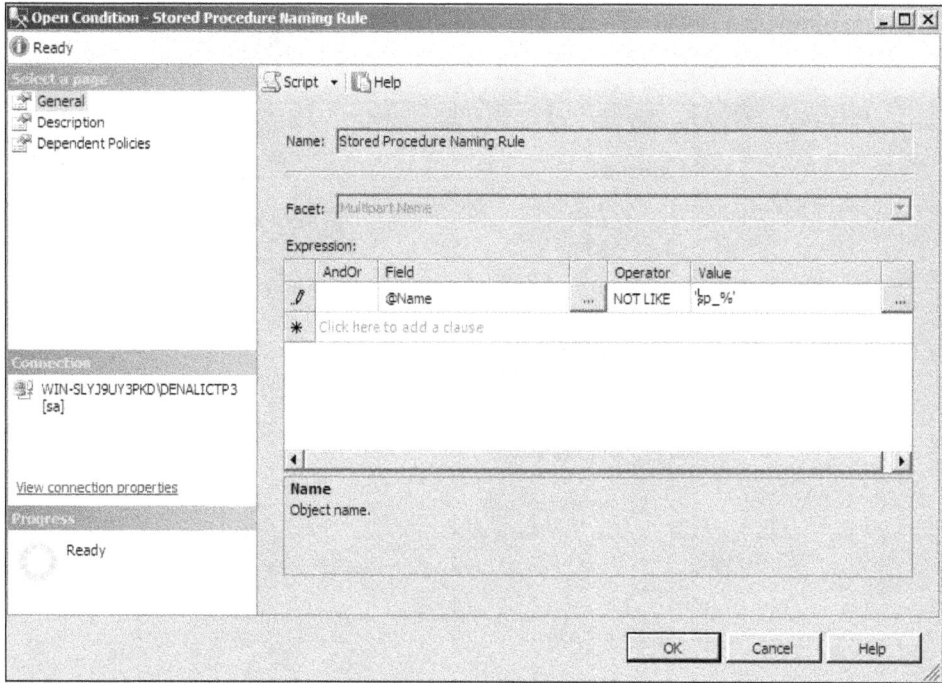

4. Now, in the **Create New Policy** dialog box, select the **On change: prevent** option from the **Evaluation Mode** drop-down menu of. Check the **Enabled** checkbox and click on the **OK** button, as shown in the following screenshot:

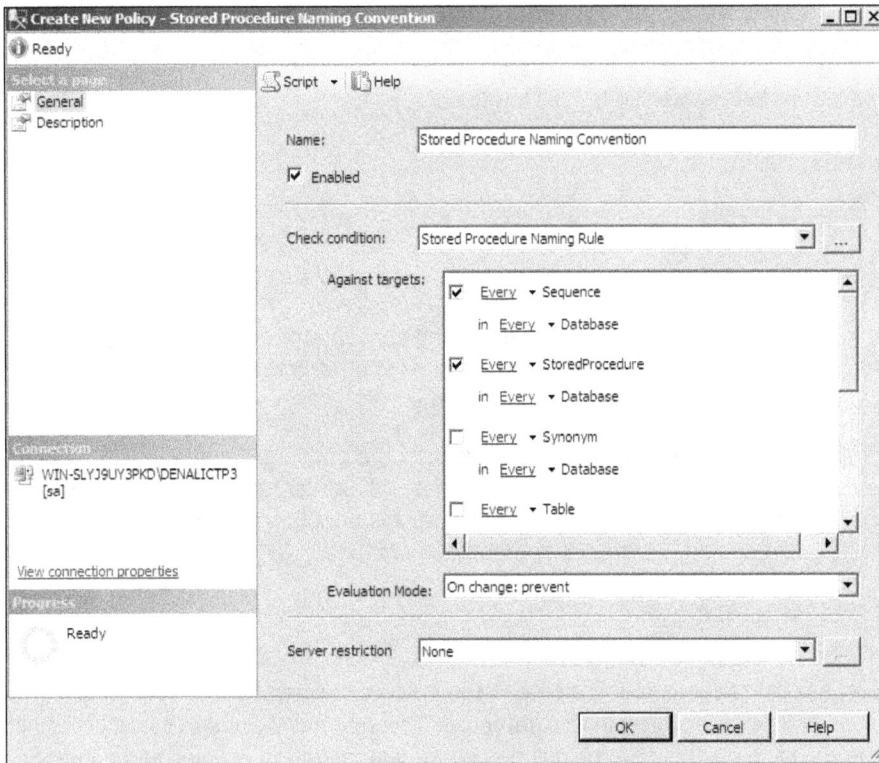

5. Try to create a procedure in the `AdventureWorks2012` database with the following T-SQL script:

```
Create Procedure sp_SelectProc
AS
SELECT 1
GO
```

6. As we are violating the policy we just created, you will be greeted with the error shown in the following screenshot:

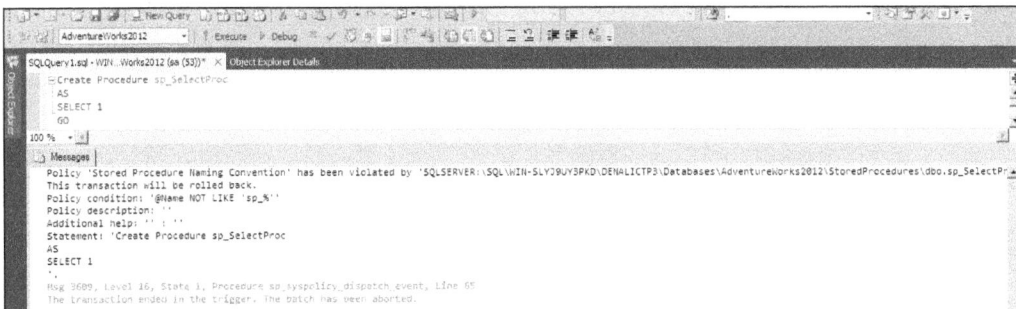

7. Now, create the stored procedure using the name that does not violate the naming policy we have created, and you will not find any error.

```
Create Procedure usp_SelectProc
AS
SELECT 1
GO
```

How it works...

We have mentioned the importance of the naming convention rules. Accordingly, we have tried to prevent the developer from using the sp_ prefix—whether intentionally or unintentionally—for the stored procedure, by creating a policy in the PBM.

In the PBM, we have created conditions that restrict the prefix sp_ and apply that condition to all the stored procedures to all databases in the SQL Server instance. We set **On Change: Prevent** as **Evaluation Mode** to so that SQL Server will not allow any stored procedure to be created with the prefix SP_, if the policy created is enabled.

There's more...

Administering PBM requires membership in the PolicyAdministratorRole role in the msdb database as policies are stored in this database. This role has complete control over all policies on the system. This control includes creating and editing policies and conditions, and enabling and disabling policies.

19
Resource Management with Resource Governor

In this chapter we will cover:

- ▶ Configuring Resource Governor with SQL Server Management Studio
- ▶ Configuring Resource Governor with T-SQL script
- ▶ Monitoring Resource Governor

Introduction

In previous chapters, you saw how you can improve the database server's performance in different ways. You have learnt how to improve the performance of queries by implementing proper indexes and keeping statistics updated, using query hints and plan guides, implementing optimum physical database design, and changing server configuration settings.

It is natural that you try your best to get the maximum out of your database server by tuning your databases in different ways as just described, even though you may be left with a few stored procedures/queries, which run slowly, if you do so; you also won't be able to do much about that, due to some hardware limitations. For example, your database server is supposed to support multiple applications, and one of these is a reporting application that executes expensive, calculated queries that are essential for the reporting application in your environment. Despite knowing that your database server has hardware limitations, you don't have the luxury of adding more hardware resources to it, and yet you are still expected to manage available CPU and memory resources in the most efficient manner among your applications. Along with this resource limitation, you need to tackle those long-running queries that consume resources and cause other priority applications to suffer. How would you handle this type of situation?

Well, prior to SQL Server 2008, you could not have done much, except for just setting server-level parameters, such as query governor, that can control and prevent long-running queries for a whole SQL Server instance. But what if you want to set resource restrictions on particular queries coming from a particular application or from a particular user?

Since SQL Server 2008, we have had Resource Governor to address this situation. Resource Governor is also present in SQL Server 2012, which you can use to manage the CPU and memory resources on your server, based on different types of requests. These "different types of requests" can be classified based on the source of the request, the login accounts / request user, and role of the request user.

The functionality of Resource Governor can be divided into the following three components:

- ▸ Classification
- ▸ Workload group
- ▸ Resource pool

Here is a basic functional/architectural diagram of Resource Governor:

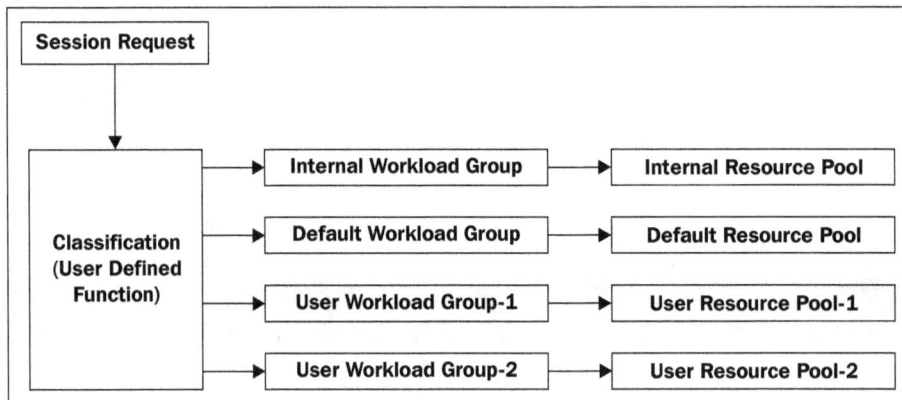

The **classification** component defines a user-defined scalar function that is to be registered with Resource Governor as a **classifier function**. Every time a request is made, the classifier function gets executed. It identifies source requests and routes those requests to a particular workload group, as per the rules defined in classifier function.

A **workload group** defines the workload by grouping multiple source requests into a single logical unit to which the resource rules are to be applied for execution, as specified by a particular resource pool. SQL Server creates two default workload groups, named *internal* and *default*. A workload group is mapped to a resource pool in order to route incoming query requests to its mapped resource pool.

A **resource pool** contains the definition of resource rules that are to be applied to incoming query requests being routed by a particular workload group to which a resource pool is mapped. SQL Server creates two default resource pools, named *internal* and *default*. A resource pool is mapped to a workload group to apply resource rules to incoming query requests routed by its mapped workload group.

Configuring Resource Governor with SQL Server Management Studio

Before we look at configuring Resource Governor, we will first set up a real-life scenario.

Let's suppose that AdventureWorks2012 is our production database and it has billions of records. The database supports multiple applications. One of the applications supported by the database is a web application, which is an OLTP database application that consumes AdventureWorks2012 database. The normal functioning of the web application is very important compared to any other applications consuming the database server resources.

Another application is the reporting application that is used to generate reports. To fulfil reporting requirements, this application runs queries with heavy calculations. Because of heavy calculations, queries take longer to execute and consume a high percentage of CPU and memory resources, which leaves less room for other query requests, made by the web application, to execute efficiently. Due to this, the web application faces performance issues.

To solve this problem, we will configure the Resource Governor in such a way that, even in conditions of resource contention caused by multiple application requests, query requests coming from the web application get a minimum of 50 percent of CPU and memory resources, and query requests coming from the reporting application get a minimum of 25 percent of CPU and memory resources. This way, by restricting resources for the reporting application, the web application can have more room to execute its queries smoothly.

In this recipe, we will learn how to set up and configure Resource Governor with SQL Server Management Studio.

Getting ready

To address the mentioned problem, we will create two pairs of a resource pool and a workload group each; one of these pairs is associated with the web application and the other with the reporting application.

The resource pool associated with the web application will be configured such that it has at least 50 percent of CPU and memory resources available at the time of resource contention.

The resource pool associated with the report application will be configured such that it has at least 25 percent of CPU and memory resources available at the time of resource contention.

For both the applications, we will create a separate, dedicated login account and user, in the `AdventureWorks2012` database, for each application that should be used to connect to SQL Server by respective application.

A separate username will be helpful in distinguishing the source of request in the classifier function. Based on username of the current request, the classifier function will route the request to the appropriate workload group, and the resource pool associated with that particular workload group will be used to execute the request.

The following are the prerequisites for this recipe:

▶ An instance of SQL Server 2012 Developer or Enterprise Evaluation edition.

▶ An SQL Server login account with administrative rights.

▶ A sample `AdventureWorks2012` database on the SQL Server instance. For more details on how to install the `AdventureWorks2012` database, please refer to the *Preface* of this book.

How to do it...

To configure Resource Governor with SQL Server Management Studio, perform the following steps:

1. Open SQL Server Management Studio and connect to an instance of SQL Server containing the `AdventureWorks2012` database.

> Make sure that the login account you are using to connect to SQL Server is an administrative account, so that it can create new login accounts and Resource Governor objects without any hassle! However, this is not mandatory, as any account with ALTER LOGIN and CONTROL SERVER will work. But for the sake of simplicity, an administrative account is recommended.

2. First, in order to set up our scenario, we need to create two login accounts and their corresponding users, one of which is supposed be used by our web application and the other by the report application. To create these logins and users, execute the following T-SQL script in a query window:

```
USE [master]
GO

--Creating new login AW_WebAppUser in SQL Server
--and its associated user in AdventureWorks2012
CREATE LOGIN [AW_WebAppUser] WITH PASSWORD=N'AW_WebAppUser123',
```

```
DEFAULT_DATABASE=[AdventureWorks2012]
GO

USE [AdventureWorks2012]
GO

CREATE USER [AW_WebAppUser] FOR LOGIN [AW_WebAppUser]
GO
ALTER ROLE [db_owner] ADD MEMBER [AW_WebAppUser]
GO

--Creating new login AW_ReportAppUser in SQL Server
--and its associated user in AdventureWorks2012
CREATE LOGIN [AW_ReportAppUser] WITH PASSWORD=N'AW_
ReportAppUser123',
DEFAULT_DATABASE=[AdventureWorks2012]
GO

USE [AdventureWorks2012]
GO

CREATE USER [AW_ReportAppUser] FOR LOGIN [AW_ReportAppUser]
GO
ALTER ROLE [db_owner] ADD MEMBER [AW_ReportAppUser]
GO
```

3. After the login/users are created, we will need to create a scalar function that will be used as a classifier function by Resource Governor. The following script will create a classifier function named `dbo.RGClassifier()`:

```
USE [master]
GO

--Creating Classifier Function in master
--database to be used with Resource Governor.
CREATE FUNCTION dbo.RGClassifier() RETURNS SYSNAME
WITH SCHEMABINDING AS
BEGIN

    DECLARE @Workload_GroupName SYSNAME

    IF SUSER_SNAME() = 'AW_WebAppUser'
        SET @Workload_GroupName = 'rg_WebApp'

    ELSE IF SUSER_SNAME() = 'AW_ReportAppUser'
        SET @Workload_GroupName = 'rg_ReportApp'

    ELSE
        SET @Workload_GroupName = 'default'

    RETURN @Workload_GroupName
END
```

4. In SSMS, expand the **Management** node under the root connection node. Right-click the **Resource Governor** node, under **Management** node, and select **Properties**. You should see a **Resource Governor Properties** dialog box, as shown in the following screenshot:

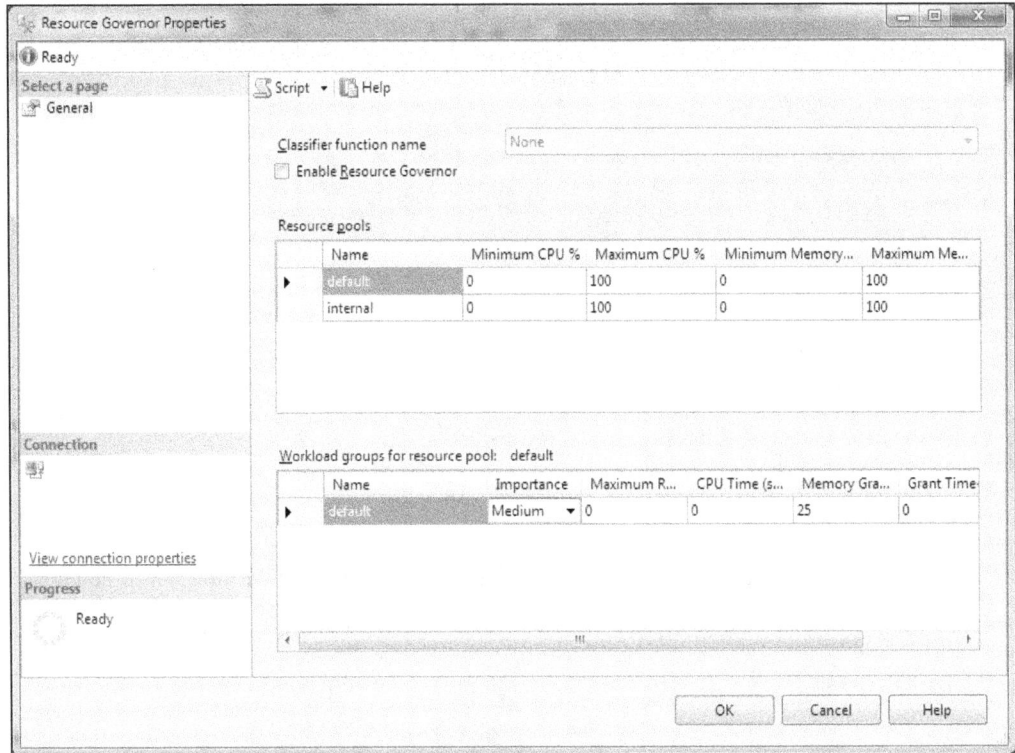

5. In this dialog box, check the **Enable Resource Governor** checkbox.

6. For the **Classifier function name** drop-down menu, select our function dbo. RGClassifier() to designate it as the classifier function name.

7. In the **Resource pools** grid, you will find two resource pools, named **default** and **internal**. In this grid, add a new resource pool named rp_WebApp with the following specified configuration values at the end of the list and leave the other configuration values with their default settings:

   ❑ **Minimum CPU %**: 50

   ❑ **Minimum Memory %**: 50

> The total for **Minimum CPU %** across all resource pools should not exceed 100 percent. The same is true for **Minimum Memory %** as well.

8. Keep the row for the new resource pool selected, and in the grid for **Workload groups for resource pool: rp_WebApp**, create a new workload group named `rg_WebApp` with following specified configuration value:

   ❑ **CPU Time (sec)**: 300

9. In the **Resource pools** grid, add another new resource pool named `rp_ReportApp` with the following specified configuration values, at the end of the list, and leave the other configuration values at the default:

   ❑ **Minimum CPU %**:25

   ❑ **Minimum Memory %**:25

10. With the row of new resource pool selected, create a new workload group named `rg_ReportApp`, in the grid for **Workload groups for resource pool: rp_ReportApp**, with following specified configuration value:

    ❑ **CPU Time (sec)**: 300

11. After you create these resource pools and workload groups, your **Resource Governor Properties** dialog box should look like the one shown in the following screenshot:

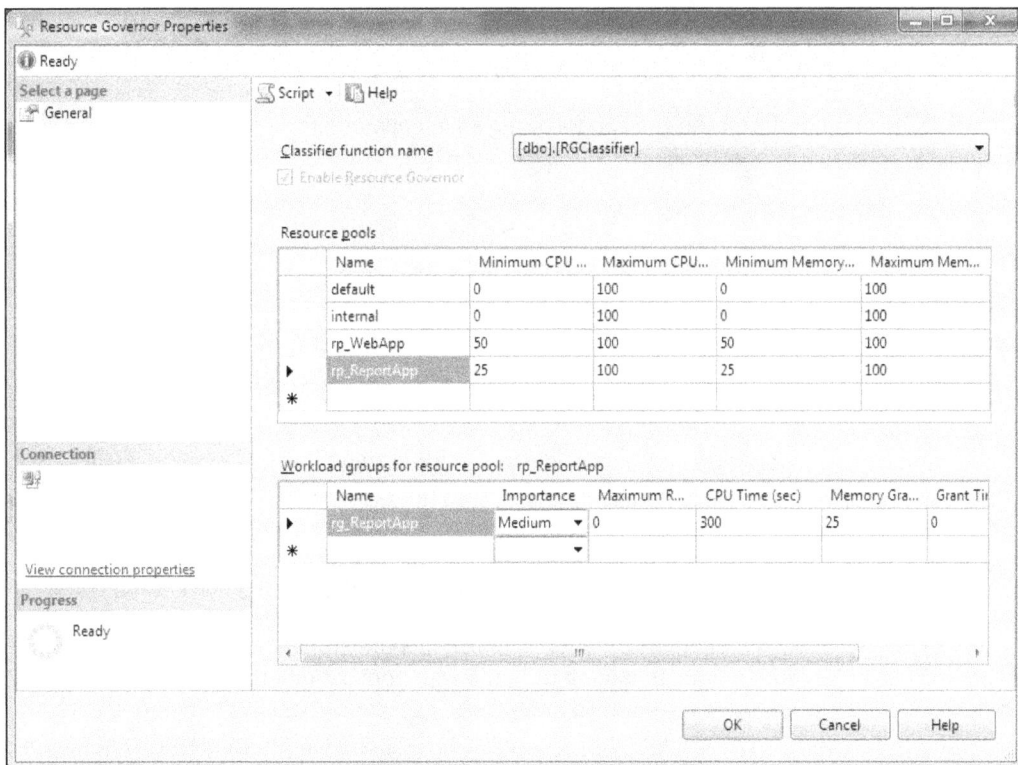

12. Expand the **Resource Governor** node under the **Management** node in **Object Explorer**. After creating the resource pools and workload groups, you will see them in **Object Explorer**, as shown in following screenshot:

How it works...

After connecting to the SQL server, we first executed a script, which by using the CREATE LOGIN T-SQL command, created the two following login accounts for web application and reporting application, respectively:

- ▶ AW_WebAppUser
- ▶ AW_ReportAppUser

The script also created corresponding users for these two login accounts in the AdventureWorks2012 database by using the CREATE USER T-SQL command. The new users were added to the db_owner database role by executing the ALTER ROLE [db_owner] command.

After creating the required login accounts and users in the AdventureWorks2012 database, we executed a script that created a user-defined scalar function—dbo.RGClassifier(). The purpose of this function is to identify the incoming session requests, classify them on the basis of their current user, and route them to their appropriate workload groups. Note that we used the SUSER_SNAME() system function, which returns the user initiating the current request.

In the SUSER_SNAME() function, a condition is checked against the current user. If the user is AW_WebAppUser (query request coming from the web application), the workload group name rg_WebApp is assigned to the variable @Workload_GroupName. If the user is AW_ReportAppUser (query request coming from the reporting application), the workload group rg_ReportApp is assigned to the variable @Workload_GroupName. In all the other cases, the default workload group name is stored in the @Workload_GroupName variable.

Finally, the value of `@Workload_GroupName`, which will be the workload group to which the classifier function will route the current request, is returned.

Thus, if a request comes from the web application, the request will be routed to the `rg_WebApp` workload group and the `rp_WebApp` resource pool will be used. If the request comes from the reporting application, the request will be routed to the `rg_ReportApp` workload group and the `rp_ReportApp` resource pool will be used. As both resource pools specify the limit on resources, SQL Server manages resource allocation accordingly, in case of resource contention. This will guarantee that the web application will get its allocated 50 percent of CPU and memory resources, even if the reporting application executes heavy and long-running queries. Also, if there is no resource contention, the application will not be limited to using only 50 percent of the available resources.

> Remember that you may frequently see requests consuming more resources than what they have been assigned by a resource pool. This is normal behaviour and can happen when there is no resource contention (no other requests are executing) at the time of executing a request.

After creating the classifier function `dbo.RGClassifier()`, we open the **Resource Governor Properties** dialog box by right-clicking the **Resource Governor** node in **Object Explorer** and choosing **Properties**. There, we enable the **Resource Governor** and specify `dbo.RGClassifier()` as our classifier function.

> **Enabling Resource Governor**
>
> By default, Resource Governor is disabled. In order to work with Resource Governor, you must enable it. You can enable Resource Governor from the **Resource Governor Properties** dialog box in SSMS or by executing the ALTER RESOURCE GOVERNOR RECONFIGURE command as well.

In the **Resource Governor Properties** dialog box, we first created the **rp_WebApp** resource pool, and the **rg_WebApp** workload group under this resource pool, by assigning a minimum of 50 percent of CPU and memory resources to be used by the web application.

We then created the **rp_ReportApp** resource pool, and the **rg_ReportApp** workload group under this resource pool, by assigning a minimum of 25 percent of CPU and memory resources to be used by the reporting application.

> Requests that are not routed to any specific workload group are always routed to the **default** workload group and use the **default** resource pool.
>
> Internal system requests generated by SQL Server are routed to the **internal** workload group and use the **internal** resource pool.
>
> Also, remember that a Dedicated Administrator Connection (DAC) is not affected by Resource Governor Classification.

Finally, we see the Resource Governor objects created in **Object Explorer**, under the **Resource Governor** node.

There's more...

In the real world, before implementing Resource Governor, you should do a trend analysis on resource requirements for various applications. This will help you in setting proper resource pool parameter values.

Resource pools are configured based on the following parameters:

- ▸ `MIN_CPU_PERCENT`
- ▸ `MAX_CPU_PERCENT`
- ▸ `MIN_MEMORY_PERCENT`
- ▸ `MAX_MEMORY_PERCENT`

The percentage of resources specified by MIN parameters is not shared by multiple resource pools, and the MIN parameter values for CPU and memory specify the minimum percentage of resources guaranteed. There can be multiple resource pools in Resource Governor. This is the reason why the total of all MIN percent values across all resource pools cannot exceed 100.

On the other hand, the percentage of resources as specified by MAX parameters is shared across multiple resource pools, and the effective MAX values are adjusted if the MIN values for any resource pools are increased or decreased.

> In SQL Server 2012, Resource Governor introduced a new parameter called `CAP_CPU_PERCENT`. The value of this parameter specifies a hard cap for CPU bandwidth and it limits the maximum CPU usage to the specified value for all the requests in the resource pool.

Configuring Resource Governor with T-SQL script

In the previous recipe, we learnt how to enable/configure Resource Governor and create workload groups and resource pools, using SQL Server Management Studio.

However, DBAs always love to work with scripts. The reason is that scripts are scalable and reusable. They can be executed on different servers to create identical objects. They can even be executed without opening SQL Server Management Studio, with a utility such as **SQLCMD**.

As a DBA, you must know how to work with Resource Governor using T-SQL commands. In this recipe, we will implement Resource Governor rules for the same scenario that we came across in our previous recipe. In this example, we will see how to achieve the same functionality with T-SQL scripts.

Getting ready

We will use the same scenario of the web application and the reporting application that we covered in our previous recipe. In this recipe, we will create required the resource pools and workload groups using T-SQL script, such that the web application gets minimum 50 percent of CPU and memory resources and the reporting application gets minimum 25 percent of CPU and memory resources, in case of resource contention.

It is assumed that you have completed the previous recipe as a part of the prerequisites for this recipe. Therefore, we are not going to repeat the part about creating the login accounts and users AW_WebAppUser and AW_ReportAppUser, for web application and reporting application, respectively.

We will also not recreate the classifier function and will use the same function that we had already created in the previous recipe.

The following are the prerequisites for this recipe:

▶   An instance of SQL Server 2012 Developer or Enterprise Evaluation edition.

▶   An SQL Server login account with administrative rights.

▶   A sample AdventureWorks2012 database on the SQL Server instance. For more details on how to install the AdventureWorks2012 database, please refer to the *Preface* of this book.

▶   You should have completed the previous recipe, *Configuring Resource Governor with SQL Server Management Studio*.

How to do it...

To configure Resource Governor with T-SQL, perform the following steps:

1.   Open SQL Server Management Studio and connect to an instance of SQL Server containing the AdventureWorks2012 database.

> Make sure that the login account you are using to connect to SQL Server is an administrative account, so that it can create Resource Governor objects. However, this is not mandatory, as any account with CONTROL SERVER permission will work. But for the sake of simplicity, an administrative account is recommended.

2. Run the following script to drop the existing Resource Governor objects that were created by the previous recipe:

```
USE [master]
GO
--Dropping the resource pools and
--workload groups created previously.

DROP WORKLOAD GROUP rg_WebApp
DROP RESOURCE POOL rp_WebApp
DROP WORKLOAD GROUP rg_ReportApp
DROP RESOURCE POOL rp_ReportApp
ALTER RESOURCE GOVERNOR RECONFIGURE
GO
```

3. Now, we will create the following Resource Governor objects:

   - Resource pool: `rp_WebApp`
   - Workload group: `rg_WebApp`
   - Resource pool: `rp_ReportApp`
   - Workload group: `rg_ReportApp`

   Next, execute the following T-SQL script to create these Resource Governor objects:

```
USE [master]
GO

--Creating resource pool to be
--used for web application.
CREATE RESOURCE POOL [rp_WebApp]
WITH
(
    min_cpu_percent=50,
    max_cpu_percent=100,
    min_memory_percent=50,
    max_memory_percent=100
)
GO

--Creating workload group to be
--used for web application.
CREATE WORKLOAD GROUP [rg_WebApp]
WITH
(
    group_max_requests=0,
    importance=Medium,
```

```
    request_max_cpu_time_sec=300,
    request_max_memory_grant_percent=25,
    request_memory_grant_timeout_sec=0,
    max_dop=0
) USING [rp_WebApp]
GO


--Creating resource pool to be
--used for report application.
CREATE RESOURCE POOL [rp_ReportApp]
WITH
(
    min_cpu_percent=25,
    max_cpu_percent=100,
    min_memory_percent=25,
    max_memory_percent=100
)
GO


--Creating workload group to be
--used for report application.
CREATE WORKLOAD GROUP [rg_ReportApp]
WITH
(
    group_max_requests=0,
    importance=Medium,
    request_max_cpu_time_sec=300,
    request_max_memory_grant_percent=25,
    request_memory_grant_timeout_sec=0,
    max_dop=0
) USING [rp_ReportApp]
GO


--Registering Classifier Function.
ALTER RESOURCE GOVERNOR
WITH (CLASSIFIER_FUNCTION = [dbo].[RGClassifier]);
GO


--Applying the in-memory changes
--in order for them to take effect.
ALTER RESOURCE GOVERNOR RECONFIGURE;
GO
```

4. To check whether Resource Governor objects have been created, run the following script to query DMVs `sys.dm_resource_governor_resource_pools` and `sys.dm_resource_governor_workload_groups`:

```
SELECT
    pool_id
    ,name
FROM sys.dm_resource_governor_resource_pools
GO

SELECT
    group_id
    ,name
    ,pool_id
FROM sys.dm_resource_governor_workload_groups
GO
```

5. The preceding query should give you output similar to that shown in the following screenshot:

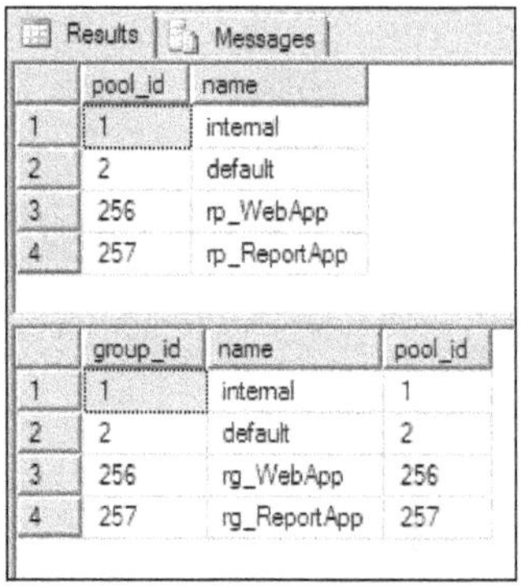

	pool_id	name
1	1	internal
2	2	default
3	256	rp_WebApp
4	257	rp_ReportApp

	group_id	name	pool_id
1	1	internal	1
2	2	default	2
3	256	rg_WebApp	256
4	257	rg_ReportApp	257

How it works...

After getting connected to SQL Server, we started by dropping the Resource Governor objects that we created in the previous recipe. Because we were to recreate the same objects with T-SQL commands, we dropped the following, previously created objects:

- Resource pool: `rp_WebApp`
- Workload group: `rg_WebApp`
- Resource pool: `rp_ReportApp`
- Workload group: `rg_ReportApp`

Observe that after dropping these objects, the command `ALTER RESOURCE GOVERNOR RECONFIGURE` was executed.

Next, we executed the script that created the required resource pools and workload groups. To create resource pools, we used the CREATE RESOURCE POOL command, and to create workload groups we used the CREATE WORKLOAD GROUP command.

We first created the rp_WebApp resource pool and the rg_WebApp workload group using the rp_WebApp resource pool. This resource pool is used by the web application.

We then created the rp_ReportApp resource pool and the rg_ReportApp workload group, using the rp_ReportApp resource pool. This resource pool is used by the reporting application.

The script also registered the [dbo].[RGClassifier] function as a classifier function with the ALTER RESOURCE GOVERNOR syntax. At the end of script, we executed the ALTER RESOURCE GOVERNOR RECONFIGURE command for the applied changes to take effect.

> If you make any changes in the Resource Governor configuration, you must execute the ALTER RESOURCE GOVERNOR RECONFIGURE command for new changes to take effect.

Finally, we verified that the script created the Resource Governor objects required, by querying dynamic management views sys.dm_resource_governor_resource_pools and sys.dm_resource_governor_workload_groups.

There's more...

While configuring workload groups, the following parameters should be kept in mind:

- **IMPORTANCE**: It specifies the relative importance of the requests in a workload group. The value can be LOW, MEDIUM, or HIGH.
- **GROUP_MAX_REQUESTS**: It specifies the maximum number of requests that can be executed in parallel in a workload group.
- **MAX_DOP**: It specifies the maximum degree of parallelism for parallel requests in a workload group.
- **REQUEST_MAX_MEMORY_GRANT_PERCENT**: It is the maximum memory in percentage that a single request in a workload group can use.
- **REQUEST_MAX_CPU_TIME_SEC**: It is the maximum amount of time in seconds that a single request can use in a workload group.
- **REQUEST_MEMORY_GRANT_TIMEOUT_SEC**: It is the maximum amount of time in seconds that a query can wait for, for memory.

For more information on Resource Governor, refer to the product documentation for SQL Server 2012 at http://msdn.microsoft.com/en-us/library/bb933866.aspx.

Monitoring Resource Governor

After you are done with configuring Resource Governor as per your applications' resource requirements, you will need to monitor your Resource Governor. You may want to monitor how resource pools are utilized and how many session requests are routed to a particular resource pool. You may also want to monitor the internal and default pool activity.

In this recipe, we will execute required sample queries from different connections, with different logins (`AW_WebAppUser` and `AW_ReportAppUser`), and monitor the CPU and memory resource usage for each resource pool in Reliability and Performance Monitor.

Getting ready

This recipe extends our previous recipe and assumes that you have already completed previous recipes in this chapter.

Taking further the scenario of the web application and the reporting application in the context of monitoring Resource Governor, we will execute sample queries with login accounts `AW_WebAppUser` and `AW_ReportAppUser`, to simulate the scenario of incoming requests from the web application and the reporting application. This causes the appropriate resource pool to be used while executing a query request. We monitor resource usage by the resource pool in Reliability and Performance Monitor.

The following are the prerequisites for this recipe:

► An instance of SQL Server 2012 Developer or Enterprise Evaluation edition.

► An SQL Server login account with administrative rights.

► A sample `AdventureWorks2012` database on the SQL Server instance. For more details on how to install the `AdventureWorks2012` database, please refer to the *Preface* of this book.

► You should have completed the previous recipe, *Configuring Resource Governor with T-SQL Script*.

How to do it...

To monitor Resource Governor, perform the following steps:

1. Start Reliability and Performance Monitor. To do this, press the Windows + R key combination to display the **Run** dialog box. In this dialog box, type `perfmon.exe` and press *Enter*.

2. When Reliability and Performance Monitor is started, to switch to **Performance Monitor** view, click on the **Performance Monitor** node under the **Monitoring Tools** node, in left-hand side console tree.

3. Click on the **+** button in the toolbar to add counters.

4. In the **Add Counters** dialog box, type the name of the computer or let it be **<Local computer>** under the **Select counters from computer:** drop-down list, if you are monitoring a local machine.

5. In the list of available performance counter objects, expand **SQLServer:ResourcePoolStats** and select **CPU usage %**.

6. In the list under **Instances of selected object:**, you will see resource pools that have been created previously. Select **<All instances>** and then click on the **Add > >** button. This will add the **CPU usage %** counter to the list of **Added counters** on the right-hand side.

7. After adding the performance counter object, your screen should look as shown in the following screenshot:

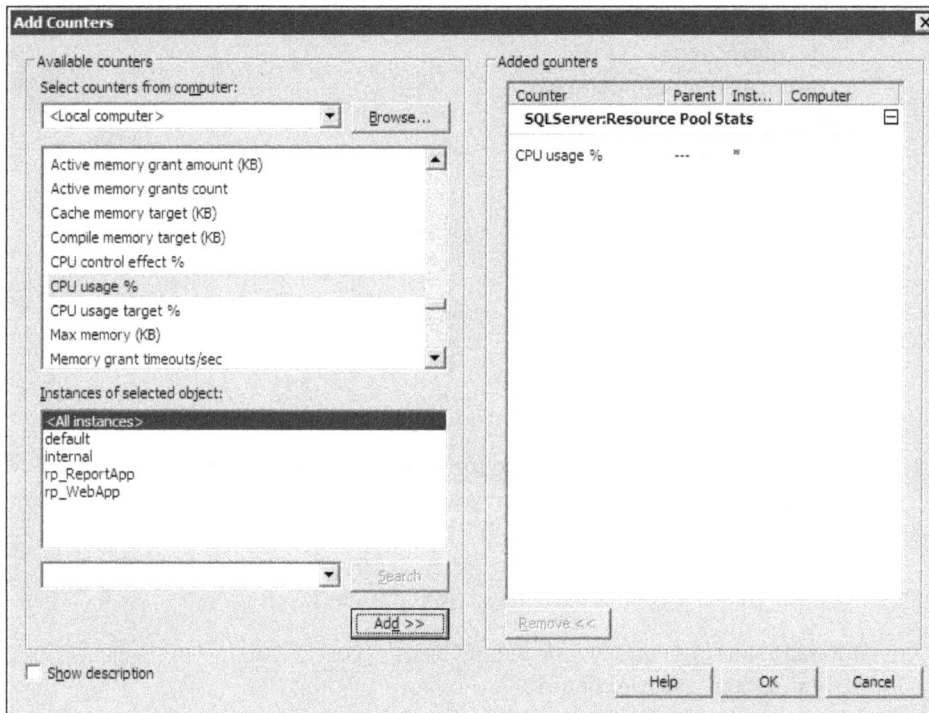

8. Open SQL Server Management Studio and connect to an instance of SQL Server containing the `AdventureWorks2012` database, by using the `AW_WebAppUser` login account (Connection-1).

9. Open another instance of SQL Server Management Studio and connect to another instance of SQL Server containing the `AdventureWorks2012` database, by using `AW_ReportAppUser` login account (Connection-2).

10. Now, from Connection-1, type and execute the following sample queries:

```
USE AdventureWorks2012
GO

--Connection-1 with Login AW_WebAppUser

--Running sample query to create a table
--tbl_TEMPSalesOrderDetail and populating
--it with the data of Sales.SalesOrderDetail
IF OBJECT_ID('tbl_TEMPSalesOrderDetail') IS NOT NULL
    DROP TABLE tbl_TEMPSalesOrderDetail

GO

SELECT
    SalesOrderID
    ,SalesOrderDetailID
    ,CarrierTrackingNumber
    ,OrderQty
    ,ProductID
    ,SpecialOfferID
    ,UnitPrice
    ,UnitPriceDiscount
    ,LineTotal
    ,rowguid
    ,ModifiedDate
INTO tbl_TEMPSalesOrderDetail
FROM Sales.SalesOrderDetail
```

11. From Connection-2, type and execute the following sample queries:

```
USE AdventureWorks2012
GO

--Connection-2 with Login AW_ReportAppUser

--Running sample query to fetch data from
--of Sales.SalesOrderDetail

SELECT
    SalesOrderID
    ,SalesOrderDetailID
    ,CarrierTrackingNumber
    ,OrderQty
    ,ProductID
    ,SpecialOfferID
```

```
    ,UnitPrice
    ,UnitPriceDiscount
    ,LineTotal
    ,rowguid
    ,ModifiedDate
FROM Sales.SalesOrderDetail
ORDER BY SalesOrderID

GO

SELECT
    SalesOrderID
    ,SUM(LineTotal)
    ,ROW_NUMBER() OVER (ORDER BY SUM(LineTotal) desc,SalesOrderID)
FROM Sales.SalesOrderDetail
GROUP BY SalesOrderID
```

12. Switch to Reliability and Performance Monitor; you will notice that there are spikes for the **rp_WebApp** and **rp_ReportApp** resource pools, as shown in following screenshot:

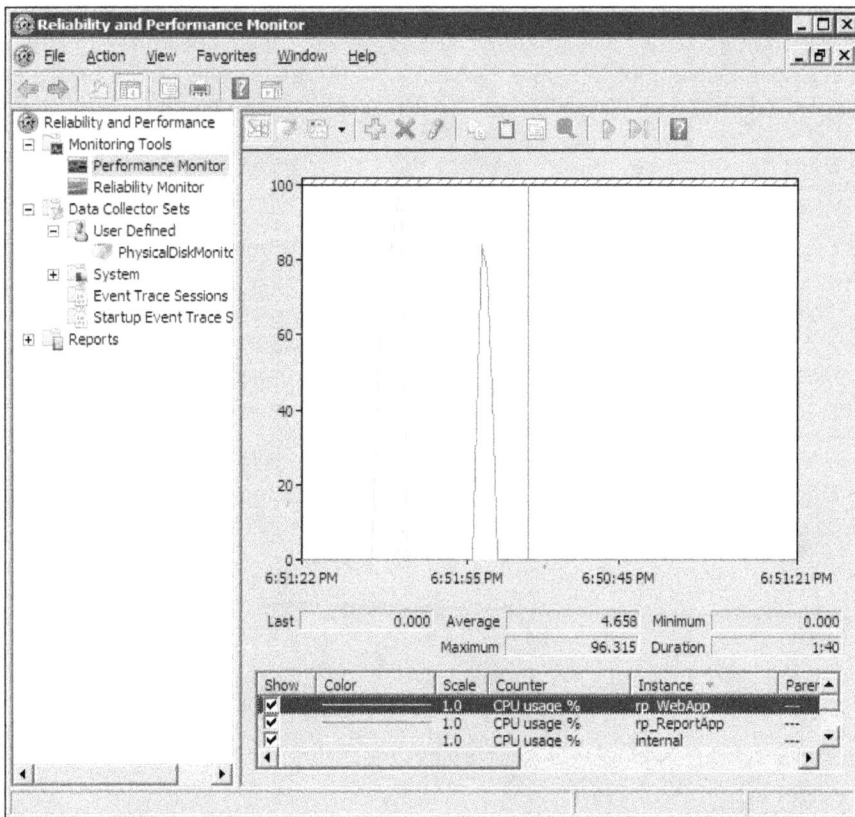

How it works...

Because we wanted to monitor the resource usage statistics for the available resource pools, we started Reliability and Performance Monitor and added the following performance counter for monitoring:

> ▸ **SQLServer:ResourcePoolStats:CPU usage %**

We added **<All instances>**, so that we can monitor all the available resource pools, not only a single one.

We then opened two instances of SQL Server Management Studio (two connections—Connection-1 and Connection-2).

We logged in with the `AW_WebAppUser` login account for Connection-1, while we logged in with the `AW_ReportAppUser` login account for Connection-2.

From both the connections, we executed sample queries on the `AdventureWorks2012` database and monitored the performance counter we had added in Reliability and Performance Monitor. Note that the query executed from Connection-1—using the `AW_WebAppUser` login account—used the `rp_WebApp` resource pool, and the query executed from Connection-2—using the `AW_WebReportUser` login account—used the `rp_ReportApp` resource pool. Examine the peaks of CPU resource usage for both the resource pools in Performance Monitor, which are represented there in different colours.

There's more...

If you want to map a particular session with a workload group, you can join the DMV `sys.dm_exec_sessions` with the DMV `sys.dm_resource_governor_workload_groups`, on the `group_id` column. You can further join DMV `sys.dm_resource_governor_workload_groups` to the DMV `sys.dm_resource_governor_resource_pools`, on the `pool_id` column, to learn the name of the resource pool for a particular session.

DMVs `sys.dm_resource_governor_resource_pools` and `sys.dm_resource_governor_workload_groups` provide various detailed statistics of Resource Governor. Just explore the different columns of these DMVs on your own. For more information on Resource Governor, refer to the product documentation for SQL Server 2012.

Index

[PACKT] PUBLISHING **enterprise** 🞰
professional expertise distilled

Thank you for buying
Microsoft SQL Server 2012 Performance
Tuning Cookbook

About Packt Publishing

Packt, pronounced 'packed', published its first book "*Mastering phpMyAdmin for Effective MySQL Management*" in April 2004 and subsequently continued to specialize in publishing highly focused books on specific technologies and solutions.

Our books and publications share the experiences of your fellow IT professionals in adapting and customizing today's systems, applications, and frameworks. Our solution-based books give you the knowledge and power to customize the software and technologies you're using to get the job done. Packt books are more specific and less general than the IT books you have seen in the past. Our unique business model allows us to bring you more focused information, giving you more of what you need to know, and less of what you don't.

Packt is a modern, yet unique publishing company, which focuses on producing quality, cutting-edge books for communities of developers, administrators, and newbies alike. For more information, please visit our website: www.PacktPub.com.

About Packt Enterprise

In 2010, Packt launched two new brands, Packt Enterprise and Packt Open Source, in order to continue its focus on specialization. This book is part of the Packt Enterprise brand, home to books published on enterprise software – software created by major vendors, including (but not limited to) IBM, Microsoft and Oracle, often for use in other corporations. Its titles will offer information relevant to a range of users of this software, including administrators, developers, architects, and end users.

Writing for Packt

We welcome all inquiries from people who are interested in authoring. Book proposals should be sent to author@packtpub.com. If your book idea is still at an early stage and you would like to discuss it first before writing a formal book proposal, contact us; one of our commissioning editors will get in touch with you.

We're not just looking for published authors; if you have strong technical skills but no writing experience, our experienced editors can help you develop a writing career, or simply get some additional reward for your expertise.

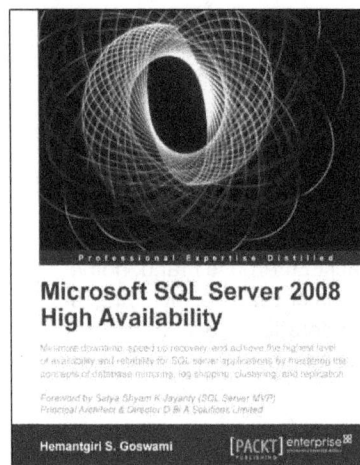

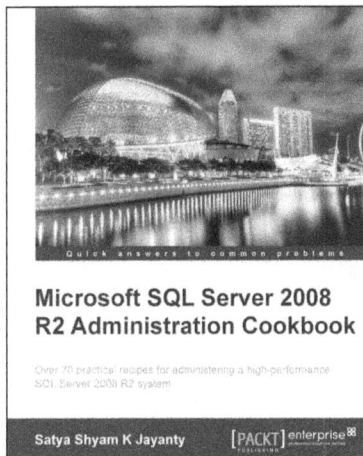

Microsoft SQL Server 2008 R2 Administration Cookbook

ISBN: 978-1-84968-144-5   Paperback: 468 pages

Over 70 practical recipes for administering a high-performance SQL Server 2008 R2 system

1. Provides Advanced Administration techniques for SQL Server 2008 R2

2. Covers the essential Manageability, Programmability, and Security features

3. Emphasizes important High Availability features and implementation

4. Explains how to maintain and manage the SQL Server data platform effectively

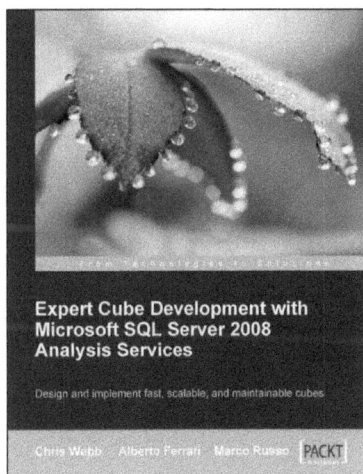

Expert Cube Development with Microsoft SQL Server 2008 Analysis Services

ISBN: 978-1-847197-22-1   Paperback: 360 pages

Design and implement fast, scalable, and maintainable cubes

1. A real-world guide to designing cubes with Analysis Services 2008

2. Model dimensions and measure groups in BI Development Studio

3. Implement security, drill-through, and MDX calculations

4. Learn how to deploy, monitor, and performance-tune your cube

www.ingramcontent.com/pod-product-compliance
Lightning Source LLC
Chambersburg PA
CBHW080128220326
41598CB00032B/4988